Andrew B. Davidson

The book of Job, with notes, introduction and appendix

Andrew B. Davidson

The book of Job, with notes, introduction and appendix

ISBN/EAN: 9783337736279

Printed in Europe, USA, Canada, Australia, Japan

Cover: Foto ©ninafisch / pixelio.de

More available books at **www.hansebooks.com**

The Cambridge Bible for Schools and Colleges.

GENERAL EDITOR:—J. J. S. PEROWNE, D.D.
BISHOP OF WORCESTER.

THE BOOK OF JOB,

WITH NOTES, INTRODUCTION AND APPENDIX

BY

THE REV. A. B. DAVIDSON, D.D., LL.D.

PROFESSOR OF HEBREW AND OLD TESTAMENT EXEGESIS IN THE
NEW COLLEGE, EDINBURGH.

EDITED FOR THE SYNDICS OF THE UNIVERSITY PRESS

Cambridge:
AT THE UNIVERSITY PRESS.
1891

PREFACE
BY THE GENERAL EDITOR.

THE General Editor of *The Cambridge Bible for Schools* thinks it right to say that he does not hold himself responsible either for the interpretation of particular passages which the Editors of the several Books have adopted, or for any opinion on points of doctrine that they may have expressed. In the New Testament more especially questions arise of the deepest theological import, on which the ablest and most conscientious interpreters have differed and always will differ. His aim has been in all such cases to leave each Contributor to the unfettered exercise of his own judgment, only taking care that mere controversy should as far as possible be avoided. He has contented himself chiefly with a careful revision of the notes, with pointing out omissions, with suggesting occasionally a reconsideration of some question, or a fuller treatment of difficult passages, and the like.

Beyond this he has not attempted to interfere, feeling it better that each Commentary should have its own individual character, and being convinced that freshness and variety of treatment are more than a compensation for any lack of uniformity in the Series.

DEANERY, PETERBOROUGH.

CONTENTS.

		PAGES
I. INTRODUCTION.		
Chapter I.	Contents of the Book................	ix—xii
Chapter II.	The nature of the Composition......	xiii—xxii
Chapter III.	The Idea and Purpose of the Book	xxiii—xxix
Chapter IV.	The Integrity of the Book............	xxix—liv
Chapter V.	The Age and Authorship of Job ...	lv—lxviii
II. TEXT AND NOTES	....	1—290
APPENDIX.		
Additional Note on ch. xix. 23—27	....	291—6
INDEX	....	297—300

⁂ The Text adopted in this Edition is that of Dr Scrivener's *Cambridge Paragraph Bible*. A few variations from the ordinary Text, chiefly in the spelling of certain words, and in the use of italics, will be noticed. For the principles adopted by Dr Scrivener as regards the printing of the Text see his Introduction to the *Paragraph Bible*, published by the Cambridge University Press.

INTRODUCTION.

CHAPTER I.

Contents of the Book.

The Book of Job is so called from the name of the man whose history and afflictions and sayings form the subject of it. As it now lies before us it consists of five parts:—

1. The prologue, written in prose, ch. i.—ii. This introduces to us a man named Job, living in the land of Uz; and describes in rapid and dramatic touches his piety and wealth and the successive and extraordinary calamities that befell him. This man was "perfect and upright, and one that feared God, and eschewed evil"; and his piety was reflected in the great prosperity that attended him, in his family felicity and wide possessions. A trait from his ordinary life is given which illustrates the happiness and affection to one another of his children, and the father's scrupulous godliness (ch. i. 1—5). Then the narrative describes how the disinterestedness of Job's piety was called in question in the Council of Heaven by the Satan, or Adversary, that one of God's ministers whose office is to try the sincerity of men, and oppose them in their pretensions to a right standing before God. This angel insinuated that Job's religion was insincere, and only the natural return for the unprecedented blessings showered on him by God; if these blessings were withdrawn he would disown God to his face. The Satan receives permission to afflict Job, with the reservation that he must not touch him in his person. In one day Job is stripped of all his possessions and bereaved of his children: robber hordes carry away his asses and camels, and slay his servants with the sword; the fire

of heaven falls on his flocks and consumes them; and his children are buried beneath the ruins of the house where they were feasting. When the calamitous tidings are brought to him, Job manifests the liveliest tokens of grief, but his reverent submission to God remains unshaken—"In all this Job sinned not nor ascribed wrong to God" (ch. i. 6—22).

Again the heavenly Council convenes, and again the Satan is present. The Lord speaks of His servant Job with approval and with compassion, and upbraids the Adversary with instigating Him to bring undeserved suffering upon him. The Satan's answer is ready: the trial did not touch Job close enough; let the hand of God touch him in his own bone and flesh and he will disown Him to His face. The Adversary receives permission to afflict Job himself, with the reservation that he shall spare his life. Straightway Job is smitten with sore boils, the leprosy called Elephantiasis; and he flings himself down among the ashes, taking a potsherd to scrape himself withal. The deeper affliction only reveals greater deeps in Job's reverent piety. In his former trial he blessed God who took away the good He had added to naked man; this was strictly no evil: now he bows beneath His hand when He inflicts positive evil: "We receive good at the hand of God, and shall we not also receive evil?" In all this Job sinned not with his lips: he let no sinful murmur against God escape him (ch. ii. 1—10).

Then the narrative informs us how Job's three friends, Eliphaz the Temanite, Bildad the Shuhite, and Zophar the Naamathite, having heard of his great misfortunes, come to condole with him. They are struck dumb at the sight of his terrible calamity, and sit with him upon the ground seven days and seven nights, none of them speaking a word. Moved by the presence and the sympathising gestures of his friends, Job loses his self-control, and breaks out into a passionate cry for death (ch. ii. 11—ch. iii.).

2. The debate between Job and his friends, ch. iv.—xxxi., written in poetry. This comprises a series of speeches in which the problem of Job's afflictions, and the relation of external evil to the righteousness of God and the conduct of men, are

brilliantly discussed. The theory of the friends is that affliction implies previous sin on the part of the sufferer, though in the case of a good man such as Job it is chastisement meant to wean him from evil still cleaving to him; and they exhort him to repentance, and hold up a bright future before him. Job denies that his sufferings are due to sin, of which he is innocent; God wrongly holds him guilty and afflicts him. And, taught by his own history, he is led to look more narrowly at the course of providence in the world, and he fails to perceive that inseparable connexion in every instance between sin and suffering which the three friends insisted on : the providence of God is not in fact administered on such a principle. The discussion between Job and his friends consists of three circles of speeches, (1) ch. iv.—xiv.; (2) ch. xv.—xxi.; and (3) ch. xxii.—xxxi. Each of these three circles comprises six speeches, one by each of the three friends in succession, with a reply from Job. In the last round, however, Zophar, the third speaker, fails to come forward. This is a confession of defeat; and Job, left victor in the strife, resumes his "parable," and carries it through a series of chapters, in which, with a profound pathos, he contrasts his former greatness with his present humiliation, protests before heaven his innocence of all the offences that have been insinuated or may be suggested against him, and adjures God to reveal to him the cause of his afflictions.

3. The speeches of Elihu, ch. xxxii.—xxxvii. A youthful bystander, named Elihu, who had been a silent listener to the debate hitherto, here intervenes, not without manifold apologies for presuming to let his voice be heard in the midst of such wise and venerable counsellers, and expresses his dissatisfaction both with Job and his friends. He is shocked at Job's impious demeanour and the charges which he has made against God, and indignant with the three friends because they have allowed themselves to be brought to silence by Job, and failed to bring home to him the wrong against God of which he has been guilty. Job ought not to have been allowed to carry off the victory: he may be shewn to be in the wrong, though with different arguments from those employed by the three friends.

Elihu then in a long discourse expresses his abhorrence of the sentiments uttered by Job, controverts his views in regard to God's providence and the meaning of afflictions, and on this latter point suggests a theory in some respects different from that advanced by Job's friends.

4. The speeches of the Lord out of the storm, ch. xxxviii.—xlii. 6. In answer to Job's repeated demand that God would appear and solve the riddle of his life, the Lord answers Job out of the storm. The answer is altogether unlike what Job had expected. The divine speaker does not condescend to refer to Job's individual problem, He makes no charge of sin against his former life, and gives no account of his afflictions. The intellectual solution of problems can never be the question between Jehovah and His servants; the question is the state of their hearts towards Himself. He asks of Job, "Who am I?" and "What art thou?" In a series of splendid pictures from inanimate creation and the world of animal life He makes all the glory of His Being to pass before Job. Job is humbled and lays his hand upon his mouth in silence; such thoughts of God as he had never had before fill his heart; his former knowledge of Him was like that learned from hearsay, dim and imperfect, now he saw Him eye to eye, and he repents his former words and demeanour in dust and ashes.

5. The epilogue, also in prose, ch. xlii. 7—17. This describes how Job, having thus humbled himself before God, is restored to a prosperity double that which he enjoyed before; his former friends and acquaintances again gather around him; he is anew blessed with children; and dies, old and full of days.

With the exception of the discourses of Elihu, the connexion of which with the Poem in its original form may be liable to doubt, all these five parts appear essential elements of the work as it came from the hand of the author, although it is possible that the second and fourth divisions may betray in some parts traces of expansion by later writers.

CHAPTER II.

THE NATURE OF THE COMPOSITION.

UNDER the enquiry as to the nature of the composition two questions may be embraced: (1) the question, Is the Book historical, or is it a pure creation of the mind of the writer? and (2) the question, To what class of literature does the Poem belong? may we call it a drama, or assign it to any understood class of writing?

On the former question various opinions have prevailed and are still entertained. (1) The Book has been considered by some to be strictly historical, both in the narrative and poetical portions. (2) Others have maintained a view directly opposed, regarding the work as wholly unhistorical and in all its parts a creation of the Poet's mind, and written with a didactic purpose. (3) And a third class assumes a middle position between these two extremes, considering that, though mainly a creation of the author's own mind, the Poem reposes on a historical tradition, which the writer adopted as suitable for his moral purpose, and the outline of which he has preserved.

Among the Jews in early times the Book appears to have been considered strictly historical. This was probably the opinion of Josephus, who, though he does not quote Job in any of his works[1], appears to embrace it among the thirteen prophetical books forming one division of his Canon[2]. The same was the generally received opinion among the Rabbinical writers. There were exceptions, however, even anterior to the age of the Talmud. A certain Rabbi Resh Lakish sitting in the school before Samuel bar Nachmani gave expression to the opinion that "a Job existed not, and was not created; he is a parable." To this Bar Nachmani replied, "Saith not the

[1] Bleek, Introduction, ii. p. 309.   [2] *Contra Apion.* i. 18.

scripture, There was a man in the land of Uz, whose name was Job?" Resh Lakish answered, "But how is it then with that place 2 Sam. xii. 3, The poor man had nothing, save one little ewe-lamb which he had bought, &c.? What is that but a common similitude? and so Job is a simple parable." Bar Nachmani could but reply that not only the name of Job but that of his country was mentioned, an answer that probably did not go far to convince his opponent[1]. Resh Lakish was most likely not alone in his opinion, though his view appears to have given scandal to others. A later scholar, Rabbi Hai, the last who bore the title of Gaon (died 1037), maintains that the Talmudic passage reads, "Job existed not and was not created except in order to be a parable (or type, i.e. a model to the children of men), for that he actually existed the passage of scripture proves" (Ezek. xiv. 14)[2]. With this view Rashi agrees, and Ibn Ezra in the beginning of his commentary refers to the passage in Ezekiel as evidence that Job was a real person. Maimonides (died 1204) refers to the difference of opinion existing on the question whether Job was "created," that is, was a real person, and advances the opinion that "he is a parable meant to exhibit the views of mankind in regard to providence[3]." The historical existence of Job appears thus to have been to some extent an open question among the Jewish scholars, though probably up to recent times the belief that the Book was strictly historical continued to be the prevailing one.

The same appears to have been the general view of Christian writers up till the time of the Reformation, when Luther with his usual freedom and sound instincts expressed another opinion. The Reformer was far from denying the existence of Job himself, nor did he doubt that there was history in the Book; it was history, however, poetically idealised. In his Table-talk he expresses himself to that effect: "I hold the Book of Job to be real history; but that everything so happened and was so done I do not believe, but think that some ingenious, pious and

---

[1] Talmud, Baba Bathra, fol. 15, in Magnus, *Comm. on Job*, p. 298.
[2] Ewald and Dukes, *Beiträge*, ii. p. 166.
[3] *Moreh Nevochim*, part iii. ch. 22.

INTRODUCTION.

learned man composed it as it is[1]." Even during the preceding centuries some dissentient voices had let themselves be heard. More than a thousand years before Luther's day a much freer judgment than his had been passed upon the Book by Theodore bishop of Mopsuestia in Cilicia (died 428), a great name in the Antiochean school of Exegesis, and a man who resembled Luther in some points, especially his free handling of the Canon, though he was without the Reformer's geniality and sound hermeneutical instincts. Theodore, equally with Luther, believed in the existence of Job himself, but he regarded the Book as a fiction, written in imitation of the dramas of the heathen by an author familiar with the Greek wisdom, and nothing short of a slander upon the godly Patriarch. The dialogue between the Almighty and Satan in the Prologue gave offence to Theodore; but much worse was what he found in the Epilogue, where according to the Sept., from which alone the bishop derived his knowledge of the Book, Job names his third daughter "Horn of Amalthea" (see on ch. xlii. 14). Such a name must have been invented by the author of the Book from love to the heathen mythology, for what could an Idumean like Job know of Jupiter and Juno and the heathen gods? And if he had known would he have bestowed upon a child given him in such circumstances by God a name borrowed from the history of the deities of Greece, or thought it any distinction to her? The whole cast of the Book, however, gave offence to Theodore, as injurious to Job, a godly man whose history was in every mouth and known far beyond the borders of Israel, and whose fame the Prophet (Ezekiel) had further enhanced. Hence he condemned alike the irreverent language put into Job's mouth, the unjust attacks made on him by his friends, and the injurious and insulting speeches of Elihu. The whole, in his opinion, gave a distorted view of Job's character, detracted from the moral value of his history, and gave occasion to blame not only the pious sufferer but also the Book[2]. Theodore, though not

[1] *Works*, Walch, xxii. p. 2093. The passage appears to exist under various forms.
[2] Kihn, *Theodor von Mopsuestia*, p. 68 *seq*.

without insight, as his rejection of the headings to the Psalms indicates, was apt to be hasty and narrow in his judgments. His views naturally compelled him to remove the Book of Job from the Canon. Though condemned as a heretic after his death, the censure does not seem to have fallen upon him for his critical opinions; he fell under suspicion from his exegetical writings, in which the seeds of the Nestorian heresy were detected, as some of the chief adherents of that error were his pupils and friends.

The comparatively free judgment of Luther regarding the Book naturally gave a handle to the Catholics which they were not slow to seize, and was not appreciated by Protestant writers in the succeeding ages. In his Commentary concerning the Antiquity, &c. of the History of Job (1670) Fred. Spanheim maintains that if Job be not history it is a fraud of the writer, *ni historia sit, fraus scriptoris.* Such a judgment would condemn as wilful frauds not only the majority of modern compositions but the dramas and parabolic writings of all ages. It is hard to see even how an exception could be made in favour of the parables of our Lord. Happily a juster conception of the nature of scripture now prevails, and we are prepared to find in it any form of literary composition which it is natural for men to employ. The view of Spanheim was shared by Albert Schultens, and defended by him in various writings, particularly in his great Commentary on Job (1736). Schultens was prepared to accept even the speeches of Job and his friends as literal transcriptions of what was said, appealing to the remarkable skill in improvising at all times exhibited by the Arabs and other Eastern peoples. The same opinion was maintained by J. H. Michaelis, professor at Halle (died 1738). According to him Job was descended from Nahor, and everything narrated in the Book is literal history, as taught in James v. 11—notwithstanding the Talmud, the Rabbins and Luther. The Patriarch lived between the death of Joseph and the Exodus; and the Book was written by Moses in Midian[1].

[1] *Adnotationes in Hagiog. Vet. Test. Libros*, vol. ii. p. 5 *seq.*; comp. Diestel, *Hist. of the O. T. in the Christian Church*, p. 417.

Yet even those times were not left without a witness in favour of different views. Grotius (died 1645) reproduced the opinion of Luther that the history in Job was poetically handled, *res vere gesta, sed poetice tractata*. And another Michaelis, John David, grand nephew of John Henry and the most distinguished of his name, professor of Oriental Languages at Goettingen (1750), expressed a judgment regarding Job very different from that of his older relative, and one which shews that critical opinions are scarcely subject to the law of heredity. According to him Job is a pure poetical creation : "I feel very little doubt that the subject of the poem is altogether fabulous, and designed to teach us that 'the rewards of virtue being in another state, it is very possible for the good to suffer afflictions in this life; but that, when it so happens, it is permitted by Providence for the wisest reasons, though they may not be obvious to human eyes[1].'" The rise in this age of the critical spirit, which indeed had been partially awakened to life in the preceding century by the publication of Richard Simon's *Critical History of the Old Testament* (1678), naturally led to free discussion of the Book and prepared the way for the comparatively unanimous verdict regarding it of modern times. The history of this discussion need not be pursued here. There are perhaps few scholars now who consider the Book strictly historical in all its parts. The prevailing view, which is no doubt just, is that it reposes on a historical tradition, which the author has used and embellished, and made the vehicle for conveying the moral instruction which it was his object to teach. There are still some, however, who regard the Poem as wholly the creation of the author's invention ; and this view is not confined to any critical school, for it numbers among its adherents men so widely apart from one another in their critical positions as Hengstenberg and Reuss.

That the Book is not literal history appears, (1) from the

---

[1] See his note in Gregory's *Trans. of Lowth on the Sacred Poetry of the Hebrews*, Lect. 32. Lowth himself (1753) adhered to the view of Luther and Grotius.

scenes in heaven exhibited in the Prologue (ch. i., ii.), and from the lengthy speeches put into the mouth of the Almighty (ch. xxxviii. *seq.*). (2) From the symbolical numbers three and seven used to describe Job's flocks and his children; and from the fact that his possessions are exactly doubled to him on his restoration, while he receives again seven sons and three daughters precisely as before. (3) From the dramatic and ideal nature of the account of the incidence of Job's calamities (ch. i. 13 *seq.*), where the forces of nature and the violence of men alternate in bringing ruin upon him, and in each case only one escapes to tell the tidings. (4) From the nature of the debate between Job and his friends. Both the thought and the highly-wrought imagery of the speeches shew that, so far from possibly being the extemporaneous utterances of three or four persons casually brought together, they could only be the leisurely production of a writer of the highest genius.

On the other hand, it is probable that the Book is not wholly poetical invention, but that it reposes upon a historical tradition, some of the elements of which it has preserved. (1) The allusion of the prophet Ezekiel to Job, where he mentions Noah, Daniel and Job (ch. xiv. 14), appears to be to a tradition regarding him rather than to the present Book. The prophet's knowledge of Daniel must have been derived from hearsay, for the present book of that name cannot have been known to him. And the manner of his allusion suggests that the fame for piety of the three men whom he names was traditional and widely celebrated. (2) Pure literary invention on so large a scale is scarcely to be looked for so early in Israel. Even considerably later the author of Ecclesiastes attaches his work to the name of Solomon; and later still the author of the book of Wisdom does the same. (3) The author of Job has a practical object in view. He does not occupy himself with discussing theories of providence that have only philosophic interest. He desires to influence the thought and the conduct of his generation. And this object would certainly have been better gained by making use of some history that lay slumbering in the popular mind, the lesson of which, when the story was awakened and set living before men, would commend itself more to the mind from not being altogether unfamiliar.

When we enquire, however, what elements of the Book really belong to the tradition, a definite answer can hardly be given. A tradition could scarcely exist which did not contain the name of the hero, and the name "Job" is no doubt historical. A mere name, however, could not be handed down without some circumstances connected with it; and we may assume that the outline of the tradition included Job's great prosperity, the unparalleled afflictions that befell him, and possibly also his restoration. Whether more was embraced may be uncertain. A vague report may have floated down that the mystery of Job's sufferings engaged the attention of the Wise of his country and formed the subject of discussion. It may also be argued that no reason can be suggested for making Uz the country of Job unless there was a tradition to that effect; and that the names of his friends, having nothing symbolical in them, must also belong to the story. This is doubtful. Eliphaz is an old Idumean name, and Teman was famed for wisdom; and "Eliphaz of Teman" might suggest literary combination. The other two names, not occurring again, do not awaken the same suspicions. They might be part of the tradition; but it is equally possible that they are names which the author had heard among the tribes outside of Israel. Even more liable to doubt is the episode of Job's wife, and the malady under which the Patriarch suffered. We can observe three threads running through the Book. One is that of the original tradition; another is the poetical embellishment of this tradition in the Prologue and Epilogue, Job being still treated as an individual. To this belong, for example, the names of Job's daughters, a touch of singular geniality from the hand of a writer who employs such sombre colours in the rest of the Book, and shewing that though crushed under the sorrows of his time he was not incapable on occasions of rising above them. In many places, however, Job appears to outgrow the limits of individual life; his mind and language reflect the situation and feelings of a class, or even of a people. He is the type either of the class of suffering righteous men, or of that afflicted, godly kernel of the people (Is. vi. 13), to which the nationality of Israel was felt still to adhere, and which is known in the Exile under the name of the Servant of the Lord. The history of this suffering remnant under the trials of the Exile has not been written; but that it had a history, marked by great trials and great faith, commanding the attention and kindling the enthusiasm of prophetic men, appears abundantly from the latter part of the Book of Isaiah. It is not easy to say with any certainty to which of these three elements any particular episode or point in the Book ought to be referred. The story of Job's wife may be thought to be just the kind of trait which the popular imagination would retain, or what is the same thing, which it would invent; the inference being that it should be considered part of the tradition. On the other hand, it is possible that her falling away under her sorrows may be but the reflection of the apostasy of many of the people under their trials, the sight of which put so severe a strain upon the faith of those still remaining true. And when we read in Deuteronomy, "The Lord will smite thee with the botch of Egypt...the Lord shall smite thee in the knees and in the legs, with a sore botch that cannot be healed, from the sole of thy foot unto the top of thy head" (ch. xxviii. 27, 35), and then in Job that Satan "went forth and smote Job with sore boils, from the sole of his foot unto his crown" (ch. ii. 7); and when further we find in Isaiah (ch. lii.—liii.) the Servant of the Lord represented as afflicted with leprous defilement, the impression can hardly be resisted that the three representations are connected together. Even in Deuteronomy the threat has ideal elements in it; in the Prophet the representation becomes wholly ideal; and the same is probably the case also in the Poet. In Deuteronomy the subject threatened is the people of Israel; in Isaiah the subject is the same, though with the modifications which history since the Exile had introduced, being the godly kernel of the people in captivity, to which the nationality and name and idea of Israel still belonged. And though we may not go so far as to say that Job is Israel or the Servant of the Lord under another name, it can scarcely be doubted that the sufferings of Israel are reflected in those of Job, and that the author designed that the people should see their own features in his, and from his history forecast the issue of their own. These are considerations that make us hesitate to regard Job's malady as part of the tradition regarding him, even though that view be supported by names so distinguished as that of Ewald.

The Book of Job has been called an Epic by some, by others a Drama, or more specifically a Tragedy, and by others still a Didactic Poem. That the Poem has a didactic purpose is unquestionable. It is equally evident that it contains many elements of the drama, such as dialogue, and a plot with an entanglement, development and solution. The action, however, is internal and mental, and the successive scenes are representations of the varying moods of a great soul struggling with the mysteries of its fate, rather than trying external situations. Much in the action may rightly be called tragic, but the happy conclusion is at variance with the conception of a proper tragedy. Any idea of representing his work on a stage never crossed the author's mind; his object was to instruct his countrymen and inspire them with hope in the future, and it is nothing to him that he detracts from the artistic effect of his work by revealing beforehand in the Prologue the real cause of Job's afflictions, the problem which is the subject of the dialogue, and the cause of the successive tragic phases of Job's feeling, in which the action chiefly consists. A more skilful artist according to western ideas might have concealed the explanation of Job's afflictions till the end, allowing it to transpire perhaps in the speeches of the Almighty. If he had allowed God to explain to Job the meaning of the sufferings with which He afflicted him, whatever addition to his literary renown he might have won, the author would have shewn himself much less wise and true as a religious teacher, for the experience of men tells them that they do not reach religious peace through the theoretical solution of the problems of providence; the theoretical solution comes later, if it comes at all, through their own reflection upon their history and the way in which God has led them. And if Job ever knew the meaning of his afflictions he learned it in this way, or he learned it through the teaching of some other man wiser than himself, as we have learned it from the author of this Book.

The Book of Job can hardly be named a drama, though it may justly be called dramatic. The dramatic movement is seen in the varying moods of Job's mind, and in his attitude towards Heaven. The dialogue with his friends partly occasions these moods and partly exhibits them. The progressive advance of the debate, however, is not to be considered as constituting the dramatic action. The commencement, culmination, and exhaustion of the debate do not run parallel with the rise, the increase and climax, and the composure of Job's perplexity of mind and war with Heaven. It is in the latter that the dramatic movement lies, in which the debate is a mere episode, for the state of Job's mind, twice signalised in the Prologue, lies before it, and the perfect composure to which he is brought by the divine speeches lies far behind it. Such a representation therefore as that of Delitzsch can hardly be accepted, who says "the Book of Job is substantially a drama, and one consisting of seven divisions: (1) ch. i.—iii., the opening; (2) ch. iv.—xiv., the first course of the controversy, or the beginning of entanglement; (3) ch. xv—xxi., the second course of the controversy, or the increasing entanglement; (4) ch. xxii.—xxvi., the third course of the controversy, or the increasing entanglement at its highest; (5) ch. xxvii.—xxxi., the transition from the entanglement to the unravelling; (6) ch. xxxviii.—xlii. 6, the consciousness of the unravelling; (7) ch. xlii. 7 *seq.*, the unravelling in outward reality".[1] This representation confuses two things quite distinct, and which do not move parallel to one another, namely the gradual thickening of the conflict between Job and his friends, ending at last in their directly imputing heinous offences to him, and the religious tension of Job's mind under his trials. It is not till the last round that the climax of the debate is reached (ch. xxii.), but the perplexity and violence of Job attain their height in the first round (ch. ix.—x.). Already in ch. xiv. the strain is considerably relieved, and it decreases still more in the speeches culminating in ch. xix., being wholly removed by the interposition of the Almighty.

[1] *Trans.* i. p. 15.

CHAPTER III.

THE IDEA AND PURPOSE OF THE BOOK.

THE Book of Job, as we possess it, conveys the impression that it is a finished and well-rounded composition. Its form, Prologue, Poem and Epilogue, suggests that the writer had a clear idea before his mind, which he started, developed and brought to an issue in a way satisfactory to himself. The Book has not the appearance of a mere fragment, or what might be called a contribution to the ventilation of a great problem, on which the author feels that he has something that may be useful to say, though nothing very definite or final; although this is a view of the Book that some have taken. The author being assumed, however, to have a distinct idea, this idea still remains so obscure, and the question, What is the purpose of the Book? has been answered in so many ways, that a judgment regarding it must be put forth with the greatest diffidence. Almost every theory that has been adopted has found itself in collision with one or more of the parts of which the Book now consists, and has been able to maintain itself only by sacrificing these parts upon its altar. With the exception of the speeches of Elihu there is no great division of the Book to which valid objections can be made, except on the ground that it does not harmonise with the idea of the Poem. The Elihu speeches occupy their right place between the discourses of the friends and the answer of Jehovah. They maintain the ground of the former, though they perhaps advance and refine upon it; and they prepare for the speeches of the Almighty, being the expression from the reverent religious consciousness of man of that which the Almighty expresses, if such language may be used, from His own consciousness of Himself. Whether, therefore, these speeches be held original or considered a later insertion they import no new principle into the Book, and may be neglected when the general conception of the Poem is being sought for. It seems fair, however, to take into account all the remaining divisions of the Book.

1. Though the author of the Book does not identify himself with Job, whom, on the contrary, he allows to assume positions which are extreme, and to utter language which is unbecoming, Job is undoubtedly the hero of the piece, and in the sentiments which he expresses and the history which he passes through combined, we may assume that we find the author himself speaking and teaching. Even the exaggerated sentiments which he allows Job to utter are not to be considered mere extravagances; they are not incoherencies which Job flings out in one line, and retracts in the next; they are excesses, which men under trials such as he suffered are driven to commit, and with which the author, amidst the questionings in regard to providence which the terrible sufferings of the time forced on men, was no doubt too familiar, if he had not himself perhaps fallen into them; and as we observe Job's mind gradually and naturally approaching the state in which he commits them, so we see it naturally recovering its balance and effecting a retreat. The discussion of the question of suffering between Job and his friends runs through a large part of the Book (ch. iv.—xxxi.), and in the direction which the author causes the discussion to take we may see revealed one of the chief didactic purposes of the Poem. When the three friends, the representatives of former theories of providence, are reduced to silence and driven off the ground by Job (ch. xxi. xxiii., xxiv.), we may assume that it was the author's purpose to discredit the ideas which they support. The theory that sin and suffering are in all cases connected, and that suffering cannot be where there has not been previous sin to account for the measure of it, is a theory of providence which cannot be harmonised with the facts observed in the world. Job traverses this theory on both its sides. He himself is an instance of suffering apart from previous sin; and the world is full of examples of notoriously wicked men prospering and being free from trouble till the day of their death. Job offers no positive contribution to the doctrine of evil; his position is negative, and merely antagonistic to that of his friends. Now without doubt in all this he is the mouthpiece of the author of the Book.

Is it natural now to suppose that the author contemplated only this negative result? Would he have thought his task sufficiently fulfilled by pulling down the old fabric under which men had found friendly shelter and comfort for ages, and strewing its ruins on the ground, without supplying anything in its place, beyond perhaps the good advice which he is supposed to give in ch. xxxviii. *seq.*? So far as the rest of the Poem is concerned no further light is cast on the question. Job is left in darkness, and the divine speeches do not touch the point. The author exhibits Job reaching the conclusion that the righteousness of God, as he in common with his friends had always understood it, cannot be detected in the world as God actually rules it. And he exhibits the terrible perplexity into which the discovery threw him. To miss God's righteousness in the world was equivalent to missing it in God Himself, and Job's idea of God threatened to become wholly transformed. He is filled with terror and despair, and in his wrestling with the question he forces his way across the confines of this world, and first demands (ch. xiv., xvi.—xvii.) and then assures himself (ch. xix.) that, if not in his life here, beyond his life here, God's righteousness shall be manifested. By allowing Job to rise to such a thought the author probably meant to signalise it as one of the solutions to which men or himself had been forced. But the time was not yet come, and the darkness that overhung all beyond this life was too thick for men to find repose in this great thought. Hence Job is made to renew his demand for a solution in this life of the riddle of his sufferings (ch. xxxi. 35—37). Does then the author offer no solution? He does not, and no solution is offered to us, unless the Prologue supplies it. This passage, however, when naturally read, teaches that Job's sufferings were the trial of his righteousness. If then we bring the Prologue and the debate into combination we perceive that it was the author's purpose to widen men's views of God's providence, and to set before them a new view of suffering. With great skill he employs Job as his instrument to clear the ground of the old theories, and he himself brings forward in their place his new truth, that sufferings may befall the innocent, and be not a chastisement for their sins but a trial of their righteousness.

This may be considered one great purpose of the Book. This purpose, however, was in all probability no mere theoretical one, but subordinate to some wider practical design. No Hebrew writer is merely a poet or thinker. He is always a teacher. He has men before him in their relations to God. And it is not usually men in their individual relations, but as members of the family of Israel, the people of God. It is consequently scarcely to be doubted that the Book has a national scope. The author considered his new truth regarding the meaning of affliction as of national interest, and to be the truth needful to comfort and uphold the heart of his people in the circumstances in which they were.

2. But the direct teaching of the Book is only half its contents. It presents also a history—deep and inexplicable affliction, a great moral struggle, and a victory. Must not this history also be designed to teach? Is it not a kind of apologue the purpose of which is to inspire new conduct, new faith, and new hopes? In Job's sufferings undeserved and inexplicable to him, yet capable of an explanation most consistent with the goodness and faithfulness of God, and casting honour upon His faithful servants; in his despair bordering upon apostasy, at last overcome; in the higher knowledge of God and deeper humility to which he attained, and in the happy issue of his afflictions—in all these Israel may see itself, and from the sight take courage, and forecast its own history. What the author sets before his people is a new reading of their history, just as another new reading is set before them by the Prophet in the latter part of Isaiah. The two readings are different, but both speak to the heart of the people. Job, however, is scarcely to be considered Israel, under a feigned name. He is not Israel, though Israel may see itself and its history reflected in him. It is the elements of reality in his history common to him with Israel in affliction, common even to him with humanity as a whole, confined within the straitened limits set by its own ignorance; wounded to death by the mysterious sorrows of life; tortured by the un-

certainty whether its cry finds an entrance into God's ear; alarmed and paralysed by the irreconcileable discrepancies which it discovers between its necessary thoughts of Him and its experience of Him in his providence; and faint with longing that it might come unto His place, and behold Him not girt with His majesty but in human form, as one looketh upon his fellow—it is these elements of truth that make the history of Job instructive to the people of Israel in the times of affliction when it was set before them, and to men in all ages[1].

The manifold theories of the purpose of the Book that have been put forth cannot be mentioned here. The construction of Ewald, brilliant and powerful though it be, has not been accepted by any other writer. Bleek, unable to find any single idea giving unity to the Book, contents himself with stating three truths which the Book appears to teach. (1) That even a pious man may be visited by God with heavy and manifold afflictions without it being necessary to consider these as punishment on account of special sinfulness and as a sign of special divine displeasure; that it is wrong to reproach such a one with his sufferings as if they had their origin in the divine displeasure, seeing they may rather be inflicted or permitted by God in order that his piety may be tried and find suitable opportunity of approving itself (Prologue). (2) That it is foolish presumption on the part of men to strive with God on account of the sufferings befalling them, and to seek to call Him to a reckoning, seeing no man is in a position to fathom the wisdom and counsel of God, man's true wisdom being rather to fear the Lord and eschew evil (Poem). (3) That Jehovah will at last surely have compassion on the pious sufferer and bless and glorify him, if he perseveres in his piety and cleaves to God, or if, having transgressed in his impatience, he repents (Epilogue)[2].

An attractive theory, in some degree a modification of that of Hupfeld and others, has more recently been put forth by some acute writers in Holland. It is to the effect that the author's

---

[1] *Encyclop. Britann.* Art. "Job."
[2] Introduction, 4 Ed. p. 534, Trans. ii. p. 277.

design is merely to cast some light upon an acknowledged *problem*. The problem is the sufferings of the innocent—how they are to be reconciled with the righteousness of God. This problem is presented in the Prologue, which exhibits a righteous man subjected to great calamities. The Prologue gives no explanation of these calamities; Job's demeanour under his successive troubles merely shews his rectitude: here is undoubtedly a righteous man. In Job's person the problem is embodied and presented. Even the debate between him and his friends has no further effect or purpose than to set the problem in a strong light. The friends attempt an explanation of Job's afflictions, and if they had succeeded the problem would have been at an end. By their failure it is only seen more clearly to be a problem. Job contributes no solution, but his perplexity and despair and danger of apostasy shew how terrible the problem is. The whole point of the Book, therefore, lies in the divine speeches. All the rest is mere fact, or brilliant exhibition of a fact, that there is a terrible problem. The divine speeches do not solve the problem, for the problem is insoluble, but they give some satisfaction: they teach why it is insoluble, namely, because God and His ways are inscrutable. They say in effect two things: man cannot do what God does; and he cannot understand why He does what He does. And the conclusion is that nothing remains for him but acquiescence in the unsearchable providence of God. This is the great lesson which the author designed to teach his generation and mankind[1].

There are difficulties in the way of this theory. 1. Besides that the line of thought found in the Book is rather modern, the reader has difficulty in believing that the author's purpose went no further than to present a problem, pronounce it insoluble, and recommend resignation. 2. The reading of the Prologue which finds in its language no *explanation* of Job's afflictions is unnatural; and this reading of it leaves the function of the Satan entirely unexplained, who becomes a mere "evil spirit",

---

[1] Kuenen, *Onderzoek*, III. 125. More fully and genially Matthes in his excellent commentary, *Het Boek Job*, Deel I.

in no connexion with the providence of God. 3. According to this theory Job's afflictions narrated in the Prologue, and these are all his afflictions, have merely the purpose of shewing his righteousness, which only comes to light by them. But in this way the author becomes guilty of a strange inconsequence. He meant to put forward the terrible problem of the sufferings of a righteous man; but these sufferings were necessary to shew that the man was righteous, and thus they are explained, and there is no problem. 4. The reading of the divine speeches is narrow and not natural. 5. The epilogue is an irrelevancy, or hangs in the loosest way to the Poem. It is added merely because "poetic justice" demanded it, or because the author "could not" let his hero die in misery, or for some similar sentimental reason.

CHAPTER IV.

The Integrity of the Book.

WITH the exception of the speeches of Elihu there is none of the five great divisions of the Book (Introd. ch. i.) against which, as a whole, serious objection can be brought, though some portions of the second and fourth divisions may be liable to doubt. The idea or purpose of the Poem has been very differently understood, and objections to particular parts of the Book have generally arisen from the feeling that these parts were not in harmony with the idea of the author as the main body of the Poem revealed it. One of the latest writers on the Book has found it necessary to amputate every limb from the Poem, leaving it a mere trunk, consisting of ch. iii.—xxxi., and even this trunk is so misshapen that its shoulders are found in the region of its bowels[1].

---

[1] Studer, who brings forward ch. xxix. xxx. to the beginning of the Poem.

1. *The Prologue and Epilogue.*

It may be remarked in general that without some introduction the discussion between Job and his friends would not have been intelligible, just as without some conclusion such as the Epilogue the Poem would have been left in a condition very unsatisfactory and incomplete. Some introduction and conclusion must have accompanied the Poem, and there is no evidence or probability that any others, different from those now found, ever existed.

1. Several of the objections urged against the Prologue and Epilogue are of no weight, such as the following: that the Prologue and Epilogue are written in prose, while the body of the Book is poetry; that the name Jehovah is employed in the Prologue while other names are used in the Poem; and that sacrifices are referred to in the Prologue and Epilogue but never in the body of the Book.

All narrative in Hebrew is in prose. The author writes in prose when introducing the speakers even in the body of the Poem, e.g. ch. xxxviii. 1. Even in the episode of Elihu the passage of some length (ch. xxxii. 1—5) which brings that speaker upon the stage is prose. As to the divine names, the author, an Israelite, employs the name usual in Israel; the speakers whom he introduces, belonging to the patriarchal time, use the divine names more current then. That this is part of the antique disguise maintained by the author appears from his allowing the name Jehovah to escape from Job's mouth on more than one occasion (ch. i. 21, xii. 9), and from his own use of this name even in the Poem when introducing a new speaker (ch. xxxviii. 1). The sacrifice referred to in the Prologue and Epilogue is the patriarchal burnt-offering, and that Job himself offers it is in keeping with the usages of that early time. There is no evidence that the Prologue has a more ritualistic colour than the Poem, for even in the Poem priests (ch. xii. 19) and vows (xxii. 27) are referred to.

2. Hardly of more consequence is the averment that the Prologue and Epilogue are in disagreement with the Poem.

first, in regard to Job's children, whom the Prologue represents as perishing, while in the Poem they are spoken of as alive; and secondly, in regard to the Almighty's treatment of Job, whom He commends in the Epilogue, but severely blames in the Poem.

Not only in the Prologue but twice in the Poem Job's sons are referred to as having perished (ch. viii. 4, xxix. 5). The passage ch. xix. 17 is of doubtful meaning (see notes). Even if we felt compelled to assume that the children of Job's body there referred to were his sons, the writer would merely be guilty of an inconsequence (no great matter in a Poem which is not strict history), no inference could be drawn against the originality of the Prologue, because the same argument would remove two chapters from the Poem.

The Lord blames Job in the Poem (ch. xxxviii. *seq.*) and commends him in the Epilogue (ch. xlii. 7). But He does not blame and applaud him at once and for the same reason. In the speeches out of the storm Job is reproved for the irreverence towards God into which he had been betrayed; and in the Epilogue he is commended for perceiving that the theory upheld by the three friends was no true theory of God's providence as it is in fact administered, and for maintaining at all hazards and under every obloquy what he perceived to be the truth. Neither is there any weight in the allegation that Job's unsubmissive behaviour in the Poem contradicts what is said of his godly patience in the Prologue. Job is able to exhibit pious resignation to the will of God on the first incidence of his calamities, but under the prolonged agony of his sufferings and in the sympathising presence of his friends he loses his self-control and breaks out into a despairing cry for death. The transition from the one mood to the other is made in the most natural manner.

3. Of more importance is the objection that the doctrine of the Satan in the Prologue belongs to an age later than that to which the Poem can be referred.

It is very difficult to say to what age the Poem ought to be referred. It is true that the name, the Satan, occurs here for the first time; that in 1 Kings xxii. 19, where a scene in heaven somewhat similar to that in the Prologue is presented, mention is made only of "the spirit"; and that in Zech. iii., a post-exile writing, where the name again occurs, the Adversary performs a part very similar to that which he plays in Job, and probably the two books do not stand at a very great distance from one another. There is, however, a certain difference between the representations in Job and Zechariah. In the prophet the Satan appears in somewhat darker colours, and in somewhat stronger opposition to the merciful purposes of God in regard to men; hence while in Job he is merely reproached by God for setting Him on against His servant, he is rebuked by Him in Zechariah. We must be careful not to impose upon the Book of Job or this prophet conceptions belonging to a more advanced period. The Satan of these books is no mere "evil spirit," the real enemy of God though His unwilling subject. There is no antagonism between God and the Satan. The idea that the "attacks of Satan are aimed primarily at the honour of God"; that his purpose is to deny that God is "ever disinterestedly served and sincerely loved by any being whatever"; and that "the object of the trial of Job is precisely to demonstrate to him the contrary[1]"—such an idea is altogether at variance with Old Testament conceptions. The Satan is the servant of God, representing or carrying out His trying, sifting providence, and the opposer of men *because* he is the minister of God; hence Job's afflictions, represented as inflicted by the Satan in one place, are spoken of as due to the hand of God in another, "thou hast set me on against him to destroy him" (ch. ii. 3), just as Job's friends "came to condole with him over all the evil which the Lord had brought upon him" (ch. xlii. 11), and of course everywhere in the Poem the Almighty is assumed to be the author of Job's calamities both by the sufferer and his friends. The angels and Satan among them are the ministers of God's providence. The Satan being the minister of God's trying providence, which is often administered by means of afflictions, it was an easy step to take to endow him with the spirit of

---

[1] Godet, *Biblical Studies*, p. 229.

hostility to man which such afflictions seemed to reflect. This step is taken in the Book, though not very decidedly. It was another and natural step to take, though in a somewhat different direction, to represent him as acting in opposition to the gracious mind of God towards men. This is little more than if a conflict had been imagined between God's attribute of mercy and His resolution to try. A movement towards this step is made in Job, and a certain further advance in the direction is observable in Zechariah. But all this is very far short of a conflict between God and Satan. The Satan is a mere instrument in the economy of God's providence, and though represented as a person, his personal standing is only of the slightest consequence. Hence he does not appear in the Epilogue. His part was, in the service of God, to try Job; that done he disappears, having no place assigned to him among the *dramatis personæ* of the Poem. There is nothing, therefore, in this conception of the Satan which implies a very late age, or which brings the Prologue into disagreement with the Poem.

4. It is objected to the Prologue that it gives an explanation of Job's calamities, while no such explanation is known in the Poem, being alluded to neither in the divine speeches nor those of any other speaker, nor yet even in the Epilogue; and that in fact the idea of an explanation of calamities such as Job's is opposed to the whole drift of the divine speeches, which teach that God's ways are inscrutable, and instead of offering an explanation to man demand from him submission and faith.

It is evident that this objection hangs by a particular conception of the idea or purpose of the Book. This idea is assumed to be revealed in the speeches of the Almighty, for no doubt the author puts into the mouth of the highest speaker the ultimate truth; and this truth is considered to be that just stated, namely, that God's ways are incomprehensible, and that man must believe in His righteousness though he cannot perceive it, and find refuge from his doubts in faith. But first, this reading of the meaning of the divine speeches is certainly not natural; they have a broader purpose than to teach that God's providence is inscrutable, or what does Job mean when he says,

"Now mine eye seeth thee"? Does he mean that now he saw Him to be wholly incomprehensible? Secondly, the fact that in the Epilogue, which no one has ever doubted to come from the same hand as the Prologue, no reference is made to the cause of Job's calamities, is a warning against making much of the silence of Job or the other speakers. How could they refer to the cause of Job's sufferings of which they were entirely ignorant, and when their ignorance was the very condition of their disputing the question? The explanation of Job's calamities is the secret of the author alone, and is the truth which he erects on the ruins of the old theory of providence, which he causes Job to demolish. And if Job's afflictions were a trial of his righteousness, it belongs to the very idea of a trial that he should be in perplexity why he is afflicted. And thirdly, it would have been altogether unbecoming that God should enter upon a discussion of His particular providences with Job, and contrary to His manner of teaching men, which is not to communicate immediate intellectual light to them, but to fill their minds with such a sense of Himself that even amidst the darkness they will take their right place before Him. The object of the divine speeches is not primarily to teach, but to impress. The panorama of creation brings before Job's mind so vividly what God is that he feels he now "sees" Him, and the sight leads him back to the position which he had been able to maintain at the end of each of his first trials; or perhaps with his higher knowledge of God and his deeper humility now attained his position was securer than before.

5. It is objected to the Epilogue that it is in contradiction with the Poem, because in crowning Job with a double prosperity the author falls back into the old doctrine of retribution, the falsehood of which is demonstrated in the Poem.

The author, however, does not desire to question the general doctrine of retribution, but to shew that there are cases or at least one case which it does not explain. He desires to add another explanation of afflictions to those existing.

If the drama be the trial of the righteous, the author must bring it to some conclusion. Job's faith projected a vindication for himself after death, but it was impossible for the author, even if he had wished, to bring this to view. Such an idea as that which we now possess of "heaven" did not exist in his day. In the consummation of the Church's history, when God and His people are in perfect fellowship, they are not translated into heaven to be with God, God comes down to earth and abides with men. The author had no stage for concluding his drama on the "other side." The most that the efforts of pious spirits had attained in his day was in occasional flights of faith to pierce the darkness beyond this life, and assure themselves that their life with God here should not be interrupted there. But there was no such clearness of knowledge as to afford room for a scene between God and the pious soul. Job presented such a scene to himself as a necessity, because he was assured that he should die under his malady. The religious truth contained in Job's anticipation the author causes to be realized, though he does it on this side of death.

Moreover, though Job be an individual, he is more than an individual. The national history reflects itself in his. And his restoration, if it was to set forth that of the people, must be to worldly prosperity.

2. *The Passage ch. xxvii. 7—ch. xxviii.*

This passage has been the source of great perplexity to commentators. The difficulties in connexion with it are two: first, to reconcile the sentiments expressed by Job in these two chapters with those expressed by him both before this passage and after it; and secondly, to discover any link of connexion between chaps. xxvii. and xxviii. On the one hand, while no doubt the state of Job's feeling towards God fluctuates, or rather gradually changes, he consistently maintains throughout the same view of providence and the same opinion as to the issue of his own afflictions, and to impute to him contradictory extravagances, or as one writer says even "incoherences," on these two points is out of the question. On the other hand, the reader is very averse to entertain the idea of a later addition to the Book at this point;

any way of overcoming the difficulties that is possible is to be preferred.

In ch. xxvii. 11 *seq.* Job undertakes to *teach* his friends regarding the fate of the wicked what they had always affirmed; and in giving them this lesson he entirely retracts what he had formerly said in regard to the prosperity of the wicked till their death, and expresses himself in a way which implies that at the moment he takes a view of his own sufferings different from the view taken by him both before this chapter and after it.

Three solutions of the difficulty have been proposed: (1) It has been thought that the speeches in this part of the book have suffered some dislocation, and that the passage in ch. xxvii., now attributed to Job, is really the missing third speech of Zophar. (2) Others think that in this passage Job is not expressing his own sentiments, but parodying or representing those of his friends, —" Why are ye thus altogether vain, *saying*, This is the portion of the wicked man with God" &c. (ch. xxvii. 12 *seq.*). (3) The passage is a later insertion into the Book.

It may be confidently said that if the passage do not express the proper sentiments of Job there is no alternative but to consider it a later addition, from ch. xxvii. 7 onwards. For as to (1), although the argument that the party addressed here is spoken to in the *plural* while Job is always addressed in the singular[1], may not go for much, as the statement is not quite exact (ch. xviii. 2—3, xxxv. 4), the brevity of the speech put into Bildad's mouth (ch. xxv.) shews that the author designed to indicate that the arguments on the side of the friends were exhausted; and therefore another reply from Zophar is not to be expected. This natural exhaustion of the controversy is what brings it to an end, not any modification of his views by Job, without which it has been said that it might have gone on for ever[2]. The dispute on the side of the friends comes to an end because they can find nothing more to urge against Job—such at least Elihu understands to be the state of the case (ch. xxxii. 5); and it comes to

---

[1] Kuenen, *Onderzoek*, III. 143.
[2] Umbreit, quoted with approval by Delitzsch.

an end *before* Job makes the modification which he is understood to make, for the place left vacant by the missing reply of Zophar lies between chaps. xxvi. and xxvii.

Then as to (2). The assumption that Job is here reciting the theories of his friends is supposed both to remove the difficulty of the language ch. xxvii. 13 *seq.*, and to afford a connexion with ch. xxviii., which then attaches itself to the words, " I will teach you concerning the hand of God " (ch. xxvii. 11-12). There is nothing, however, in the passage to suggest that the sentiments are not those of the speaker himself. On the contrary, when he undertakes to teach concerning the hand of God, it cannot be doubted that the following verses contain the lesson, namely, God's way of dealing with the wicked. If *vv.* 11-12 be connected with ch. xxviii. the teaching must be sought in that chapter. But there is really no teaching regarding the " hand " of God in ch. xxviii., though much regarding the ingenuity of men. The intermediate passage, ch. xxvii. 13—23, hides the incongruity of this view; but if these verses be removed and ch. xxviii. read in connexion with ch. xxvii. 11—12, what Job says to his friends is this: "I will teach you regarding the hand of God! —It is simply incomprehensible"!

In regard to (3) these remarks may suffice :—

1. Job's protestation of innocence, ch. xxvii. 2—6, is quite in place, but the connexion between *vv.* 2—6 and *v.* 7 *seq.* appears loose, and the change of *tone* in the two passages is difficult to account for (see on ch. xxvii. 7).

2. The meaning suggested by *vv.* 7—10 is difficult to reconcile with the condition of Job at this stage of his history, or with the view which he takes of the meaning of his afflictions, and of the certain issue of them, both before and after the present chapter (see on ch. xxvii. 10—12).

3. The supposition is made by most writers that in ch. xxvii. 13 *seq.* Job is modifying his former extravagant expressions regarding the wicked, and conceding that *as a rule* they come to a disastrous end at the hand of God. The limitation, however, " as a rule " under which the passage has to be read is conveyed into it; the language is as absolute as that of Zophar or any of the three.

Besides, far too much is made of the extravagances of Job. He has really nothing to retract *except* his unbecoming words in regard to God (ch. xl. 3—5, xlii. 1—6). He never said anything so absurd as that the wicked were always happy, it was enough for his purpose to give instances of their happiness. His contention from beginning to end, stated with perfect plainness, ch. xxi. 22 *seq.*, and ch. xxiv. 1 with the illustrations that follow, was that in God's rule of the world no clear distinction was to be observed between the lot of the righteous and that of the wicked. And it is the undoubted purpose of the author to allow Job successfully to maintain this contention. The consideration urged so universally that Job, though here modifying his former extreme statements about the felicity of the wicked, abates not one jot of his own claim to rectitude, is rather beside the point. It is not Job altogether but the author of Job with whom we have to do. Job is merely his instrument, and he has used him with the advance of the dispute to raise a much more general question than that involved in his own case, namely, the question of God's providence on the whole as it is observed in the lot of men. Job's innocence is merely one key of the situation, the prosperity of the wicked is the other; and it is highly improbable that the author should allow Job to evacuate either of his positions, for it is the maintenance of these very positions to which he sets the seal of God's approval in the Epilogue (ch. xlii. 7 *seq.*).

Even assuming that Job should desire to modify his former language in regard to the wicked, his modification is now more exaggerated on the one side than his former statements were on the other. He is to the full

as extreme in submission
As in offence.

Ewald puts in a caution against taking the words "too slavishly." But this representation of Job as indulging first on one side in extravagant language, which he retracts only to indulge in language more extravagant on the opposite side, can scarcely be true to the author's conception. In addition, the language of ch. xxvii. 13 *seq.* presents what might be called a psychological difficulty. When describing the fate of the wicked at God's hand, Job uses the same figures and even the same words as he employs when speaking of his own destruction by God (see on ch. xxvii. 21 *seq.*). There is something unlikely in this.

On the other hand, two things must be remembered: first, there is nothing in the literary character of the passage which suggests another speaker than Job; and second, it was not the author's design to deny the doctrine of the retributive righteousness of God out and out, and he might have allowed Job to modify his statements.

Ch. xxviii. suggests some points for reflexion, apart from its loose connexion with ch. xxvii.

1. The Poet appears more conscious of his art here than the author of the preceding chapters has hitherto shewn himself to be, and we have a daintier piece of work from his hand than any we have yet met with. Job's fierce moral earnestness, too, seems to have deserted him; he is diverted by the activities and ingenuities of mankind, while before he was fascinated by the overwhelming thought of God, and spoke of man chiefly as God's terrible power exhibited itself upon him (ch. ix., xii. and often).

2. The meaning of the speaker here can be no other than that stated in the notes, namely that to understand the principles that rule in the world and the histories of men is beyond the reach of man's mind. Man has his wisdom, which is to fear the Lord; that Wisdom, which is comprehension of the world, is beyond him. This is very unlike the spirit of Job. He shews no such contentment in the face of the problems of his history. He demands knowledge. He is a chained eagle, who spreads his wings and dashes himself against the bars of his cage; he would soar unto God's place and pluck the mystery out of the darkness (ch. xxiii. 3). And, though with less of passion, this continues to be his temper to the end (ch. xxxi. 35 *seq.*). That he should here acquiesce in the incomprehensibility of God's way and a little further on again demand to comprehend it is very strange.

3. Such a subdued and reflective frame of mind at this stage

anticipates the effect produced by the manifestation of God and His words on Job (ch. xxxviii. *seq.*), and it is hardly to be thought that the author would have allowed him to descend from his previous agitation into such calm apart from the influence of the Almighty's interposition. Besides, the passage seems to go beyond the teaching of the divine speeches, for these hardly contain the formal doctrine of the inscrutableness of God's ways, though they teach that submission to God is due from men even when they cannot comprehend them. And there is another point. The ironical tone of the divine speeches is unsuitable if adopted towards one in the frame of the speaker in this chapter. This tone is hard enough to understand in any case, but it is doubly hard if assumed towards one who avows with such devoutness his intellectual bankruptcy.

After all the efforts that have been made to relieve the difficulties of these two chapters they still to a considerable extent remain.

3. *The Speeches of Elihu.*

A brief review of these speeches is necessary in order to understand the reasons that have been adduced for believing that the passage does not belong to the original cast of the Book. There are three points that require to be looked at: (1) the motive which Elihu has for speaking; (2) the position which he takes towards the three friends and their doctrine; and (3) the position which he takes towards Job and his sentiments.

(1.) That which moves Elihu to speak and the purpose he has in his discourses are described by the writer who introduces him, and repeated by himself. The three friends left off speaking because Job was right in his own eyes: they could not move him from his assertion that God afflicted him wrongly. Therefore the anger of Elihu was kindled against both Job and his friends—against Job because he made himself in the right at the expense of the rectitude of God; and against the friends because they had allowed themselves to be silenced, and had failed to convict Job of the wrong of which he was guilty against God. In other words, indignation at the position towards God which Job had assumed was what moved Elihu to speak, and of course the purpose of his speech was to shew Job to be in the wrong. His anger against the friends arose simply from their failing to do what they ought to have done. He was disappointed in their arguments; he had looked for something better from their gray hairs. He does not appear to express dissatisfaction with them on any other ground. Hence, after giving vent to his indignation that "they found no answer to condemn Job" (ch. xxxii. 3), that "there was no answer in the mouth of these three men" (ch. xxxii. 5, 12), and his astonishment that they had allowed themselves to be silenced by Job (ch. xxxii. 15), and after excusing himself for venturing to let his youthful voice be heard among such venerable counsellors (ch. xxxii. 6 *seq.*), he no more alludes to them. His contention is with Job alone, and his purpose is to justify God against his unbecoming charges.

Elihu is of a very devout nature; his reverence of God and awe and fear before Him are very great. It is this feeling that makes him come forward to meet the assertions of Job: he "will ascribe right to his Maker" (ch. xxxvi. 3). The irreverence of Job shocks him; the hardihood with which he confronts the Almighty marks him out to his mind as the most godless of men—"who is a man like Job, drinking in scorning like water"? (ch. xxxiv. 5—7). This feeling is not strange, for undoubtedly the speeches of Job exceed in boldness almost anything that has ever been written (ch. vii., ix—x). To judge Job fairly, it is true, his other expressions of ineradicable faith in God must be taken into account. But these being allowed their due weight, his language still remains an offence to reverent feeling. How much it does so in our own day may be inferred from the painful assiduity with which it is toned down in modern commentaries. This reverent sensitiveness in regard to God constitutes the chief charm of Elihu's speeches, and the Book would be decidedly poorer for the want of them. At the same time the contrast between it and the spirit of Job's speeches, in which the human conscience asserts its equality with God or even its superiority over Him, may suggest a doubt whether both conceptions be the creation of the same author. It is in this spirit of reverence that Elihu addresses himself to the refutation of Job's charges. Hence he usually meets them first by an appeal to that which is "becoming" God, to the common reverent thoughts of Him inherent in the human mind. To Job's assertion that God displayed an arbitrary hostility to him, he replies, "Nay, God is greater than man"; "God is great and despiseth not any" (ch. xxxiii. 12; xxxvi. 5, cf. xxxvi. 24—25, xxxvii. 24). But his whole contention with Job is in defence of God's righteousness against his imputations. Having this great general object before him, Elihu does not enter much into Job's circumstances. He makes a general question out of Job's complaints, which he argues on general considerations. This is particularly the case in his first three speeches (see the headings to ch. xxxiii. xxxiv. xxxv.); it is only in the last that his argument assumes a more directly practical tone.

(2.) So far as Elihu's relation to the three friends is concerned, it is not easy to find any great difference between his conceptions and theirs, or almost any difference whatever in principle; and when his sharp censure of the friends is considered this apparent agreement with them in principle suggests the question whether his speeches have yet been clearly understood. Perhaps the explanation may be that to the ancient mind different details, which we should refer to one principle, may have seemed as large and distinct as different principles now do to us. 1. Elihu agrees with the three comforters, in opposition to the Prologue and Epilogue, in referring all suffering or affliction to sin. He quotes Job's claims to innocence with marks of admiration (ch. xxxiii. 9, 10), and says that "he adds rebellion to his sin," for which he was afflicted (ch. xxxiv. 37). Any sufferings not having reference to sin he does not recognise. God afflicts, and if in the midst of affliction there be an angel to shew man "what is right," then He is gracious and says, "save from going down to the pit," and the ransomed sinner sings before men and says, *I sinned and perverted right* (ch. xxxiii. 23—27). Again, in another passage on affliction, it is said that God "sheweth unto them their (evil) deed, *and their transgressions, that they deal proudly*" (ch. xxxvi. 9). 2. Elihu agrees with the friends further in insisting on the rectitude of God, and on the principle that His dealings with men everywhere illustrate it: "Far be it from God that He should do wickedness, *for the work of a man shall He render unto him, and cause every one to find according to his ways*" (ch. xxxiv. 10, 11). And if the prayer of the righteous be not answered it is because sin impairs its effect: "None saith, Where is God my Maker"! "Surely God heareth not vanity" (ch. xxxv. 10—13). And again: "He preserveth not the life of the wicked, but giveth his right to the poor" (ch. xxxvi. 6). Though Elihu be in these passages defending the rectitude of God in general, he nowhere gives any intimation that he considers affliction employed by God except in connexion with sin. 3. Elihu is certainly also at one with the friends in his judgment on Job. Though in the main directing his attention to Job's demeanour under his trials, he goes behind these when he says that Job adds rebellion *to his sin* (ch. xxxiv. 37), and when he represents God's chastisements as meant to allure him out of the jaws of distress (ch. xxxvi. 16). He no doubt drew Job's afflictions, for he must have explained them in some way, under his general principle, enunciated in his last speech, "if men are bound in the cords of affliction He sheweth unto them their deed and their transgressions, that they deal proudly" (ch. xxxvi. 9). And he is equally in agreement with the friends in regard to the issue of afflictions, which depends upon the sufferer's behaviour under them: "If they hear, they spend their days in prosperity; if they hear not, they perish by the sword" (ch. xxxvi. 8—12). 4. Finally, Elihu is in agreement with the friends in regarding afflictions as chastisement, inflicted with the gracious design of weaning the sufferer from his evil (ch. iv. v.). This is the great purpose of God when speaking to men by or in afflictions: "Lo, all these things worketh God oftentimes with man, *to bring back his soul from the pit, to be enlightened with the light of life*" (ch. xxxiii. 29, 30; cf. *v.* 19 *seq.*). If men are bound in the cords of affliction, God is shewing them their transgressions, *and commanding them that they return from iniquity* (ch. xxxvi. 8—10). And this is the meaning of Job's distresses (ch. xxxvi. 16 *seq.*) and of God's purpose in them—"Who is a teacher like Him"? (ch. xxxvi. 20—22).

It is at this last point that whatever difference exists between the views of Elihu and those of the three friends begins to appear. The difference does not amount to much, and is apt to be exaggerated. Elihu in propounding his views has not the friends but Job present to his mind, and his theory of suffering is intended to be set in contrast with what he conceives to be the tenets of Job. The latter had complained that God persecuted him and counted him as His enemy (ch. xix. 11, 22); that He tore him in His anger (ch. xvi. 9), and had resolved upon his death (ch. xxiii. 14, xxx. 23); in other words he regarded his afflictions as the expression of the divine *wrath* and meant for his destruction. The theory of Elihu meets this view directly in the face: affliction is the expression of the divine goodness, designed to save man's soul from the pit (ch. xxxiii. 29 *seq.*), into which but for God's gracious interposition his sins would have cast him. This, however, though in distinct opposition to Job's contention, is virtually what the friends had always maintained. Their exhortations to Job all proceeded on the supposition that God was shewing His mercy towards him, and smiting only in order to heal. It is true that the friends, more and more convinced of Job's sins by his hardened demeanour under his afflictions, tend to drift away from this position, and begin to express the fear that God's final judgment on him may be visible in his calamities; yet they do not altogether desert their first ground, to which Eliphaz returns in his last speech (ch. xxii.). It is possible, however, that in one or two points Elihu makes an advance on the doctrine of the three. They appear to regard afflictions as always following sins committed, while he perhaps regards them as sometimes divine warnings to men against sins into which they are in danger of falling. In the one case suffering would be exclusively curative, in the other it might be preventive. This would certainly widen the idea of the friends by multiplying the points in the sinner's life at which the divine interposition through affliction might fall. The passage, ch. xxxiii. 17, may express this idea: "that he may withdraw man from his deed, and hide pride from man"—the deed being only meditated or in danger of being perpetrated. The words, however, might bear the sense, "that man may put away a deed"; and in all the other passages where Elihu's view is stated, the evil against which the sinner is warned by God appears to be already at least begun. The term "pride" might suggest to the reader that Elihu has a more inward conception of evil than the three friends, that while they speak of "sins" he refers to "sinfulness" of heart, and spiritual self-confidence and presumption. There may be something in this, but when Old Testament phraseology is considered there is less than might be supposed. "Pride, in the Old Testament, stands as the distinctive characteristic of ungodliness, in opposition to humility, the distinctive trait of true piety, nor is there anything to shew that it is used otherwise here (ch. xxxiii. 17). To 'deal proudly' (ch. xxxvi. 9) is to manifest in daring acts of rebellion against God the inward spirit of resistance to His will, a very different thing from a vain conceit of perfect conformity to it"[1]. In all this, therefore, Elihu occupies in principle the same ground with the friends, and his views may be regarded as the legitimate expansion of theirs.

In another point Elihu may differ from Job's friends. His great principle that afflictions are the expression of God's goodness seems to be a universal theory of providence, embracing the incidence of evil both on the righteous and the wicked. This idea may be closely connected with his profoundly reverential and devout conceptions of God. The point is not very clear, but he does not anywhere refer to afflictions which are strictly penal and intended to destroy; they become destructive only when the sinner "lays up wrath," that is, rebels against them. The three friends, while taking this view of the afflictions of the righteous (ch. iv—v), insist upon a kind of calamity which in its first purpose is penal and judicial.

(3.) It has been seen that Elihu agreed with the other speakers in explaining Job's sufferings by his sins (ch. xxxiv. 7, 8, 36,

---

[1] Conant, *Job*, Introd. p. xxvi.

37). In his reply to Job there are two things to be noticed, his arguments in behalf of the divine rectitude, and his positive explanation of the sufferings that befall men. The former are given chiefly in ch. xxxiv.—xxxv; and the latter in ch. xxxiii., xxxvi. (see the headings to these chapters). His explanation of afflictions, as stated above, is to the effect, that they are the expression of the divine goodness, designed to warn men from their sin and save them from death. Along with this principle has to be taken the very interesting passage in ch. xxxv., in which an answer is given to the difficulty that the righteous often cry to God in vain. The answer is, that sin in them or in their supplication impairs its efficacy, and there is none that answereth. If now the two questions be put, Is this theory of affliction and of unanswered prayer a theory that will admit of universal application and comprehend every particular? and, Is there anything in what Elihu advances that ought to bring Job to silence or compose the troubles of his heart? an affirmative answer can hardly be given. The sinfulness of man is such that in a multitude or in the majority of cases afflictions may be supposed due to it, but the Prologue teaches that the connexion is not invariable. In a multitude of instances prayer may be unanswered because the suppliant prays amiss. But to say that this is always the case is extremely harsh, and is to measure providence by a very narrow gauge. The arguments of Elihu just like those of the three friends are general principles of wide application; they are considerations which if a man would weigh them and apply them *to himself* would perhaps prevent such complaints as those into which Job fell. But when put forth, as they are here, as an all-sufficient measure of God's providence, they are obviously defective. Again, although the prominence given by Elihu to the goodness of God when He afflicts might have given another turn to Job's thoughts, there is no reason why he should have acquiesced in Elihu's view more than in that of the friends. For both views agreed in connecting his sufferings with his sin, and Job instinctively felt that he was not afflicted for his sin. If Elihu differs from the friends in considering affliction an instance of

INTRODUCTION.

preventing grace, while they regarded it as a medicine intended to cure, the difference is not essential. There was no reason to suppose that Job meditated evil or was in danger of falling into it more than to suppose that he was already guilty of it. He would have resented the one insinuation as equally unjust with the other.

The arguments that have been used to shew that the episode of Elihu did not form part of the original Poem are chiefly the following :

1. That Elihu is unknown both to the Prologue and Epilogue.
2. That Job makes no reply to him.
3. That he addresses Job by name, and that his citations from the Book are so minute as to betray a reader of the Poem rather than a listener to the debate.
4. That his speeches destroy the connexion between the challenge of Job and the reply of the Almighty, and weaken the dramatic effect of the divine manifestation.
5. That the language of the piece betrays signs of deterioration, marking a later age; and that both Elihu and his speeches are characterized by a mannerism too great to be the creation of the author of the rest of the Poem.
6. That Elihu virtually occupies the same ground with the friends, and there is no probability that the original author would have created a fourth speaker to say in effect what the three had already said. And further that where Elihu differs from the friends it is rather in deeper reverence and a somewhat more advanced view of sin, both things betraying a later age, and suggesting that the original Book perplexed pious minds by its extraordinary boldness.

Some of these arguments have little weight, while others are of considerable force.

1. The argument that Elihu does not appear in the Prologue has little value. The author introduces the speaker with ample details when he has need of him, and certainly at the right place. He was not one of Job's friends, calling for mention along with them, but a bystander. On the other hand, it is

remarkable that his name does not appear in the Epilogue. It is urged that there was nothing in his discourses calling for mention : he did not discover the truth, and could not therefore be praised; but his views being just so far as they went, he could not be included in the censure pronounced upon the three friends. The answer is not quite satisfactory, for on that point in regard to which the friends are condemned for not speaking "that which was right" Elihu shared their opinions.

2. The author of the speeches of Elihu certainly means them to be such an answer to Job that he cannot reply to them (ch. xxxiii. 32, xxxiv. 35, xxxv. 16, xxxvi. 4). The question is, Would the author of the rest of the Poem have regarded them as a conclusive answer to Job? This question. however, runs into objection 6.

3. There is not much weight in the argument that Elihu addresses Job by name, though the name of "Job" is certainly so often in his mouth as to constitute a peculiarity of his manner (ch. xxxiii. 1, 31, xxxiv. 5, 7, 35, 36. &c.). Elihu interposes as a third party and addresses Job or speaks of him in distinction from the three friends. The other speakers do not do so, for they have not the same reason ; and although the Lord does not appeal to Job by name in addressing him from the storm, He speaks of "my servant Job" when He has to distinguish him from the three friends (ch. xlii. 7, 8). On the other hand, the full and *verbatim* reproduction of Job's words at the head of the several speeches of Elihu does suggest that he was the reader of a book rather than the listener to a debate, though the argument does not amount to much.

4. The words of the Lord, "Who then is obscuring counsel by words without knowledge?" addressed to Job without naming him, naturally suggest that Job had just been speaking, or that the divine voice broke in upon him before he had ceased ; they are not natural if Job had been long silent, while another speaker had been proceeding with a discourse extending through six chapters. The feeling has been expressed by some thoughtful writers that it would not have been becoming for the Lord to

reply to Job's challenge without the intervention of some pause. This observation may be perfectly just, but it does not meet the point of the objection, which is that the words of the Almighty suggest that the connexion between His reply and Job's challenge was immediate. And perhaps if the author allowed Jehovah to reply to Job in any manner, he might not have been sensible of any incongruity in His replying immediately.

5. The body of the Poem, though undoubtedly exhibiting some Aramaisms, is comparatively pure in language and lucid in expression, notwithstanding the obscurity of a few passages, in some of which the text may probably be corrupt. The style is terse, nervous and pointed, and hardly anywhere marked by such breadth as to be enfeebled or become prolix. The speeches of Elihu are marked by a deeper colouring of Aramaic; are frequently very obscure; and not seldom descend almost to the level of prose. The touches of the author's hand in the other parts of the Poem, particularly in the divine speeches, are easy, vigorous and graphic; in the speeches of Elihu the figures are laboured and the thought strained. Renan says, not without truth, that "in the other parts of the Poem the obscurity arises from our own ignorance; here it arises from the style itself"[1], though his further remark, that we might almost believe that Elihu's speeches belong to a time when Hebrew had become a dead language, goes rather far. The difficulties of other parts of the Poem arise from the occurrence of words which, owing probably to the small compass of the literature, are not found again, and from allusions which we have not the means of understanding, such as the astronomical references in the speeches from the storm, though it must be confessed that some parts of ch. xxx. are obscure for other reasons. In Elihu's speeches there are not only unknown words, there is an unknown use of known words, as well as a manner of joining familiar words together to form phrases which have no parallel —in short, the author speaks a language which in some parts is not quite that of any other Old Testament writer.

[1] *Le Livre de Job, Étude,* p. 54.

The deeper Aramæan colour has been supposed intentional on the part of the author, who makes Elihu, "of the family of Ram," speak a more decidedly Aramæan dialect than the others. It is not certain, however, that Ram is the same as Aram; and even if it were so, it is to ascribe to the author a proficiency in the dramatic art scarcely probable in his age, to imagine that he makes Elihu talk Aramæan as Shakespeare makes Captain Jamy talk something supposed to be Scotch. If this were the case, however, the older dramatist would appear to have the advantage of the modern one.

The circumstantial way in which Elihu is introduced (ch. xxxii. 2) is unlike the curt and general statements regarding the other three speakers (ch. ii. 11), and his somewhat self-confident and boisterous manner of comporting himself differs greatly from the bearing of Job's other antagonists. This dissimilarity is so great as to suggest that Elihu is the creation of a writer of less severe taste and feebler dramatic power than the author of the other characters manifests. Some of those, indeed, who consider Elihu the creation of the original author suppose that he intended the character for a burlesque. But this is altogether improbable. When we consider the devout nature of Elihu, the purpose which he sets before him in his speeches, "to ascribe right to his Maker," and the many lofty thoughts to which he gives expression in regard to God, it is impossible to believe that the original Poet, unparalleled for religious boldness though he be, would have set such a character upon the stage to play a burlesque part and provoke ridicule. This would have been to mock religion, when his design went no further than to shew the insufficiency of certain religious opinions current among men. The conclusion to which these objections have led the majority of modern writers on the Book is, that the author of the Elihu speeches was one who was not endowed with the brilliant powers of the writer who composed the body of the Poem, or, to use the more appropriate language of Delitzsch, that he was "one whose *charisma* did not come up to that of the older poet."

6. If the analysis given above of the general meaning of

Elihu's speeches be moderately correct, this objection has considerable force. It is natural to suppose that in the *three* speakers whom he introduces, whether the number three be his own creation or came down to him in the tradition, the author found sufficient means for expressing all that he desired to bring forward on the side opposed to Job. It may be said that the three friends all advance one and the same opinion. This would only shew that this opinion was what the author intended to set forth in its most persuasive form, with the view of proving that even when presented to the best advantage it could not be sustained. At all events, a fourth speaker would be introduced only if he were to occupy ground entirely distinct from the other three. And it cannot be said that Elihu does so. See above, p. xlvi.

Some positive arguments have been presented in favour of the originality of the speeches of Elihu. It is argued, for instance, that the close and natural connexion between the last speech of Elihu and the answer of the Lord from the storm appears in this, that the rising thunder-cloud which Elihu graphically describes, and at the sound from which his heart leaps up out of its place, is just the storm out of which Jehovah speaks. If this were the case it might merely indicate that the later writer skilfully took advantage of the elements of the original poem to make a frame to set his own piece within. It is not certain, however, that Elihu in referring to the storm, has any thought of the storm out of which Jehovah speaks. If he had he ought to have closed his speech with the description of it, but instead of doing this he passes away from it to other celestial marvels, such as the balancing of the cloud, the sultry stillness of the earth from the south wind, the burnished summer sky like a molten mirror, and the dazzling light in the clear heavens (ch. xxxvii. 16 *seq.*).

What is really the greatest difficulty in the way of considering these speeches a later insertion is just one of the facts which has been adduced to shew that they are an insertion, namely the opposition between them and the Prologue. If Elihu spoke like the three friends in ignorance of the Prologue and the cause of Job's calamities which it reveals, his position is natural. But if he was a reader of the Book, the way in which he completely ignores the Prologue with its view of affliction and substitutes a theory radically different is extraordinary. In such a case his censure would extend to the whole cast of the Book[1]. The motive of this censure might be twofold, namely, partly his profound conviction of the sinfulness and presumption of the human mind (too well illustrated in Job's demeanour under his afflictions), which made him dislike the conception of a perfectly "righteous" man presented in the Book; and partly his exalted idea of the *goodness* of God, which could not reconcile itself to the view that God might afflict a man merely to try his righteousness, and though He found no sinfulness in him.

The question certainly occurs to any reader of the Poem whether Job's afflictions did not stand in some relation to his religious state. The Book itself suggests the question. When Job is represented as falling into sin, when he attains to a higher knowledge of God and a deeper humility, and when he is crowned with blessings twofold greater than he enjoyed before, all through his afflictions or in connexion with them, we can perceive that they served wider purposes than merely to try. The trials of the righteous are not mere barren experiments made on them by God for His own satisfaction, or that He may derive glory from their stedfastness to Him to the confusion of the powers of Evil, they are fruitful of good to the minds of those who are tried (Rom. v. 3 *seq.*, Jam. i. 2, 12). At the same time this view has not received much elaboration from the author of the Book, and, though it be the view to which our minds most readily turn, we must beware, when constructing a theory of the Book, of giving it greater prominence than the author has assigned it, and especially of allowing it to push his idea that Job's afflictions were a trial altogether out of sight.

---

[1] This is felt by Delitzsch, who characterizes his speeches as "less a criticism of Job than of the Book in general." Art. "Hiob," in Herzog.

4. *The Speeches of the Almighty.*

Objection has been taken to these speeches as a whole, and particularly to the long passage which describes Behemoth and Leviathan.

The passage referred to may raise some suspicions, but it may be said with certainty that the divine speeches belong to the original form of the Book, and that they come from the hand of the author of the Prologue. In fact, if we could obliterate from our minds the dialectical conflict between Job and his friends, and carry with us nothing but the general impression that under his prolonged sufferings Job had been betrayed into sinful murmuring against God and doubts of His righteousness and impatient demands to know the cause of his afflictions, we should be in the best position to understand the divine speeches, which would then follow the Prologue at an interval occupied by the impression produced on us by Job's altered demeanour. At the end of his first trial the author says, "In all this Job sinned not nor imputed wrong to God" (ch. i. 21). At the end of the second trial Job says, "We receive good at the hand of God, and shall we not receive evil?" (ch. ii. 10), and the author adds, "In all this Job sinned not with his lips." Job's reverent thought of God was such that amidst his complete darkness he let no murmur against Him escape his lips. This is what the author demands of men in the name of religion. This is the idea of true religion suggested by the suspicion of the Satan, namely, that men should cleave to God, from their sense of what God Himself is, though receiving nothing from His hand. As another sufferer expresses himself in circumstances similar to those of Job, "Nevertheless I am continually with thee. Whom have I in heaven? and on earth I desire nought beside thee" (Ps. lxxiii. 23—25). The following chapters exhibit Job drifting away from this position maintained on the first incidence of his calamities, wrestling with doubts of God's righteousness, and ready to disown Him, though ever coming back to

Him, and assured that His righteousness will yet reveal itself. It is the object of the divine speeches to bring Job back to that position which he was able to occupy at the beginning. Obviously, according to the author's view of religion, this could be effected by nothing but a revelation of God, filling Job's mind with such a sense of Him that he should quiet his heart before Him, even amidst the intellectual darkness that remained around him. Such a revelation of God is given in the divine speeches: "Now mine eye seeth thee!"

The objections that have been made to the long passage ch. xl. 15—xli. 34, describing Behemoth and Leviathan, are briefly such as these: that the description of these animals would have been in place in the first divine speech beside the other animal pictures, but is out of harmony with the idea of the second speech; that the description swells the second speech to a length unsuitable to its object, which is fully expressed in ch. xl. 6—14; and that the minuteness and heaviness of the representation betray a very different hand from that which drew the powerful sketches in ch. xxxviii., xxxix.

The last-mentioned point is not without force. The rapid, light and expressive lines of the former pictures make them without parallel for beauty and power in literature; the two latter belong to an entirely different class. They are typical specimens of Oriental poems, as any one who has read an Arab poet's description of his camel or horse will feel. These poets do not paint a picture of the object for the eye, they schedule an inventory of its parts and properties. So the poet of Leviathan says, "I will not be silent concerning his parts" (ch. xli. 12). There is a certain awkwardness in these words, coming from the mouth of the divine speaker, which has led some scholars to miss here the artistic power and dexterity of the former poet. Other writers, however, are at a loss to find language to express their admiration of the beauty and poetical grace of these descriptions. The maxim, *De gustibus*, absolves from the obligation of arguing the point.

CHAPTER V.

THE AGE AND AUTHORSHIP OF JOB.

As there is nothing in the Book which fixes its date at once with certainty, a great variety of opinion has prevailed upon the question. There is almost no age of the world, from the patriarchal times down to the period after the Captivity, to which the Book has not been assigned. The juster conceptions, however, which now prevail regarding the history of Israel and the advancement in the ideas of the people, occasioned in part by the progress of this history and accompanying it, have considerably narrowed the limits within which such a work can reasonably be supposed to have appeared. And a more careful examination of the allusions which, in spite of the antique and patriarchal colour thrown over the Book, may be detected in it to the circumstances and events of later times, has still further reduced the range of plausible conjecture. The Book can hardly have been written before the decline and fall of the northern kingdom, nor later than the return of the exiles of Judah from Babylon.

The question of the age of the Book must not be confounded with that of the age of Job himself. Job is represented as living in the patriarchal times. The author has skilfully thrown the colours of this age over his composition and preserved its general features. Thus, though employing the Israelitish name Jehovah himself, he allows the speakers in the Book to use the divine names peculiar to patriarchal times, as *El, Elôah* (Arab. *ilâh*, God), *Almighty*. No doubt he betrays his own nationality, which he has no desire to conceal, by letting the name Jehovah escape two or three times from the mouth of Job, in current formulas into which the name entered (ch. i. 21, xii. 9; cf. xxviii. 28). Again, like the great forefathers of Israel, Job is represented as rich in cattle and flocks (ch. i. 3, xlii. 12, comp. Gen. xii. 16, xxiv. 35, xxvi. 13, xxx. 43). In like manner Job, the head of the family, is also its priest and offers sacrifice (ch. i. 5, xlii. 8; comp. Gen. xxii. 13, xxxi. 54), although in another place he is made to say of God that "He leadeth priests away stripped" (ch. xii. 19). Further, the sacrifice in use is the "burnt-offering", as in ancient times, before the more developed ritual in Israel came into operation. The great age, too, to which Job attains is patriarchal (ch. xlii. 16; comp. Gen. xxv. 7, xxxv. 28), though Bildad speaks as if the age of men of his day was greatly reduced in comparison with former standards (ch. viii. 8). The money referred to is the ancient *kesitah* (ch. xlii. 11; comp. Gen. xxxiii. 19, Josh. xxiv. 32); and the musical instruments named are the simple ones of primitive times (ch. xxi. 12, xxx. 31; comp. Gen. iv. 21, xxxi. 27). And, to mention no more, historical allusions of any directness are usually to the great events of the patriarchal world (ch. xviii. 15, xxii. 15 *seq.*).

Nevertheless, the features of the author's own time may often be perceived beneath this patriarchal disguise. Job betrays familiarity with the Law, or at least with the social customs and moral ideas of Israel. When he refers in his speeches to pledges (ch. xxiv. 9, see on xxii. 6), and to landmarks (ch. xxiv. 2; comp. Deut. xix. 14, xxvii. 17, Hos. v. 10, Prov. xxii. 28, xxiii. 10); or when he alludes to judicial procedure against those guilty of special forms of idolatry, such as adoration of the sun and moon (ch. xxxi. 26, comp. Deut. iv. 19, xvii. 3—7, Ezek. viii. 16), or against those guilty of adultery (ch. xxxi. 9, comp. Deut. xxii. 22), the voice is the voice of a godly child of Israel although the hands may be those of a son of Edom. The allusions to judicial practices found only as legal enactments in Deuteronomy are remarkable. There is even verbal coincidence in the two passages, ch. xxxi. 26 and Deut. iv. 19; and those who consider Deuteronomy a late book might feel justified in fixing the eighteenth year of Josiah (620) as the

INTRODUCTION. lvii

point above which the composition of Job cannot be carried[1]. At all events there is abundant evidence to shew that the age assigned to Job and the age of the author of the Book lie widely apart. The statements of Renan that "not one allusion is made to Mosaic customs, nor to beliefs peculiar to the Jews," that "the atmosphere of the Book is not more specially Hebrew than Idumean or Ishmaelite," and that "in a very real sense these precious pages have transmitted to us an echo of the ancient wisdom of Teman[2]", are exaggerations and part of the romance with which this brilliant writer delights to invest the sacred subjects which he treats. The author of Job is a true Israelite, and betrays himself to be so at every turn, however wide his sympathies be with the life of other peoples, and however great his power of reanimating the past. The idea that the Poem is a production of the Desert, written in another tongue and translated into Hebrew, is more than destitute of a shadow of probability, it is absurd. The Book is the genuine outcome of the religious life and thought of Israel, the product of a religious knowledge and experience possible among no other people.

The date of such a Book as Job, which deals only with religious ideas and general questions of providence, and contains no direct allusions to the events of history, can be fixed only approximately. Any conclusion on the subject can be reached only by an induction founded on matters that do not afford perfect certainty, such as the comparative development of certain moral ideas in different ages; the pressing claims of certain problems for solution at particular epochs of the history of the people; points of contact which the Book may offer with other writings the age of which may with more certainty be determined; and indirect allusions which may betray a condition of the national life known to be that of a particular period of its history. These are all lines of reasoning more or

---

[1] Comp. Job ii. 7 with Deut. xxviii. 35; v. 14 with xxviii. 29; v. 18 with xxxii. 39; vii. 4 with xxviii. 67; viii. 8 with iv. 32; xx. 4 with iv. 32.
[2] *Le Livre de Job, Étude*, p. 16, 27.

less precarious. Only when several of them unite in pointing to the same result can we feel much confidence in its justness. The comparison of passages in different books is apt to be rather barren of fruit. There is such a general unity of thought and language pervading the books of Scripture that similar expressions or even identical phraseology in two writers cannot in all cases be held evidence of literary dependence. The writers of Scripture are for the most part men of the people and speak the popular language, and the same phrase in several books may be original in them all. And even when we cannot escape the conviction that there is dependence, it is usually very difficult to decide which is the original and which the imitator. The argument, on the other hand, founded on the connexion of the thought and literature of Israel with the successive developments of its history, though still a delicate one, is more solid. The mind of the people was intensely national, and the spirit of its literature is for the most part national rather than individual. This is no doubt less true of the poetry and the wisdom. But the truth holds even of a very great part of the poetry, it reflects the consciousness of the nation; and it holds of the wisdom to this extent, that the vicissitudes of the people's history suggested the successive aspects under which the questions reflected on by the Wise presented themselves to their minds.

The opinion expressed in the Talmud, and followed by some writers, that Moses was the author of Job is unworthy of any attention. The thin antique colour of the Book suggested to uncritical minds that it was an ancient composition, and such minds, impatient of uncertainty, everywhere seek to satisfy themselves by ascribing any great anonymous work to some well-known name. But the conjecture is more than improbable. It is the part of the founder of a constitution like Moses to project principles and ideas which are of general truth, and to sketch an outline which succeeding ages may be left to fill up; it is scarcely his part to subject the general principles upon which his constitution is founded to questionings which would undermine them, or to introduce alongside of them the modifications which future generations or society in altered conditions may find needful to make on them. Neither the author of the Law which describes God as "visiting the iniquity of the fathers upon the children unto the third and fourth generation" (Ex. xx. 5), nor any of his contemporaries was likely to have written the words of Job (ch. xxi. 19),

> God (say ye) layeth up his iniquity for his children.—
> Let Him recompense it unto himself that he may know it;
> Let his own eyes see his destruction.

The principle enunciated in the Law may have raised difficulties in some minds at an early time, but the first expression of dissatisfaction with it in any composition to which we can assign a date appears in the prophecies of Jeremiah (ch. xxxi. 29; comp. Ezek. xviii. 2).

The centuries after the Exodus down to the end of the reign of David, times of stirring enterprize and warfare and conquest, were not favourable for the production of a work of deep reflection like Job. Nor, in spite of the repeated humiliations to which the nation was subjected in those ages, can the spirit of the people ever have sunk to that state of exhaustion and despair which appears in this Book. There is evidence too in the Poem that the author was familiar with some of the writings usually ascribed to the Davidic age. There is a distorted reflection of the ideas of Ps. viii. in the passage ch. vii. 17, which is scarcely due to coincidence.

The earliest period to which the Book can be assigned with any propriety is the age of Solomon. A good many general considerations suggest this period. Unless history and tradition are to be alike discredited (1 Kings iv. 29 *seq.*) a strong current of thought sprang up in this age in the direction of reflexion upon human life and the laws of man's well-being, upon God and the ways in which His providence rules the destinies of men. These are the questions which, in a particular form, are discussed in Job. Again, it was at this period that Israel became to some extent a commercial people, and entered into relations with distant lands, with Egypt, the farther East and even the West; and these relations might seem reflected in many allusions in the Book, the author of which is familiar with foreign countries and their products, with the arts and customs of many strange peoples, and draws his illustrations from many distant sources. These considerations have led a number of writers of distinction, such as Delitzsch, to conclude that the Book is a production of this age; and such appears to have been the view of Luther.

If, however, we examine the Book of Proverbs, much in which may be referred to the age of Solomon, particularly the sayings in ch. x.—xxii., though much even in this division may be later, we find scarcely a trace of the problems and questionings that fill the Book of Job. The same general subjects are treated in both books, but in Job they have entered upon a new phase. In Proverbs the teaching on God's providence is still entirely positive. The law stated with such beauty and simplicity in Ps. i., that it is well with the righteous and ill with the wicked, is insisted on in a thousand forms, but not once subjected to doubt. In the settled, well-ordered life of Israel in this peaceful time the general principles of man's well-being were receiving their brightest illustration, and it was the delight of the wise to recognise them and give them expression in compressed and polished aphorisms. Such problems as burn in the pages of Job, the miseries of the just, the prosperity and peaceful end of the ungodly, appear unknown. They were not likely to attract men's attention at such a time. Only later, when the state began to stagger under the blows which it received from without, and when through revolution and civil discord at home great and unmerited sufferings befell the best citizens in the state, would such problems arise, or at least present themselves with an urgency which demanded some solution. It is only in those parts of Proverbs which are later than the great central division that we find allusion to disquietude occasioned to the righteous by the prosperity of the ungodly, and even these references are slight; the difficulty hardly engages a moment's attention (Prov. iii. 11, 31, xxiii. 17 *seq.*; xxiv. 19).

The relation of Job to most parts of the Book of Proverbs

is close[1]. The elements of that Book probably belong to different ages. Part of it at least was not published earlier than the days of Hezekiah (ch. xxv. *seq.*); and the first division, ch. i.—ix., though its date may be difficult to determine with exactness, can hardly be earlier than this age, if so early. But even this division as well as the central portion, ch. x.—xxii., appears to be anterior to the Book of Job. A pair of instances may suffice as examples. In Prov. xiii. 9 we read, "the lamp of the wicked shall be put out"; and the same formula appears again in another division, ch. xxiv. 20. The principle is stated in all its generality, and nowhere modified in the Book. In this form it continues to be upheld by Bildad, the representative in Job of theories of Providence which the author considers cannot any longer be maintained (ch. xviii. 6). Job, therefore, comes clean athwart it with his demand (ch. xxi. 17),

> How often is the lamp of the wicked put out?
> And how often cometh their destruction upon them?

Again in Prov. i.—ix. Wisdom earnestly presses herself upon men: she loves them that love her. Even when she rises to the highest conception of herself as architect of the world she still offers herself to men and may be embraced by them (ch. viii. 32). But the speaker in Job xxviii. despairs of wisdom: it can nowhere be found, neither in the land of the living nor in the place of the dead, neither by man nor by any creature. The divine thought in creation, the world-plan, effectuating itself in nature and human life, lies beyond the intellectual reach of man. Two such opposing representations can hardly be contemporaneous; that in Job shews an approach towards the position taken by the Preacher (Eccles. iii. 11), and is no doubt the later of the two. Great difficulty, it is true, has been felt in fitting ch. xxviii. into the Book, and it may belong to a time somewhat further down. But even in Job xv. 8 *seq.* the per-

---

[1] Comp. Job v. 17 with Prov. iii. 11; xi. 8 with ix. 18; xv. 7 with viii. 25; xviii. 6 and xxi. 17 with xiii. 9 and xxiv. 20; xxii. 28 with iv. 18; xxviii. 18 with iii. 14 and viii. 11; xxviii. 28 with i. 7; xxxviii. 10 with viii. 29. There are also some peculiar terms common to the two books; see Davidson's Introduction, Vol. II. p. 193.

sonification of Wisdom in Prov. viii. seems alluded to, or at least there is allusion to personifications similar. Such personifications mark the highest point to which Hebrew thought on the world rose, and cannot belong to an early age. Wisdom, pausing in the work of expounding providence and the laws of human happiness, which she had long instinctively pursued with self-forgetful fascination in her task, becomes self-conscious, and, turning her eyes upon herself, displays her own graces and beauty before the eyes of men. They who attain to her and live as she directs attain to the thought of God Himself and fulfil His purpose; human thought and life coincides with or even coalesces in the divine thought and will. In Proverbs the fear of the Lord is the beginning of wisdom, in Job xxviii. it is all the wisdom possible to man.

The conclusion to which the remarks just made would lead is that the Book of Job cannot be assigned to an earlier date than the 7th century. The coincidences between the Book and the earlier prophets are not very conclusive, though perhaps they confirm the inference just drawn. The phraseology in several passages is so similar to that in Amos that some have concluded that the author like this prophet was a native of the south of Judah[1]; but the similarities hardly justify any inference as to the priority of either book. The same may be said of most of the coincidences between Job and the prophets Hosea and Isaiah. The passage Is. xix. 5, however, compared with Job xiv. 11, perhaps affords some evidence of the priority of Isaiah. In Job the verse reads,

> The waters fail from the sea,
> And the stream decayeth and drieth up;

and in Isaiah, "and the waters shall fail from the sea, and the stream shall decay and dry up." In the prophet the "sea" is the Nile, and the "stream" the same or its larger branches, and the verse is closely connected with the context, which contains a threat against Egypt. In Job the term "sea" is used of any

---

[1] Stickel, *Iliob*, p. 263. Comp. Job ix. 8 with Am. iv. 13; ix. 9 with v. 8; xii. 15 with ix. 6; xviii. 16 with ii. 9; xxx. 31 with viii. 10.

INTRODUCTION.

inland water, and the words are made to express a general fact of experience, which finds a parallel in the complete extinction of the life of man. In Isaiah the term rendered "fail" is somewhat unusual, while in Job there stands for "fail" a word which, though not greatly more in use in the Bible, would certainly be much more common in the mouths of the people in the later period of their history[1].

The most weighty arguments, however, for assigning the Book to an age not earlier than the 7th century are the two facts, closely related together, first, that questions of providence have entered upon a new phase: its laws are no longer calmly expounded but subjected to doubt; from being principles securely acquiesced in they have become problems painfully agitated; and secondly, that a condition of great disorder and misery forms the background of the Poem. These two circumstances naturally go together, and they both point to the same comparatively late period. Even in some of the Psalms which treat of these questions the "ungodly" oppressor, whose felicity occasions disquietude to the religious mind (comp. Job xii. 6), is probably the heathen conqueror. But these shorter pieces in all likelihood preceded in time the more elaborate treatment to which such problems are subjected in Job. But the situation reflected in these pieces and in Job alike is one of suffering and despondency. When we read such words as, "Wherefore giveth He life to the bitter in soul, who long for death and it cometh not, and search for it more than for hid treasures?" (ch. iii. 20); "Is there not a time of hard service to man upon the earth? are not his days also like the days of an hireling?" (ch. vii. 1); "The earth is given into the hand of the wicked: he covereth the faces of the judges thereof" (ch. ix. 24); "The tabernacles of robbers prosper, and they that provoke God are secure, they who carry their god in their hand" (ch. xii. 6; cf. Hab. i. 11, 16); "Out of the city the dying groan, and the soul of the wounded crieth out, yet God regardeth not the wrong" (ch. xxiv. 12)—we feel that the points in the picture are too distinct and in too

---

[1] Other similarities are Job xii. 24 with Is. xix. 13; xvii. 12 with v. 20.

full relief to be the mere reflection of the gloom that hangs over the mind of the sufferer even in an ordinary condition of society. The passage ch. xii. 17 *seq.* is remarkable,

> He leadeth counsellors away stripped,
> And maketh the judges fools.
> He looseth the bond of kings,
> And girdeth their loins with a girdle.
> He leadeth priests away stripped,
> And overthroweth the long-established caste, &c.

Such a passage might have been written by an eyewitness of the captivity, or as Job says that he learned such details from "ancient" men (ch. xii. 12), it might have been written by one who had heard the harrowing events of that time described by one who had himself seen them. Behind the author's time there probably lay some great public calamity, which reduced multitudes of men to a wretchedness more unendurable than death, and forced the questions of evil and the righteousness of God upon men's minds with an urgency that could not be resisted. Such a calamity could be nothing short of deportation or exile. The question remains whether it was the exile of the northern nation or of Judah.

Some writers, as Hitzig, think that the author of Job, from his bold handling of questions of providence, must have belonged to the northern kingdom, where the attitude of men's minds towards religion was freer. There is not, perhaps, much in this; but some of the ablest writers on the Book, such as Ewald, connect it more or less closely with the fall of the northern state. This judgment might be acquiesced in at once were there not several things which suggest the question whether the Book may not rather reflect the circumstances of the Babylonian Captivity. These points briefly are: (1) the extremely developed form both of the morality and the doctrine of God in the Book; (2) the points of contact which it presents with Jeremiah and the ideas of his age; and (3) the strange parallel existing between Job and the "Servant of the Lord" in the second part of Isaiah.

The first point can hardly be drawn out in detail, but the teaching of Eliphaz regarding human nature (ch. iv. 17 *seq.*) and the inwardness of the moral conceptions of Job (ch. xxxi.) are very surprising. The doctrine of God is much the same in principle throughout the whole Old Testament, the later writers differing from the earlier more in the breadth with which they express the common conceptions. In Job these conceptions are expressed with a breadth and loftiness without parallel, except in the second part of Isaiah and some of the later psalms (e.g. Ps. cxxxix.). It is true it is chiefly what might be called the natural attributes of God that are dwelt upon, and this has created in some minds the feeling that the God of the Book of Job is not the God of the Old Testament[1]. He is certainly without some of the attributes ascribed to Him in such prophets as Hosea and the later chapters of Isaiah. He is God and not man—so entirely not man that He seems not altogether God. The author's conception of God is austere and lofty, and we readily understand how its features in a particular light cast that spectral shadow before Job's eye which he calls God and which he is in danger of renouncing.

Apart from the Psalms, the date of which is uncertain, the problems discussed in Job first shew themselves in the prophets of the Chaldean age. Jeremiah says, "Let me talk with thee of thy judgments: wherefore doth the way of the wicked prosper? wherefore are all they happy that deal very treacherously?" (ch. xii. 1; cf. Hab. i. 13 *seq*.). Similarly, the other question of visiting the sins of the fathers upon the children occupies the minds of the people (Jer. xxxi. 29; Ezek. xviii.). The history of the nation and its sufferings forced these questions on the attention, and there is a certain probability that a Book like Job devoted to their discussion is the creation of this time. The parallels in thought and language between Job and Jeremiah are numerous, but they strike different minds very differently. Most writers have felt that Job iii. and Jer. xx. 14 *seq*. are not altogether independent of one another, but the question of priority is difficult to settle. The argument that the passage in Job is fresher, more vivid and powerful, and therefore the original has little force. The author of Job was cer-

---

[1] Luzzatto, quoted in Del.

tainly a greater literary artist than Jeremiah, as Shakespeare was superior to the earlier dramatists whose materials he used, but the possible analogy neutralizes the argument for priority. If the author of Job used Is. xix. 5, as is probable, he has recast some of the expressions into the more strict poetical form, and he may have dealt with the language of the other prophet in the same way. Job iii. is highly elaborate and finished, while the impression which the passage in Jeremiah makes on the reader, just on account of its disjointed character and defect in literary grace, is that it is independent. The strong positive statements in Ezekiel that "the soul that sinneth shall die", and that the children shall no more be visited for their fathers' iniquity, might seem to imply that the question had advanced a stage beyond that of debate in which it appears in Job. This is less certain, because it is the peculiarity of the Book of Job that all its new truths are presented through the medium of controversial dialogue[1].

The affinity of the Book of Job to Is. ch. xl. *seq.* is remarkable, and appears in two points, coincidences of expression and thought, and the parallel between the figure of Job and that of the Servant of the Lord. Thus the same lofty conception of God is expressed in both in identical words, *who spreadeth out the heavens alone* (ch. ix. 8, Is. xliv. 24; cf. xlv. 12). Again comp. ch. xxvi. 12—13, "He quelleth the sea with His power, and by His understanding He smiteth through Rahab," with Is. li. 9, "Art thou not it which hath cut Rahab and pierced the dragon?" Compare also Job xiii. 28 with Is. l. 9; xv. 35 with lix. 4; xxx. 21 with lxiii. 10. These similarities of phraseology might be due to dependence of the one writer upon the other. There are, however, many conceptions common to the two writers not expressed in the same phraseology, and the more probable explanation is that they lived surrounded by the same atmosphere of thought.

---

[1] Comp. Job iii. with Jer. xx. 14; vi. 15 with xv. 18; ix. 19 with xlix. 19 (Is. l. 8); xii. 4 with xx. 7; xix. 23 with xvii. 1; Job xix. 18 with Lam. iii. 15; xvi. 9 with iii. 46; xvi. 13 with iii. 12; xix. 8 with iii. 7; xxx. 9 with iii. 14.

The similarities between the figure of Job and that of the Servant are numerous and striking. Both are innocent sufferers—"my servant Job, a perfect and upright man" (Job i. 8), "my righteous servant" (Is. liii. 11); both are afflicted in a way that strikes horror into the beholders, and causes them to deem them smitten of God (Is. lii. 14, liii. 4, Job *passim*); both are forsaken of men and subjected to mockery and spitting (Job xix. 4 *seq.*, xvi. 10, xxx. 9 *seq.*; Is. l. 6, liii. 3); both are restored and glorified and receive "double", as they both continued faithful, assured that He was near that should justify them (Job xiii. 18, xvi. 19, xix. 25; Is. l. 8). The points of agreement might be greatly multiplied[1], and, notwithstanding the important differences in the two representations, they suggest some relation between the two figures. The difficulty is to ascertain whether the relation be one of similarity merely or of identity. If Job were the type of the righteous individual sufferer or of the class of individuals, and the servant the suffering righteous Israel, that is, the godly remnant to which the nationality and name belonged, seeing these two subjects are virtually the same under different conceptions, the author of the one picture might have transferred some features from the canvas of his predecessor to his own[2]. The probability is as great that the two authors worked up common conceptions into independent creations; and there are many parts of Job that appear to reflect national feeling and conditions, though of course the author could not allow the formal conception of the nation to appear.

The question enters a region here which is not that of argument but of impressions; but upon the whole probabilities point to the age of the captivity of Judah as that to which the Book belongs.

[1] See Dr Cheyne's interesting Essay, *Isaiah*, II. p. 244. Kuenen has an exhaustive paper on the subject in the *Theolog. Tijds.*, 1873.

[2] This is the later opinion of Kuenen, who considers that the collective or national representation in Isaiah has served in some respects as the model of the individual portrait in Job. In this case Job would be later than the Restoration. It is difficult, however, to believe that the solution of the problem of suffering innocence given in Job could be posterior to the more profound solution found in the prophet.

As to the Author of the Book we are in complete ignorance. He has been supposed to be Job himself, Elihu, Moses, Solomon, Heman the Ezrahite, author of Ps. lxxxviii., Isaiah, Hezekiah, author of the hymn Is. xxxviii., Baruch the friend of Jeremiah, and who not? There are some minds that cannot put up with uncertainty, and are under the necessity of deluding themselves into quietude by fixing on some known name. There are others to whom it is a comfort to think that in this omniscient age a few things still remain mysterious. Uncertainty is to them more suggestive than exact knowledge. No literature has so many great anonymous works as that of Israel. The religious life of this people was at certain periods very intense, and at these periods the spiritual energy of the nation expressed itself almost impersonally, through men who forgot themselves and were speedily forgotten in name by others.

THE BOOK OF JOB.

THERE was a man in the land of Uz, whose name *was* 1
Job; and that man was perfect and upright, and one

CH. I. 1—3. JOB'S NAME AND ABODE; HIS PIETY, AND CONSE-
QUENT FAMILY FELICITY AND WORLDLY PROSPERITY.

1. *the land of Uz*] This word occurs several times in the Old Testament: (1) as the name of a son of Aram, Gen. x. 23; (2) as the name of the eldest son of Nahor, the brother of Abraham, Gen. xxii. 21; and (3) as that of a descendant of Seir, Gen. xxxvi. 28. These references would point either to Syria on the north-east of Palestine or to the region of Edom, further south. From the Book itself we learn that Job's flocks were exposed on the east to inroads on the part of the Chaldeans, the tribes between Syria and the Euphrates, i. 17; and in another direction to attacks from the Sabeans, i. 15. The most prominent man among his friends was from Teman, which belonged to Edom, ii. 11 (comp. Gen. xxxvi. 15; Jerem. xlix. 7, 20), and he himself is named the greatest of all the children of the East, i. 3. In Lam. iv. 21 it is said: Rejoice O daughter of Edom that dwellest in the land of Uz. These words do not imply that Uz is identical with Edom, but they imply that Edomites had possession of Uz, which could not have been the case unless the lands bordered on one another. The land of Uz, therefore, probably lay east of Palestine and north of Edom. This general position is already assigned to it in the Sept. which, in some verses added to the end of the Book, and embodying the tradition of the time, says that the land of Uz lay "on the borders of Edom and Arabia."

There is nothing in Scripture that defines the position of Job's home more precisely. An interesting tradition, as old at least as the early centuries of the Christian era, has been investigated by Wetzstein. This tradition places the home of Job in the Nukra, the fertile depression of Bashan at the south-east foot of Hermon. Near the town of Nawa, about 40 miles almost due south of Damascus, a little to the west of the pilgrim route from this city to Mecca, and about the latitude of the north end of the sea of Tiberias, there still exist a *Makâm*, that is, *place*, or tomb, and monastery of Job. Wetzstein assigns the building to the end of the third century. See his Excursus at the end of Delitzsch's Comm. on Job.

whose name was Job] The Heb. form of the name is *Iyyôb*, which does not occur again in the Bible. There is no play on the name or *that feared God, and eschewed evil. And there were born*

allusion to its significance in the Book. It does not seem, therefore, to have been coined by the Author of the Poem, but probably came down to him with other fragments of the tradition on which he worked. The way in which Ezekiel alludes to Job, in company with other renowned names such as Noah and Daniel, seems to imply that this prophet drew his information regarding Job from a more general source than the present Book: "Though these three men, Noah, Daniel and Job were in it (the sinful land), they should deliver but their own souls by their righteousness," xiv. 14. The tradition regarding Job and his sufferings was probably well known in the East, and the name of the suffering hero was part of the tradition. It is of little consequence, therefore, to enquire what the name means of itself. If the word be Hebrew it might mean the "assailed" or "persecuted," that is, by Satan (or God). In Arabic the form of the word is *Ayyûb*, and if derived from this dialect the name might mean the "returning," that is, *penitent*, or more generally, the "pious." Job is several times spoken of in the Kor'an. In Sur. xxxviii. 44 he is called *awwâb*, which means "ever returning to God," i.e. pious rather than penitent, but there seems no allusion in the term to the etymology of his name, for in the same chapter both David and Solomon receive the same epithet.

that man was perfect] The term "perfect" means properly "complete," without defect. It does not imply that the man was sinless, for Job never puts forward any such pretension, but that he was a righteous man and free from specific sins such as were held to bring down the chastisement of heaven. That he was so is the very foundation of his trial and the first principle of the Book. Job's "perfection" is affirmed in heaven: "Hast thou considered my servant Job...a perfect and an upright man?" i. 8, ii. 3 ; it is understood by his wife: Dost thou still hold fast thy perfection? ii. 9; and it is persistently claimed for himself by Job, not only in moments of excitement when stung by the insinuations of his friends: I *am* perfect, ix. 21 (see notes), but also when the heat of the conflict is over and under the most solemn oaths: As God liveth who hath taken away my right,...I will not remove my perfection from me; my righteousness I hold fast, xxvii. 2, 5, 6. The word occurs again, xxxi. 6, and in another form, xii. 4: The just, perfect man is laughed to scorn. Even the three friends admit Job's perfectness in general, although they are under the impression that he must have been guilty of some serious offences to account for his calamities, and they urge it upon Job as a ground of confidence in his ultimate recovery: Is not thy hope the perfectness of thy ways? iv. 6; and again: "God will not cast away a perfect man," viii. 20. One of the objects the writer of the Book had in view was to teach that sufferings may fall on men for reasons unconnected with any sin on their own part; and using the history of Job for this purpose, it was necessary that he should lay emphasis in all parts of the Book upon Job's perfection. The term "perfect" is used of Noah in the same sense: Noah, a just man, was perfect in his generation; that is, he was righteous and exempt from the sins of his contemporaries, Gen. vi. 9.

unto him seven sons and three daughters. His substance 3

feared God] Job was not only just and upright, with a high morality, he was also godfearing. These two things are never separated in the Old Testament. For as God was the author of all the movements in the world and human history, so right thoughts of Him and right relations to Him lay at the foundation of all right human conduct. The fear of the Lord is the beginning of wisdom; and wisdom includes both just thinking and right conduct.

2, 3. Job's family and wealth. A first principle in the Oriental Wisdom, which corresponds in part to our Ethics, was, that it is well with the righteous and ill with the wicked, Is. iii. 10, 11. This principle is set at the head of the Psalter in Ps. i., and is reiterated in many shapes as an unalterable law in the Book of Proverbs. According to this principle Job and all acquainted with him would see his piety reflected in his worldly prosperity, and regard this as God's blessing upon him on account of it. It is not the intention of the writer of the Book to break with this principle absolutely. On the contrary when he lets Job at the end of his trials be restored to a prosperity double that which he enjoyed before, he gives in his adhesion to the principle in general. If he had not done so his position would have been more false than that of Job's friends, who asserted that the principle prevailed in the world without exceptions. The Author's design goes no further than to teach that the principle is subject to great modifications, and that sufferings may arise from causes more general than any connected with the sufferer's own life. His object, however, in teaching this doctrine cannot have been the limited one of correcting a false theory of Providence, he must have had before him the wider purpose of sustaining individuals or most probably his nation under severe and inexplicable trials and encouraging them with brilliant hopes of the future.

The round numbers 7, 3, 5, by which Job's children and his flocks are described, express, according to the ideas connected with such numbers in the East, their perfection and complete sufficiency. They teach at the same time that what we have before us here is not actual history, but history idealized by the Poet and Teacher, that he may convey by it more vividly the moral lessons which he desires to inculcate. Job's sons were seven and his daughters three, for sons were more esteemed in the East than daughters, partly for reasons connected with the state of society, one of which is alluded to in the Psalm: "They shall not be ashamed, they shall speak with the enemies in the gate," Ps. cxxvii. 5. Mohammed expresses the feelings of the Arabs when he says: For when any one of them is informed of the birth of a daughter a black shadow falls upon his face and he is wroth, and withdraweth himself from men because of the evil tidings, uncertain whether he shall keep it with disgrace or bury it (alive) in the dust, Kor. xvi. 60; and even the modern Jew in his prayers gives thanks in this way: Blessed art thou, O king of the universe, who hast not made me a woman.

1—2

also was seven thousand sheep, and three thousand camels, and five hundred yoke of oxen, and five hundred she asses, and a very great household; so that this man was the 4 greatest of all the men of the east. And his sons went and feasted *in their* houses, every one his day; and sent and called for their three sisters to eat and to drink with them. 5 And it was so, when the days of *their* feasting were gone

As a great Eastern Emeer, Job was rich in camels. These were used for riding when the journey was long, and for transporting produce and merchandise to the distant cities. They were also eaten by the Arabs. She-asses, the price of one of which is said to be three times that of a male, were esteemed not on account of their milk, but for the sake of their foals. In a country where wheeled carriages are unknown, they were used not only for riding, but for all purposes of home and agricultural carriage. Oxen were used for labouring the fields, for which the horse is not employed in the East. The amount of arable land was measured by the number of yoke, that is, *pairs*, of oxen required to cultivate it. Job's rich and extensive fields were plowed by a thousand oxen, *v.* 14. Such wide possessions implied a very great "household," that is, body of servants. And the writer finishes his picture of Job by saying that he "was the greatest of all the men (lit. children) of the East." His "greatness" did not lie in his wealth alone, but in the respect in which he was held and in his influence. See the pathetic picture which he draws of his own former estate, ch. xxix. On the general phrase "children of the East" see Gen. xxix. 1; Jud. vi. 3, vii. 12, viii. 10; 1 Kings iv. 30; Jer. xlix. 28; Ezek. xxv. 4, 10.

4, 5. A TRAIT FROM JOB'S ORDINARY LIFE, ILLUSTRATING THE HAPPINESS AND UNITY OF HIS CHILDREN AND THE FATHER'S SCRUPULOUS PIETY.

4. *in their houses, every one his day*] lit. *made a feast at the house of each on his day*, or, *at the house of him whose day it was*. The seven sons had homes of their own. The daughters probably lived in the house of their father. It does not appear with certainty from the Book whether any of Job's children were married. Each son made a feast at his house on his day, to which the other six brothers and the three sisters were invited. When the cycle of seven feasts had gone round, the father sent and purified his children and offered sacrifice on their behalf. What seems meant is that, as there were seven sons, there was a feast at the house of one of them in succession each day of the week, and that at the end of the week, when all the seven had given their feast, the father sent, possibly on the morning of the first day of the week, and sanctified them. Thus week after week was passed; their life was a continual feast. It is to be remembered that we do not stand on the ground of mere history here. The idea shapes its materials to its own ends; and what is presented to us is the highest earthly joyousness and affection combined with the most sensitive piety.

about, that Job sent and sanctified them, and rose up early
in the morning, and offered burnt offerings *according to* the
number of them all: for Job said, It may be that my sons
have sinned, and cursed God in their hearts. Thus did
Job continually.

5. *sent and sanctified them*] that is, most likely, sent *for* them. The
sanctification or purification consisted probably in washings and change
of garments, Gen. xxxv. 2, and similar rites, and was preparatory to the
sacrifice or religious service immediately to be engaged in, as Samuel
said to the family of Jesse, "Sanctify yourselves and come with me to the
sacrifice," 1 Sam. xvi. 5. The act of worship was the sacrifice. As was
customary in the Patriarchal age, to which Job belonged, and even far
down in the history of Israel, the father was priest of the family, and the
sacrifice offered was the burnt-offering. This offering contained in it the
germs which afterwards expanded into the various distinct kinds of
sacrifice, such as the sin-offering. Job used it as a sacrifice of atone-
ment.

number of them all] Whether Job offered ten burnt-offerings, including
his daughters in his atoning sacrifice, which would seem likely, or only
seven, one corresponding to each feast day, is a point that cannot be
settled with certainty.

sinned, and cursed God in their hearts] Rather, **sinned and disowned
God**, that is, sinned by disowning or renouncing God in their hearts.
Job himself was not present at the youthful festivities. He did not any
longer care for such things, but he did not wish to impose his own gravity
upon those whose years it did not suit. His desire was to see his children
happy, provided their happiness was innocent. What he feared in them
was not any open excess, or outbreak into coarse vice, but a momentary turning away of the heart from God in the midst of social enjoyment,
as if they felt that this enjoyment was better than religion or might fill
its place in one's life.

The word translated "curse" means in usage *to bless*, hence to *salute*,
1 Sam. xxv. 14, either at meeting or parting, as the Oriental wishes the
peace (salâm) or blessing of God upon one whom he meets or parts from,
Gen. xlvii. 7, 10. From this use of the word in taking leave it may have
come to mean, to bid farewell to, and hence to disown or renounce. A
similar secondary use is found in our own and the classical languages.
Thus:

    Valeat res ludicra.
    Good bye the stage. HOR.
    Farewell faint-hearted and degenerate King,
    In whose cold blood no spark of honour bides.
                            K. Henry VI.

Si maxime talis est Deus, ut nulla gratia, nulla hominum caritate
teneatur, *valeat*. Cic. *Nat. Deor.* I. 44. See Aesch. *Agam.* 572; Plat.
Phaedr. 58. These and other examples will be found in the commentaries.
Others, assuming that the radical sense of the word is *to kneel*, Ps. xcv.

6 Now there was a day when the sons of God came to

6, have supposed that the sense of *curse* might arise from a person's kneeling to imprecate evil. But this is a far-fetched idea. Besides, the sense of *curse* is unsuitable in this passage as well as in the other places where the word occurs. Some such sense as "renounce" suits all the passages in Job and the only other passage where the sense of the word must be similar, 1 Kings xxi. 10.

It is curious that the sin which Job feared in his children as the consequence of drinking too deeply of the joys of life was the sin to which he himself was almost driven by the acuteness of his misery. So surrounded are we of God on every side.

6—12. THE DISINTERESTEDNESS OF JOB'S PIETY BROUGHT UNDER SUSPICION BY THE ADVERSARY IN THE COUNCIL OF HEAVEN.

After the scene of happiness and piety presented by Job's home on earth, the Poet draws the veil aside and shews us a scene in heaven. The Council of the Most High convenes. Around the throne of the King, whose subject and servant Job is, stand "his ministers that do his pleasure," Ps. ciii. 21. Their offices are various. The office of one of them is to try the sincerity of men, and put their religion to the proof. Job's piety is commended on the part of God, but suspicions regarding its disinterestedness are insinuated on the part of this angel. He receives permission to try Job, with the reservation that he must not afflict him in his person.

6. *Now there was a day when*] lit. *now it fell on a day that the sons of God presented themselves...and Satan came.* The meaning is not that there was a set time for the sons of God presenting themselves, but that they did on a certain day convene and Satan came among them. He came because one of them—not, although not one of them. The phrase is the same in i. 13; ii. 1; 2 Kings iv. 18.

the sons of God] Rather perhaps, *sons of the Elohim*, i.e. angels. The word *Elohim* usually means God, but this is scarcely its meaning here. The angels are not called "sons of God" as if they had actually derived their nature from Him as a child from its father; nor in a less exact way, because though created they have received a nature similar to God's, being spirits; nor yet as if on account of their stedfast holiness they had been adopted by grace into the family of God. These ideas are not found here. The name *Elohim* or *sons* (i.e. members of the race) *of the Elohim* is a name given directly to angels in contrast with men. The word means probably "powers," "mights," and the name is given to God and angels in common; He is the Elohim preeminently, they are Elohim in an inferior sense. The name describes their nature or standing in contrast to what is human; the name angels, that is, messengers, is descriptive of the duties which they fulfil. The same Beings are called "sons of Elîm," Ps. lxxxix. 6 ("sons of the mighty"), and Ps. xxix. 1 ("ye mighty"), and there as here they stand in the temple or palace of the Lord, xxix. 9; lxxxix. 6—8. Angels are referred to several

present themselves before the LORD, and Satan came also
times in the Book of Job. In v. 1 the supposition is put that men might
appeal to them for sympathy or a hearing amidst sufferings judged to be
undeserved. In xxxiii. 23 they fulfil the office of interpreter between
God and men. They form the Council of God, xv. 8. They are not
said to have been created, but were present when the earth was formed,
xxxviii. 7. They are called the "holy ones," v. 1; xv. 15, where, however, "holy" is not a moral term, but means attending on God. Though
pure like the heavens and all contained in its sphere, in contrast with
God they are impure and unwise, iv. 18; xv. 15; xxv. 5.

For a scene in heaven similar to that presented in this verse see
1 Kings xxii. 19 *seq.*; Comp. Is. vi.; Ps. lxxxix. 6 *seq.*, also Zech. iii.

and Satan came also] Or, **and the Adversary**, or **Opposer**, as in the
margin. The Heb. is *the Satan*, where the presence of the article shews
that the word has not yet become a proper name. The word Satan
means one who opposes another in his purpose, Numb. xxii. 22, 32, or
pretensions and claims, Zech. iii. 1; 1 Kings xi. 14, 23, 25, or generally.
The Satan is that one of God's ministers whose part it is to oppose men
in their pretensions to a right standing before God, Zech. iii. 1, and
here; that is, who represents God's trying, sifting providence. He is one
of God's messengers and presents himself before God to report, or to
receive commissions, parts of God's will which he is to execute.

God's providence is over all; He doeth whatsoever is done in heaven
or on earth. But He makes use of agents in His operations. Hence the
same act, such as instigating David to number the people, may be in
one place ascribed to God directly, 2 Sam. xxiv. 1, and in another to
Satan, 1 Chron. xxi. 1. God's purposes are usually beneficent and
gracious, hence the angels are comprehensively designated as "ministering spirits, sent forth to minister for the sake of them who shall be heirs
of salvation," Heb. i. 14. But He has also purposes of judgment and
chastisement, which are executed by those called the "destroyers,"
Job xxxiii. 22; Ex. xii. 23. In all these operations, whether of mercy
or of judgment, the angels are simply servants. They do God's behests.
Their own moral character does not come into question. They are
neither good nor bad angels. The spirit from the Lord that troubled
Saul is called "evil," 1 Sam. xvi. 14 *seq.*, not in reference to its own
character, but to the effect produced on Saul's mind. In like manner
the spirit that came forth and undertook to delude Ahab to his destruction, was not a false spirit in himself, he merely became a lying spirit in
the mouth of Ahab's prophets, 1 Kings xxii. 19 *seq.* In all such cases
the spirit is characterized according to the influence which he exerts.
Neither is the Satan represented here as a fallen or evil spirit. Yet
undoubtedly a step towards this is taken. He shews an assiduity slightly
too keen in the exercise of his somewhat invidious function. He rather
usurps the initiative in marking out Job for trial, even though he might
feel sheltered under his general commission. The Author lets us know
that this is his view of him when he puts into God's mouth the words:
Thou didst set me on against him, ii. 3. And in the parallel passage
Zech. iii. his cold-blooded cruelty in the exercise of his office against the

7 among them. And the LORD said unto Satan, Whence comest thou? Then Satan answered the LORD, and said, From going to and fro in the earth, and from walking up 8 and down in it. And the LORD said unto Satan, Hast thou considered my servant Job, that *there is* none like him in the earth, a perfect and an upright man, one that feareth 9 God and escheweth evil? Then Satan answered the LORD, 10 and said, Doth Job fear God for nought? Hast not thou made a hedge about him, and about his house, and about all that he hath on every side? thou hast blessed the work of his hands, and his substance is increased in the land. 11 But put forth thine hand now, and touch all that he hath,

miserable and in a moral sense the somewhat ragged Church of the Restoration stands rebuked before the spirit of Divine compassion: "The Lord rebuke thee Satan, is not this a brand plucked from the burning?" Subsequent revelation made advances on the doctrine of Satan, the discussion of which, however, does not belong here.

7. *From going to and fro*] As the word is used by the Satan of himself there is, naturally, no shade of self-condemnation in it: rather the reverse, he speaks with a certain consciousness of his assiduous faithfulness. The term is used of "the eyes of the Lord, that go to and fro," 2 Chron. xvi. 9. What is suggested is the swiftness and ubiquity of his survey of men. Similarly *walking up and down* is said of those benevolent emissaries sent forth from heaven in the interest of the suffering righteous of the earth, Zech. i. 10, 11; vi. 7. The growing light of revelation cast the figure of Satan into deeper shade, and his restless activity receives a corresponding deepness of tint, "Your adversary, as a roaring lion, walketh about, seeking whom he may devour," 1 Pet. v. 8.

8. The integrity and godliness attributed to Job by the author of the Poem are confirmed by God Himself.

9. *for nought*] Satan does not dispute Job's piety; only, the devotion of the rich landowner to the Bountiful Giver of all good is not ill to understand! A different estimate of what true religion is and of the things that are difficulties in the way of it was formed by Another, who said: "How hardly shall they that have riches enter into the kingdom of God!" A subtle turn is given to the words of Satan by Godet in his Essay on Job, who thinks that while they are openly a slur upon man, they are covertly a sarcasm on the Most High Himself, implying that no one truly loves Him, He is served only for the benefits He confers. The Essayist may do no injustice to Satan, but he does to the Old Testament conception of him. The Satan of this Book may shew the beginnings of a personal malevolence against man, but he is still rigidly subordinated to heaven, and in all he does subserves its interests. His function is as the minister of God to try the sincerity of man; hence when his work of trial is over he is no more found, and no place is given him among the *dramatis personæ* of the poem.

and he will curse thee to thy face. And the LORD said unto 12 Satan, Behold, all that he hath *is* in thy power; only upon himself put not forth thine hand. So Satan went forth from the presence of the LORD.

And there was a day when his sons and his daughters 13 *were* eating and drinking wine in their eldest brother's house:

11. *curse thee to thy face*] that is, renounce thee openly. See on vers. 5. The phrase *and he will curse thee* has the form of an oath in the Heb. Satan so little believes in the sincerity of human religion that he is not afraid to take his oath that it is hollow.

12. Satan receives permission to try Job, but the length he can go is rigidly bounded by the will of the Most High. Having received his commission he immediately "goes forth," glad to appearance in the opportunity of doing mischief and confident in the result.

13—22. JOB'S FIRST TRIAL; AND ITS ISSUE: HIS REVERENCE TOWARDS GOD REMAINS UNSHAKEN.

Between *vv.* 12 and 13 there is an interval, an ominous stillness like that which precedes the storm. The poet has drawn aside the curtain to us and we know what is impending. Job knows nothing. His children are about him and he thinks the Almighty is yet with him, xxix. 5. The earth smiles to him as it was wont by day; and by night the Bear, Orion and the Pleiades come forth in their silent procession, and the Dragon trails his glittering folds across the heavens overhead, and he looks with wonder into the deep chambers of the South. All is glorious with a constant glory because it is an unchanging hand that leads them forth, the hand of the Holy One from whose words he has never declined, vi. 10, and whose candle as he deems still shines upon his head, xxix. 3. He does not know that he is being played for like a pawn. Suddenly the catastrophe overtakes him. Messenger after messenger, each taking up his tale of ruin before the other has concluded his, announce that all he had has been taken from him. Heaven and earth have combined to overwhelm him. The forces of nature and the destructive violence of men have united to strip him bare.

The description has many features of the ideal. First, the catastrophe befell on the day when Job's children were feasting in their eldest brother's house, *v.* 13, the day on the morning of which Job had sent for his children and sanctified them and offered sacrifices on their behalf. Job's godliness and his calamity are brought into the closest contrast. He felt this, and as he regarded every event as wrought by the hand of God immediately, his afflictions threw his mind into the deepest perplexity regarding the ways of God. Again, while heaven and men alternate their strokes upon him, these strokes follow one another with increasing severity, and in each case only one escapes to bring the grievous tidings. The rapid touches of the Author do not suggest any struggle or rising rebelliousness in Job's mind. He manifests the liveliest grief, but maintains his self-control. And the scene closes

14 and there came a messenger unto Job, and said, The oxen
15 were plowing, and the asses feeding beside them: and
the Sabeans fell *upon them*, and took them away; yea, they
have slain the servants with the edge of the sword; and
16 I only am escaped alone to tell thee. While he *was* yet
speaking, there came also another, and said, The fire of
God is fallen from heaven, and hath burnt up the sheep,
and the servants, and consumed them; and I only am
17 escaped alone to tell thee. While he *was* yet speaking,
there came also another, and said, The Chaldeans made out
three bands, and fell upon the camels, and have carried
them away, yea, and slain the servants with the edge of the
18 sword; and I only am escaped alone to tell thee. While
he *was* yet speaking, there came also another, and said,
Thy sons and thy daughters *were* eating and drinking wine
19 in their eldest brother's house: and, behold, there came a
great wind from the wilderness, and smote the four corners
of the house, and it fell upon the young men, and they are
20 dead; and I only am escaped alone to tell thee. Then

upon the sufferer, a solitary man, worshipping God amidst the waste
where his rich possessions once had lien.

14, 15. The first stroke, the loss of the oxen and she-asses, with
the slaughter of the servants. Job's servants were probably armed, as
is usual in the East, and offered resistance, for the Bedawin do not
usually shed blood unless opposed. The Sabeans were an Arab tribe,
or possibly different tribes bore the name (Gen. x. 7, 28; xxv. 3). In
vi. 19 they are represented as trading with caravans. They are mentioned in connexion with Dedan, and probably detachments of them
encamped on the borders of Edom, and these would be the assailants
of Job's servants. The raid came from the direction of the South, and
the fact that the oxen were plowing indicates that the disaster befell in
winter.

16. The second stroke. The fire of God can hardly have been the
sultry, poisonous Samoom, or hot wind of the desert, nor any rain of
sulphur such as destroyed Sodom, but was most likely lightning; see
1 Kings xviii. 38; 2 Kings i. 12.

17. The third stroke. The name Chaldeans was perhaps given
generally to the tribes that roamed between the cultivated land on the
east of the Jordan and the Euphrates. Dividing an attacking force into
several bands, so as to fall on the enemy on several sides, was a common
piece of Oriental tactics, Judges vii. 16, ix. 43; 1 Sam. xi. 11.

18, 19. The fourth stroke, the death of Job's children. The wind
struck the four corners of the house, being a whirlwind. It came from
the side or region of the desert.

Job arose, and rent his mantle, and shaved his head, and
fell down upon the ground, and worshipped, and said,   21
  Naked came I out of my mother's womb,
  And naked shall I return thither:
  The LORD gave, and the LORD hath taken *away;*
  Blessed be the name of the LORD.
In all this Job sinned not, nor charged God foolishly.   22

20, 21. Job's demeanour under his sorrows. As became a man of his rank Job had received the messengers sitting. When the full extent of his misery came home to him he arose and gave way to the liveliest expressions of grief. He rent his mantle, in token that his heart was rent with sorrow, as Joel ii. 13 says, "Rend your heart and not your garments;" he shaved his head, putting off, in token of his mourning, every adornment, even that which nature had supplied; and he cast himself upon the ground, laying his forehead on the dust, in deepest submission before God. Grief has its rights, which religion stands by to see fulfilled, and then comes forward to hallow it and cast its peace over it.—The "mantle" (me'eel) was not a detached garment as the word might suggest, but a tunic, the uppermost of the garments proper. It was worn by women of the higher rank, 2 Sam. xiii. 18, as well as men; was of linen or later of cotton, with arms, and reaching to the ankles. It was often either richly embroidered or perhaps made up of pieces of cloth of various colours, Gen. xxxvii. 3.

21. *naked shall I return thither*] The general sense is plain, though the precise idea is obscure. The words "my mother's womb" must be used literally, and *return thither* somewhat inexactly, to describe a condition similar to that which preceded entrance upon life and light. Or, as growth in the womb is described, Ps. cxxxix. 15, as "being curiously wrought in the lowest parts of the earth," the womb and the bosom of the earth, "the mother of all," may be compared together. "We brought nothing into the world, and it is certain we can carry nothing out," 1 Tim. vi. 7. All that man has is a gift of God which He may recall. Job blesses God alike who gave and who recalled.

the name of the Lord] The Author here lets the Israelitish name Jehovah fall from the lips of his hero, contrary to his usual habit of putting the names God, Almighty, which were not distinctively Hebrew, into the mouths of the speakers. Perhaps the phrase was a general one which alteration would have spoiled; or more likely, the writer was so much in sympathy with the sentiment put into Job's mouth that it escaped him for the moment that it was not himself or his nation but one foreign to Israel that was uttering it.

22. The Writer's judgment on Job's demeanour.

In all this] Both in what he suffered and in what he said and did. Job's expressions of grief were no sin.

charged God foolishly] Rather as margin, **attributed folly to God.** The word "folly" hardly expresses the idea, though a better word is

2 Again there was a day when the sons of God came to present themselves before the LORD, and Satan came also
2 among them to present himself before the LORD. And the LORD said unto Satan, From whence comest thou? And Satan answered the LORD, and said, From going to and
3 fro in the earth, and from walking up and down in it. And the LORD said unto Satan, Hast thou considered my servant Job, that *there is* none like him in the earth, a perfect and an upright man, one that feareth God, and escheweth evil? and still he holdeth fast his integrity, although thou

not easy to find. The adj. signifies *insipid*, without savour, vi. 6 (unsavoury), and the term here means moral impropriety; Job attributed no want of right moral savour to God's actions in His dealing with him. Others prefer the meaning: Gave God no cause of displeasure; a sense less suitable to the meaning of the word and to the connexion, for the action of the poem turns immediately on the estimate which Job will form of God, and whether in consequence he will renounce Him, and only indirectly on what God shall find in Job. But comp. ii. 10.

The confident predictions of the Satan are wholly falsified.

CH. II. 1—10. JOB'S SECOND TRIAL AND ITS ISSUE: HE SINNED NOT WITH HIS LIPS.

How long time intervened between Job's first trial and the second is not stated. The Targum seems to conjecture a year. The new trial is introduced like the first by a scene in heaven. The Council of God convenes. His ministers stand before Him, and among them the one whose office is, as the Targum says, to scrutinize the deeds of men. The Lord speaks of His servant Job with approval and with compassion, reproaching the Satan with instigating Him to bring undeserved affliction upon him. Satan's answer is ready: the trial did not touch Job near enough; safe himself, his children may perish; if the hand of God would touch him in his own bone and flesh, he would renounce Him to his face. Satan receives permission to afflict Job himself, with the reservation that he shall spare his life. Straightway Satan goes forth and smites Job with sore boils, the leprosy called Elephantiasis or botch of Egypt, Deut. xxviii. 27, 35. The deeper affliction only opens or reveals greater deeps in Job's reverent piety. In his former trial he blessed God who took away the good He had added to naked man; this was strictly no evil: now he bows beneath His hand when He inflicts positive evil, "We receive good at the hand of God and shall we not also receive evil?" And again the Writer sums up the issue of the trial with the words, "In all this Job sinned not."

3. *still he holdeth fast his integrity*] Or, **his perfectness**, see on i. 1. Satan had insinuated that Job's religiousness was interested, he served

movedst me against him, to destroy him without cause. And Satan answered the LORD, and said, Skin for skin, yea, 4 all that a man hath will he give for his life. But put forth 5 thine hand now, and touch his bone and his flesh, and he will curse thee to thy face. And the LORD said unto Satan, 6 Behold, he *is* in thine hand; but save his life. So went 7 Satan forth from the presence of the LORD, and smote Job with sore boils from the sole of his foot unto his crown.

God for the benefits He conferred. That he maintained his godly fear when the benefits were taken away refuted the suspicion, and shewed that his trials were without cause.

4. The Satan's reply is that the trial was not sufficiently close, it left the man himself untouched.

Skin for skin, yea, all] Rather, **skin for skin, and all that a man hath will he give for himself.** The second half of the sentence is an application to the subject in hand of the general truth expressed in the words, Skin for skin. These words seem proverbial, though the origin of the proverb is obscure. The meaning seems to be, Like for like, so all &c. Others take the expression in a less general sense. The Targum translates, Member for member, one member of the body in behalf of, or to cover another member, as the arm the head. The word *skin* is used in our Book once or twice for the body, xviii. 13, xix. 26. If this sense could be adopted here the meaning would be, Skin or body of others for one's own, all that a man has &c., in which case the second clause would merely repeat the first. This is prosaic, though adopted by Jerome, pro corio suo coria obtulit filiorum. The verse would then run: Others for oneself, all that a man hath will he give for himself. See the different interpretations discussed at length in Conant's Job, p. 8 *seq.*

7. *with sore boils*] It is generally agreed that the disease of Job was the leprosy called Elephantiasis, so named because the swollen limbs and the black and corrugated skin of those afflicted by it resemble those of the elephant. It is said by ancient authors, as Pliny, to be peculiar to Egypt, but it is found in other hot countries such as the Hijâz, and even in northern climates as Norway. It is said to attack the limbs first, breaking out below the knees and gradually spreading over the whole body. We are probably to consider, however, that Job was smitten "from the sole of his foot unto his crown" all at once. Full details of its appearance and the sensations of those affected may be gathered from the Book, though, being poetically coloured, they will hardly bear to be read like a page from a handbook of Pathology. The ulcers were accompanied by an itching so intolerable that a piece of potsherd was taken to scrape the sores and remove the feculent discharge, ii. 8. The form and countenance were so disfigured by the disease that the sufferer's friends could not recognise him, ii. 12. The ulcers seized the whole body both without and inwardly, xix. 20, making the breath fetid, and

8 And he took him a potsherd to scrape himself withal; and
9 he sat down among the ashes. Then said his wife unto

emitting a loathsome smell that drove every one from the sufferer's presence, xix. 17, and made him seek refuge outside the village upon the heap of ashes, ii. 8. The sores, which bred worms, vii. 5, alternately closed, having the appearance of clods of earth, and opened and ran, so that the body was alternately swollen and emaciated, xvi. 8. The patient was haunted with horrible dreams, vii. 14, and unearthly terrors, iii. 25, and harassed by a sensation of choking, vii. 15, which made his nights restless and frightful, vii. 4, as his incessant pains made his days weary, vii. 1—4. His bones were filled with gnawing pains, as if a fire burned in them, xxx. 30, or as if his limbs were tortured in the stocks, xiii. 27, or wrenched off, xxx. 17. He was helpless, and his futile attempts to rise from the ground provoked the merriment of the children who played about the heap where he lay, xix. 18. The disease was held incurable, though the patient might linger many years, and his hopelessness of recovery made him long for death, iii. 20 and often. Delitzsch and Dillmann refer to various treatises on the subject, in particular, to one published at the cost of the Norwegian Government, Danielsen et Boeck, *Traité de la Spédalskhed ou Éléphantiasis des Grecs* (with coloured plates), Paris, 1848.

8. *and he sat down among the ashes*] Rather, **as he sat among**. By the "ashes" is possibly meant (as the Sept. already understands, which translates ἐπὶ τῆς κοπρίας) the Mázbalah, the place outside the Arabic towns where the *zibl*, that is, dung and other rubbish of the place is thrown. "The dung which is heaped up upon the *Mezbele* of the Hauran villages is not mixed with straw, which in that warm and dry land is not needed for litter, and it comes mostly from solid-hoofed animals, as the flocks and oxen are left over night in the grazing places. It is carried in baskets in a dry state to this place before the village, and usually burnt once a month...The ashes remain... If the village has been inhabited for centuries the Mezbele reaches a height far overtopping it. The winter rains reduce it into a compact mass, and it becomes by and bye a solid hill of earth... The Mezbele serves the inhabitants for a watchtower, and in the sultry evenings for a place of concourse, because there is a current of air on the height. There all day long the children play about it; and there the outcast, who has been stricken with some loathsome malady, and is not allowed to enter the dwellings of men, lays himself down, begging an alms of the passers-by by day, and by night sheltering himself among the ashes which the heat of the sun has warmed. There too lie the village dogs, perhaps gnawing a fallen carcase, which is often flung there." Wetzstein in Delitzsch, Comm. on Job, 2 Ed. p. 62 (Trans. vol. II, p. 152).

9. *Then said his wife*] The incident related of Job's wife is not introduced for her sake, but for the purpose of exhibiting through it the condition of Job's mind, around which the drama turns. The author did not indicate the impression which Job's personal affliction produced upon him. What thoughts he had are concealed; he is represented

him, Dost thou still retain thine integrity? curse God, and

as sitting silent in his seclusion. The full impression of his miseries is brought home to him reflected from the mind of another, that other being the one fitted to influence him most powerfully. It is probable that the episode of Job's wife is brought in with a double purpose, first, to shew how all around Job, those nearest to him, gave way under the severity of his trial, and thus by contrast to enhance the strength of his faith and the grandeur of his character; and second, to shew how, though subjected to the keenest trial from the example and representations of his wife, he still remained true.

The name Dinah given to Job's wife by the Targum or Chaldee Translation most probably rests on no tradition, but is a mere child's fancy. The Sept. introduces her speech, which it gives in a greatly amplified form, with the words "when a long time had passed." The amplification is not unsuitable to the circumstances, but the curt phrases of the original are truer to art and nature, for grief is possessed of few words. Much animated dispute has taken place over the character and conduct of the woman. The Ancients were not favourably impressed by her. Augustine calls her roundly *Diaboli adjutrix*. The Geneva Version discerns a sad and universal principle in her conduct, "Satan useth the same instrument against Job as he did against Adam." As was to be expected the present age has espoused her cause, and labours hard to put a face upon her words. The only question of importance is, what sense the Author intended her words to convey; and the key to this is found in the way in which her husband takes them up. He does not directly call her a "fool," that is, a godless person (Ps. xiv. 1), but with mild circumlocution says that she speaks as one of the foolish women speaks. The Eastern writer lets the woman act in character (Eccles. vii. 26 *seq.*). He would have probably smiled at the elaborate analysing of the female mind to which Westerns devote themselves, thinking it a waste of time. As the weaker Job's wife fell first into the snare of the Devil, and used her influence, as in the beginning of history, to draw her husband after her. Her story, however, is not told for her sake, but to shew how those around Job fell away, and to set in a strong light the strain to which his faith was put by such an example and the solicitations that accompanied it.

curse God, and die] Rather as before, *renounce God and die*. From a modern point of view many extenuations may be pleaded for Job's wife, but her religion is represented here as precisely of the kind which Satan said Job's was of. She wonders that Job still maintains his pious resignation; and counsels him, as he gets no good from God but only evil, even the extreme evil of death, to renounce an unprofitable service, and die, as he must, for nothing else awaits him. This is probably the meaning of the words "and die." The words might have a different meaning. When two imperatives come together the second often expresses the consequence of the first, as *do this and live*. And, "renounce God and die" might mean, renounce Him and bring down His final stroke of death at once. The other is more probable.

10 die. But he said unto her, Thou speakest as one of the foolish *women* speaketh. What? shall we receive good at

> 10. *one of the foolish women*] The fear of the Lord is the beginning of wisdom. "Wise" is less an intellectual than a moral term; and its opposite "foolish" means godless, Ps. xiv. 1. To "work folly in Israel" is to infringe any of the sacred laws of natural or consuetudinary morals, Judg. xix. 23; 2 Sam. xiii. 12.
> *what? shall we receive*] Or, *we receive good...and shall we not also receive* (i.e. accept) *evil?* Job's words might mean, we receive much good at the hand of God, shall we not also out of thankfulness for the good, accept evil when He sends it? But this hardly goes to the root of the counsel given by his wife. Therefore rather: we receive good from God, not due to us, but in which we see the gift of His sovereign hand (i. 21), shall we not also do homage to His absoluteness when He brings evil upon us? Here Job reaches the utmost height of the religious feeling. He is in danger of drifting away from this feeling under the irritation of his friends' misdirected counsels, but he is led back again to it with a deeper peace through the appearance and words of the Lord (ch. xxxviii. *seq.*). The Author lets us know what in his view true religion is, whether in a man or in a nation, and doubtless amidst the troubles and perplexing darkness of his time he had seen it exemplified both in individual men and in that godly kernel of the nation which kept up the true continuity of Israel and conserved its true idea.
> The Writer adds his emphatic testimony to Job's sinlessness. *In all this*, under this severe affliction of body, and exposed to this searching temptation on the part of his wife, *Job did not sin with his lips*, that is, in any particular. Thinking and speaking hardly differ in the East, and the words mean, let no sinful murmur escape him; comp. Ps. xvii. 3.
> Though the Writer professedly paints the sufferings and mental troubles of an individual, and though it may be certain that he has the sorrows of individuals before his mind, it is scarcely possible to doubt that he is writing history also on a large scale. He has his nation with its calamities and the various impressions these made upon the religious mind in his view. The national calamity could be nothing less than deportation or exile. As not one but several successive and diverse waves of feeling pass over Job's mind in regard to his afflictions, we may assume that the Writer did not stand close behind the great blow that fell upon his people, but lived at a considerable distance from it. The people had not only been stripped of their possessions, but subjected to severe treatment themselves, and the apostasy of many was a sore trial to the faith of those who remained constant, and the evil had lasted long enough to produce various impressions on men's minds and give rise to many attempts to solve the problem which it raised. These solutions are reflected in the debate between Job and his friends. The Author has a solution which is new, to the effect, namely, that the calamity is not a punishment or chastisement on account of sin, as others held, but a trial of righteousness. This view he invests in all the dramatic splendour that distinguishes the Prologue. Though living long after the calamity had

the hand of God, and shall we not receive evil? In all this did not Job sin with his lips.

Now when Job's three friends heard of all this evil that 11 was come upon him, they came every one from his own place; Eliphaz the Temanite, and Bildad the Shuhite, and Zophar the Naamathite: for they had made an appointment together to come to mourn with him and to comfort him. And when they lift up their eyes afar off, and knew him not, 12

befallen his fellow-citizens, the Author must have written previously to the happy turn of affairs that restored them to prosperity and to a higher plane of religious life. This restoration was the great hope he desired to inspire. Such a hope was the counterpart of the other half of his theory of evil. If suffering be the trial of righteousness, the trial, if patiently borne, must bring an accumulation of spiritual gain. This part of the theory was necessary also in another view, in order to justify the ways of God in subjecting the innocent to trial.

11—13. JOB'S THREE FRIENDS, HAVING HEARD OF HIS MISFORTUNES, COME TO CONDOLE WITH HIM.

How long time intervened between Job's second affliction and the arrival of his friends cannot be accurately ascertained. From the allusions in chaps. vii., xix., and xxx., it is probable that a considerable time elapsed. A man of Job's rank would not choose his friends from the men of inferior station around him; they would be, like himself, Eastern princes, all but his equals in rank and influence. Their abodes would therefore be distant from one another, and more distant from his, and travelling in the East is slow. The tone of Job's mind, too, as reflected in ch. iii., has undergone a change, the effect, no doubt, of protracted sufferings.

Eliphaz is an old Idumean name (Gen. xxxvi. 4), and Teman, the place of his abode, is frequently mentioned in connexion with Edom. The place was famed for the wisdom of its inhabitants (Am. i. 12; Obad. 8; Jerem. xlix. 7; Ezek. xxv. 13). Shuah was a son of Abraham by Keturah. The descendants of this wife were sent by Abraham to the East (Gen. xxv. 2, 6). Bildad may be connected by the Author with this family. Naamah, the dwelling-place of Zophar, means, perhaps, pleasant abode (*Beauséjour*, Reuss). A place of this name is mentioned, Josh. xv. 41, but this, being in Palestine, can hardly have been the home of Zophar. The place is doubtless supposed by the Writer to lie east of the Jordan.

11. *for they had made an appointment*] Or, *and they met together*. They came each from his own place and met at one point to go to visit Job together.

to mourn with him] Or, condole with him, and shew their sympathy with him in his sufferings.

12. *knew him not*] He was so altered and disfigured by the disease.

they lifted up their voice, and wept; and they rent every one his mantle, and sprinkled dust upon their heads toward
13 heaven. So they sat down with him upon the ground seven days and seven nights, and none spake a word unto him: for they saw that *his* grief was very great.

As Job perhaps lay outside the town they may have seen him at a distance.

sprinkled dust upon their heads] that is, they threw dust upwards towards heaven, which fell upon their heads, the gesture intimating perhaps that they were laid in the dust by a calamity sent from heaven; comp. Josh. vii. 6; 1 Sam. iv. 12; Lam. ii. 10. See on i. 20.

13. *none spake a word*] Being overwhelmed by the affecting sight before them; as the Author adds: they saw that the *grief*, i.e. the pain or affliction, was very great. Comp. Ezek. iii. 15. The length of time during which they sat in silence, seven days and seven nights (the time of mourning for the dead, Gen. l. 10; i. Sam. xxxi. 13), shews the profound impression made upon them.

CH. III. MOVED BY THE SYMPATHISING PRESENCE OF HIS FRIENDS, JOB LOSES HIS SELF-CONTROL, AND BREAKS OUT INTO A PASSIONATE CRY FOR DEATH.

The expressive gestures of Job's friends betokened the liveliest sympathy, and their silence of seven days indicated how awful they felt his calamity to be. And we often learn how to estimate our own situation from the countenances of others, and the passing movements on the faces around us rule the tide of feeling in our own breasts. From the sentiments which the three friends gave utterance to afterwards we know that very mixed feelings may have led to their silence and dismay, but if so, such a thing was unsuspected by Job. He was so conscious of his own innocence that he never supposed that others could suspect it, and he saw only sympathy and friendship and the reflection of his great misery in his friends' demeanour. Formerly he was able to rebuke the suggestions of the woman, his wife, and restrain himself. But now he is in the presence of men his fellows, the companions of his former prosperity, and his self-control deserts him, and he breaks out into a passionate cry that he might die.

This cry of misery is thrice repeated in the chapter:
1—10. Would God I had never been conceived or born.
11—19. Would God I had died from my birth.
20—26. Why does God continue life to the wretched, who long for death?

1—10. WOULD GOD I HAD NEVER BEEN CONCEIVED OR BORN.

This is the idea really expressed when Job curses his day and wishes it blotted out of existence. First he curses the day of his birth and the night of his conception together, *v.* 3, and then each separately, the day in two verses and the night in four. Let darkness seize that

After this opened Job his mouth, and cursed his day. 3
And Job spake, and said, 2
Let the day perish wherein I was born, 3
And the night *in which it was* said,
There is a man child conceived.
Let that day be darkness; 4
Let not God regard it from above,
Neither let the light shine upon it.
Let darkness and the shadow of death stain it; 5
Let a cloud dwell upon it;
Let the blackness of the day terrify it.

day; let not God from above seek after it; let thick darkness and the shadow of death claim it as part of their heritage; let clouds and all that maketh black the day, eclipses, ominous obscurations, affright it, *vv.* 4, 5. Let darkness swallow up that night that it be not reckoned nor come in among the joyful troop of nights in their glittering procession; while other nights ring with birth-day gladness let it sit barren; let enchanters curse it; let it be endless, waiting always for a dawn that never breaks, *vv.* 6—10.

1. *cursed his day*] The day of his birth. Reverent minds have always found difficulty in accommodating themselves to the religious boldness of the Book of Job. A curious instance of this is given in the Catena of Greek interpreters on Job, where one writer interprets Job's "day" to be the day when man fell from righteousness to sin. The same feeling has influenced the translation of xiii. 15 and xix. 25.

3. *night in which it was said*] Rather, **the night which said.** The night is personified and cursed as a conscious agent, responsible for Job's existence, comp. *v.* 10.

There is a man child conceived] Rather, **a man**; "A woman when she is in travail hath sorrow; but as soon as she is delivered of the child she remembereth no more the anguish, for joy that a man is born into the world," John xvi. 21.

4. *regard it*] lit. *seek after it*, or care for it. Let it perish from His mind that He cause no sun to rise upon it.

5. *shadow of death stain it*] Rather, **claim it**, lit. *redeem it*. Let it become part of the possession of darkness. The word, however, does not mean *re*claim, as if the idea were that the day had been won from darkness by light and was to be reconquered. The translation "shadow *of death*" possibly rests on a false etymology; at the same time it is perhaps the best that can be given, and Hitzig's conjecture that the Hebrews themselves came to see the word "death" in the termination of the form may not be far astray, comp. Job xxxviii. 17. The word originally means "deepest darkness."

the blackness of the day] lit. *blacknesses*. The word probably means "all that makes black the day," eclipses, supernatural obscurations and the like—all ominous darknesses that terrify a day.

6   *As for* that night, let darkness seize upon it;
    Let it not be joined unto the days of the year,
    Let it not come into the number of the months.
7   Lo, let that night be solitary,
    Let no joyful voice come therein.
8   Let them curse it that curse the day,
    Who are ready to raise up their mourning.
9   Let the stars of the twilight thereof be dark;

6. *let it not be joined unto*] Rather, **let it not rejoice among**. Let it not enter the joyful troop of days, glad in its existence and its beauty. Another way of spelling the word gives the meaning, let it not be joined unto.

7. *be solitary*] Rather perhaps, *barren*, as Is. xlix. 21. Let it not experience a parent's joy, and let nought that lives date its birth from it. *no joyful voice*] of birthday rejoicing.

8. The most probable sense of this verse is,

> Let them that curse days curse it,
> Them that are skilled to rouse up the Dragon.

They that curse days or the day are enchanters and magicians, who were believed to have power to cast their spells upon a day and overwhelm it with darkness and misfortune. Perhaps, however, the first half of the verse is explained by the second, and only one species of enchantment referred to, namely, rousing up the Dragon. The Heb. word is *leviathan*. This name is given in ch. xli. to a sea or river monster, probably, the crocodile, but it is difficult to find any logical connexion between rousing up the crocodile and cursing days. The word leviathan means twisted or having folds, and is an epithet for a serpent. In Is. xxvii. 1 we read: In that day Jehovah with his sore and great and strong sword shall visit leviathan the fleeing serpent, and leviathan the serpent with coils. The key to the meaning of the verse, however, is found in Job xxvi. 13, which rightly rendered means,

> By His breath the heavens become bright,
> His hand pierceth the fleeing serpent.

Here piercing the fleeing serpent and making the heavens clear are parallel acts. The fleeing serpent, therefore, was the cause of the darkness. In both passages in Job there is an allusion to the popular mythology, according to which the darkening or eclipse of the sun and moon was caused by the serpent throwing its folds around them, or swallowing them up. In its origin this mythology is probably nothing more than a stroke of the poetic imagination, which turned the dark cloud or eclipsing shadow into a huge Dragon. Enchanters were supposed to have power to set this Dragon in motion, and cause the lights of day or night to be swallowed up.

9. *the twilight thereof*] that is, the morning twilight of that night. Let its morning stars, that should herald its day, go out—as the next clause explains: let it look for the light of a day that never breaks.

Let it look for light, but *have* none;
Neither let it see the dawning of the day:
Because it shut not up the doors of my *mother's* womb, 10
Nor hid sorrow from mine eyes.
Why died I not from the womb? 11
Why did I *not* give up the ghost when I came out of the belly?
Why did the knees prevent me? 12
Or why the breasts that I should suck?
For now should I have lien *still* and been quiet, 13
I should have slept: then had I been at rest,
With kings and counsellers of the earth, 14
Which built desolate places for themselves;

see the dawning of the day] lit. *behold the eyelids of the morning*. This beautiful figure looks like an idea from Western poetry, just as the chamber of the Sun, Ps. xix. 5. All commentators quote the parallel from Sophocles, χρυσέας ἁμέρας βλέφαρον, Antigone, 103.

10. *the doors of my mother's womb*] to hinder conception or fruitfulness, Gen. xx. 18; 1 Sam. i. 5. The crime of the night is deferred to the last, and the curse closes with the mention of it.

11—19. WOULD GOD I HAD DIED FROM MY BIRTH.

If he must be born, Job asks, Why he did not die from the womb? his eye turning to the next possibility and chance of escaping sorrow. Had he died he would have been at peace; and the picture of the painless stillness of death fascinates him and he dwells long on it, counting over with a minute particularity all classes, kings and prisoners, slaves and masters, small and great, who there drink deep of a common peace, escaping the unquietness of life, for life upon the earth, however lived, is full of a painful restlessness. The thought of this stillness of death brings a certain calm to the sufferer's mind, and the passionateness of his former words subsides.

12. *the knees prevent me*] Rather, **receive**, or meet me. The reference may be to the father's knees, on which the new born child was laid, or more general. As to the expression, see Gen. l. 23; Is. lxvi. 12. The sufferer's eye runs over all the chances of death which he had miserably lost, when he came from the womb, was laid upon the knees, and pressed to the breasts. The sorrow of his later years transmutes (as it does still with others) the tender affections and solicitudes lavished on his infancy, and makes them seem bitter cruelties.

13. The words receive their pathos from the contrast of his present anguish, *v.* 26.

14. *which built desolate places*] The expression seems to be that which occurs several times in Scripture, e.g. Is. lviii. 12, lxi. 4; Ezek. xxxvi. 10, 33; Mal. i. 4, and means to build up or rebuild ruins, i.e.

15 Or with princes that had gold,
    Who filled their houses *with* silver:
16 Or as a hidden untimely birth I had not been;
    As infants *which* never saw light.
17 There the wicked cease *from* troubling;
    And there the weary be at rest.
18 *There* the prisoners rest together;
    They hear not the voice of the oppressor.

cities or habitations desolated or abandoned, and make them again inhabited. If this be the meaning the phrase must be used in a general way to indicate the greatness of those kings and counsellors when they were alive and the renown they won. To this idea the words in *v*. 15, princes who had gold, form a parallel. The speaker wishes to indicate that instead of lying in squalor and being the contempt of the low-born race of men as he now is (ch. xxx.), if he had died he would have been in company of the great dead who played famous parts in life. This appears to be the general idea of the words, but the phrase "built desolate places for themselves" is too vague in such a connexion, and the words "for themselves" suggest something definite and well-known as that which they built, as does the parallel expression "who filled their houses with silver." The Hebrew word "desolate places" has a distant resemblance in sound to the Egyptian word Pyramids, and some adopt this sense here. There may be some corruption of the Text.

15. *their houses with silver*] There is no reason for supposing that "houses" means mausoleums or tombs. The reference is not to the practice of burying treasures along with the dead, nor to the idea that the pomp of riches could thus be perpetuated in death. It is those who were famous in this life with whom Job, had he died, would have been in company in death.

16. With strong revulsion from the anguish of life Job desires even if possible a deeper death than to have died when born, even the death of having been dead born, scarcely to be distinguished from non-existence itself. Comp. Eccles. iv. 2, 3, with Plumptre's notes and citations from the classics.

17. *cease from troubling*] That is, probably, not from troubling others, but from the unquiet of their own evil. Verses 17—19 contain the two main ideas, first, that all, evil and good, great and small, are the same in the place of the dead; and second, that this common condition is one of profound rest. Even the wicked there are no more agitated by the turbulence of their passions. Comp. Is. lvii. 20.

the weary] lit. *the wearied as to strength*, the exhausted.

18. *the prisoners rest together*] The "prisoners" are not those immured in prison, but captives driven to forced labour.

the oppressor] The taskmaster, Ex. iii. 7. The prisoners are there all together, and they hear not the voice, the shouts and curses of the driver (ch. xxxix. 7).

The small and great *are* there; 19
And the servant *is* free from his master.
Wherefore is light given to him that is in misery, 20
And life unto the bitter in soul;
Which long for death, but it *cometh* not; 21
And dig for it more than for hid treasures;
Which rejoice exceedingly, 22
And are glad, when they can find the grave?
Why is light given to a man whose way is hid, 23
And whom God hath hedged in?

19. *small and great are there*] i.e. are there alike, the same.

20—26. WHY DOES GOD CONTINUE LIFE TO THE WRETCHED, WHO LONG FOR DEATH?

The vision of the peacefulness of death passes away, and Job awakens again to the consciousness of his real condition, and his words, which had sunk into calmness as he contemplated the peace of death, now seem to rise again like the storm after a lull, Wherefore gives He light to him that is in misery? He does not name though he alludes to God, and the indirect reference though partly due to reverence betrays a rising alienation in his heart. His question is one of anguish and impatience. His own condition throws its gloom over all human life, and he puts the question first generally, *vv.* 20—22; there are many like him seeking death and unable to find it, who would exult for joy if they could find the grave. Then he comes to the individual, *v.* 23, meaning himself; Wherefore gives He life to the man whose way is hid? the man who cannot see and cannot move, who can discover no solution of the riddle of his life, and find no course of action to relieve himself, who lies in the grasp of a calamity which has too surely come from God, and which has introduced confusion among all the principles of religion which he has hitherto held and into the relation to God in which he has hitherto stood, *v.* 23. And finally he adds some touches to the picture of his misery, his constant moaning, and the unbroken succession of troubles that afflict him, which come so thick that he has no respite from one before another overtakes him, *vv.* 24—26.

20. *Wherefore is light given*] This is a possible translation, but more probably we should render, **wherefore gives He light?** the Author of light and life being alluded to obliquely and not named. *The bitter* is plur., those that are bitter in soul. Job's eye looks over mankind and sees many in the same condition of misery as himself. Comp. ch. vii. 1 *seq.*

22. *rejoice exceedingly*] lit. *rejoice even to exultation*, Hos. ix. 1.

23. *whose way is hid*] Job now narrows his view from the general sorrows of mankind to himself. His way is hid or lost, the clear path of his former life has suddenly broken off, or as the second clause of the verse expresses it, has been shut in by a hedge, set by God across it.

24 For my sighing cometh before I eat,
And my roarings are poured out like the waters.
25 For the thing which I greatly feared is come upon me,
And *that* which I was afraid of is come unto me.
26 I was not in safety, neither had I rest, neither was I quiet;
Yet trouble came.

The reference is not merely to his physical calamities, but much more to the speculative and religious perplexities which his calamities wove about his mind, and from which he can find no outlet, cf. xix. 8.

24. *before I eat*] lit. *before my meat*, as margin. The temporal meaning of *before* gives no sense here. In 1 Sam. i. 16 the same expression occurs, "Count not thine handmaid *for* a daughter of Belial." Therefore render, my sighing cometh *for* (instead of, or, like) my meat; it is his constant, daily food.

like the waters] Rather, **like water**, i.e. a broad, unbroken stream.

25, 26. *the thing which I feared*] These two verses read thus,

    For let me fear an evil, and it cometh upon me,
    And whatsoever I dread, it overtakes me;
    I have no ease, neither quiet nor rest,
        But trouble cometh.

The whole passage from *v.* 20 describes Job's present condition. The speaker says, if he but imagines an evil, if he but "'fears a fear," it is immediately upon him. The words are put hypothetically in the past tense: Have I feared a fear, it cometh upon me; but the reference cannot be to the real past, as in the English Version, because it would be contrary to the idea of the poem to suppose that Job even in the days of his golden prime was haunted with indefinite fears of coming misfortune. On the contrary the picture he gives of himself, ch. xxix., shews that his piety reflected itself in a full and trustful peace of mind; see his own words ch. xvi. 12, xxix. 18 *seq.*

Verse 26 means that Job has no pause between the waves of his affliction, no time to recover from one before another overwhelms him. "Trouble" here is the fit or paroxysm of trouble.

Job's three friends sat silent before him seven days. Then Job spake and cursed his day. His speech opened his friends' mouths and probably also their eyes. Job's language and demeanour were not what they would have looked for from one in his condition. His violent complaints and his indirect allusions to Heaven were not only unbecoming in themselves, but cast an unwelcome light upon his past life. Job speaks no doubt with the passion of despair and in the bitterness of his misery, and his indirect allusions to God betray impatience and are uttered with a tone of resentment, though there is as yet no direct charge of injustice against God, only an impatient demand why He continues life to one in such misery. His tone of mind is very different from that exhibited when his trials had newly befallen him or when he replied to the suggestions of his wife. And it is this tone, suggesting so much more than it expressed, that the three friends lay hold of and attach their exhortations to, and which is thus the point out of which the whole succeeding debate developes itself.

CH. IV.—XXXI. THE DEBATE BETWEEN JOB AND HIS FRIENDS ON THE QUESTION OF HIS SUFFERINGS AND ON THE MEANING OF EVIL IN GENERAL.

This Debate occupies the whole body of the Book. It attaches itself to Job's passionate cry for death and his impatient allusions to Heaven in ch. iii. The tone of this speech the friends cannot refrain from reprobating—they must speak (ch. iv. 2); and thus the warfare of words commences. The subject to begin with is Job's sufferings, but naturally the discussion widens out, so as to embrace the whole question of the meaning and purposes of calamity or evil in general. As the debate on the meaning of suffering occupies so large a portion of the Book, we must assume that one of the main intentions of the Author in writing his poem was to let light in upon this question from various sides and present ancient and current as well as new views regarding it. And as he allows the three friends to be brought to silence by Job, we may be sure that it was his purpose to discredit the theories which they represented and to teach that they could not any longer be maintained. Job in his speeches has no theory, he contributes nothing positive. The part he plays is merely negative and destructive. But in confuting the friends he clears the ground of the old encumbrances, and in their place the Author himself brings forward his new truth regarding the meaning of suffering, which he exhibits in a highly dramatic form in the Prologue. Both Job and his friends debate the question ignorant of the real cause of Job's calamities, and neither they nor he approach the true solution. The Author allows us who watch the debate to know that Job's sufferings were a trial of his righteousness. Thus the Prologue serves the same purpose as the prologue in the Greek drama, it introduces the actors, and supplies the spectators with the information needful to understand the action.

The Author allows three persons to confront Job and maintain against him the traditional beliefs. It is possible that the number as well as the names of Job's friends may belong to the tradition upon which the Author worked. If not, he may mean to indicate by the number three the widespread currency and general acceptance of the views they advocate. The friends have each a well-marked individuality, and represent distinct aspects of religious conviction among mankind. Eliphaz, who on each occasion opens the debate, is the most dignified, the calmest and most considerate, and perhaps the oldest of Job's friends. He is a man almost of Prophetic rank, who speaks with the composure and authority and clear eye of a seer, as one to whom revelations by vision have been granted from Heaven (iv. 12 *seq*.). Bildad, a man of less consideration, is a representative of the class of the Wise (Jerem. xviii. 18; Prov. i. 6); an observer of life, one who generalizes on the ways of God to man, whose mind is stored with the priceless moral precedents of past ages, and who reposes upon the conclusions of thoughtful men of all times (ch. viii.). While Zophar is the private religious man of strong personal conviction, who doubtless lives by the truth he believes, and cannot imagine how any one should question it; who gets irritated and indulges in unworthy imputations against any one who disputes the truth of his principles. All three were sincere men, though their sincerity had never perhaps been put to the proof as Job's had been.

The three friends come to the contemplation of Job's sufferings, and to the discussion of the meaning of them, with a principle which they all agree in holding. Like all Shemitic thinkers they have no idea of what we call second causes. In their view God is in immediate relation to the world and the lives of men, and does all directly that happens. Evil and Good come immediately from His hand; and being a righteous ruler every event of His providence must be either a reward of good or a retribution on evil. It is invariably well with the righteous and ill with the wicked, or perhaps more strictly, it is invariably well with righteousness and ill with wickedness. For even the righteous may do evil, for what man is he that sinneth not? and his evil will bring down punishment upon it. But God is far from being an impersonal moral balance, weighing out happiness and adversity according to the deserts of men, with no interest in their fate. On the contrary, His eyes are on the righteous, and though He chastens them for their sin, His chastisement is not in order that they may perish (iv. 7), it is correction, meant to wean them from their evil and turn them again in humility and repentance unto righteousness. Therefore "happy is the man whom God correcteth" (ch. v. 17); such correction is an arrest laid upon him in his way of evil. Calamity therefore is not in itself decisive of the character of a man, though it is decisive of the fact that he has sinned. The issue of calamity only can shew what a man really is. If he is a righteous man, he accepts it as the warning of God and turns from his evil, and his future life is filled with blessings from God, and he shall enjoy length of days and all prosperity (v. 19—27). If he is evil he murmurs and rejects the divine correction, and brings wrath upon himself and perishes (v. 2). These principles explain the course pursued by the three friends towards Job. However strange it might seem to them they had no help but to conclude that Job, though a righteous man as they had always thought him, and continued to think him, had been guilty of acts of sin very displeasing unto God. And the temper he displayed under his afflictions alarmed them: it was the very temper of the ungodly (v. 2). Hence one after another they earnestly warn and exhort him to turn in humility and repentance unto God; and they draw bright pictures of the happy future which he shall yet enjoy.

As for Job he agreed with his three friends in believing that all events occurred through the immediate agency of God; good and evil came directly from His hand. Further he agreed with them that evil or suffering was inflicted by God on those whom He held guilty of having sinned. But Job's consciousness of his own innocence forbad his drawing the conclusion with his friends that he had been guilty of great and specific offences. He knew he had not. He was driven therefore to the conclusion that, though he was not guilty, God had resolved to hold him guilty (ix. 29 and often), and treat him as if he were so. Hence he is led to charge God with injustice. This feeling shines dimly through his words in ch. iii., and his friends detected it, but under their provocations and insinuations of his guilt he boldly avows his conviction of God's injustice, and throws it out with a passionate fury appalling to a reverent mind. This however is but one side of the conflict going on in his mind. There are other currents of feeling that run side by side with this one. The action of the drama is nothing else than the progress of feeling in Job's mind under his sufferings and the views regarding them presented by his friends. This progress, however, will be better understood when the chapters are read.

It is evident that the alienation of Job's mind from God was increased and his feelings embittered by the insinuations and the misdirected advice of his friends. We should be deviating, however, from the line of the Author's conception if we were to regard the provocations of the friends as a third or separate temptation. Job's trial was merely his afflictions, narrated in the prologue. This trial continued. The friends only set it in a particular light. Before they arrived, or at least before they spoke, Job's mind had already drifted away from the attitude of reverent submission which he took up when his afflictions newly befell him. The friends add to his perplexity, but they are little else than voices that give body to the thoughts that must have risen and struggled in his own mind. It is to be noticed that the Satan no more appears. With the infliction of Job's calamities his part is ended. The supernatural agencies of the Prologue are no more called into requisition. It is plain indeed that the scenes in the Prologue are nothing but a splendidly dramatic form adopted by the Author for putting before us his new truth that calamities may befall the righteous not for any evil they have done but in order to try their righteousness and through the trial to perfect it.

The great debate is divided into three circles of speeches: (1) ch. iv.—xiv.; (2) ch. xv.—xxi.; (3) ch. xxii.—xxxi. Each of these three circles contains six speeches, one by each of the three friends in succession, with a reply from Job. In the last round, however, the third speaker, Zophar, fails to come forward. This is a confession of defeat; and Job, resuming the thread of his reply to Bildad, carries it through a series of chapters, in which, with a profound pathos, he contrasts his former greatness with his present misery, protests his innocence before Heaven, and adjures God to reveal to him the cause of his afflictions.

CH. IV.—XIV. THE FIRST CIRCLE OF SPEECHES.

CH. IV. V. THE SPEECH OF ELIPHAZ.

Eliphaz attaches his speech to Job's despairing cry in ch. iii. The tone of Job's words and his state of mind seem to him strange and very far from right. And though he would gladly be silent and spare one in Job's condition, yet he is constrained to speak (iv. 2). Proceeding to speak, Eliphaz gives expression to *three* thoughts, each of which

4 Then Eliphaz the Temanite answered and said,
2 *If we* assay to commune with thee, wilt thou be grieved?

bears on the tone and temper displayed by Job in his cry of despair (ch. iii.).

1—11. First, Eliphaz wonders that Job, who had comforted so many in trouble, and who was a righteous man, should fall into such despair under his afflictions, forgetting the great principle that the righteous never perish under affliction. Calamity destroys only the wicked; the affliction of the righteous is designed to have a very different issue.

12.—V. 7. Second,—proceeding with deeper earnestness—he must advert to Job's murmurs against Heaven and warn him from them. For can any man have right on his side in complaining of God? Only the ungodly resent the dealing of God with them. By their impatience under affliction they bring down God's final anger upon them, so that they perish.

8—27. Third, surely instead of despairing and murmuring under his afflictions Job should follow a very different way. I, says Eliphaz, putting himself in Job's place, would seek unto God, all whose doings are directed to the saving of the meek and disappointing the devices of the evil. When He smites, He smites only that He may the more profoundly heal. Happy should the man count himself whom God corrects, for his correction is meant to awaken him out of his dream of evil and lead him into a broader, clearer life, rich in blessings, and to be crowned with a ripe and peaceful end.

This beautiful speech consists of three parts, of which the first contains a single division, ch. iv. 1—11; the second, two divisions, ch. iv. 12—21, and ch. v. 1—7; and so also the third, ch. v. 8—16, and ch. v. 17—27.

CH. IV. **1—11.** ELIPHAZ WONDERS THAT JOB, WHO HAD COMFORTED SO MANY IN TROUBLE, AND WAS A RIGHTEOUS MAN, SHOULD FALL INTO SUCH DESPAIR UNDER HIS AFFLICTIONS.

Eliphaz would gladly have kept silence in the circumstances of his friend, but the tone of Job's words constrains him to speak (*v.* 2). He wonders at the despondency of Job, one who had shewn himself so skilful in comforting other good men in affliction (*vv.* 3, 4), and who was himself a righteous man. He should place confidence in his righteousness, and remember that the righteous never *perish* under affliction. God does not send trouble upon them to destroy them, but for very different ends (*vv.* 6, 7). It is only the wicked whom He chastises unto death, and causes to reap the trouble which they sow (*vv.* 8, 9), and perish like beasts of prey (*vv.* 10, 11). Eliphaz's doctrine of the meaning of suffering or evil comes out in the very forefront of his remonstrance with Job.

2. *If we assay to commune*] lit. *if one should assay a word with thee*.
be grieved] This word is rendered *thou faintest, v.* 5. It means *to be weary;* this may be equivalent either to *be impatient,* Is. i. 14, or to

But who can withhold himself from speaking?
Behold, thou hast instructed many, 3
And thou hast strengthened the weak hands.
Thy words have upholden him that was falling, 4
And thou hast strengthened the feeble knees.
But now it is come upon thee, and thou faintest; 5
It toucheth thee, and thou art troubled.
Is not *this* thy fear, thy confidence, 6
Thy hope; and the uprightness of thy ways?
Remember, I pray thee, who *ever* perished, being in- 7
nocent?

be exhausted. It is difficult to decide here. We may render, leaving the ambiguity, *will it be too much for thee?* Eliphaz speaks unwillingly, and would spare Job, but he is compelled by the frame of mind in which he sees his friend.

3. *the weak hands*] lit. the hands hanging down, a sign of helplessness and despondency, 2 Sam. iv. 1; Is. xiii. 7. Comp. Job's words of himself, ch. xxix. 15, 16.

4. *the feeble knees*] lit. as margin, *the bowing*, or tottering, *knees;* the figure being that of one tottering under a heavy load, which he is ready to sink beneath. See Is. xxxv. 3, 4; Heb. xii. 12.

5. *it is come upon thee*] Rather, it cometh. *It* is the calamity, which Eliphaz does not care further to particularize.

art troubled] Or, *art confounded*, losest self-possession, as Job had indeed described himself as one wholly perplexed, "whose way was hid," iii. 23.

We must beware of supposing that there is any flavour of sarcasm in the words of Eliphaz, as if he hinted that Job found it an easier thing to administer comfort to others than to take home the comfort to himself. Such a thing is wholly foreign to the mood of Eliphaz at starting, who, though he does find something to blame in Job's state of mind, is perfectly sincere and friendly. It is equally irrelevant to the connexion.

Those whom Job had consoled are to be supposed pious men under trials. Job, as a man of deep religious experience, was able to set before them such views of providence, and of the uses of adversity in God's hand, and open up such prospects to them, that he upheld and confirmed them. The verses 3—5 are incomplete, and form the foreground to *vv.* 6, 7, which express the real point of the statement of Eliphaz.

6. *Is not this thy fear?*] This verse should read,

Is not thy fear of God thy confidence?
And thy hope, is it not the perfection of thy ways?

When Job comforted others he no doubt would refer to their god-fearing life as a ground of hope that God would give them a happy issue out of their afflictions. Eliphaz desires that Job should apply the same medicine to himself. He assumes that Job is a god-fearing man.

Or where were the righteous cut off?
8 Even as I have seen, they that plow iniquity,
And sow wickedness, reap the same.
9 By the blast of God they perish,
And by the breath of his nostrils are they consumed.
10 The roaring of the lion, and the voice of the fierce lion,
And the teeth of the young lions, are broken.
11 The old lion perisheth for lack of prey,
And the stout lion's whelps are scattered abroad.

7. Eliphaz would have Job remember that the afflictions of the righteous are disciplinary, and not designed for their destruction—who ever perished being innocent? He puts his principle first negatively, the righteous do not perish under affliction; and then positively, it is the wicked, they who plough iniquity that reap it, *v.* 8 *seq.*
8. *even as I have seen*] Rather, **as I have seen**. The words might be also rendered, *when I saw those that ploughed iniquity...they reaped it*. Eliphaz draws a distinction between two classes of men, on both of whom affliction may come—the righteous, who may no doubt sin and be chastised for their sin, but who do not perish under their chastisements (see ch. v. 17 *seq.*), and the wicked, whose sinning is, so to speak, a business which they practise as the tiller ploughs and sows his field, and whose harvest is unfailing. The words *iniquity* and *wickedness* may mean also *affliction* and *trouble*. The two pairs of things correspond to one another. That which the wicked plough and cast into the ground may be iniquity and wickedness, they reap it in the form of affliction and trouble. For the figure comp. Hos. viii. 7; x. 13.
9 *by the blast of God*] Better,

By the breath of God they perish,
And by the blast of his anger are they consumed.

The destructive judgment of God upon the wicked is described as a fiery breath coming from His mouth, as the hot wind of the desert withers and burns up the grass, cf. Is. xl. 7; Am. i. 2.
10, 11. The sudden destruction of the wicked is thrown by Eliphaz into another graphic figure, the breaking-up and dispersion of a den of lions. There are five words used for lion in these verses, some of which are epithets taken from the characteristics of the lion; they are: lion, roaring lion (rather than, fierce lion), young lion, *v.* 10, and strong (or, old) lion, and lioness—the whelps of the lioness, *v.* 11. Between the lion and the wicked whom Eliphaz describes there are two points of resemblance; first, their strength or power; and second, their inherent violence of nature. This is the kind of men on whom afflictions fall that are final. The picture of the breaking-up of the lion's home is very graphic; in the midst of the strong lion's roaring and tearing of his prey by a sudden stroke his roaring is silenced and his teeth dashed out; thus disabled he perisheth for lack of prey; and the whelps having no

provider are scattered abroad. The reality of the figure is seen in the breaking-up of the home of the wicked, ch. v. 2—5.

12.—V. 7. TURNING TO JOB'S MURMURS AGAINST HEAVEN, ELIPHAZ POINTS TO THE UNAPPROACHABLE PURITY OF GOD AND THE IMPERFECTION OF ALL CREATURES, AND WARNS JOB AGAINST SUCH COMPLAINTS.

Having expressed his wonder that a righteous man like Job should fall into such utter despair under afflictions, forgetting that to the righteous affliction is but a discipline, Eliphaz seeks to draw Job back to consider what is the real cause of all affliction. This is the imperfection of man, an imperfection which he shares indeed with all created beings, in the highest of whom to God's eye there is limit and possible error. And this being so, murmuring can only aggravate his affliction by provoking the anger of God.

The passage falls into two divisions. In the first, *vv.* 12—21, Eliphaz contrasts the holiness of God with the imperfection of all creatures, even the pure spirits on high, and much more a material being like man, and thus indirectly suggests to Job the true secret of his troubles. In the second, ch. v. 1—7, having laid this broad foundation, he builds on it a warning to Job against his murmurs. Only the wicked resent God's dealing with them, and by doing so bring increased wrath upon themselves till they perish.

With great delicacy and consideration Eliphaz, instead of impressing the imperfection of man on Job directly, narrates how this truth was once impressed upon himself by a voice from heaven. It was in the dead of night, when all around were in deep sleep. His mind was agitated by perplexing thoughts arising out of visions of the night. Suddenly a great terror fell upon him. Then there passed before his face a breath. And there seemed to stand before him a form, too dim to discern, from which came forth a still voice, which said, Can man be righteous with God? Or, Can a man be pure with his Maker? Even to the holy angels He imputeth error, how much more to frail and earthly man? *vv.* 12—21.

Applying to Job this truth, so impressively taught to himself, Eliphaz asks, If Job appeals against God, whether any of the holy beings, who minister between God and men, will listen to his appeal? (ch. v. 1). Nay, it is only the wicked who resent the afflictions of God, and by their rebellious impatience increase their afflictions till they are destroyed. Such an instance he had himself seen. He saw a fool, a rebellious murmurer against Heaven, spreading forth his roots and giving promise for a moment of prosperity. But suddenly destruction came upon him. His harvest was seized by the hungry robber; the rights of his children were trampled upon; and his home was broken up and desolate (*vv.* 2—5). And finally, Eliphaz condenses into a vivid aphorism his teaching in this section: *for trouble springs not out of the ground*—it is not accidental nor a spontaneous growth of the soil. *But man is born unto trouble*—it is his nature so to act that by his evil deeds he brings trouble upon himself. Out of his heart rises up evil as naturally as the fire sends forth sparks (*vv.* 6, 7).

12 Now a thing was secretly brought to me,
And mine ear received a little thereof.
13 In thoughts from the visions of the night,
When deep sleep falleth on men.
14 Fear came upon me, and trembling,
Which made all my bones to shake.
15 Then a spirit passed before my face;
The hair of my flesh stood up:
16 It stood still, but I could not discern the form thereof:
An image *was* before mine eyes,
There was silence, and I heard a voice, *saying*,

12. *Now a thing*] Or, **and a word.** Eliphaz proceeds to another point, but he introduces it calmly, though with deepening earnestness in his tone; it is something additional, and he appends it by the simple *and*.

a little thereof] Rather, **the whisper thereof.** His ear caught it all, but the whole of it was but a whisper.

13. This revelation which came to him secretly or "stealthily," as the word means, was given in the dead of night. He had had visions on his bed, and perplexing, tangled thoughts filled his heart. God's providence and ways to man, no doubt, were the subject of his thoughts.

The night was recognised of old as favourable to deeper thought from its stillness. Then the mind was less distracted and ranged more freely in the regions of higher truth. And revelations from heaven often came to men in the night-season; cf. Zech. i. 8, and the story of Nathan's oracle to David in regard to building the Temple, 2 Sam. vii. 3, 4; also the words of the Psalmist, "My reins also instruct me in the night-seasons," Ps. xvi. 7.

14. Eliphaz depicts graphically the circumstances in which he received the message from heaven. In the dead night, in the midst of his perplexing thoughts upon his bed, a supernatural terror suddenly seized him. Then he was conscious of a breath passing before him, *v.* 15. Then he seemed to perceive a figure in his presence, too dim, however, to be discerned; and at last a whisper of a voice gave utterance to the awful words that expressed the relations of man to God, *v.* 16. So awful were the impressions of that night, that Eliphaz in recalling the circumstances almost feels himself in the midst of them again, and he falls into the present tense in describing them: a breath passeth before my face...an image is before mine eyes...and I hear a voice, &c.

15. *then a spirit*] Rather, **a breath.** It was something which he felt; that which he saw follows in *v.* 16. The word *spirit* does not seem used in the Old Testament in the sense of an apparition.

16. *it stood still*] *It* is the mysterious object in his presence.

there was silence, and I heard a voice] lit. *stillness and a voice I heard*, i.e. probably, **I heard a still voice**; cf. "whisper," *v.* 12.

Shall mortal man be more just than God? 17
Shall a man be more pure than his Maker?
Behold, he put no trust in his servants;
And his angels he charged with folly:
How much less *in* them that dwell in houses of clay, 19
Whose foundation *is* in the dust,
Which are crushed before the moth?

17. *be more just than God*] This translation is possible. It is very unnatural, however; for though, if a man were found complaining of God's ways, the immediate inference might be that he was making himself more righteous (at least in the perception of moral rectitude) than God, such an inference does not seem drawn by any of the speakers, the idea of a man being *more* righteous than God being too absurd to suggest itself. The charge brought against Job was that he made God unrighteous, not that he claimed to be more righteous than He. Two senses seem possible, either,
   Can man be righteous before God?
   Can a man be pure before his Maker?
a sense which the phrase has Numb. xxxii. 22, and is adopted by the Sept.; or, *can man be in the right in his plea against God?* a meaning which the phrase has in the speeches of Elihu, ch. xxxii. 2. This latter sense is less suitable to the second clause of the verse. The first and more general sense is the more probable because, of course, the vision appeared to Eliphaz before Job's calamities befell him and had no direct reference to them. This sense also suits the scope of the following verses, and the general aphorism ch. v. 6, 7 with which Eliphaz sums up this paragraph of his speech, and is most in harmony with the studiously general tone of Eliphaz's first discourse.

18. *he put no trust*] Better, **he putteth.**
he charged with folly] Rather, **he chargeth with error.** The "servants" of God are here His heavenly ministers, as the parallel, "angels", indicates. The word "folly" (*tohŏlah*) does not occur again in Heb., and its meaning must be in some measure conjectural. Dillmann has drawn attention to an Ethiopic root *tahala, to err*, and the word may be connected with this stem and mean *error*.

19. *houses of clay*] The verse refers to men, and their "houses of clay" are their bodies, which are of the dust, Gen. ii. 7; iii. 19; 2 Cor. v. 1.
whose foundation] Men's bodies being compared to houses are now spoken of as, like houses, having a foundation. They are not only of earth, they are founded on earth—of the earth earthy. They are built of earth, derived from earth, limited to earth. The accumulation of terms enhances the material nature of man in opposition to the spirits on high. Yet even these spirits are limited, and, as creatures, not absolute in their holiness, and to God's eye even erring. No words could more strongly express God's unapproachable holiness.
before the moth] The words may mean: sooner, easier, than the moth

20 They are destroyed from morning to evening:
    They perish for ever without *any* regarding *it*.
21 Doth not their excellency *which is* in them go away?
    They die, even without wisdom.

is crushed. They can hardly mean in the connexion, *by* the moth; although the moth is usually elsewhere spoken of as the destroyer, ch. xiii. 28; Is. l. 9; li. 8, and not as the object of destruction. The phrase *before* might have a sense similar to what it has in ch. iii. 24, *like* the moth; so the Sept.

20. *from morning to evening*] i.e. from a morning to an evening, in the course of a single day, cf. Is. xxxviii. 12. They are short-lived as ephemerids.

without any regarding] i.e. without any one noticing it; so insignificant and of no account are they, that they pass away unobserved, like ephemeral insects. The words might mean, *without any of them laying to heart;* they are thoughtless in their sinful levity, an idea parallel to "without wisdom" in the next verse. Verse 19 described how *easily* men are destroyed, this verse describes how *soon*. All is meant to widen the chasm between men and God, and by giving Job right thoughts of God, and of himself a man, to bring back his mind to a becoming attitude towards Heaven.

21. *their excellency go away*] This verse is obscure. The word rendered *go away* means to *pull out*, as a pin or the posts of a gate, Judg. xvi. 3, 14 (English version, went away with), or the stake of a tent, Is. xxxiii. 20 (be removed). This is probably the original meaning. Then the word is used in a secondary, more general sense, to break up an encampment, to remove or journey, to depart, e.g. very often in Numb. xxxiii. In the present verse the verb is *pass.*, and probably has its original sense, plucked up, or torn out. The word translated *excellency* has that meaning, e.g. Gen. xlix. 3; Prov. xvii. 7. In other places the word means a *cord*, Judg. xvi. 7—9, the string of a bow, Ps. xi. 2; and similarly Job xxx. 11. The *figure* in the Poet's mind here is the pulling down of a tent, to which the death of man is compared; so in Is. xxxviii. 12, where the meaning is, my habitation is removed. The meaning *cord* suits this figure better than *excellency*, and the sense would be, *their tent-cord is torn away*. As to the relation of the two clauses of the verse to one another, the construction is probably the same as in ch. iv. 2, if one should venture...wilt thou be grieved? Therefore,

If their tent-cord is torn away in them,
Do they not die, and not in wisdom?

There is an emphasis on *die;* the moment the tent falls, through the tearing-away of the cord that upheld it, the inhabitant wholly perishes. It is not necessary to ask what the tent-cord is. The cord belongs to the figure, and is scarcely to be interpreted of the soul.

They die without attaining unto wisdom. This trait heightens the

> Call now, if there be *any* that will answer thee; 5
> And to which of the saints wilt thou turn?
> For wrath killeth the foolish man, 2
> And envy slayeth the silly one.

darkness of the picture of man's condition. He is not only frail, his frailty is but another side of his moral imperfection, and this cleaves to him to the very end.

There is something very wise and considerate as well as profoundly reverential in these words of the aged speaker. He does not touch Job's murmurs directly, but seeks to reach them by suggesting other thoughts to Job. First, he speaks of the exalted purity of God, to awaken reverence in Job's mind. Then he descends to the creatures and seeks to look at them as they appear unto God. In His eyes, so sublime is He in holiness, all creatures, angels and men, are erring. Thus Eliphaz makes Job cease to be an exception, and renders it more easy for him to reconcile himself to his history and acknowledge the true cause of it. He is but one where all are the same. There is nothing strange in his having sinned (ch. v. 6, 7). Neither, therefore, are his afflictions strange. But it will be something strange if he murmurs against God.

Ch. v. 1—7. Having laid this broad ground, Eliphaz proceeds to apply the principle to Job.

1. *Call now, if there be any*] Rather, **call then, is there any...?** The imperative *call then* is not ironical, but merely a very animated way of putting a supposition: if thou appeal then against God is there any that will hear thee or aid thee?

which of the saints] Better, **the holy ones**, that is, the angels, as ch. xv. 15; Ps. lxxxix. 6—7; will any of these exalted beings receive thy complaint against God? In ch. xxxiii. 23 the angels are interpreters, conveying the meaning of God's providences to men. But the converse idea that they convey men's representations to God or intercede for them with Him is not found here, because the reference is to a complaint against God. There underlies the passage the idea that the angels are helpful to men, and the question is asked, If Job appeals to any of them against God will they hear his appeal and aid him? The question is only a vivid way of saying that they would turn away from him, abhorring his folly. Being holy, they know, for that very reason, the unapproachable holiness and rectitude of God, and the distance of all creatures from Him.

2. Verse 1 asked, Will any one answer thy complaint? will complaining bring any deliverance? This verse gives the other side—nay, rather, such murmuring betrays a mind "most incorrect to heaven," and such a fool will by his impatience but bring upon himself increased calamity till he altogether perish.

> Nay, rather, the foolish man impatience killeth,
> And the silly one his passion slayeth.

The meaning, of course, is not that the fool and silly one vex them-

3 I have seen the foolish taking root:
But suddenly I cursed his habitation.
4 His children are far from safety,
And they are crushed in the gate, neither *is there* any to deliver *them*.

selves to death, but that their rebellious impatience and resentment of the chastisements of heaven bring down upon them more grievous chastisement, under which they perish. There are several words for "fool" in the Old Testament. Two characteristics of the fool here spoken of are mentioned: he rejects instruction or correction, Prov. i. 7; xii. 15; and he openly exhibits his chagrin or angry impatience, Prov. xii. 16 (*ka'as* as here). The last word describes impatient bearing under affliction, or under that which offends, such as an affront. These words of Eliphaz hurt Job deeply, and in the very first sentence of his reply he alludes to them, "Oh that my impatience (*ka'as*) were weighed and laid in the balances against my affliction," ch. vi. 2. The word in the second half of the verse means properly *heat*, hence any strong passion, as jealousy, the wild ardour of battle, Is. xlii. 13, and the like. On the use of "fool" and similar words in a moral sense to denote wicked, that is, without true insight into the ways of God and right feeling towards Heaven, see on ch. ii. 10.

3. *the foolish*] Rather perhaps, **a foolish man**, the same word as in *v.* 2. Eliphaz cites an instance from his own experience confirming the truth stated in *v.* 2. He saw a man of this character taking root, and for the moment appearing to give promise of prosperity.

but suddenly I cursed] The meaning is not that Eliphaz cursed his habitation before-hand, foreseeing that destruction would certainly overtake him; but that, though this fool appeared prosperous and seemed preparing for enduring happiness, suddenly God's judgment fell on him, and Eliphaz, seeing his desolation and knowing the true meaning of it, pronounced his habitation accursed; and this he did "suddenly," so speedily in the midst of his apparent luxuriance did the curse of God wither up the prosperity of the fool.

4, 5. These verses describe the desolation that befell the home and family of the man who hardened himself against God. The speaker falls here into the present tenses because, though he is describing an instance which he saw, the instance illustrates a general truth.

4. *they are crushed in the gate*] The gate of the town is the seat of the Oriental court of law, where justice is administered, ch. xxix. 7, xxxi. 21; Ps. cxxvii. 5. The words *are crushed* might be reciprocal, "crush one another;" more likely the word means exactly, "must let themselves be crushed," as the last clause indicates: having none to deliver them. In the East he has right who has power (ch. xxii. 8), and the poor, who cannot bribe the judge or find powerful men to speak for them, go to the wall.

The iniquity of the father is visited upon the children, Exod. xx. 5, a law of providence which does not quite meet Job's approval, ch.

Whose harvest the hungry eateth up,   5
And taketh it *even* out of the thorns,
And the robber swalloweth up their substance.
Although affliction cometh not forth of the dust,   6
Neither doth trouble spring out of the ground;
Yet man is born unto trouble,   7
As the sparks fly upward.

xxi. 19, 20. That this principle created difficulty to thoughtful men about this time appears also from Ezek. xviii. 19 *seq*.

5. *even out of the thorns*] i.e. from within the enclosed field, protected by the thorn-hedge. The roving, hungry Bedawin carry their thievish depredations up to the very homestead and in-fields of the ruined estate of the wicked man.

the robber] This word occurs again ch. xviii. 9, in the certain meaning of *snare*; and the sense would thus be, *and the snare gapes for their substance*, the general idea being that their substance falls a prey to the greed of every crafty and cunning one. This is rather vague and colourless. The ancient versions by alteration in the punctuation give the meaning of *the thirsty*. This agrees with the parallel "the hungry" in the preceding clause, and therefore naturally suggested itself. While "the thirsty" suits "gapes" very well, it is less suitable to "substance." On the whole, as the meaning *snare* is assured from ch. xviii. 9, it is safer to rest content with this sense. The whole forms a very graphic picture of desolation.

6, 7. Eliphaz now sums up into an aphorism the great general principle which he seeks to illustrate in this section of his speech, ch. iv. 12—v. 7. It is that affliction is not accidental, nor a spontaneous growth of the earth, but men acting after the impulses of their evil nature bring it on themselves.

6. *Although affliction*] Rather, **for affliction.** The foregoing examples, the general evil and imperfection of man, ch. iv. 12 *seq*., and the particular rebelliousness of the fool, ch. v. 2 *seq*., shew how affliction arises, and Eliphaz confirms the whole with his general maxim, *for*...... Eliphaz reverts here to his principle already enunciated, They that sow trouble reap the same, ch. iv. 8. Affliction does not spring out of the earth like weeds, it is not a necessary product of the nature of things, turned out by the friction of the universe, it is due to the evil nature of men.

7. *Yet man is born unto trouble*] Rather, **but man.** The true explanation of affliction is now given, as the false explanation was denied in *v.* 6. The words "man is born unto trouble" mean, it is his nature through his sin to bring trouble upon himself; evil rises up out of his heart as naturally as the sparks fly up out of the flame. Cf. the words of Christ, "Out of the heart proceed evil thoughts," and the appalling list which follows. Eliphaz is severe on human nature, but the broad generality of his doctrine is fitted to enable Job to find himself in his history and let himself be led back to a more devout demeanour. See the concluding remark to ch. iv.

8   I would seek unto God,
    And unto God would I commit my cause:
9   Which doeth great *things* and unsearchable;
    Marvellous *things* without number:
10 Who giveth rain upon the earth,

8—27. Eliphaz, in Job's place, would seek unto God, all whose ways are marked by one purpose, to do good, and whose chastisements, therefore, but open the way to a richer blessing.

The passage attaches itself to the picture of man's evil nature just given, and suggests where man should find refuge from himself, even in God. Eliphaz in Job's place would seek unto God for help—God who is so great in power, and wonderful in His ways (*vv.* 8, 9). His ways are not only surpassingly wonderful, but one purpose of goodness runs through them, for even the thirsty wilderness where no man dwells He satisfies with rain, and sets the humble on high (*vv.* 10, 11). So on the other hand He disappoints the devices of the crafty and delivers the poor from their hand, and the end is reached towards which all His working tends: the poor hath hope, and evil, ashamed, shuts her mouth (*vv.* 12—16).

And under this general purpose of universal goodness fall even the chastisements of God, and in this light happy should Job consider himself in being afflicted, for God afflicts only that He may be able the more richly to bless (*vv.* 17, 18). And, anticipating that his afflictions will "yield the peaceable fruit of righteousness," Eliphaz draws a brilliant picture of Job's restoration and happy future,—the divine protection (*vv.* 18, 19), the plenty and security (*vv.* 20—23), the peaceful homestead (*v.* 24), the offspring numerous as the grass (*v.* 25), and the ripe and peaceful end of all (*v.* 26).

The passage like the preceding section has two divisions, *vv.* 8—16 describing the purpose of goodness running through all God's ways; and *vv.* 17—26 applying this to Job's calamities and painting his restoration; to which is added a concluding verse, in which Eliphaz beseeches Job to ponder his words (*v.* 27).

8. *I would seek unto God*] Rather, **But** I would seek; i.e. in humility, and for help and light.

9. This description of God as great in power and wonderful in working supports the implied exhortation in *v.* 8. Eliphaz in Job's place would commit his cause, or exactly as we say colloquially, his *case*, unto God, for He, being great and wonderful in His ways, is capable of dealing with it, perplexed and mysterious though it be. A touch of humanity seems here almost to get the better of the moral and religious severity of Eliphaz.

10. *upon the earth*] lit. *upon the face of the earth;* and so next clause, *upon the face of the fields.* He watereth the earth when it is thirsty, with a universal goodness.

And sendeth waters upon the fields:
To set up on high those that be low; 11
That those which mourn may be exalted *to* safety.
He disappointeth the devices of the crafty, 12
So that their hands cannot perform *their* enterprise.
He taketh the wise in their own craftiness: 13
And the counsel of the froward is carried headlong.
They meet with darkness in the daytime, 14
And grope in the noonday as in the night.
But he saveth the poor from the sword, 15
From their mouth, and from the hand of the mighty.

11. *to set up*] If this construction be adopted, the watering of the earth, *v.* 10, must be regarded as the means to this which is effected in *v.* 11. He watereth the fields, giving abundant pasture and harvest, that the humble may be set on high. God's operations in the lower creation, though instances of goodness to it, have the wider end of blessing man in view. The words, however, may mean, *setting up*, and be another operation of benevolence parallel to that in *v.* 10. This view is rather confirmed by the second clause of the verse.

that those which mourn may be] Or, *and those which mourn are*.

12—16. Verses 10, 11 describe how the stream of God's goodness acts when it moves directly, bearing up upon it the humble and those that mourn towards safety or salvation. These verses describe how the stream moves when it meets with obstacles, such as craft and evil.

he disappointeth] The same word is rendered, *he frustrateth*, Is. xliv. 25.

their enterprise] A difficult word to translate. It is a technical term of the Hebrew Wisdom or Philosophy, and, except in Is. xxviii. 29, Mic. vi. 9, occurs only in Job and Proverbs. It seems to mean that which is essential. Hence it is said of a state or action when it corresponds to the idea; and conversely of thought when it corresponds to the reality, as ch. xi. 6, xii. 16. It is used here in the former sense (cf. ch. vi. 13), and the words mean, their hands perform nothing effectual (Sept. *true*), or nothing to purpose.

13. *in their own craftiness*] Quoted by St Paul, 1 Cor. iii. 19. This is the only quotation from the Book of Job in the New Testament, though Rom. xi. 35 seems a reminiscence of Job xli. 11. Phil. i. 19 contains language similar to ch. xiii. 16.

carried headlong] lit. *hastened*, i.e. precipitated before it be ripe, and so frustrated.

14. A picture of the perplexity and bewilderment of those crafty men whose counsels God has come athwart, *v.* 13.

15. *but He saveth*] Rather, **so He saveth**. The salvation of the poor is the consequence of defeating the devices of the crafty, as it is the object in view.

from the sword, from their mouth] It is evident that this verse wants the usual balance of clauses, and probably there is some cor-

16 So the poor hath hope,
   And iniquity stoppeth her mouth.
17 Behold, happy *is* the man whom God correcteth:
   Therefore despise not thou the chastening of the Almighty:
18 For he maketh sore, and bindeth up:
   He woundeth, and his hands make whole.
19 He shall deliver thee in six troubles:
   Yea, in seven there shall no evil touch thee.
20 In famine he shall redeem thee from death:
   And in war from the power of the sword.
21 Thou shalt be hid from the scourge of the tongue:
   Neither shalt thou be afraid of destruction when it cometh.
22 At destruction and famine thou shalt laugh:
   Neither shalt thou be afraid of the beasts of the earth.
23 For thou shalt be in league with the stones of the field:

ruption in it. Some MSS omit *from* before mouth, "from the sword of their mouth." The omission wants support, but the sense is probably that of the words as they stand: from the sword (which cometh) from their mouth; or the two expressions may be in apposition: *from the sword* even *from their mouth*. Others have proposed to point the word *from-the-sword* differently, making it to mean *the desolate*. This restores balance to the verse: thus he saveth the desolate from their mouth, and the poor from the hand of the mighty. The word "desolate" occurs Ezek. xxix. 12, said of cities, and the verb is often applied to lands, mountains, &c., but does not seem used of persons.

16. The end contemplated and reached by the all-embracing sweep of God's benevolent purpose and providence.

17—27. The imagination of Eliphaz himself kindles as he contemplates the universal goodness of God. And Job seems to him happy in being made the object even of God's afflictions, for He afflicts only with the purpose of more abundantly blessing.

17. The idea of this verse occurs often in Scripture, cf. Ps. xciv. 12, Prov. iii. 11, Heb. xii. 5.

18. *maketh sore and bindeth up*] Maketh sore in order to bind up, smiteth in order more perfectly to heal. If this physician induce disease, it is in order to procure a sounder health.

19. "Six" and "seven" are round numbers meaning "many" or "all," like "three" and "four" and other numbers, elsewhere, cf. Prov. vi. 16; see Am. i. 3 *seq.*, Mic. v. 5. Eliphaz assumes that God's afflictions will have their due effect on Job, he will turn unto the Lord, whose hands will "make him whole," and the care and protection specified in this and the following verses shall mark his restored life.

vv. 23—27.]				JOB, V.				41

And the beasts of the field shall be at peace with thee.
And thou shalt know that thy tabernacle *shall be in* peace; 24
And thou shalt visit thy habitation, and shalt not sin.
Thou shalt know also that thy seed *shall be* great, 25
And thine offspring as the grass of the earth.
Thou shalt come to *thy* grave in a full age, 26
Like as a shock of corn cometh in in his season.

23. When man is at peace with God he is at peace with all God's creation, he has a league with all nature and every creature: "We know that all things work together for good to them that love God," Rom. viii. 28.

24. Verses 19—23 describe the immunity which Job himself, restored to peace with God, would enjoy from every evil, the evils specified being those which God in His judgments brings upon men or a people, cf. Ezek. v. 17, xiv. 21; this verse describes the safety and peace of his homestead, or rather the perfect confidence which he would feel in regard to his possessions,—*thou shalt know* that thy tent is in safety.

tabernacle shall be in peace] Or, *tent* (i.e. dwelling) *is* in peace.

visit thy habitation] Or, perhaps, *muster, look over*, thy homestead; the reference is to his cattle and possessions.

shalt not sin] lit. *shalt not miss* or *fail;* that is, probably, he shall find that his actual possessions correspond to what he expected. The general meaning is, thou shalt miss nothing.

25. Another much-desired joy he shall feel that God has given him, a numerous offspring.

26. And finally he shall receive the crowning blessing of man on earth, to live long and die old and full of years; cf. Ps. cii. 24; Is. xxxviii. 10; Numb. xxiii. 10. The *Speaker's Comm.* quotes the following from Milton,

> So mayest thou live, till, like ripe fruits, thou drop
> Into thy mother's lap; or be with ease
> Gathered, not harshly plucked; for death mature.

The speech of Eliphaz is one of the masterpieces of the Book. The surprising literary skill of the Author is hardly anywhere so conspicuous. (See remark at the end of ch. iv.)

Nevertheless, if we follow the clue which the Author himself puts into our hand in the reply which he causes Job to make, we must infer that Eliphaz erred in two particulars. If his religious tone was not too lofty, it was at least too cold, and too little tempered with compassion for the sufferings of men. The moral impropriety of Job's murmurs and despair so engrosses his mind that he forgets the unbearable misery of the sufferer before him, and the just claims of sentient life not to be put to the torture. The consequence is that he will have to hear from Job language still more shocking to his religious feeling (ch. vii. 17 *seq.*). This error was due to another, his theory of suffering (see prelimi-

27   Lo this, we have searched it, so it *is*;
     Hear it, and know thou *it* for thy good.

nary remarks to ch. iv.—xiv.). This theory gave a full explanation to his mind of Job's afflictions and compelled him to take the tone towards him which he did. However true his theory might be as a general principle of moral government, it was not universal and did not include Job's case. Job's conscience told him this. Hence the admonitions of Eliphaz fell wide of the mark, and he only aggravated the evil which he sought to heal.

CH. VI.—VII. JOB'S REPLY TO ELIPHAZ.

Job's reply to the first of his three friends falls into *three* great sections:—

First, vi. 1—13. He defends against the remonstrances of Eliphaz the bitterness of his complaining and his despair.

Second, vi. 14—30. He laments with sorrowful disappointment the attitude his friends have taken up towards him.

Third, ch. vii. He falls anew into a bitter lamentation over his sorrowful destiny, and appeals against God's treatment of him in language much more direct and keen than that used in ch. iii.

CH. VI. 1—13. JOB DEFENDS THE VIOLENCE OF HIS COMPLAINTS AND HIS DESPAIR.

Eliphaz had made no reference directly to sin on Job's part; but he drew dark pictures of the evilness of human nature before the eye of his friend, and for his advantage. Job shews a dislike to touch this point. His dislike is that of a man conscious of his innocence, and who can hardly believe that his friends seriously mean what their indirect allusions seem to imply. Hence he attaches his reply to what Eliphaz had openly expressed, namely, his wonder at the despair of Job and his blameable impatience. The idea of his having sinned he touches only in passing and with strong repudiation of it (ch. vi. 28—30).

Eliphaz had used the word "confounded" of Job's hopeless despair (ch. iv. 5); he had spoken of "impatience," and "passion"; and had referred to the "fool" or godless man, as shewing this kind of temper under affliction (v. 2). All this wounds Job deeply, and he first of all replies to it, justifying the bitterness of his complaints by the overwhelming heaviness of his sorrow.

First, he wishes that his impatience and his calamity were laid against one another in the balance. His calamity is heavier than the sand of the sea. For that which gives it its terror is that it is from God. The arrows of the Almighty are in him, and his spirit drinks in their poison and is paralysed, *vv.* 1—4.

Second, a more kindly judgment, he thinks, would have reasoned the other way from his friends, namely, from the violence of his complaints to the greatness of his sufferings. So men reasoned with regard to beasts even. No creature complained if it had no want or no pain;

But Job answered and said,   6
  Oh that my grief were throughly weighed,   2
  And my calamity laid in the balances together!
For now it would be heavier than the sand of the sea: 3
  Therefore my words are swallowed up.
For the arrows of the Almighty *are* within me,   4
  The poison whereof drinketh up my spirit:
  The terrors of God do set *themselves* in array *against* me.

neither would he complain if what was unbearable were not thrust upon him, *vv.* 5—7.

Third, so far he goes in his defence. But so keenly does he realize as he describes it (*vv.* 6, 7) the misery and loathsomeness of his state that here he breaks out into a passionate cry for death, his mind passes into a momentary frenzy, and he says he would leap for joy in the midst of unsparing pain, if it brought death with it. This is the consolation that he seeks. And this consolation he can look for, for he has never denied the words of the Holy One. And no other can he look to, for his flesh is not brass that it should resist his exhausting afflictions; and what issue has he to expect that he should be patient? *vv.* 8—13.

2. *my grief*] Rather, **my impatience** (ch. iv. 2). The word expresses the whole demeanour which in ch. iii., and to the eyes of his friends, he shews under his trouble. He desires that it were weighed and also his calamity. Naturally he wishes them weighed against one another. It is not certain that this is expressed in the word *together;* that word may mean, and my *whole* calamity laid in the balances.

3. *the sand of the sea*] A frequent figure for that which is infinite in weight, Prov. xxvii. 3, or number, Gen. xxxii. 12, or measure, Jer. xxxiii. 22.

are swallowed up] Rather, **have been wild**, or perhaps *vain* or idle. Probably the word is allied to an Arabic root that signifies to speak, and also, to speak wrongly and foolishly. Job with transparent simplicity concedes a certain extravagance in his language, although he excuses it (*v.* 4 *seq.*). Elsewhere he says in reference to himself that the words of one that is desperate go into the wind (*v.* 26).

4. *the arrows of the Almighty*] This explains his bearing and excuses it. Everywhere Job says that it is not his afflictions in themselves that terrify him, it is that they come from God ; it is the moral problem that lies under his calamities and that God has become his enemy that makes his heart "soft" (ch. xxiii. 15 *seq.*). The "arrows" of God are the plagues, diseases and pains with which He assails men, ch. xvi. 12 *seq.*; cf. Ps. xxxviii. 2 *seq.*; Deut. xxxii. 23. So Hamlet,

  The slings and arrows of outrageous fortune.

the poison whereof drinketh] Rather, **the poison of which my spirit drinketh in**. God's arrows are poisoned arrows, the poison of which the spirit sucks in and becomes enervated and paralysed. This is the

5   Doth the wild ass bray when he hath grass?
    Or loweth the ox over his fodder?
6   Can that which is unsavoury be eaten without salt?
    Or is there *any* taste in the white of an egg?
7   The things *that* my soul refused to touch
    Are as my sorrowful meat.
8   O that I might have my request;
    And *that* God would grant *me* the thing that I long for!
9   Even *that* it would please God to destroy me:
    That he would let loose his hand, and cut me off!
10 Then should I yet have comfort;
    Yea, I would harden myself in sorrow; let him not spare:
    For I have not concealed the words of the Holy One.

idea, rather than maddened. The figure in the end of the verse is that of a beleaguering army; this host is composed of "terrors" from God. The reference is again not to Job's mere physical pains, but to the perplexing thoughts and fears which they occasioned.

5, 6. Job's complaints are proof of his pain, for does any creature complain when it has what its nature desires? The "braying" and "lowing" here are those expressing discontent or want.

be eaten without salt] Rather, **can that be eaten which is unsavoury and saltless?**

the white of an egg] This is the traditional interpretation and is perhaps the most probable. Others think of some insipid herb, and render: the slime (broth) of purslain. The reference in the passage is to Job's afflictions, which he compares here to an insipid, and in next verse to a loathsome, food, cf. ch. iii. 24. Others have thought that the reference was to the insipid harangues of the friends. But such a reference entirely breaks the connexion.

7. This verse may be rendered not quite literally,

My soul refuseth to touch them!
Such things are like loathsome food to me.

Literally, *like my corrupted*, or, *diseased food*. Job does not name his afflictions but refers to them indirectly as "they" and "such things." He compared his sufferings to food in ch. iii. 24.

8, 9. So keenly does Job realize the loathsomeness of his sufferings that he forgets his defence and breaks out into a passionate cry for death, which he calls the thing that he longs for.

10. This verse reads,

And I should yet have my comfort,
And I would leap (for joy) amidst unsparing pain;
For I have not denied the words of the Holy One.

His comfort or consolation that he would have is death, the only one he seeks or can receive (*v.* 11). The second clause betrays a rising

What *is* my strength, that I should hope? 11
And what *is* mine end, that I should prolong my life?
Is my strength the strength of stones? 12
Or *is* my flesh of brass?
Is not my help in me? 13
And is wisdom driven *quite* from me?

frenzy in the sufferer's mind. The third clause is thrown in almost in parenthesis. It expresses Job's feeling that there is nothing that would impair his comfort or mar his joy in death, for he has never denied or disobeyed the words, or commands, of the Holy One. Perhaps the words may be flung out also against a thought which Job felt might rise in the minds of his friends. They serve at least to give an emphatic contradiction to their suspicions, by shewing how fearlessly he looks at death.

Others render the verse somewhat differently: *and it should still be my consolation...that* I have not denied, etc., making his consolation in death to consist in the thought that he had never disobeyed the words of the Holy One, cf. ch. xiii. 16; xxvii. 8 *seq*. But this gives a prominence to the innocence of Job which is not suitable in this place, and makes his words too reflective and self-possessed for the rest of the passage.

11—13. With more calmness Job proceeds to describe his hopeless condition, carrying out in this indirect way his defence of his despair.

11. This verse should read,
> What is my strength that I should wait?
> And what is mine end that I should be patient?

His impatient cry for death and his despair are justified by his condition. "Mine end"—i.e. what can the end of my afflictions be but death? Why then should I wait?

12. Unless his strength were that of stones or his flesh brass he could not hold out against the exhausting afflictions which he has to bear, or recover from them.

13. This verse reads something as follows,
> Is not my help within me gone,
> And recovery driven away from me?

Both clauses seem to refer to the exhaustion caused by his disease. He feels that all resource within himself and all possibility of recovery is gone. The word "recovery" is that used in ch. v. 12, "anything effectual" (see notes), and probably signifies substance, or powers of recovery. The word might also be applied, as in ch. xi. 6, to a condition of the mind and signify mental resource, but this sense does not seem to suit the connexion.

14—30. JOB'S SORROWFUL DISAPPOINTMENT AT THE POSITION TAKEN UP TOWARDS HIM BY HIS THREE FRIENDS.

Job had freely expressed his misery in ch. iii., believing that the sympathies of his friends were entirely with him. He is

14   To him that is afflicted pity *should be shewed* from his friend;
But he forsaketh the fear of the Almighty.

> a brother noble,
> Whose nature is so far from doing harms
> That he suspects none.   *Lear*, i. 2.

And more sorrowful to him than any cold, critical words which they have uttered is the feeling that his friends have taken up such a position against him. This was what he had not looked for. And his disappointment is like that of the thirsty caravan that finds the long-looked-for waters dried up in the heat. Every emotion seems now to find a place in Job's mind in succession. First, his disappointment, expressed in this beautiful figure, is mixed with the feeling how unworthy his friends' conduct was. They had not acted to him as men do to one who is, as he describes himself, "despairing" and "losing hold of the fear of the Almighty." Kindness is due to such a one, but they had turned against him from sheer feebleness of spirit, because they saw that his calamity was from God, *vv.* 14—21.

Second, this mixed sadness and contempt passes into sarcasm when he tells them that he could have understood their fear if he had asked anything from them—even one's friends must not be put under that strain—but he sought only sympathy, *vv.* 22, 23.

Third, this sarcasm then gives place to a direct appeal of great severity, in which he demands that they should shew him the sins at which they had indirectly hinted, and wonders at their superficial captiousness in fastening on the mere excited words of a man in despair; adding in terms of bitter invective that their disposition was so hard that they would cast lots for the orphan and make market of their own friend, *vv.* 24—27.

Finally, he challenges them to seek the explanation of his afflictions on other principles than the supposition of his guiltiness, asking them whether, in asserting his innocence, he would lie in their faces, and if he was not able to say whether his calamities were deserved or not? *vv.* 28—30.

14. The most probable sense of the verse is this:—

> Kindness from his friend is due to him that is despairing,
> To him that is forsaking the fear of the Almighty.

The sense of the second clause proposed by some, *else he will forsake the fear*, is good in itself, but the language hardly admits it. The word "kindness" has the sense of *reproach*, Prov. xiv. 34 (the verb, Prov. xxv. 10, put to shame), and some adopt this sense here: *if reproach from his friend fall upon him that is despairing, he will forsake the fear*, &c. The word, however, is not used elsewhere in the Book of Job in this sense, and the interpretation destroys the strong antithesis between this verse and the opening words of the next, *my brethren*, &c.

My brethren have dealt deceitfully as a brook, 15
And as the stream of brooks they pass away;
Which are blackish by reason of the ice, 16
And wherein the snow is hid:
What time they wax warm, they vanish: 17
When it is hot, they are consumed out of their place.
The paths of their way are turned aside; 18
They go to nothing, and perish.
The troops of Tema looked, 19
The companies of Sheba waited for them.
They were confounded because they had hoped; 20
They came thither, and were ashamed.
For now ye are nothing; 21

15. *they pass away*] Better, **that pass away**, cf. ch. xi. 16. The other sense, *that overflow* (their banks), is improbable.

16. *are blackish*] Rather, **are black**, that is, turbid.
is hid] lit. *hides itself*, that is, dissolves.

> Pleasures are like poppies spread,
> You seize the flower, its bloom is shed;
> Or like the snow-falls in the river—
> A moment white, then melts for ever.

18. *they go to nothing*] Rather, **they go up into the waste.** The expression *go up* in Heb. is used when no ascent in the strict sense is meant; it signifies to go inland, into the interior of a region. The streams of these brooks flow out and wind into the desert and are consumed by the heat or lost in the sand. A somewhat different sense is drawn from the words by many writers. The word *paths, v.* 18, is the same as *troops* or caravans, *v.* 19, and they assume that the reference to the caravans is already made in *v.* 18, rendering : *the caravans that go by the way of them* (the streams) *turn aside, they go up into the desert and perish*. In favour of this interpretation it is urged that there is something unnatural in the use of the same word in different senses in two consecutive verses; and that it is customary in the Poets to express a general idea first (*v.* 18) and then to particularize and exemplify it (*v.* 19). On the other hand Ibn Ezra has already remarked that it is not usual for caravans to leave the route and "turn aside" in search of water, a route is selected and formed rather because water is found on it. The danger of the caravan is that it be exhausted before it reach the place where water is known to be, or, as here, that the water may be found dried up.

19. Tema lies in the northern highlands of Arabia, towards the Syrian desert, Is. xxi. 14 ; Jer. xxv. 23. On Sheba see i. 15.

21. *ye are nothing*] Or, **are become nothing**. Job applies his comparison. Another reading is : *ye are become it*, i.e. the deceitful, disappointing brook. The general sense remains the same.

Ye see *my* casting down, and are afraid.
22 Did I say, Bring unto me?
Or, Give a reward for me of your substance?
23 Or, Deliver me from the enemy's hand?
Or, Redeem me from the hand of the mighty?
24 Teach me, and I will hold my tongue:
And cause me to understand wherein I have erred.
25 How forcible are right words!
But what doth your arguing reprove?

my casting down] lit. *ye see a terror.* Job's comparison of his friends to the brook is graphic and telling. In winter these brooks are full, but in summer when the thirsty caravan needs them and looks for them they are found to have disappeared before the heat. And Job's friends may have been effusive in their offers of friendship when friendships were abundant, but now when he needs their aid, the sight of his terrible affliction, like the summer heat, dissipates their sympathy and makes them "nothing," without power to help. In the words "ye see a terror and are afraid" Job insinuates more than that his friends are paralysed at the sight of his calamity, he means probably that, judging his calamity to be from God, they have not courage to shew him sympathy, cf. xiii. 7 *seq.*

22, 23. He had not asked anything very great from his friends, which would have been too severe a strain on their friendship, only sympathy, and straightforward dealing, and that they should consider him the truthful man whom they knew him to be.

22. *a reward*] Rather, **a gift.**

23. *hand of the mighty*] that is, the powerful robber, who held his captives to ransom.

24—27. In answer to their covert insinuations Job demands that they should bring home to him the sins of which they suspected him.

25. *how forcible are right words*] Or, *words of uprightness*, that is honest, straightforward, close dealing with a man about himself, or his offences, sign of true friendship, Ps. clxi. 5; cf. ch. xxxiii. 3, where Elihu claims to speak out of this rectitude of mind. The word rendered *forcible* is of rather uncertain meaning. It occurs again 1 K. ii. 8, a *grievous* curse, Mic. ii. 10, a *sore* destruction, and in Job xvi. 3, what *emboldeneth* thee that thou answerest? The fundamental sense of the word is assumed to be *to be sharp*, hence, to be strong, vehement. This is conjectural. What may be but another form of the word occurs in Ps. cxix. 103, *how sweet* are thy words unto my taste! And many prefer that meaning here : *how sweet are words of uprightness.*

your arguing reprove] lit. *what doth reproving from you*, the kind of reproving that comes from you, insinuations and captious laying hold of more excited language, *reprove?* In *v.* 24 Job demanded to know from his friends directly what sins they laid to his charge. He would welcome straightforward dealing that went into his circumstances.

Do ye imagine to reprove words, 26
And the speeches of one that is desperate, *which are* as wind?
Yea, ye overwhelm the fatherless, 27
And you dig *a pit* for your friend.
Now therefore be content, look upon me; 28
For *it is* evident unto you if I lie.
Return, I pray you, let it not be iniquity; 29
Yea, return again, my righteousness *is* in it.

26. *do ye imagine*] that is, is it your purpose? think ye?
and the speeches...which are *as wind*] Rather, **though the speeches of one that is desperate go into the wind.**
27. This verse probably reads,

Yea, ye would cast lots upon the fatherless,
And bargain over your friend.

A strong invective against their unfeeling behaviour. The words are severe; the preceding passage, however, in which their refusal of sympathy (*vv.* 22, 23), and their petty faultfinding with Job's language (*vv.* 25, 26), are referred to, naturally leads up to the idea. The same phrase *to cast lots* occurs 1 Sam. xiv. 42, and the phrase, *bargain over* or make merchandise of, occurs again, Job xli. 6 (Heb. xl. 30), "will the partners bargain over him?" The "fatherless" is probably the child of the debtor. After his death the ruthless creditors cast lots for possession of the child as a slave.
28. The verse means as a whole,

Now, therefore, be pleased to look upon me,
I will not surely lie to your face!

"Be pleased," or, as we say, be good enough. "To your face," as in ch. i. 11. Job desires that instead of speaking at him with averted faces they would look him in the face, and judge from his countenance whether he would lie directly in asserting his innocence—a test that only conscious honesty would propose.
29. *Return, I pray you*] The verse means,

Turn, I pray you, let there be no injustice;
Turn again, I say; my cause is righteous.

The word "turn" appears to mean not "begin anew," but "adopt another course," that is, proceed on other suppositions than that of my guiltiness, and seek another explanation of my calamities. Hence, he adds, let there be no injustice, or wrong, that is, on the part of his friends in imputing guilt to him. The phrase "my cause is righteous" means literally *my right is in it*, that is, is here, is present; in other words, I have a righteous cause. *In it* can hardly mean, in the matter under discussion, as if the meaning were: the question is one that concerns my rectitude. By his right or righteous cause Job means his plea

30   Is there iniquity in my tongue?
    Cannot my taste discern perverse things?

against God in reference to his afflictions; in this plea he has right on his side.

30. In *v.* 28 Job asseverated that he spoke truth in affirming his innocence. In *v.* 29 he affirmed that he had right on his side in his plea against God, in other words that he was wrongly afflicted. This verse, therefore, can hardly be a new assertion that he speaks the truth when he affirms his innocence; it must refer to a point further back, and be, in the form of a question, an affirmation of his ability to say whether he is innocent or not, and to judge rightly regarding the nature of his afflictions. The question, Is there iniquity in my tongue? means Is my tongue perverted that it cannot distinguish? In the second clause "taste" or "palate" is not referred to as an organ of speech but of perception (ch. xii. 11).

The expression "perverse things" may mean *wickednesses*. This may be used generally and the question in the second clause have the same meaning as that in the first, viz. whether Job had lost moral sense and could not distinguish wrong from right? And the whole would be an affirmation of the soundness of his moral judgments, meant to support the asseveration of his innocence and the righteousness of his cause (*vv.* 28, 29). The phrase "perverse things" is that rendered "calamity" *v.* 2, and this might be the meaning here: "cannot my taste discern calamities?" i.e. the true nature of my afflictions, and perceive that they are undeserved and unjust?

Either of the above meanings forms a fitting and pathetic transition to the renewed cry of despair in ch. vii. For that which makes Job's condition so crushing to him is that though innocent he feels himself in the hands of a ruthless and arbitrary fate, which, regardless of his innocence, is bent on destroying him. For this fate he has no other name but God; cf. ch. ix. 22 *seq.*, xxiii. 13 *seq.*

Ch. VII.   Renewed outburst of despair at the thought of his sorrowful destiny.

With a deeper pathos than any that had gone before, this innocence of his and this capacity to form true moral judgments regarding his history (ch. vi. 28—30) being his starting-point, Job turns to the broad world, to contemplate how helpless man is with these qualities against that fated, inexorable misery called human life. His view is general, though he himself is the centre of it, and his own history gives colour to that of man.

First, *vv.* 1—10, his complaint is that human life is short and evil, inexorably short and arbitrarily evil. It is a soldier's "campaign," and a hired labourer's "day," a time of heavy, forced toil at the stern will of another, in which one longs for discharge, and pants for the shadow, —the release and the night of death. The toil of this time and the fated compulsion of it Job chiefly describes in *vv.* 2—5; its brevity and

Is there not an appointed time to man upon earth?   7

the regrets that accompany having lived and ceasing to live, in *vv.* 6—10.

Second, *vv.* 11—21. It is dangerous dwelling on misery, it usually but adds to it. The misery of feeling we are miserable is exquisite. With too fertile a fancy Job had heaped images together to picture out the fatal brevity of life,—the motion of the shuttle (*v.* 6), the wind (*v.* 7), the glance of the eye (*v.* 8), the cloud of vapour gorgeous for a moment but dissolved by the very light that illuminates it (*v.* 9)—and the inexorable "nevermore" that death writes on things, on one's "home" and "place" (*v.* 10) when he is carried from it; and these regrets combine with that impatience of coercion natural to the mind and drive him on with a certain recklessness to utter his feelings in the face of that Power whose irresistible constraint presses upon him. He is not unconscious of the meaning of what he is going to do, for that which binds him in such chains of misery is not a power but a Person. Nevertheless he will not be deterred—I also will not refrain my mouth (*v.* 11).

Thus commences a remonstrance with God, who disposes all, which is only saved, if it be saved, from being too bold by that reverential hesitation and half pause which marks the commencement of it. First, he asks if he be dangerous to the peace and stability of the universe that he needs to be so restrained and subdued with plagues by God? In the description of these plagues his tone rises into the sharpest despair and he begs for death, desiring only that God would leave him alone and give him a little respite before he departs, *vv.* 11—16.

Then he asks whether man is not too mean a thing for God to torment? appealing to the Almighty's sense of His own greatness and the unworthiness of distressing so slight a thing as man; and travestying with a surprising acuteness of mind and bitterness of irony the admiring gratefulness of the Psalmist that God "made so much "of man (Ps. viii.), *v.* 17—19.

Finally he comes to that to which perhaps he would rather not come at all, the supposition, which he will hazard though scarcely concede, that he has sinned, and asks, If so, what can I do unto thee? how can I by my sin injure thee? Even in hazarding this supposition he casts a side-glance of discontent on God, naming Him *watcher* or spy *of men*, as if it was due to Him if not that sin was at least that it was raked to the surface. And he concludes with asking why God does not take away his sin and spare him—for soon it will be too late, *vv.* 20, 21.

1. The connexion is with the preceding verses ch. vi. 28—30, which express the thought of Job's innocence, and the thought that in spite of his innocence he is miserably plagued. Under this feeling he throws his eye over all mankind, and sees them also doomed by an inexorable destiny to a life that is brief and filled with pain.

an appointed time] Or, *a time of service*. The reference is to the hard service of the soldier, in which there are two elements, the fixed

Are not his days also like the days of a hireling?
2 As a servant earnestly desireth the shadow,
And as a hireling looketh for the reward of his work:
3 So am I made to possess months of vanity,
And wearisome nights are appointed to me.
4 When I lie down, I say,
When shall I arise, and the night be gone?

period and the hard toil of the campaign. Both are laid on man by a power to which he is subject; cf. Isai. xl. 2; Job xiv. 14.

days of a hireling] The "hireling" might be the mercenary soldier, whose fate, far from home and at the disposal of an alien power, might be thought harder even than that of the ordinary soldier. The word is used in this sense, Jer. xlvi. 21, and the verb, 2 Sam. x. 6. In *v*. 2, however, the word has its ordinary sense of a hired labourer, and this is probably its meaning here.

2. With slight change the verse reads,

> As a slave who panteth for the shadow,
> And as an hireling who looketh, &c.

The slave in the heat and under his hard toil pants for the shadow of evening, the day's end; and the hireling looks for his wages, that is, the close of the day; cf. Prov. xxi. 6.

3. *made to possess*] lit. *made to inherit*. They are laid on him by the will of another. Job narrows his view here from the lot of men in general to his own. He is one of an afflicted race, but the universal misery does not alleviate his own, it rather increases it.

> That loss is common would not make
> My own less bitter, rather more;
> Too common! Never morning wore
> To evening, but some heart did break.

A sorrowing Arab poet gives expression to a different feeling:

> Did not a common sorrow console me I would not live an hour among men,
> But whenever I will, they in like condition with myself respond to me.   *Hamasa*, p. 389, 396.

The point of comparison between Job's life and the day of the hireling lies in their common toil and their common longing for the end of it. Job describes his day as "months of vanity" and "nights of trouble," indicating that his disease had already endured a long time. He refers to "nights" perhaps because his pains were severest then (cf. *v*. 4, 14, ch. xxx. 17); although in the East the method also of counting by nights instead of days was common.

4, 5. A graphic account of his condition under his malady. Verse 4 should probably be rendered,

> When I lie down I say, When shall I arise?
> And the night stretches out, and I am full of tossings, &c.

vv. 5—9.]   JOB, VII.   53

And I am full *of* tossings to and fro unto the dawning of the day.
My flesh is clothed with worms and clods of dust; 5
My skin is broken, and become loathsome.
My days are swifter than a weaver's shuttle, 6
And are spent without hope.
O remember that my life *is* wind: 7
Mine eye shall no more see good.
The eye of him that hath seen me shall see me no *more:* 8
Thine eyes *are* upon me, and I *am* not.
As the cloud is consumed and vanisheth away: 9
So he that goeth down *to* the grave shall come up no more.

At evening he longs for morning (Deut. xxviii. 67), but the night seems to him to prolong itself, and he tosses restlessly till the daybreak.

5. *with worms and clods of dust*] His ulcers bred worms; and the hard earthy-like crust of his sores he calls lumps of dust.

is broken, and become loathsome] Rather, **my skin closes and breaks afresh**—the allusion being to the alternate gathering and running of his sores, which went on continually.

Verses 1—5 describe the pain of life; the following verses, 6—10, its brevity and utter extinction in death. There is no break, however, in the connexion, for it is the exhausting pains described in *vv.* 3—5 that naturally suggest the hopeless brevity of his life. Job has been thought inconsistent in complaining that life being evil is also brief. But in his view life itself is the highest good; it should be free of evil and prolonged. And his complaint is that human life has been made by God *both* evil and brief; cf. ch. xiv. 1 *seq.*

6. By his "days" is meant his life as a whole, not his individual days, which are far from passing quickly (*v.* 4); and "are spent" means, have been consumed (as *v.* 9), or, are come to an end (Gen. xxi. 15). He regards his life as near a close, for his disease was incurable; this is expressed by "without hope," i. e. hope of recovery or relief.

7. This feeling of the hopeless brevity of his life overwhelms the sufferer, and he turns in supplication to God, beseeching Him, the Everlasting, to think how swiftly his mortal life passes, cf. Ps. cii. 11.

see good] i.e. happiness or prosperity. He means in this life; but then the state of the dead, though not extinction, was not to be called life, it was but a dreary, dreamy shadow of life, having no fellowship with the living, whether men or God; cf. ch. x. 21 *seq.*; Ps. vi. 5; Eccles. ix. 5 *seq.*; Is. xxxviii. 18.

8. *are upon me, and I am not*] Perhaps rather, **shall be upon me and I shall not be**; God will look for him, enquiring, it may be, after the work of His hands, but he shall be gone; cf. *v.* 21.

9. *goeth down to the grave*] Heb., *down to She'ôl,* the place of departed persons. This is never in the Old Testament confounded with

10   He shall return no more to his house,
     Neither shall his place know him any more.
11   Therefore I will not refrain my mouth;
     I will speak in the anguish of my spirit;
     I will complain in the bitterness of my soul.
12   Am I a sea, or a whale,
     That thou settest a watch over me?
13   When I say, My bed shall comfort me,
     My couch shall ease my complaint;

the grave, although, being an ideal place and state, the imagination often paints it in colours borrowed from the grave and the condition of the body in death; cf. ch. iii. 13 *seq.*, x. 21 *seq.*

11. Job heaps image upon image to set before himself and the eye of God the brevity of life, the weaver's shuttle (*v.* 6), the wind (*v.* 7), the morning cloud (*v.* 9, Hos. vi. 4), ending with a pathetic reference to his home which shall see him no more (*v.* 10). These regrets altogether overmaster him and, combining with his sense of the wrong which he suffers and his impatience of the iron restraints of human existence, hurry him forward, and he resolves to open the floodgates to the full stream of his complaint (*v.* 11): *Therefore I will not refrain my mouth*, i.e. therefore *I also, I on my side*, will not refrain.

12. First, he asks with bitter irony if he is *the sea or the monster of the sea*, that he must be watched and subdued with plagues lest he prove dangerous to the universe? The proud waves of the sea must be confined and a bound which they cannot pass set to them (ch. xxxviii. 8 *seq.*; Jer. v. 22); has he a wild, untameable nature like this? The monster of the sea here is no real creature such as the crocodile, "sea" being used in the sense of the *river*. The connexion shews that the reference is to the half poetical, half mythological conception of the raging sea itself as a furious monster, for it is God that sets a watch over it. Studer boldly renders, "am I the sea, or the sea serpent?" His sea serpent, however, is not that of the modern mariner and the mythology of our own day, but that of a more ancient mythology. The serpent of the sea—which was but the wild stormy sea itself—wound himself around the land and threatened to swallow it up, as the serpent of the sky swallowed up the heavenly luminaries (ch. xxvi. 12, see on iii. 8). God sets a watch upon the one, as His hand pierces the other, lest the fixed order of the world be disturbed and land and sea or light and darkness be confused. Job enquires if he must be watched and plagued like this monster lest he throw the world into disorder?

13, 14. Further description of the plagues employed to subdue him.

ease my complaint] *Complaint* always means complaining, not malady; ch. ix. 27, x. 1, xxi. 4, xxiii. 2. When he looks for sleep

      That knits up the ravelled sleeve of care,
      Balm of hurt minds,

instead of finding it he is scared with dreams and terrified through

Then thou scarest me with dreams, 14
And terrifiest me through visions:
So that my soul chooseth strangling, 15
And death rather than my life.
I loathe *it;* I would not live alway: 16
Let me alone; for my days *are* vanity.
What *is* man, that thou shouldest magnify him? 17
And that thou shouldest set thine heart upon him?
And *that* thou shouldest visit him every morning, 18
And try him every moment?

visions. Such distressing dreams and terrors in sleep are said to be one of the symptoms of Elephantiasis.

15. Consequence of the preceding, *v.* 14.

chooseth strangling] A sense of choking is one of the accompaniments of the disease, which is said to end sometimes in actual suffocation. Job refers to this symptom, saying that he is driven to desire that it might be really fatal. The parallel word *death* in the next clause shews that this is what he is driven to wish for, but he selects this form of death as one incidental to his disease, and one with which he had perhaps felt himself more than once threatened.

death rather than my life] lit. *death rather than* these *my bones*. So he describes the emaciated skeleton to which he was reduced.

16. So keenly does he realize the misery of his condition and the intolerable painfulness of his life, that he breaks out into a passionate cry that he hates and is weary of life—*I loathe* it. The object of his loathing is not expressed, but it is rather life in general, as the words, *I would not live alway*, indicate, than what he calls his "bones," cf. x. 21. No emphasis falls on *alway*, the phrase "I would not live alway" is rather an exclamation of revulsion, meaning *I desire not life*.

let me alone] i.e. cease from paining me with such afflictions. Job like his friends regarded his sufferings as inflicted directly by the hand of God, and if God would leave him his pains would cease. The words here are hardly a prayer, but something like an imperious command, to such a height of boldness is the sufferer driven by the keenness of his pains. The last words, "for my days are vanity," support his demand that God would let him alone, by a reference to the shortness of his life; he seeks a little respite ere he die, cf. x. 20 *seq.* This reference to his life as "vanity" or a *breath* forms the natural transition to the next question.

17—19. Second, Job asks, If man be not too mean a thing for God thus to busy Himself with and persecute? cf. ch. xiv. 3.

set thine heart] that is, thy *mind;* as *magnify* means, to think great, to consider of importance.

18. The words of this verse recall Ps. viii. 5, cxliv. 3, the former of which passages at least must have been in the Author's mind. The admiring gratefulness of the Psalmist that God condescended to visit

19 How long wilt thou not depart from me,
    Nor let me alone till I swallow down my spittle?
20 I have sinned; what shall I do unto thee,
    O thou preserver of men?

man and gave him such a place in His estimation is parodied by Job, and the Psalmist's words are made with bitter irony to express his wonder that God should occupy Himself continually with so slight a thing as man, and make him the object of His unceasing persecution.

19. *depart from me*] lit. *look away from me;* an impatient demand that God would turn away His plaguing glance; cf. "watcher of men," *v.* 20.

swallow down my spittle] A proverbial phrase like "twinkling of an eye," signifying *a moment*, as we might say "till I let over"; cf. "draw my breath," ch. ix. 18. To let one swallow his spittle is to give him a moment's respite or time. The phrase is not unusual among the Arabs. In De Sacy's Notes to Hariri, p. 164, a person tells the following: "I said to one of my Sheichs (teachers), Let me swallow my spittle; to which he replied, I will let you swallow the two Confluents"(the Tigris and Euphrates).

20, 21. Third, Job makes the supposition that he has sinned, and asks, how such a thing can affect God? and, why He does not take away his sin instead of plaguing him unto death because of it?

20. The first half of the verse reads,

Have I sinned: what do I unto thee, O thou watcher of men?

I have sinned] Rather as above, **have I sinned**; the words being put as a supposition, equivalent to, *if I have sinned*. Job makes the supposition, he hardly concedes the fact, which is not meantime the point. His object is to pursue the idea that even sin (supposing it) on man's part cannot affect God, and ought not to be the reason for such unsparing pains as man has to suffer. In ch. xiv. 3, 4, where Job is calmer and more self-possessed, the same argument occurs, but is there supported by a reference to the universal sinfulness of mankind, which descends to the individual by inheritance and makes him more excusable and pitiable. Here the moral relations of men and God are less before his mind, it is God's natural Greatness in contrast with the natural littleness of man that engages his attention, and he thinks that in this there is a reason why men even if sinful should be less severely reckoned with.

what shall I do unto thee?] Rather, **what do I unto thee?** that is, how do I affect thee by my sin? The idea is repeatedly expressed in the Poem that God is too high to be affected by men's actions, whether sinful or righteous, cf. ch. xxii. 2 *seq.*, xxxv. 5 *seq.*

thou preserver of men] Rather, **thou watcher**, or **keeper**, of men. "Watcher" or keeper, elsewhere a word of comfort to the godly (Deut. xxxii. 10; Ps. xxxi. 23, cxxi. 4), is here used in an invidious sense to express the constant espionage exercised by God over men, that He may detect their sin and bring them to a reckoning, cf. ch. xiii. 27, xiv. 16.

Why hast thou set me as a mark against thee,
So that I am a burden to myself?
And why dost thou not pardon my transgression,   21
And take away mine iniquity?
For now shall I sleep in the dust;
And thou shalt seek me in the morning, but I *shall not be.*

a mark against thee] lit. *unto thee.* The word *mark* here does not mean a target at which to discharge arrows (ch. vi. 4, xvi. 4), but a stumbling-block or obstacle against which one strikes. Job feels that he is continually in the way of God, an obstacle against which the Almighty is always of set purpose striking Himself. The thought is one of unprecedented boldness.

am a burden to myself] Or, *am become* a burden, &c., that is, weary of myself and of my life, cf. 2 Sam. xv. 33. The Septuagint seems to have read, "a burden *unto thee*"; and according to Jewish tradition this was the original reading, but was corrected by the scribes as savouring of impiety.

21. *seek me in the morning*] Rather, **seek me**, simply, or, **seek me earnestly**; the addition "in the morning" (just as "betimes," ch. viii. 5) rests upon a mistaken etymology. Job concludes his speech by a pathetic reference to what must be the speedy issue of God's stringent watching of him: he will lie down in the dust and even should God enquire for him it will be too late.

There is something very open and engaging in the character of Job as it appears in this speech. He confesses the impatience that Eliphaz found fault with, though he excuses it by the incalculable weight of his affliction (ch. vi. 2). He admits that his words have been wild, though he thinks this was but natural when a creature found himself in conflict with God (ch. vi. 4). He even suggests to his friends the worth at which to estimate his language when he says that the words of one that is desperate go into the wind (ch. vi. 26). And he goes so far as to speak of himself as losing hold of the fear of the Almighty under the trial of his calamities (ch. vi. 14). There is something simple too and childlike in his defence of his cry of despair by the example of the lower creatures, which also express their pain or want by cries of distress (ch. vi. 5).

In keeping with this openness in regard to himself is his impatience and resentment of the covert insinuations of his friends through their first spokesman. He demands that they should shew him what they are hinting at by the pictures they are drawing and the blind parables they are narrating at him (ch. vi. 24); he himself will look them in the face and affirm his innocence (ch. vi. 28). And even the one bitter sentence which he utters against their hard-heartedness (ch. vi. 27) is quite in harmony with the honest directness of the rest of his words.

The state of Job's mind in ch. vii., when he turns away from his friends and casts his eye over the life of man as a whole, is more difficult to estimate. It appears to him that God has made man's condition upon the earth full of painfulness and bounded within iron limits. The world wears many aspects according to the eye that beholds it. It was natural for one in Job's condition to view it on its dark side. His view, however, has deeper grounds than mere subjective feeling. The view which Eliphaz presented of a scheme of universal goodness linking all events into a unity and making good the end even of ill may be the view which we ultimately rest in. Yet we believe in such a scheme rather than observe it. And the reasons of our belief, though various, are instinctive and ideal oftener than inductive. There are moments when another view forces itself upon the mind. And Scripture has here given this experience a place in its picture of man's life. It may be said that Job spoke under a mistake. Men so often make mistakes even in the highest things. It may also be said that enough was revealed to Job to correct his false impressions. But men so often are either unable or unwilling to receive that which is revealed.

There is this difference between us and Job: where we can say "the world," he was obliged to say "God." In this chapter he regards God almost exclusively on the physical side of His Being. He speaks out of the agony of suffering and from the abjectness of his own whole condition, and contrasts these with the natural Greatness of the Being who has plunged him into them. It is the physical claim of sentient life, which he urges, not to be tortured on any grounds whatsoever they be. In this mortal agony of the creature, and in view of the Greatness of God, moral considerations are almost mocked at, and sin is sneered out of reckoning as an irrelevancy.

CH. VIII. THE SPEECH OF BILDAD.

Bildad passes over in complete silence both Job's defence of his despairing cry (ch. vi. 1—13) and his assault upon the cruel behaviour of his friends (ch. vi. 14—30), and comes directly to the main issue, viz. Job's plea against God. The first speaker who thinks it necessary to defend the attitude taken up by the three friends towards Job is Eliphaz, who, in his second discourse (ch. xv.), speaks of their advices to Job as "the comforts of God and a word gently spoken" (ch. xv. 11), to which Job retorts, "miserable comforters are all of you" (ch. xvi. 2).

Bildad attaches his speech to what seemed the general drift of Job's words, particularly to two points where his drift more plainly shewed itself: first, his assertion that he had right on his side against God (ch. vi. 29), which implied a denial of the rectitude of God in his own case; and second, his assertion that the race of mankind were bound within the chains of a cruel force which bore upon them universally with an iron pressure (ch. vii. 1 *seq.*, *v.* 17 *seq.*). In the last point Job went far beyond his own individual instance. To meet these assertions Bildad affirms the rectitude of God, not merely in general but on both its sides, as a *discriminating* rectitude, which rewards the righteous and punishes the wicked.

Then answered Bildad the Shuhite, and said, 8
How long wilt thou speak these *things*? 2
And *how long shall* the words of thy mouth *be like* a strong wind?
Doth God pervert judgment? 3
Or doth the Almighty pervert justice?

This double-sided action of the divine rectitude, its discrimination as opposed to Job's cruel force that bore on mankind as a whole, is the chief point in Bildad's discourse.

The other point of importance is that he supports his doctrine not as Eliphaz did from revelation and religious feeling, but from the moral traditions of the fathers of humanity and the wisdom of the ancients.

The speech has three short sections:

First, *vv.* 1—7. Bildad's affirmation of the discriminating righteousness of God, one side of which was illustrated in the destruction of Job's children for their sin, and the other (as all good men hope) will be seen illustrated in the restoration of their father (for God is no respecter of persons) for his righteousness' sake to a prosperity greatly surpassing what he before enjoyed.

Second, *vv.* 8—19. This doctrine, especially that side of it which bears on the destruction of the wicked, is supported from the proverbial Wisdom of the Ancients. The moral maxims of the ancient time are thrown into gorgeous similes drawn from the rank and luxuriant vegetation of the swamps and river brakes of the semi-tropical East. The downfall of the wicked when God turns away from him is as rapid and complete as the sinking and withering of the stately reed when water is withdrawn from it.

Third, *vv.* 20—22. Bildad finally repeats his principle on both its sides, drawing from the beneficent side of it the assurance of a happy future for Job.

1—7. THE DISCRIMINATING RECTITUDE OF GOD.

2. Before coming to his principle and by way of introducing it Bildad expresses his wonder that Job should allow himself to speak such things as his discourse contained. *These things* are such things as ch. vi. 29, vii. 1, 2, 12—21, and perhaps even ch. vi. 10. He refers to the general drift of Job's speech, which appears to him to be an assertion that God was unjust (*v.* 3).

a strong wind] Violent, and empty, cf. ch. xv. 2, xvi. 3.

3. *doth God pervert*] Or, *will God pervert…will the Almighty, &c.?* This is what Bildad means by his reference to *these things.* Job's speech put briefly is an assertion that God perverts justice. God is referred to in his character of ruler of the world. By the question Bildad expresses his astonishment and abhorrence of what seems the drift of Job's language. The words "God" and "Almighty" stand first in the sentence for the sake of emphasis, will *God…?* and the same word "pervert" is also used in both clauses with an intonation of astonishment.

4   If thy children have sinned against him,
    And he have cast them away for their transgression;
5   If thou wouldest seek unto God betimes,
    And make thy supplication to the Almighty;
6   If thou *wert* pure and upright;
    Surely now he would awake for thee,

4—7. In opposition to Job's impious principle Bildad brings forward his doctrine of the Divine rectitude on both its sides, the one illustrated in the fate of Job's children (*v.* 4), the other, as he hopes, to be illustrated in the history of Job himself (*vv.* 5—7).

4. The construction of the English version is possible, which makes the whole of *v.* 4 the supposition or protasis and begins the second member of the sentence with *v.* 5. But more probably *v.* 4 is complete in itself: *if thy children have sinned so* (or, then) *he hath, &c.*

cast them away for] Rather lit., **he hath sent them away**, or, let them go, **into the hand** of their transgression. The idea is that evil carries its own retribution with it, and that a sinner is destroyed by the very sin which he commits, a common idea in the Book, cf. ch. iv. 8, xv. 31, 35, xviii. 7, 8, xx. 12 *seq*. Though Bildad puts his reference to the children of Job hypothetically there is great harshness in the allusion, and we may understand how the father would smart under it from his own reference later in the Book to the time when his children were yet alive: "When my boys were about me," ch. xxix. 5. A wiser and more human-hearted Teacher than Bildad has instructed us from the instances of the affliction of blindness (John ix. 2—3) and the accident in the tower of Siloam (Luke xiii. 4) that calamity is no proof of guilt in those on whom it falls, and that evil may serve in the hand of God wider uses than the chastisement of individuals. This is the very lesson of the Book of Job, though it seems that men in the days of our Lord had not yet learned it. The verse refers back to ch. i. 19, and is evidence that the Prologue forms an integral part of the Book.

5. Bildad saw in the fate of Job's children not only proof that they had sinned but that their sin was deadly. He saw in Job's afflictions proof equally decisive that he had sinned, but the fact that he was still spared, however severe his afflictions, gave a different complexion to his sin, and also suggested a different meaning for his afflictions. They were chastisements meant for his good, and Bildad is enabled to hope the best for Job, if he will rightly lay his trials to heart.

wouldest seek unto God betimes] Rather, **if thou wilt seek earnestly unto God**. *Thou* is emphatic in antithesis to "thy children," *v.* 4.

6. *if thou* wert *pure*] Or, *if thou be pure*, cf. subjunctive in ch. xi. 15.

surely now he would awake] Rather, **surely now he will awake**. The words, *if thou wilt seek, v.* 5, suggest the right point of view from which to look at the words, *if thou be pure, &c.* The whole passage refers to the conduct which Bildad hopes for from Job. The meaning, therefore, does not seem to be, If thou be pure, as thou sayest, and as

And make the habitation of thy righteousness prosperous.
Though thy beginning was small, 7
Yet thy latter end should greatly increase.
For inquire, I pray thee, of the former age, 8
And prepare *thyself* to the search of their fathers:
(For we *are but of* yesterday, and know nothing, 9
Because our days upon earth *are* a shadow:)
Shall not they teach thee, *and* tell thee, 10
And utter words out of their heart?

we have supposed thee; but rather, If thou become pure, through penitence, and by letting afflictions work the fruits of righteousness, cf. ch. xi. 13 *seq.*

make the habitation of thy righteousness prosperous] Or, *restore thy righteous habitation,* that is, restore the lost prosperity (cf. Joel ii. 25) of thy habitation, now become the abode of righteousness. Bildad comes out with his suspicions of Job's guilt much more explicitly than Eliphaz did; and similarly Zophar, ch. xi. 13.

7. *thy beginning*] i.e., thy former estate, before affliction; similarly "latter end" (read: thy latter end **shall** greatly increase) is said of his future condition of prosperity; see the same use of the words ch. xlii. 12. The verse means that his former estate shall seem small in comparison with the splendour of his renewed prosperity. It is curious that the Author here allows Bildad to utter a prophecy, the literal fulfilment of which, though not through the means suggested by Bildad, he takes care expressly to chronicle.

8—19. THE MORAL WISDOM OF THE ANCIENTS.

Bildad, having laid down his moral principle, invites Job to reflect that it is a principle resting on the research and the generalized experience of men of generations long past, whose long lives enabled them to weigh and balance and infer from the multitude of cases the general truth. It is no new theory of his or of the short-lived men of to-day, who are but of yesterday and know nothing. These maxims of the ancient world are clothed in rich and gorgeous similes drawn from the luxuriant plant-life of the sultry East.

8. *prepare thyself to the search*] i.e., give heed to the research, or, to that which their fathers have searched out. By referring to a former age, and then to the fathers of that age or generation, Bildad intimates that his truth was recognised through all antiquity backwards till history loses itself in the beginnings of time.

10. *words out of their heart*] Words not the result of hasty and superficial generalizing, but of an experience which the lengthened lives of these men had enabled them to pass through, and the principles learned in which had sunk into their heart. The "heart" is in Heb. the deepest part of human nature, whether intellect or feeling. There is an implied condemnation in all this of the new principles which Job was

11 Can the rush grow up without mire?
Can the flag grow without water?
12 Whilst it *is* yet in his greenness, *and* not cut down,
It withereth before any *other* herb.
13 So *are* the paths of all that forget God;
And the hypocrite's hope shall perish:
14 Whose hope shall be cut off,
And whose trust *shall be* a spider's web.
15 He shall lean upon his house, but it shall not stand:
He shall hold it fast, but it shall not endure.

setting forth, what a subsequent speaker calls his "doctrine," ch. xi. 4, principles based on nothing but his own single experience and instance.

11. The ancient wisdom itself. This wisdom is plainly not that of the Arabs or Idumeans, but is Egyptian. The *rush* is most probably the Papyrus, which is said to attain a growth twice the height of a man. The *flag* is the Nile-reed, or Nile-grass (only here and Gen. xli. 2).

12. *and not cut down*] lit. *and not to be cut down* (or, plucked, ch. xxx. 4), that is, in its full luxuriance, not ripe nor ready for cutting, and therefore with no trace of withering or decay in it. In this state of full freshness, when water is withdrawn from it, it sinks and collapses, withering sooner than any herb.

13. Application of the simile. When men forget God, and His sustaining grace is withdrawn from them, they sink down suddenly and perish like the luxuriant water-reed.

the hypocrite] This word is difficult to translate, it means rather *the godless*, or, *profane*, cf. Jer. xxiii. 11; hypocrisy in the ordinary sense is not at all the idea of the term. The verb is rendered in the English Version mostly "defile" or "pollute," but "profane" would suit most of the passages.

14. *shall be cut off*] Perhaps rather, **goeth in sunder,** though the meaning is not quite certain. One would have expected a noun here parallel to "spider's web" in the second clause, but no efforts to find a noun have been successful. Saadia in his Arabic Translation rendered *gossamer*, the filmy thread-like substance that floats in the air, or the thread-like shimmer of the air itself when sultry and moist. This is a very suitable sense but is without sufficient support.

a spider's web] lit. spider's *house*, cf. "house" in *v.* 15. The flimsiness of the spider's house is proverbial in the East. Mohammed compares idolaters to the spider: The likeness of those who take to themselves patrons beside God is as the likeness of the spider who taketh to herself a house; and verily the frailest of houses is the spider's house, if they did but know, Kor. xxix. 40. See also Job xxvii. 18.

15. *hold it fast*] i.e. *hold fast by it.* The meaning of course is not that he tries to uphold his house, but that he tries to support himself by holding on to it. This is true both of the spider and the man.

He *is* green before the sun, 16
And his branch shooteth forth in his garden,
His roots are wrapped about the heap, 17
And seeth the place of stones.
If he destroy him from his place, 18
Then *it* shall deny him, *saying*, I have not seen thee.
Behold, this *is* the joy of his way, 19
And out of the earth shall others grow.
Behold, God will not cast away a perfect *man*, 20

16—19. A new figure of a spreading, luxuriant plant, suddenly destroyed, and leaving not a trace of itself behind.

before the sun] This scarcely means *openly*, in broad day and in the face of the sun, but, under the fostering heat of the sun.

17. *seeth the place of stones*] This translation can hardly mean that in his high growth he looks down upon the stone heap, or bends over it, but rather that he chooses it, fixes himself upon it. Others prefer the sense: *he pierces between the stones,* that is, with his roots, or, he pierces the place of stones, the word which ordinarily means *to see* having it is said in the dialect of the Hauran the sense of *cut,* or *split* (Wetzstein in Delitzsch, note, p. 120). This affords a more distinct sense. The luxuriance of the plant and its hold of the soil are graphically described. It is fresh and green under the heat of the sun; its suckers spread out and run over all the garden; its shoots clasp the heap of stones and weave themselves about it; and, finally, its roots thrust themselves down and pierce the stony soil, grasping the heart of the earth.

18. *if he destroy him*] The subject is God. The words might be rendered, *if he be* (when he is) *destroyed*. This is perhaps better, as the plant is spoken of. The point of the verse is not who destroys him, but that he is destroyed, and when destroyed utterly disappears, so that his place says, I never saw thee. In spite of his luxuriance and hold of the soil he is suddenly and wholly swept away and his place denies ever having known him.

19. *joy of his way*] *way* may be "fate," as often, and the words would be ironical; or "way" may be "course of life"—so ends what was to him the joy of his course of life.

shall others grow] Or, *do others grow*. Who the others are or what quality they are of is not the point, which is that his place is occupied by others as if he had never been. He leaves no trace, no blank, and no memory.

20—22. Finally Bildad repeats his general principle and augurs from the one side of it a happy and brilliant future for Job.

cast away a perfect man] This word "perfect" is the title given to Job by the Author, and acknowledged due to him by God, see on ch. i. 1. The phrase, God will not cast off a "perfect" man, becomes almost the text of Job's reply, cf. ch. ix. 20, 21; x. 3.

Neither will he help the evil doers:
21 Till he fill thy mouth *with* laughing,
And thy lips *with* rejoicing.
22 They that hate thee shall be clothed with shame;
And the dwelling place of the wicked shall come to nought.

help the evil doers] lit. *hold by the hand of* evil-doers, cf. Is. xli. 13, xlii. 6.
21. *till he fill*] If this rendering be adopted, the word "till" is used somewhat generally to express what God's practical rectitude, as described on both its sides *v.* 20, will issue in. Others prefer to read, he will *yet* fill—making a stop at the end of *v.* 20.
22. In his concluding words Bildad puts himself and his friends right with Job, and desires to put Job right with himself and God. By referring to Job's haters he intimates that he and his friends are none of them; and by identifying these haters with the wicked (*v.* 22), he lets Job know that he regards him as at heart one who belongs to quite a different class.

The position of Job's friends cannot be understood at all unless we consider that they assumed Job's piety at heart, but concluded from his calamities that he had been guilty of some great sins. And as Eliphaz had already brought to bear on Job's mind the influence of a revelation, the next strongest argument was the consent of mankind. And to some minds, especially in that condition of perplexity and confusion on religious experience in which Job's was, the general accord of mankind speaks with a more persuasive voice than anything called revelation. Bildad clearly enough perceived the drift of Job's words in ch. vii.; they were to the effect that the government of the world and the supreme Power in it was un-moral. And his reply, that mankind everywhere, and especially in circumstances that gave their judgment weight, had perceived a moral law ruling the universe, was conclusive as a general principle. His error lay in supposing that this was the only principle on which the universe was ruled, and in imagining that this principle operated always in a manner direct and immediate. Hence the principle lost its effectiveness in his hands by being stretched to uses which it did not cover.

Ch. IX.—X. Job's reply to Bildad.

The Discourse though formally a reply to Bildad seems to touch also upon things said in the speech of Eliphaz. It is rather difficult to divide into paragraphs, not being calm and logical but passionate and hurried and passing on by rapid steps from one point to another all more or less connected, and fusing all together in the glow of a fire the colours of which are awe before an omnipotent Power, and moral terror and indignation mixed with piteous despair at the indiscriminate severity with which it crushes men.

Job starts with a sneering adhesion to the maxim of his friends, How can man be righteous with God? by which he means, How can man make his righteousness appear, though he has it, seeing God's might will overpower him in all attempts to substantiate it? This idea is carried on throughout ch. ix. At the end of this chapter there is a pause. The sufferer has exhausted his idea in his terrible pictures of the Divine might and the hopeless paralysis of the Creature before His Majesty in any meeting with Him to vindicate its own innocence.

But now as he pauses for a moment and looks around on his condition, the idea returns with a new force and fills his mind, and pushes him out upon a new stream of complaint. And as in ch. vii. 12—21 he had exhausted possibility in speculating what it could be in man or himself that provoked the Almighty's hostility to him, he now boldly enters the Divine mind itself and explores every corner of it in the hope of discovering what thought or feeling or defect in God it could be that led Him thus to afflict and destroy him in a way in such contradiction to His former gracious treatment of him. Baffled in every effort he leaps to the desperate conclusion that His present treatment of him reveals God's real character, and that His former favour and care had been lavished on him only that at the last He might the more effectually torment him.

Thus the Discourse falls into two great sections:

Ch. ix. God's might and the terror of His Majesty will prevent man from substantiating his innocence in his plea with God.

Ch. x. Job's efforts to discover in the Divine mind the secret of the terrible afflictions with which God visited him.

CH. IX. GOD'S MIGHT AND THE TERROR OF HIS MAJESTY WILL PREVENT MAN FROM ESTABLISHING HIS INNOCENCE IN HIS PLEA WITH GOD.

Starting with the question, How can man substantiate his innocence in the face of God's overpowering might (*vv.* 2, 3), Job passes on to a delineation of this Divine power, which he conceives as a terrible irresistible Force, which moves mountains, and shifts the earth from its place; which dictates to the sun that he shine not; which made the mighty constellations of the sky; and whose workings are beyond the compass of the human mind to grasp (*vv.* 4—10).

Then passing from the material world to creatures he imagines this Power coming, say, upon himself, unseen, beyond intelligence (*v.* 11), irresistible, irresponsible (*v.* 12), and cites as an instance good for all the memorable defeat of the abettors of Rahab, *the helpers of Rahab succumbed to him, how then should I answer him?* (*vv.* 13, 14). What Job describes is a meeting of God and man that the latter may uphold his innocence against Him, or perhaps any meeting of God and man; and such a meeting has Job to face in the attempt to establish his innocence. He must be overpowered and fall though guiltless:—if I were innocent I could not assert my innocence, I must fall down and supplicate my omnipotent Opponent (*v.* 15). This feeling of helplessness before a crushing power altogether overmasters Job and rouses him to a recklessness which is that of despair, and going back upon his words, *if I were innocent*, he cries, I *am* innocent, innocent and guilty He destroys alike; the earth is given into the hands of the

9 Then Job answered and said,
2 I know *it is* so of a truth:
   But how should man be just with God?
3 If he will contend with him,

wicked, He covers the faces of the judges thereof—if it is not He, who then is it? (*vv.* 16—24).

But now the paroxysm being over Job proceeds more calmly to speak of his own condition, which is but an illustration of what is everywhere seen, but sorrow and perplexity now prevail over indignation. He describes the pitiful brevity of his life (*vv.* 25, 26). And with a touching pathos he tells how he sometimes resolves to leave off his sad countenance and brighten up, but the thought that God has resolved not to hold him innocent again crushes him, he *has* to be guilty, and all his efforts to shew himself to be clear are vain (*vv.* 27—31). And he rounds off his speech with a reference to that with which he began, the central difficulty: God is not a man that man might answer Him; there is no umpire between Him and man to impose his authority on both; but if He would lift His afflicting rod from Job and not affright him with His Majesty, he would speak without fear, for his conscience is void of offence (*vv.* 32—35).

2. It is not quite easy to see what form of the maxim of the friends it is to which Job gives his sneering assent in this verse, when he says, *To be sure I know that it is so.* In *v.* 10 he quotes words from Eliphaz, ch. v. 9, verbatim, and he may refer to the form in which this speaker put forward the principle common to them all, Shall man be righteous before God? ch. iv. 17. In this case the second member of the verse merely explains the words *that it is so*,

Of a truth I know that it is so:
How shall man be righteous with God?

Job, however, gives a different turn to the words, meaning by them, How shall man substantiate his righteousness, and make it to appear, when he has to maintain it in the face of the overpowering might of God? (*v.* 3). Or, Job may attach his reply to Bildad's question, Will God pervert right? (ch. viii. 3). To which he replies: Of course —but how shall man have right with God? God's power makes right. Job does not quibble with words. He speaks from the point of view of his own circumstances and the construction which he put on them. His afflictions were proof that God held him guilty, while his own conscience declared his innocence. But he was helpless against God's judgment of him. In the view of his friends and all men, and even himself, his afflictions were God's verdict against him. And his answer is that man must be guilty before God because he cannot contend with an omnipotent power resolved to hold him guilty.

3. *if he will contend*] Or, *if he would;* if he (man) should desire to contend with God. "To contend" is a legal term meaning to enter a plea with, the idea of a court or judge being in the mind of the speaker.

He cannot answer him one of a thousand.
He is wise in heart, and mighty in strength: 4
Who hath hardened *himself* against him, and hath prospered?
Which removeth the mountains, and they know not: 5
Which overturneth them in his anger.
Which shaketh the earth out of her place, 6
And the pillars thereof tremble.
Which commandeth the sun, and it riseth not; 7
And sealeth up the stars.
Which alone spreadeth out the heavens, 8
And treadeth upon the waves of the sea.

Here man is supposed to have a plea with God on the question of his innocency, or on any question involving his righteousness. The question in *v.* 4, " Who hath hardened himself against Him?" makes it probable that man is here considered the appellant. Others take the subject to be God: *if He were pleased to contend with him* (man), cf. *vv.* 14, 16. This suits the second half of the verse, but seems less suitable to the general connexion.

he cannot answer him] Or, *he* (man) *could not* answer him (God) one of a thousand of the questions with which in His infinite wisdom (*v.* 4) He would ply him.

4. *wise in heart*] i.e. in *mind*, corresponding to "mighty in power."
hardened himself] Probably *hardened* his neck, i.e. braved him, Prov. xxix. 1.
hath prospered] lit. *been safe*, or as we say, "with impunity."

5—10. Description of God's omnipotent power as it displays itself in the material world.
they know not] Suddenly and unexpectedly, Ps. xxxv. 8; Jer. l. 24.

6. The reference is probably to earthquakes. The earth is conceived as a structure supported on pillars, ch. xxxviii. 6; Ps. lxxv. 3. The conception was poetical; if the pillars were supposed anything actual, they were probably the roots of the great mountains which extended downwards and bore up the earth, as the part of them above the earth supported the heavens.

7. The reference may be to days when from storm and darkness the sun seems not to rise, or to eclipses and sudden obscurations of the heavenly bodies.

8. The point lies in the gigantic power of God who "alone" and of Himself stretched out the heavens; cf. the expression of the same idea of power, Is. xl. 12, xliv. 24. In Is. xl. 22 it is said that God stretches out the heavens as a curtain and spreadeth them out as a tent to dwell in. Our "firmament" is a relic of a false astronomy for which scripture is not responsible.

waves of the sea] lit. *heights* of the sea, cf. heights of the earth, Amos iv. 13. The "sea" here is scarcely the celestial waters, Ps. xxix. 3.

9   Which maketh Arcturus, Orion,
    And Pleiades, and the chambers of the south.
10 Which doeth great *things* past finding out;
    Yea, and wonders without number.
11 Lo, he goeth by me, and I see *him* not:
    He passeth on also, but I perceive him not.
12 Behold, he taketh away, who can hinder him?
    Who will say unto him, What doest thou?
13 *If* God will not withdraw his anger,

God is represented as walking on the sea when its waves mount up to heaven, and His voice may be heard in the thunder.

    9. The Hebrew names are '*âsh* ('*ayish* ch. xxxviii. 32), *keseel*, and *keemah*. These names may possibly denote the Bear, Orion and the Pleiades or seven stars; there is, however, considerable uncertainty. The word *keseel* means "fool," which is to be interpreted as the Syr. and Chal. in this place, *giant*, cf. Gen. vi. 4, that is, some heaven-daring rebel, who was chained to the sky for his impiety. Such mythological ideas belong to a time anterior to authentic history, though as still lingering in the popular mind they are alluded to in such poems as Job. In Is. xiii. 10 the word is used in the general sense of constellations. *Keemah* perhaps means *heap*, and is a natural name for the Pleiades. Others have interpreted the expressions differently (see Delitzsch Comment. p. 127).

    the chambers of the south] are probably the great spaces and deep recesses of the southern hemisphere of the heavens, with the constellations which they contain. These being known to exist, but only suggested to the eye, are alluded to generally.

    10. The description of the operation of God's might in the material world concludes with a general statement that this operation surpasses all power of comprehension by the human mind. The words are exactly those of Eliphaz ch. v. 9, but while to Eliphaz all God's operations have an ethical meaning and subserve one great purpose of goodness, to Job they seem the mere un-moral play of an immeasurable Force. This force was of course a Person, for an impersonal force is an idea unknown to the Shemitic mind. But this force seemed all the more tremendous to Job from his having no idea of second causes or of what we call laws of nature; the phenomena of the universe, even the most stupendous, were the immediate work of this mighty agent.

    11—24. From the operation of this terrible force in the physical world Job passes on to describe its display among creatures, and to shew how it paralyses and crushes them.

    11. This power is subtle and invisible in its presence, felt but impossible to grasp.

    12. It is irresistible and irresponsible.

    taketh away] Carries off, as a beast of prey its booty.

    who can hinder him] Or, *turn him back*.

    13. *if God will not withdraw*] Rather, **God withdraws not.** His

The proud helpers do stoop under him.
How much less shall I answer him, 14
And choose out my words *to reason* with him?
Whom, though I were righteous, *yet* would I not answer, 15
But I would make supplication to my judge.

fury is persistent and inexorable till it has accomplished its purpose, cf. ch. xxiii. 13—14.

the proud helpers do stoop] Rather, **the helpers of Rahab did stoop.** The "helpers" are the abettors, the partizans and company of Rahab; and the clause illustrates by an example, the highest example that could be chosen, the statement in the first clause, God withdraws not his anger; to this wrath even the aiders of Rahab succumbed. (1) "Rahab" means pride or arrogancy. But the "helpers of pride" or the "proud helpers" is an expression too indefinite to occur in the present connexion, where, in addition, the perf. *bowed* beneath him, points to a distinct historical event, adduced as an illustration. (2) In Ps. lxxxvii. 4 Rahab is a name for Egypt; so Ps. lxxxix. 10, Is. xxx. 7 (for, "their strength" read Rahab), Is. li. 9. Any historical illustration, however, from the history of Egypt in connexion with Israel is not to be looked for in this Book, the scene of which is laid in an age anterior to the Exodus. Direct allusions do not occur to the history of Israel. Allusions of any kind are rare, but such as are made are to the general history of mankind before Israel became a nation, cf. ch. xxii. 16, a reference to the flood or the cities of the Plain. (3) In Is. li. 9 the parallel clause to "cut Rahab (Egypt) in pieces," is, "wounded the *Dragon.*" Again in Ps. lxxiv. 13—14 the parallel to "didst divide the sea" is "brakest the heads of *Leviathan.*" From this it appears that Egypt was called Rahab, Dragon or Leviathan with reference to its native monster, which was taken as the symbol of the nation and its character (cf. Ps. lxviii. 30 margin). All this leads finally to the conclusion that Rahab is the monster of the sea, which is probably nothing but the sea itself, as appears from Job xxvi. 12. In the poetical nature-myth this stormy sea, assaulting heaven with its waves, was personified as a monster leading his helpers on to wage war with heaven, but was quelled (ch. xxvi. 12) by the might of God. This is the instance of God's power adduced by Job. That the Poet makes use of the floating fragments of superstition and mythology still existing in the popular mind has nothing surprising in it.

14. Job now draws an inference from this instance to his own—how much less should *he* meet God in a hostile plea?

choose out my words] In a plea against God circumspection and careful selection of language would be needful, but the self-possession and calmness requisite for this would be destroyed by His overbearing might, and the terror of His majesty.

15. *though I were righteous*] i.e. though I were in the right, though my cause was just against Him.

make supplication to my judge] Rather, **to mine adversary, or opponent.** Had Job right on his side he could not maintain it; over-

16 If I had called, and he had answered me;
　　Yet would I not believe that he had hearkened unto my voice.
17 For he breaketh me with a tempest,
　　And multiplieth my wounds without cause.
18 He will not suffer me to take my breath,
　　But filleth me *with* bitterness.
19 If *I speak* of strength, lo, *he is* strong:
　　And if of judgment, who shall set me a time *to plead?*
20 If I justify myself, mine own mouth shall condemn me:
　　If I say, I *am* perfect, it shall also prove me perverse.
21 *Though* I *were* perfect, *yet* would I not know my soul:
　　I would despise my life.

powered by the irresistible and awful might of his opponent he would desert his own just plea and supplicate his adversary.

16. In *vv.* 14, 15 the plea against God is not supposed actually entered upon; the idea of such a plea presents itself to Job's mind and he pictures the results that would follow upon himself; in *v.* 16 he assumes the plea entered upon, that he had actually cited God, who had appeared, and he describes what would follow at this stage.

if I had called] i.e. cited God as a party in my plea against Him.

that he had hearkened] Rather, **that he would hearken.** Had Job with a superhuman courage cited God, and had God appeared, Job would not believe that He would listen to him, cf. *v.* 35, ch. xiii. 21 *seq.*, xxiii. 6 *seq.*

17—21. These verses describe what would ensue in the supposed case that God had actually responded to Job's citation. He would not listen to Job's plea but would crush him with His infinite power. The words do not describe what Job actually suffers at present or has suffered, but what he would have to endure *then*, though the colours of the terrible picture are drawn from his actual sufferings.

17. *he breaketh*] Rather, **he would break.** Similarly, **and multiply.** The word translated *break* may mean to seize and swallow up, that is, *to sweep away*, cf. ch. xxx. 22.

18. *will not suffer*] Rather, **would not suffer.** And so, **but fill.**

19—21. These three verses read as follows,
　　If you speak of the strength of the mighty, Here I am! (saith He)
　　If of judgment, Who will set me a time?
　20. Were I in the right, mine own mouth would condemn me,
　　Were I perfect, He would prove me perverse:
　21. I am perfect! I regard not myself,
　　I despise my life.

The speaker in *v.* 19 is God, at least it is He who uses the words, "Here I am," and "Who will set me a time?" The rest may be words of Job, in which case the words "saith He" must be supplied to these two

> This *is* one *thing*, therefore I said *it*,
> He destroyeth the perfect and the wicked.
> If the scourge slay suddenly,
> He will laugh at the trial of the innocent.

phrases alone. It gives a more vigorous sense to suppose the whole verse spoken by God. The frightened imagination of Job with much dramatic force represents God as suddenly flinging Himself into the arena before all, with a consciousness of irresistible might and irresponsibility, ready for any encounter of strength and defying any to bring Him to law. The action of "appointing one a time" or ordaining a day, is of course not the action of the plaintiff but of a judge, and the words imply the irresponsibility and superiority to all law of the speaker.

20. In *v.* 20 Job is the speaker; he describes the effect upon him of the might of God,—though he had right on his side his own mouth would make him out wrong; out of terror he would speak at random or say the opposite of what he should say. The word *perfect* is used as in ch. i. 1, not in an absolute sense, but to mean upright and free from transgression. The subject in the second clause is more probably God than *it*, i.e. my mouth; were Job perfect the effect of God's power would be that he would appear perverse or wicked.

21. This feeling of being helpless in the hands of an overmastering might, which has no regard to his innocence, drives Job on to a reckless defiance of his adversary, and he will assert his innocence in His face though it should cost him his life. Going back upon the words, "if I were perfect," he cries, I *am* perfect, I regard not myself, I despise my life. The phrase, I regard not, care not for, myself, is lit. *I know not myself*, cf. Gen. xxxix. 6, Ps. i. 6. On the last words cf. ch. vii. 20. The speaker feels that his bold assertion of his innocence may provoke his adversary altogether to destroy him, but he proclaims his indifference.

22. This verse reads,

> It is all one, therefore I say,
> He destroyeth the perfect and the wicked,

that is, indiscriminately. Here there is not only the former statement of ch. vii. that the destiny of man at the hands of God is hard and crushing, but in addition an express denial of the position of Bildad that God's dealing with men was discriminating. An emphasis falls on *He.* It is not quite easy to decide what is meant by *it is all one*. The close connexion with *v.* 21 makes it most natural to understand: it is all one whether I live or die; so that the verses 21—24 are all one outburst, in which the Almighty is described as a crushing force that bears down on all good and bad without distinction.

23. Further illustration of this character of God.

the scourge] i.e. the plague, as pestilence, famine, war, and the like, Is. xxviii. 15.

will laugh at the trial] Or, *mocks at the despair*, cf. vi. 14.

24. The same illustrated on the widest scale. Verse 23 spoke of

24 The earth is given into the hand of the wicked:
He covereth the faces of the judges thereof;
If not, where, *and* who *is* he?
25 Now my days are swifter than a post:
They flee away, they see no good.
26 They are passed away as the swift ships:

particular calamities afflicting portions of the earth. At the despair of the innocent under these God mocks, distant and indifferent. Now Job makes the sweeping statement that the earth is one scene of injustice. The wicked prevail in it, it is given into their hand, to rule and dominate within it. Comp. ch. xxiv.

covereth the faces of the judges] that they cannot see the right, to give the innocent justice. It is God who covereth their faces; He not only does not hinder wrong, He ensures that it prevail and have the upper hand.

if not, where, and who is he] Rather, **if not He, who then is it**—who does all this (*v.* 24), if it is not He? Others besides Job have asked such questions.

In this passage Job's spirit reaches the lowest abyss of its alienation from God. From this time onwards his mind is calmer and the moral idea of God begins to reassert its place in his thoughts. Here God appears to him as a mere omnipotent power, with a bias, if He have one, to evil and cruelty, and he speaks of Him distantly as "he" (cf. ch. iii. 20). His conception is but the reflection of his own case, as he conceived it, flung over the world, though his conception of his own case was false. To a Shemitic mind who had no conception of second causes or of general laws or of a scheme of providence, but regarded God as the immediate author of every single occurrence, the danger must always have been imminent of being driven to conclude that God was the author of the misery and wrong and cruel hardship under which men groaned.

In these verses Job traverses directly the maxim of his friends in regard to the discriminating righteousness of God, and the examples which he cites he might have used to demolish their theory. But he is little concerned with their theory here; later he does use his examples to drive them from the field. But here he is occupied with himself, with the impossibility of making his innocence which he is conscious of to appear and be admitted; for, of course, to himself and to all others his afflictions were the testimony of God to his guilt. And thus, though in the last verses his view extends to the world in general, he comes back in *v.* 25 to himself.

25. *Now my days*] Better, **and my days**—under the weight of this unjust and oppressive Force (*vv.* 5—24).

than a post] i.e. a courier, 2 Sam. xviii. 22, 24.

26. *the swift ships*] *the ships of reed*. These skiffs, constructed of a wooden keel and the rest of reeds, are the "vessels of bulrushes" of Is. xviii. 2. They carried but one or two persons, and being light were

As the eagle *that* hasteth to the prey.
If I say, I will forget my complaint, 27
I will leave off my heaviness, and comfort myself:
I am afraid of all my sorrows, 28
I know that thou wilt not hold me innocent.
If I be wicked, 29
Why then labour I in vain?
If I wash myself with snow water, 30
And make my hands never so clean;
Yet shalt thou plunge me in the ditch, 31

extremely swift. The ancients were familiar with them; Plin. xiii. 11, ex ipso quidem papyro navigia texunt; and Lucan, *Phars.* iv. 36,

conseritur bibula Memphitis cymba papyro,

(quoted in Gesenius, *Com. on Is.* i. p. 577). Job as usual heaps images together to picture out the brevity of his life, cf. ch. vii. 6 *seq.* Here the images are new, a runner, a skiff of reed, an eagle swooping on his prey.

27. *my complaint*] i.e. as always, my complaining, ch. vii. 13.
my heaviness] lit. *my faces*, my sad mien, 1 Sam. i. 18.
comfort myself] lit. *brighten up*, ch. x. 20; Ps. xxxix. 13. The word in Arab. (*balija*) means to have a space clear of hair between the eyebrows, hence to have an open, bright countenance. A certain woman described the Prophet (Mohammed) as *ablaju 'lwajhi*, bright in countenance. Then the word came to mean also *to be bright*, of the dawn or the day.

28. As Job's afflictions were the proof of his guilt in the estimation of God, "to hold him innocent" means to remove his afflictions, as the first clause suggests.

29. *if I be wicked*] Rather, **I shall be guilty**, that is, I have to be, shall be held, guilty; God has resolved so to consider me. Everywhere in these verses guilt and afflictions mean the same thing, the one being the sign of the other.

30. *with snow water*] This is according to one reading (*bemê*). According to another (*bemô*), *with snow*. The latter is better; snow-water is turbid and foul, ch. vi. 16; snow is the symbol of the most perfect purity, Is. i. 18, Ps. li. 7. Locman's 23rd fable illustrates this Oriental idea very well: "A negro stripped himself of his clothes one day and began rubbing his body with snow. He was asked, Why do you rub yourself with snow? He answered, Perhaps I shall become white. A wise man passing by said to him, You fellow, don't fatigue yourself, your body may well make the snow black, but it will never make you white. The moral is &c."

make my hands never so clean] lit. *cleanse my hands with lye*, or, potash.

31. An expressive figure for, to cover again with uncleanness. The naked body (*v.* 30) is supposed plunged in the ditch, and the clothes refuse to cover so foul an object.

And mine own clothes shall abhor me.
32 For *he is* not a man, as I *am, that* I should answer him,
And we should come together in judgment.
33 Neither is there *any* daysman betwixt us,
That might lay his hand upon us both.
34 Let him take his rod away from me,
And let not his fear terrify me:
35 *Then* would I speak, and not fear him;
But *it is* not so with me.

32—34. The preceding verses described how unavailing all Job's efforts were to make out his innocence in the face of the fixed resolution of God to hold him guilty. Now Job comes back to what is the real difficulty,—God is not a man like himself.

33. *any daysman*] i.e. any umpire, or, arbiter. The word possibly comes from the Lat. *diem dicere*, to fix a day for hearing a cause.

>For what art thou
>That mak'st thyself his dayes-man to prolong
>The vengeance prest?   Spenser, *Fae. Q.* ii. 8. 28.

(Wright, *Bible Word-Book*.)

lay his hand] i.e. impose his authority on both, and do justice between the two. There is no prophecy of the incarnation in these verses. But there is a cry of the human heart amidst its troubles that it might meet and see God as a man. Then man's relations to Him might be understood and adjusted. That the cry is uttered under a misconception of God and of the meaning of His providence does not make the expression of man's need any the less real or touching, for in our great darkness here misconceptions of God prevail so much over true conceptions of Him.

34. The subject is God, not the daysman—let God remove His rod, His afflictions.

his fear terrify me] Or, *his terror affright me*. The "terror" of God is His overawing majesty, cf. ch. xiii. 21, xxxiii. 7, the last passage with direct reference to the present one.

35. If God would meet Job as a man, removing His afflicting rod and laying aside His awful majesty, Job would speak out his innocence and plead his own cause without fear.

but it is not so with me] Rather, **for I am not so in myself**—in my own consciousness I am not so, or such, that I should fear Him. "In myself" is lit. *with myself*, cf. ch. x. 13, xxiii. 14, xxvii. 11, and St Paul's *by* myself, 1 Cor. iv. 4.

Ch. X. Job's new Appeal to God, in the form of an effort to discover what in the Divine Nature it can be that will explain his terrible sufferings.

The chapter attaches itself closely to the last words of ch. ix., precisely as ch. vii. to the end of ch. vi. Ch. ix. ended with the expression

My soul is weary of my life; 10
I will leave my complaint upon myself;
I will speak in the bitterness of my soul.

of the feeling on Job's part of his own innocence, and at the same time of the feeling that God had determined to hold him guilty. Added to this was the feeling of his helplessness to make his innocence appear against God's power and majesty. After a slight pause, perhaps, these mixed feelings gather new volume in his mind and he breaks out, perplexed and baffled, *my soul is weary of my life*. Then commences an appeal unto God in which one supposition after another is hazarded as to what in God's nature it is that is the secret of Job's sufferings, each supposition being refuted by being seen to be in contradiction to God's true nature. The whole thus forms a very impassioned argument with God founded on His own nature.

First, Job appeals to God not to *make* him guilty by mere arbitrary will, but if He have cause against him to reveal it, *v.* 2. Then with a strong feeling of his own innocence he asks if it be a pleasure to God to oppress and reject the just and smile upon the wicked? Can it be that God finds pleasure in this? *v.* 3. Then he wonders if God have eyes of flesh, subject to illusion and error, so that He mistakes the innocent for the guilty; or if He be short-lived like men and must gratify His vengeance on suspicion lest His victim should escape Him—though in truth none of this could be, for He *knew* Job's innocence, and none could deliver from His hand, *vv.* 4—7.

Then the mention of His "hands" suggests to Job, and he brings it before God, the strange contradiction in God's treatment of him—His hands fashioned Him once like a precious vessel and now He reduces him to dust again! *v.* 8.

This contradiction vividly put in *v.* 8 is then enlarged upon. Job recalls God's remembrance to past times, how He wonderfully began his being in the womb, and with a careful and minute tenderness fashioned all his parts, forming him with a prodigal expenditure of skill; and then when a living man hedged him about with loving kindness and guarded his spirit with constant oversight, *vv.* 9—12. The contradiction between this gracious guidance in the past and God's present treatment of him utterly baffles Job, and he leaps to the desperate conclusion that all that he now suffers had always been designed by God, and that even while expending His greatest skill upon him He had been cherishing this deep purpose of plaguing him. With an elaborate minuteness Job goes over this divine scheme, *vv.* 13—17, and as he realizes it to himself in detailing it,

He finally cries out in despair, why God ever gave him life at all, *vv.* 18, 19? and begs for a little easing of his pain before he goes into the land of darkness, *vv.* 20, 21; concluding with some terrible touches concerning that gloomy land, where the light is as darkness, *v.* 22.

1. *leave my complaint upon myself*] Rather, **give free course to my complaint**, cf. ch. vii. 11 *seq.*

2 I will say unto God, Do not condemn me;
　Shew me wherefore thou contendest with me.
3 *Is it* good unto thee that thou shouldest oppress,
　That thou shouldest despise the work of thine hands,
　And shine upon the counsel of the wicked?
4 Hast thou eyes of flesh?
　Or seest thou as man seeth?
5 *Are* thy days as the days of man?
　Are thy years as man's days,
6 That thou inquirest after mine iniquity,
　And searchest after my sin?
7 Thou knowest that I am not wicked;
　And *there is* none that can deliver out of thine hand.
8 Thine hands have made me and fashioned me
　Together round about; yet thou dost destroy me.

2. *Do not condemn me*] Or, *make me not guilty;* that is, by mere arbitrary will. Job felt himself "made guilty" by his afflictions, which to all were proofs that God held him guilty.

thou contendest with me] Job's afflictions were proof that God had a contention or plea against him, Job desires to know the ground of it. Perhaps the afflictions themselves may be called the contention.

3. *is it good unto thee*] The usual meaning of the phrase is, Is it thy pleasure, does it seem right to thee? Deut. xxiii. 17. The words might also mean, Is it becoming thee? Ex. xiv. 12. The former sense suits the connexion better, because Job is groping after the discovery of some characteristic or quality in God to account for his afflictions.

the work of thine hands] No doubt both Job and the wicked were all the work of God's hands, but the righteous are in such a special sense the work of His hands that here they are so described in opposition to the wicked.

4. Job hazards the supposition that God has eyes like men and may see amiss, to account for His mistaken treatment of him.

5—7. Then he asks if God's life be brief like human life, that by the inquisition of chastisements He seeks to bring Job's sin to light, lest His victim should outlive Him, and hurries on his punishment lest some one should rescue His captive from His hand.

7. *thou knowest*] Rather, **though** thou knowest. All these suppositions are vain; for as to the first (*v.* 4), God knew that Job was guiltless, and as to the other, none could rescue from His hand. The suppositions are but a subtle mode of appealing from God to God Himself, from God's dealing in providence to God's inner heart and being.

8. According to the Hebrew punctuation this verse reads,

　　Thine hands have fashioned me and made me,
　　Together round about; and thou dost destroy me!

Remember, I beseech thee, that thou hast made me as 9
  the clay;
And wilt thou bring me into dust again?
Hast thou not poured me out as milk, 10
And cruddled me like cheese?
Thou hast clothed me with skin and flesh, 11
And hast fenced me with bones and sinews.
Thou hast granted me life and favour, 12
And thy visitation hath preserved my spirit.
And these *things* hast thou hid in thine heart: 13
I know that this *is* with thee.
If I sin, then thou markest me, 14
And thou wilt not acquit me from mine iniquity.

Mention of God's hand, *v.* 7, suggests how of old God's hand fashioned him with lavish expenditure of skill on all his parts, and he brings the contradiction of God's present dealing with him before God—exclaiming, Thou dost destroy me!

9. The figure is that of a potter who has lavished infinite care upon his vessel, and now reduces his work of elaborate skill and exquisite ornament into dust again.

10—12. These verses refer to the formation of the child in the womb, from conception to full growth, cf. Ps. cxxxix. 13—16.

11. *fenced me*] Rather, **woven**, or, knit me.

12. *granted me life and favour*] i.e. granted me life and shewn me loving kindness. The verse speaks of God's dealing with Job from the time he was born and became a living man.

thy visitation] i.e. thy providence.

13—17. The contradiction between this dealing with Job in the womb and since his birth and God's present treatment of him is only to be reconciled by the supposition that God's present severe treatment of Job had been resolved on from the first, and that His careful fashioning of him and care over him had been in order the better to carry out His purpose. The details of this cruel purpose are given in the following verses.

13. *and these things hast thou hid*] Better perhaps, **but these things didst thou hide.**

this is with thee] Rather, **this was with thee**,—was thy purpose, and in thy thoughts, cf. ch. ix. 35. "These things" and "this" refer to the details about to be given (*vv.* 14—17) of God's deep purpose cherished beforehand of plaguing Job.

14. *If I sin, then thou markest*] Rather, **if I sinned then thou wouldst mark.** Similarly, **wouldst not acquit.** "To sin" here appears to mean, to be guilty of trivial sins (ch. vii. 20, xiii. 26); if he sinned even venially his sin would be held in remembrance against him and not remitted. This is the first supposition included in the Divine purpose with Job.

15 If I be wicked, woe unto me;
And *if* I be righteous, *yet* will I not lift up my head.
I am full of confusion; therefore see thou mine affliction;
16 For it increaseth. Thou huntest me as a fierce lion:
And again thou shewest thyself marvellous upon me.
17 Thou renewest thy witnesses against me,
And increasest thine indignation upon me;
Changes and war *are* against me.

15. *if I be wicked*] Better, **were I wicked**—guilty of great offences. Job cannot express what would be the punishment of greater sins were he guilty of them, but indicates its incalculable severity by the exclamation, Woe unto me! This is the second supposition.

and if I be righteous] Rather, **and were I** righteous.

yet will I not lift up] Or, *yet must I not* lift up my head.

I am full of confusion] The words to the end of the verse must mean, *being filled with shame and beholding* (or, and with the sight of) *mine affliction*. Were Job righteous he must not lift up his head in the consciousness of innocence or to protest against his being held guilty. This is the third supposition, which is further illustrated in the next verse.

16. This verse reads, **and if it** (i.e. my head) **should lift itself up, thou wouldst hunt** me as a fierce lion, **and again shew** &c. Cf. the figure of a wild beast again, ch. xvi. 9. There is a touch of sarcasm in the words "shew thyself marvellous upon me,"—marvellous in the variety and nature of His plagues, and in plaguing such an object.

17. *thou renewest*] **wouldst renew.** Similarly, **and increase.** All the verbs in these verses (*vv.* 14—17) are to be translated from the point of view of God's intention cherished beforehand with regard to Job. This intention has, of course, been carried out, and has been fulfilled in Job's present condition, and this condition supplies the colours in which the intention is painted. God's "witnesses" are His plagues and afflictions, as the margin explains, which testified to Job's guilt, cf. ch. xvi. 8.

changes and war are against me] Or, *changes and a host with me.* The words are either an exclamation, in which the preceding statements of *v.* 17 are summed up; or are in apposition to "indignation," being a description of how this indignation shews itself. The expression "changes and a host" means most naturally, an ever-changing, or, renewed host, the figure being that of an attacking army which makes continually fresh and renewed assaults. This army is composed of his afflictions sent against him by God, ch. vi. 4, xvi. 14, xix. 12. Others regard the "changes" as the successive new attacks, and the "host" as the abiding old army of afflictions,—which seems artificial and puerile. The word "change" occurs ch. xiv. 14 in the sense of release, and the word "host" in the general meaning of warfare, ch. vii. 1, xiv. 14. If these meanings were adopted here the sense would be: releases and

| Wherefore then hast thou brought me forth out of the | 18 |

Wherefore then hast thou brought me forth out of the womb?
Oh that I had given up the ghost, and no eye had seen me!
I should have been as though I had not been;
I should have been carried from the womb to the grave.
Are not my days few? cease then,
And let me alone, that I may take comfort a little,
Before I go whence I shall not return,
Even to the land of darkness and the shadow of death;
A land of darkness, as darkness itself;
And of the shadow of death, without any order,
And *where* the light is as darkness.

warfare with me, i.e. brief intervals and then terrible conflict. Job, however, usually represents his afflictions as without intermission.

18, 19. Perplexed even to despair by this idea of the purpose of God Job asks, Why God ever gave him existence at all? and as in ch. iii. 11 *seq.* wishes he had never seen life.

hast thou brought] **didst thou bring.**

Oh that I had given] **I should have given.**

20—22. He begs for a little easing of his pain ere he departs to the land of darkness.

are not my days few] The same argument as ch. vii. 16.

cease then, and let me alone] Another reading is, *let him cease then*, &c. In the last case the speaker turns away from God and speaks of Him. In the rest of the chapter, however, Job everywhere addresses God.

take comfort] The same word as ch. ix. 27, *brighten up*.

22. *without any order*] There Chaos reigns; cf. the beautiful description of the effect of light upon the earth, ch. xxxviii. 12—14.

the light is as darkness] The light in that region is

> No light, but rather darkness visible.

Job's three friends, strong in their traditional theory and unobservant of facts or indifferent to them, maintained that God's rule of the world was righteous, by which they meant that He rewarded the righteous with outward good and dispensed severe suffering only to the great sinner. Job agreed with them that this *ought* to be the way in which God governed the world, and would be the way in which a just ruler would govern it. But his own experience and much that he could perceive taking place in the world convinced him that the world was not governed in this way in fact. This feeling not only disturbed but threatened to transform Job's whole idea of God. His unbearable sufferings and this thought of God's injustice together suggested to his mind the conception of the supreme Power in the world as an omnipotent, cruel Force, that crushed all, good and evil, alike, and mocked at the despair of the innocent. This is the tone of Job's mind in ch. ix., in which he does not address God but speaks of Him in a kind of agitated soliloquy, as if fascinated by the omnipotent unmoral spectre which his imagination has conjured up. The difference between Job's ways of thinking and those prevailing in our own day can readily be seen. In our day we have reached an ideal of God, to which, if there be any God, he must correspond. And even if we took the same pessimistic view of the world as Job did we should hesitate to believe that the conception was embodied in any Being; we should probably conclude that there was no God. But such a conclusion could not suggest itself to an Oriental mind. God's existence and personality were things which Job could not doubt. Hence he had no help but invest God with the attributes of evil which he thought he saw reflected in the world.

It might seem that Job is now on the high road to renounce God, as Satan had predicted he would do. But Job does not find renouncing God quite so easy a thing. And he enters upon a course in ch. x. which, though at first it appears to take him a step further in this direction, is really the beginning of a retreat. He endeavours to set before his mind as broad a view of God as he is able, in order that by thinking of all that he knows of God he may catch the end of some clue to his calamities. This makes him realize how much he is still sure of in regard to God. And first, he cannot doubt that He is all-knowing and omnipotent (x. 3—7). But he goes further. He cannot help seeing in the carefulness and lavish skill with which he was fashioned round about in all his being by the hands of God, not only wisdom, but a gracious Benevolence, and in the preservation of his spirit a Providence which was good. And he dwells on these things, not in the cold manner of a philosopher making an induction, but with all the fervour of a religious mind, which felt that it had fellowship with the Being whose goodness it experienced, and still longed for this fellowship. Yet God's present treatment of him seemed in contradiction to all this. Thus Job balances God against Himself. Others have done the same, asking the question whether the order of the world inclines to the side of benevolence or of evil; and some have professed themselves unable to answer. So strong is Job's present sense of misery that he concludes that the universal Ruler is evil. His present treatment of him displays His real nature, and His former goodness was but apparent (x. 13—17). Thus this singular method adopted by Job of balancing God against God seems to have led him further into darkness. Yet there is no other method by which he can reach the light; and though the balance inclines in one direction meantime, by and by it will incline in another. See notes on chap. xvi. 18 *seq.*

CH. XI. THE SPEECH OF ZOPHAR.

In ch. iii. Job did not assert his innocence, but only lamented his fate. And it was possible for Eliphaz tacitly to assume his guilt with-

Then answered Zophar the Naamathite, and said, 11
   Should not the multitude of words be answered? 2
   And should a man full of talk be justified?

out alluding to it, and admonish him in regard to his complaints. Even in chaps. vi. vii. Job only threw out here and there a spasmodic affirmation of his innocence, being occupied with other things, and being deterred by his own sense of rectitude from condescending to clear himself. And Bildad could suppose himself entitled to disregard Job's passing claims to innocence, they were natural but perhaps scarcely seriously meant. But in chaps. ix. x. Job had denied his guilt with a vehemence which made it impossible not to take his denial into account. Here was a new element introduced into the strife, which the three friends had to reckon with. It was plain that Job seriously believed in his own innocence. But it was equally plain from his afflictions that God regarded him as guilty. This is the state of the question as Zophar feels he has to face it. Naturally he does not range himself on Job's side. No, Job may be unaware of his sins, but the Divine Omniscience knows them and is bringing them to remembrance. And if God would appear and speak, as Job seems to wish, he too would be made to know them. This is the new application which Zophar makes of the doctrine of the three friends. Job is setting up his knowledge of himself against God's knowledge of him.

The speech falls into three short sections:—

First, *vv.* 2—6, after some preliminary personalities of a more depreciatory kind than those used by Bildad (ch. viii. 2), Zophar expresses his wish that God would appear and speak with Job, as he had desired (ch. ix. 34), and reveal to him the depths of the Divine Wisdom or Omniscience, then Job would be made to know his sins.

Second, *vv.* 7—12, this thought leads Zophar into a panegyric of the Divine wisdom; and this wisdom it is, which, detecting men's hidden sin, accounts for the sudden calamities which they suffer.

Finally, *vv.* 13—20, from this Zophar passes to an exhortation to Job to put away his evil, with a promise, if he will do so, of great prosperity and unclouded happiness in the time to come.

2. *Should not the multitude of words*] Or, *shall not*...? Zophar probably did not demand the *parole* immediately on Job's ceasing to speak. A pause was allowed to intervene, and the words with which he commences form his apology for speaking—he replies to Job only lest Job should fancy that by his much speaking he has shewn himself to be in the right, cf. Prov. x. 19.

should a man full of talk] Or, *shall* a man full of talk, lit. *a man of lips*. Zophar insinuates that Job's words come merely from his lips; they could not come, as the words of the ancients did, from the heart, ch. viii. 10; they were mere empty phrases, cf. ch. viii. 2; Is. xxxvi. 5. Job, it must be confessed, had made a long and in some parts vehement oration.

JOB 6

3   Should thy lies make men hold their peace?
    And when thou mockest, shall no man make *thee* ashamed?
4   For thou hast said, My doctrine *is* pure,
    And I am clean in thine eyes.
5   But O that God would speak,
    And open his lips against thee;
6   And that he would shew thee the secrets of wisdom,

3. *Should thy lies*] Or, *Shall thy boastings*, or, as Reuss, "ton verbiage." The reference is probably to Job's assertions of his own innocence, or perhaps the general scope of his speech. The word "men" is as we should say "people"—shall thy boastings put people to silence?

and when thou mockest] Or, **so that thou mockest, none putting thee to shame.** Job's "mockery" or irreligious, sceptical talk is summed up in *v.* 4. This mockery is called "scorning," ch. xxxiv. 6.

4. *For thou hast said*] Better, **and sayest**, explaining what his mockery consists in.

My doctrine is pure] Job had not used precisely such words. Zophar gives what he understands as the gist of his contention.

and I am clean in thine eyes] Perhaps rather, **I was clean**, when plunged into my afflictions. The words are those of Job addressed to God, which Zophar recalls, cf. ch. ix. 21, x. 7. It is probable that this clause explains what Zophar means by the preceding clause, "my doctrine is pure." Job's "doctrine," which Zophar considers an example of "mockery," is not his general principles, but this particular point, that God afflicts a man whom He *knows* to be righteous. Zophar quite justly discovers here a novel doctrine to which he certainly had not been accustomed. But connected with this particular assertion of Job's were his views on human destiny in general, ch. vii. 1, and on the character of God's government, ch. ix. 1—23. The two preceding speakers had assumed that Job's principles were identical with their own, and anticipated that a few good advices in the line of these principles would bring the man to a right mind. Zophar begins to surmise that they have a more obstinate disease to cure than they had looked for, and that Job's principles, instead of being identical with theirs, cut clean athwart them. This discovery accounts for the rather unworthy tone of his language. His irritation was natural. He had never met a man with such ideas as those of Job before, and he is driven out of patience and decorum by his new theories. Elihu is even more shocked, and thinks that such another as Job does not exist, ch. xxxiv. 6.

5. Job had expressed his readiness to meet God and plead his cause before Him, ch. ix. 25; Zophar, with reference to this, exclaims, Would that God would speak! The result would be different from what Job anticipated, his guilt would be laid before him.

6. *shew thee the secrets of wisdom*] *Wisdom* here is God's omniscience. Its *secrets* are not the things known to it, such, for example, as Job's sins, but its own profound depths and insight.

That *they are* double to that which is.
Know therefore that God exacteth of thee *less* than thine iniquity *deserveth.*
Canst thou *by* searching find out God? 7
Canst thou find out the Almighty unto perfection?
It is as high as heaven; what canst thou do? 8

that they are double to that which is] Or, **that it** (wisdom) **is double in** (true) **understanding.** By double or twofold in regard to true understanding is not meant, double of man's wisdom or that of the creature in general, but rather, twofold what Job conceived of it, in other words, that, in regard to its true insight, it far exceeded all conception. This translation presents the smallest deviation from the A. V. and is simple. It is an objection to it that it makes "understanding" a quality of "wisdom," while the former word (on which see note on ch. v. 12) would more naturally be but another name for the "wisdom," as it is in Job's reply to all this, ch. xii. 16, cf. *v.* 13. Hence others assume that the word *twofold* means "many folds," translating: that folds, complications, belong to (true) understanding,—that is, that (God's) understanding is manifold.

Know therefore] i.e. then shouldst thou know. The imperative is a more vivid way of expressing the future, see on ch. v. 1.

exacteth of thee less, &c.] This gives the general sense, though the translation seems to rest both on a false etymology and a false idea of construction. Literally the words mean: *God bringeth into forgetfulness for thee some of thy guilt,* that is, remembereth not against thee all thy guilt. Others (e.g. Hitz.): God causeth thee to forget thy guilt. The general meaning is, that if God would appear and speak and reveal His knowledge of Job's sins, Job would be brought to know that he was guilty—perhaps even that his afflictions were far below his guilt. This is a harder word than has yet been uttered against Job.

7—12. Panegyric on the Divine Wisdom or Omniscience. This wisdom cannot be fathomed by man (*v.* 7). It fills all things (*vv.* 8, 9). And this explains the sudden calamities that befall men, for God perceives their hidden wickedness (*vv.* 10, 11). But man is of no understanding (*v.* 12).

7. The verse means, Canst thou fathom or conceive God? The special side of God's being, which Zophar declares to be unfathomable, is His wisdom or omniscience. This is the point in question, for it is this which discovers Job's heart and his sins; and Zophar desires to put this omniscience before Job to bring him to take a right place before it, just as Eliphaz brought the holiness of God before him. Literally the verse reads: Canst thou find the deeps of (or, that which has to be searched out in) God, canst thou reach to the perfection (the outmost, the ground of the nature) of the Almighty? Cf. ch. xxvi. 10, xxviii. 3.

8. His wisdom is immeasurable, unfathomable. The words are an exclamation: heights of heaven! what canst thou do?—thou art impotent before it, to scale it or reach it.

Deeper than hell; what canst thou know?
9 The measure thereof *is* longer than the earth,
And broader than the sea.
10 If he cut off, and shut up, or gather together,
Then who can hinder him?
11 For he knoweth vain men:
He seeth wickedness also; will he not then consider *it*?
12 For vain man would be wise,
Though man be born *like* a wild ass's colt.

deeper than hell] i.e. than Sheol, the place of the dead—canst thou fathom it, penetrate with thy knowledge to it?
10. This omniscience in its operation among sinful men.
If he cut off] **if he pass by.** Zophar uses Job's own word and illustration, ch. ix. 11 (passeth on).
and shut up] i.e. arrest, and put in ward.
or gather together] i.e. call an assembly for judgment, which took place in full concourse of the people; cf. the graphic picture Prov. v. 3 *seq.*, esp. *v.* 14.
who can hinder him] Or, *turn him back*, again Job's own words, ch. ix. 12.
11. Job had used these words to describe God as an irresistible, unaccountable force; Zophar indicates what account is to be given of God's actions—He knoweth vain (wicked, Ps. xxvi. 4) men. His action is the reflexion of His omniscient insight.
will he not then consider it] Rather, **without considering it.** The words are closely connected with the preceding: he seeth wickedness also, without needing to consider it, that is, with a knowledge immediate and requiring no effort, cf. ch. xxxiv. 23, notes. So already Ibn Ezra. Another meaning is possible: and that which they (men) consider not. But this is a useless repetition.
12. Having finished his brilliant picture of God's omniscient wisdom, Zophar adds further brilliancy to it by contrasting it with the brutishness of man. The verse perhaps should read,

> But an empty man will become wise
> When a wild ass colt is born a man,

the one thing will happen when the other happens. The verse seems to be in the shape of a proverb, and is full of alliterations which cannot be reproduced in translation. The word "empty" is properly "hollow;" and "to become wise" is literally "to get heart," i.e. understanding or mind (ch. ix. 4, xii. 3). The last phrase was understood by Gesenius to mean "to be without heart" or understanding. Following this view, many translate: But empty man is void of understanding, yea, man is born (like) a wild ass colt. Gesenius objects to the other that it offends against dignity. The verse has been interpreted in a great variety of ways.
13—20. Zophar turns to Job in exhortation and promise.

If thou prepare thine heart, 13
And stretch out thine hands toward him;
If iniquity *be* in thine hand, put it far away, 14
And let not wickedness dwell in thy tabernacles.
For then shalt thou lift up thy face without spot; 15
Yea, thou shalt be steadfast, and shalt not fear.
Because thou shalt forget *thy* misery, 16
And remember *it* as waters *that* pass away;
And *thine* age shall be clearer than the noonday; 17
Thou shalt shine forth, thou shalt be as the morning.
And thou shalt be secure, because there is hope; 18

13. *If thou prepare thine heart*] *Thou* is emphatic, and meant by the speaker to place Job in a different class from the "hollow man" described in *v.* 12. Job hardly accepted the good intention, cf. ch. xii. 3. "To prepare the heart" may mean, to bring it into a condition of right thought and feeling towards God. The word might also mean "fix thy heart," let it no more be driven to and fro amidst false feelings and views, Pss. x. 17, li. 10, lvii. 7, lxxviii. 37.

and stretch out] In prayer, and seeking help, Ex. ix. 29; Is. i. 15; cf. Job viii. 5.

14. The reformation which Zophar impresses on Job has several steps: first, the preparation of his heart; then, prayer unto God; then, the putting away of his personal sins; and finally, those of his home. These are enumerated, one after another, but nothing lies in the order of enumeration.

15. *for then shalt thou*] Or, **surely then** shalt thou, ch. viii. 6.

lift up thy face without spot] The word *lift up* is selected to meet Job's complaint that he must not lift up his head, ch. x. 15; and the words "without spot" meet his words "filled with shame." Then he shall lift up his face in conscious innocence and disfigured with no signs of God's anger on account of his guilt.

be steadfast, and shalt not fear] Said in reference to Job's fluctuating feelings and condition as he describes them, ch. ix. 27—28.

16. *because thou shalt forget*] Or, **for thou shalt forget** trouble.

that pass away] **that are passed away.**

17. *and thine age*] Or, as we should say, and *life*, Ps. xvii. 14, xxxix. 5.

thou shalt shine forth] Rather, **if there be darkness, it shall be** as the morning. Even should temporary darkness occur it will not be utter, but light like the morning. This seems said in opposition to Job's mournful words, ch. x. 22, "where the light is as darkness." The present words might also mean that the darkness shall be not a continual obscurity but one which a morning comes to dispel.

18. *because there is hope*] In opposition to Job's desponding pictures of his life, ch. vii. 6 *seq.*, ix. 25 *seq.*, x. 20 *seq.*

Yea, thou shalt dig *about thee, and* thou shalt take thy
rest in safety.
19 Also thou shalt lie down, and none shall make *thee* afraid;
Yea, many shall make suit unto thee.
20 But the eyes of the wicked shall fail,
And they shall not escape,
And their hope *shall be as* the giving up of the ghost.

thou shalt dig about thee] Rather, **thou shalt look, or search**, about thee, cf. ch. xxxix. 29; Deut. i. 22. Job, as one naturally does before retiring to rest, will look around to see if there be any danger near or cause of disquietude, and seeing none will take his rest in safety.

19. *make suit unto thee*] The phrase means literally: shall stroke thy face, i.e. supplicate or flatter thee. Prov. xix. 6; Ps. xlv. 12.

The picture which Zophar draws of Job's restored prosperity is beautiful. (1) Trouble shall be forgotten, or remembered as waters that are passed away; and the memory of a past trouble that cannot recur but makes the present happiness greater (*v.* 16). (2) And the future shall rise brighter than noon, or, it may be, shall increase towards brightness more than the noon does, shewing an ever-growing clearness; and if it be at any time clouded, as in any life however clear there are clouds, the darkness shall only be a lesser light like that of the morning; or as the words may mean, the darkness shall only be like the fixed changes of nature and shall give place like the night to a fair and hopeful morning (*v.* 17). (3) Thus restored to the fixed order of a life with God he shall be trustful because there is hope, and he shall look about, surveying all things, and finding nothing to dread shall lie down in confidence (*v.* 18); and when lain down he shall rest peacefully. (4) And his security and prosperity shall draw to him the homage of many, who (as before) shall seek his favour (*v.* 19).

20. Zophar concludes by setting in opposition to this picture another, the fate of the wicked.

their hope shall be as the giving] Rather, **shall be the giving up** of the ghost; death is what they have to look for. Perhaps Zophar adds these words by way of warning to Job. Eliphaz allowed no streak of darkness to cloud the brightness of the prospect he anticipated for Job, ch. v. 19—26; Bildad spoke of perishing, but it was of Job's enemies, ch. viii. 22; Zophar throws out his warning more generally, and Job may accept it if it fits him.

The problems that trouble us are not new. These ancient disputants graze at least the edges of most of them. Under Zophar's speech lies the question, If the affirmations of a man's conscience or of his consciousness be contradicted by the affirmations of God, what does it become a man to do? Job's conscience declared that he had not been guilty of sins, while God by his afflictions was clearly intimating that he had.—It may be safely concluded that a real contradiction of this kind will never occur. Both Zophar and Job were under a false impression when they supposed that God by His affliction of Job was affirming his guilt. They put a wrong meaning on his afflictions. Zophar, however, thought that a man must bow to God. But as Job's consciousness spoke to a fact, which was to him indubitable, he felt that he was unable to submit. The history of Job teaches us that the wise course in such circumstances is to raise the prior question, Is this supposed affirmation of God really His affirmation? It may be that we are putting a wrong construction on His words or providence And as such supposed contradictions will not usually be, as in Job's case, in regard to simple facts but to moral judgments and the like, there is much room always to raise the prior question also on the other side, Is this affirmation of conscience, which seems opposed to the intimations of God, a true affirmation of conscience? the affirmation of an enlightened, universal conscience? As none of us, unfortunately, is in possession of this universal conscience of mankind, but only of our own particular one, which must, however, be our guide, perplexities may occasionally arise in our actual religious experience.

CH. XII.—XIV. JOB'S REPLY TO ZOPHAR.

The distinctive point in Zophar's discourse was his prominently adducing the omniscient wisdom of God against Job, before the judgments of which, as seen in the providences that befall men, anything called individual conscience ought to be silent. This led Zophar into an eulogy of God's wisdom, the greatness of which was to him the explanation of the sudden and destructive interferences of God among men (ch. xi. 10, 11). And in contrast with this insight of God Zophar spoke of men as "hollow."

All this stung Job deeply, for it implied not only ignorance of himself (ch. xi. 6), but ignorance of God, and he felt keenly the assumption over him (a thing only ventured on because he was afflicted, ch. xii. 4, 5) of these men, who thought themselves entitled to give him instructions regarding the wisdom and the power of God (ch. xii. 3, xiii. 2). Hence there runs through his reply a continual sarcasm against their assumed superiority, mixed with pathetic references to the lowness into which he had sunk—he whose past life had been one of close fellowship with God, ch. xii. 4—when such men took it on them to give him lessons; and he is never weary ringing changes on the "wisdom" which was the key-note of Zophar's unfortunate oration—No doubt! wisdom will die with you (ch. xii. 2); "I have understanding as well as you...who knoweth not such things as these?" (ch. xii. 3); "With God is wisdom" (ch. xii. 13); and, with a half-concealed reference to the proverb, he wishes at last that they would hold their tongue and it should be their "wisdom" (ch. xiii. 5). In this speech Job for the first time really turns upon his friends in earnest, and he reads them some severe lessons not only on the mental superficiality with which they took in hand his problem, which they thought to unravel by citing a few old saws and "maxims of ashes" (ch. xiii. 12), but also on the moral onesidedness which they shewed. They took the part of God against him not as true men who had really planted their feet on the bottom of things as the world presented them, but from a shallow religiosity which was but partiality for God; and, as they had invoked the rectitude and the omniscience of the Almighty against him, he sists them before the same bar, reminding them that the God before whom they shall have to answer is God of the universe, according to the facts which the universe reveals, and bidding them fear His resentment and chastisement for their very pleading in His behalf, because that pleading was made ignorantly and not in true sincerity (ch. xiii. 4—12, cf. the result, ch. xlii. 7 *seq.*).

The speech falls into three large sections, which coincide generally with the three chapters, although the limits between the second and third are not very well marked.

First, ch. xii. Job resents the assumed superiority of his three friends in regard to knowledge of the operation of the Divine power and wisdom in the world, and shews by a lofty delineation of them that he is a far greater master in this knowledge than they are.

Second, ch. xiii. 1—22. But this Divine wisdom and power do not, as the friends imagine, explain his calamities. On the contrary, it is against this very action of God in the world that he desires to appeal to God. And their defence of it is false, and from no better reason than out of servility to God. He desires to meet God on the question of his innocence, and challenges Him to appear and answer him.

Third, ch. xiii. 23—xiv. The challenge remains unanswered. And again, as before, the thought of his sad condition and of the riddles in which he is involved gets the better of Job, and he sinks into a sorrowful wail over the wretchedness of man, his weakness and God's rigid treatment of him, and the complete extinction of his life in death. But just when the folds of darkness which the mysteries and the pathos of human life wrap around him are thickest, there suddenly arises in his mind, like a star struggling through the clouds, the surprising thought that after this life there might be another, and that God, when His wrath is overpast, might call His creature back to Him again in friendship. The star comes out but for a moment, but Job has once seen it, and on every occasion when it appears again it shines with greater brilliancy.

CH. XII. IN REPLY TO ZOPHAR'S APPEAL TO THE DIVINE WISDOM AND POWER, JOB SHEWS BY A BRILLIANT DELINEATION OF THEM THAT HE IS A GREATER MASTER IN THE KNOWLEDGE OF THESE THAN HIS FRIENDS ARE.

First, *vv.* 1—6. Job gives sarcastic expression to his admiration of the wisdom of his friends (*v.* 2). Then, passing into earnestness, he laments the depth to which he has sunk when men take it on them to inflict such common places on him about God's wisdom and power—on him whose life had been lived with God. This was how men treated one, though righteous, when afflictions befell him; the prosperous wicked man was differently regarded (*vv.* 4—6).

Second, *vv.* 7—25. Coming to the matter itself, the display of God's power and wisdom in the world, especially in the world of life, with its sufferings, the knowledge of which the friends boasted of as exclusively their own (cf. shew thee the secrets of wisdom, ch. xi. 6), Job

And Job answered and said, 12
 No doubt but ye *are* the people, 2
 And wisdom shall die with you.
 But I have understanding as well as you; 3
 I *am* not inferior to you:
 Yea, who knoweth not such *things* as these?
 I am *as* one mocked of his neighbour, 4
 Who calleth upon God, and he answereth him:
 The just upright *man is* laughed to scorn.

(1) intimates that this knowledge is so common that anyone may learn it who opens his eyes and looks upon the life and fates of the lower creatures—all shew that God moves among them with an absolute power and sway (*vv.* 7—10).

(2) The same may be learned by anyone who has ears to hear what aged men tell of God's ways in the world. Thus Job introduces a brilliant picture (in which much history both of catastrophes in nature and revolutions among men is condensed) of the uncontrolled movement of God in the affairs of the world:—the natural world (*vv.* 14, 15); those highest in rank among men, the wise, the rulers, the eloquent (*vv.* 16—22); and nations (*vv.* 23—25). Zophar had sought to shew that a moral purpose directed the action of God's wisdom and might—"he knows wicked men" (ch. xi. 11); Job, on the other hand, brings out their immeasurable greatness and the absoluteness with which they dominate among men, and how they confound with an ironical destructiveness everything human that bears any likeness to themselves, "making fools" of judges, and "pouring contempt" upon princes (*vv.* 17, 21).

2. *ye are the people*] Sarcastic admiration of the wisdom of his three friends, cf. ch. xi. 6. "The people" does not seem to mean the *right* people, persons worthy of the name of "people;" rather "the people" is used as three other persons, well known to history, employed it, when they said, "We, the people of England." It means the whole people; hence Job adds, "Wisdom will die with you."

3. *But I have understanding*] Rather, **I also have understanding**, lit. *heart;* cf. on ch. xi. 12, to the depreciating words of which Job refers.

who knoweth not such things as these] lit. *with whom are not such things as these?* i.e. such knowledge as this. The reference is to Zophar's exhibition of the Divine wisdom and might, ch. xi. 7—12.

4, 5. Job laments how low he had fallen when men thought to instruct him, a man of God, with such primary truths regarding God's operation in the world. Yet it was but an illustration of the general truth—righteousness when unfortunate was held in contempt. The verses read,

4. I am to be one that is a laughing-stock to his friends,
 I, who called on God and he answered me:
 A laughing-stock the just and perfect man!

5 He that is ready to slip with *his* feet
    Is as a lamp despised in the thought of him that is at ease.
6 The tabernacles of robbers prosper,
    And they that provoke God are secure;
    Into whose hand God bringeth *abundantly*.
7 But ask now the beasts, and they shall teach thee;
    And the fowls of the air, and they shall tell thee:
8 Or speak to the earth, and it shall teach thee:
    And the fishes of the sea shall declare unto thee.

5. There is contempt for misfortune in the thought of him that is at ease,
It awaiteth them who are slipping with their foot.
Zophar's references for Job's advantage to the Divine wisdom and might implied that Job was ignorant of all this, and took no account of Job's past life spent in the fellowship of God and in meditation on His ways. It is to this last that Job refers when he says: I who called on God, &c. He feels keenly the pass he has come to when men inculcate such commonplaces upon him; this feeling he expresses by saying, I am to be, I must be, or have to be a laughing-stock.

Verse 5 means, But such is the treatment which those who fall into misfortune, even though they be righteous men, receive at the hands of those that are at ease and prosperous. The word rendered "misfortune" or calamity occurs again, ch. xxx. 24, xxxi. 29, Prov. xxiv. 22. On the slipping of the foot, cf. Ps. xxxviii. 16, lxxiii. 2.

6. The other side of the picture, the peace of the wicked.
into whose hand God bringeth abundantly] The words might also mean: *they who carry (their) god in their hand*, the idea being that their god is their own strong hand or the weapon in it; cf. what the prophet says of the Chaldeans, This their power is their god, Hab. i. 11 with *v.* 16. The commentators quote from Vergil the words of the contemptor deorum, *dextra mihi deus*, and Hitzig refers to Ammianus, 17. 12, who says of some Scythian tribes, *mucrones pro numinibus colunt*. In *v.* 5 Job said that the afflicted righteous were despised; the strict antithesis would have been that the prosperous wicked received respect; but Job, with the keen eye which he has at present for the anomalies of the Divine government, attributes the peace of the wicked to God, though they recognise no God but their own strong arm. Cf. ch. v. 24.

7—10. Such knowledge as the friends possessed of God's wisdom and power and their action in the world could be learned by any one who had eyes to observe the life and fate of the lower creatures. In all may be seen God's absolute might and sway prevailing (*v.* 10).

8. *speak to the earth*] The "earth" here includes all the forms of lower life with which it teems.

9. *in all these*] Or, *by* all these, Gen. xv. 8.

Who knoweth not in all these	9
That the hand of the LORD hath wrought this?	
In whose hand *is* the soul of every living *thing*,	10
And the breath of all mankind.	
Doth not the ear try words?	11
And the mouth taste his meat?	
With the ancient *is* wisdom;	12
And *in* length of days understanding.	
With him *is* wisdom and strength,	13
He hath counsel and understanding.	
Behold, he breaketh down, and it cannot be built *again:*	14

hath wrought this] Rather, **doeth this**, viz. as Zophar had taught and as *v.* 10 explains, rules with an absolute sway in all the world of life upon the earth, men and creatures. We should say in English here, *acts thus* (as Zophar had said), cf. Is. xli. 20, though the point prominently referred to is the infliction of suffering.

10. This verse rounds off the statement in *v.* 7 *seq.* that God moves among the living creatures upon the earth, dispensing life and death, in a way absolute and uncontrolled.

11—25. Verses 7—10 referred to what one could *see* of God's power and wisdom in the world, these verses refer to what one might learn of them by *hearing* ancient men discourse regarding them. In ch. xiii. 1, where Job looks back upon this chapter, he refers to both channels of knowledge, his eye and his ear. He does not despise knowledge learned from the observation of others when it is pertinent, cf. ch. xxi. 29. And it is obvious that the description in *vv.* 13—25 contains many allusions to catastrophes, both in nature and in human society, which Job could not have seen himself, but must have learned from tradition.

11. *and the mouth taste his meat*] Rather, **as the mouth** (lit. palate) **tasteth his meat.** Does not the understanding ear discern and appropriate sound knowledge, as the palate discerns and relishes wholesome food? The ear (as well as the eye, *vv.* 7—10) is a channel of sound information.

12. As *v.* 11 indicated the instrument, the ear, through which one learned, this verse refers to the source from which the information was to be obtained, viz. the ancients, that is, the aged men.

13. *With him is wisdom and strength*] i.e. with God, *him* being emphatic. There is no antithesis however between His wisdom and that of the aged referred to *v.* 12. The passage that follows to the end of the chapter describes God's power and wisdom as their operations had been observed by men, though naturally the picture receives its colour from the state of Job's mind. "Strength" is rather might or power to execute what wisdom devises. These attributes of God's confound and bring to nought everything bearing the same name among men.

14. *breaketh down*] e.g. fenced cities, devoting them to ruin, cf. ch. xv. 28.

He shutteth up a man, and there can be no opening.
15 Behold, he withholdeth the waters, and they dry up:
Also he sendeth them out, and they overturn the earth.
16 With him *is* strength and wisdom:
The deceived and the deceiver *are* his.
17 He leadeth counsellers away spoiled,
And maketh the judges fools.
18 He looseth the bond of kings,
And girdeth their loins with a girdle.
19 He leadeth princes away spoiled,
And overthroweth the mighty.
20 He removeth away the speech of the trusty,

shutteth up a man] In prison, as captive kings and the like, cf. Jerem. xxii. 24 *seq.*, 2 Kings xxv. 27 *seq.*
15. *withholdeth the waters*] In droughts. The second half of the verse refers to floods and cataclysms.
16. The word "wisdom" in this verse is that in ch. v. 12, xi. 6.
the deceived and the deceiver] lit. *he that errs and he that leads into error*, he that is ruled and he that rules oppressively. These are distinctions among men; to God both are the same, or both are equally in his hand, cf. Prov. xxii. 2.
17. *away spoiled*] The word is rendered "stripped" Mic. i. 8, the meaning being, deprived of their outer garments, and clothed as slaves and captives. The word might perhaps mean "barefooted" (so Sept. Mic. i. 8), also a condition of those in destitution and mourning, 2 Sam. xv. 30.
On second clause "maketh judges fools," turns them into fools, and shews them as fools, cf. Is. xliv. 25, xix. 11 *seq.*
18. *he looseth the bond of kings*] The verse probably means, he relaxes, removes the authority of kings, destroys their bond or power over men; and as a consequence their own loins are girt with a girdle, i.e. either the common girdle of the labourer, or the cord of the captive.
19. *leadeth princes away spoiled*] Rather, **priests**. In antiquity priests occupied influential places; cf. what is said of Melchizedek, Gen. xiv., of Jethro, priest of Midian, Ex. ii. 16 *seq.*, and of the influence of the priests in several crises of the history of Israel. On "spoiled" see *v.* 17.
the mighty] lit. *the established* or *perennial;* being in apposition with priests, usually a hereditary caste, the word describes those who occupied high permanent place among men.
20. *the speech of the trusty*] Eloquent men, able to recommend and carry their plans. The word "understanding" means *sense* or discretion (Prov. xi. 22).

And taketh *away* the understanding of the aged.
He poureth contempt upon princes, 21
And weakeneth the strength of the mighty.
He discovereth deep *things* out of darkness, 22
And bringeth out to light the shadow of death.
He increaseth the nations, and destroyeth them: 23
He enlargeth the nations, and straiteneth them *again*.
He taketh away the heart of the chief of the people of the 24
earth,
And causeth them to wander in a wilderness *where there
is* no way.
They grope *in* the dark without light, 25
And he maketh them to stagger like a drunken *man*.

21. *contempt upon princes*] Or, *nobles*, ch. xxxiv. 18; cf. Ps. cvii. 40.
weakeneth the strength of the mighty] lit. *looseth the girdle of the strong*. As the garments were girt up for active labour or battle, to loose the girdle means to incapacitate; Is. v. 27.
22. *he discovereth deep things*] In the A. V. to "discover" is to reveal, to bring to sight. The verse means that God through His wisdom sees into the profoundest and darkest deeps, and brings what is hidden to light. "Shadow of death" means the deepest darkness, ch. iii. 3. The reference is not to be limited to the deep and concealed plans of men, which God exposes and frustrates (ch. v. 13, Is. xxix. 15), though this may be included. The verse can hardly mean that God reveals or manifests His own profound deeps (ch. xi. 6; Is. xlv. 15), though such a sense would give the parallelism desirable to the two other commencing verses, 13 and 16.
23. God's rule among the nations and direction of their fate.
and straiteneth them again] Perhaps, *and leadeth them away*, cf. 2 Kings xviii. 17. The clause is obscure, it may not be a direct, but an inverse parallel to the first clause, and mean: *he spreadeth abroad* (or, scattereth, cf. Jer. viii. 2; Numb. xi. 32), *and giveth them settlements again*.
24. *he taketh away the heart*] i.e. the understanding; cf. on ch. xi. 12.
in a wilderness] Same word as in ch. vi. 18. The word is that rendered "without form," Gen. i. 2; Jer. iv. 23, i.e. chaos. The reference is to the confusion and perplexity into which the chiefs are thrown. The word is finely used Is. xlv. 19, I said not to the seed of Jacob seek ye me in the waste, i.e. in uncertain conditions (A. V., in vain).
25. Further description of their perplexity. Cf. ch. v. 14.
maketh them to stagger] Or, *to wander*. Cf. Is. xix. 14; Ps. cvii. 27, 40.

13   Lo, mine eye hath seen all *this*,
     Mine ear hath heard and understood it.
2   What ye know, *the same* do I know also.
     I *am* not inferior unto you.
3   Surely I would speak to the Almighty,
     And I desire to reason with God.
4   But ye *are* forgers of lies,
     Ye *are* all physicians of no value.

CH. XIII. 1—22. JOB KNOWS THE DIVINE WISDOM AND MIGHT AS WELL AS THE FRIENDS; THEIR APPLICATION OF THESE TO HIM IS FALSE. HE DESIRES TO PLEAD HIS CAUSE BEFORE GOD.

Having finished his delineation of God's might and wisdom as they act in the world, Job looks back upon his picture, saying that he knows all this as well as his friends (*vv.* 1, 2); but his calamities receive thereby no solution. In spite of this knowledge he desires to plead his cause before God (*v.* 3).

And they who sought to use this wisdom and might of God against him, were mere forgers of lies, who gave a false as well as feeble explanation of his troubles (*vv.* 4, 5). They were nothing but partizans for God. And as they had invoked the omniscience of God against him he will threaten them with the judgment of the same God, who will search out their hidden insincerity, and before whom their old maxims will be but "proverbs of ashes" (*vv.* 6—12).

With this stinging rebuke to his friends Job turns from them unto God. He will adventure all and go into His presence to plead his cause come what may (*vv.* 13—15). This courage which he feels is token to him that he shall be victorious, for a godless man would not dare to come before God. He knows he shall be found in the right (*vv.* 16—19). Only he will beg for two conditions, That God would remove His hand from him, and, That he would not terrify him by His majesty; then he is ready to answer if God will call, or to speak if God will answer (*vv.* 20—22).

1—2. Looking back to his delineation of the Divine wisdom and might as they dominate among men and in the world (ch. xii. 7—25), Job says that his knowledge of them is not inferior to that of the friends— a final answer to Zophar, ch. xi. 6; cf. as to *v.* 2 ch. xii. 3.

3. But this knowledge neither helps nor hinders him. In spite of this knowledge, if not because of it, he desires to reason with God. *surely I would speak*] Rather, **but I would** (same word in *v.* 4).

4. *but ye are forgers of lies*] The *but* in *v.* 3 had for its background the knowledge of the Divine wisdom (*vv.* 1, 2); Job knows this well, *but* for all his knowledge of it he desires to plead his cause before God, he will speak unto the Almighty. This desire and purpose, however,

O that you would altogether hold your peace, 5
And it should be your wisdom.
Hear now my reasoning, 6
And hearken to the pleadings of my lips.
Will you speak wickedly for God? 7
And talk deceitfully for him?
Will ye accept his person? 8
Will ye contend for God?

are crossed by the thought of the use which his friends make of the Divine wisdom against him, and he is diverted from his great object to administer a rebuke to them—*but* ye are forgers of lies. Verses 4—12 are therefore a digression, the main object being resumed in *v.* 13; the digression, however, is profoundly interesting. In clause one Job tells his friends that their assumptions of his guilt and the application which they made to his case of the Divine omniscience are false; in the second he compares them to ignorant physicians, who take in hand a disease which they are incompetent to treat.

5. This verse is suggested by the last clause of the preceding—their impotence to help was such that their silence would be the most helpful thing they could offer. There is a final sarcasm at Zophar's speech in the reference to "wisdom"; cf. Prov. xvii. 28, Even a fool when he holdeth his peace is counted wise; and the *si tacuisses, philosophus mansisses*, quoted by all the commentators.

6—12. Severe rebuke of the three friends, in which (1) they are charged with partiality for God, and with acting the advocate for Him (*vv.* 6—8); and (2) they are threatened with the chastisement of God for their insincerity, and for falsely pleading even in God's behalf (*vv.* 9—12).

6. *hear now my reasoning*] Rather, **hear now my rebuke**. The reference is not to Job's cause with God, this is not resumed till *v.* 13. He utters a formal indictment against his friends which he commands them to hear.

the pleadings of my lips] i.e. the *reproofs* of my lips, their pleadings against you, or their controversy with you, cf. Deut. xvii. 8. These reproofs now follow, *vv.* 7—9.

7. *speak wickedly*] Or, *wrongously*, lit. *speak iniquity*, ch. v. 16, cf. Zophar's recommendation to Job, ch. xi. 14. *For* God means in His behalf, in His defence; and the words *for God* are emphatic.

8. The same charge put more explicitly. To accept the person of one is to be partial on his side, cf. *v.* 10.

contend for God] i.e. will ye play the advocate for God? The charge made against his friends by Job is that they had no knowledge of his guilt, and merely took part for God against him out of servility to God. This servility was nothing but a superficial religiousness, allied to superstition, which did not form its conception of God from the broad facts of the universe.

9   *Is it* good that he should search you out?
    Or as *one* man mocketh another, do ye *so* mock him?
10 He will surely reprove you,
    If ye do secretly accept persons.
11 Shall not his excellency make you afraid?
    And his dread fall upon you?
12 Your remembrances *are* like unto ashes,
    Your bodies to bodies of clay.

9. *Is it good*] The words may mean, will it be well (for you) that He should search (or, when He shall search)? or as ch. x. 3, do you like that He should search you out? The second clause should read,

Or as one deceiveth a man will ye deceive Him?

When God searches you out and looks into the secret springs of your actions do you expect to be able to deceive Him by representations or demeanour or look as one imposes on a man, who cannot "read the mind's construction in the face"?

10. God's rectitude and impartiality are such that He will punish partiality shewn even for Himself—a statement which, when taken along with the imputations which Job has cast on God, shews a singular condition of his mind.

11. *his excellency*] His *majesty* affright you. They shall be paralyzed when they stand before God who searches the heart.

12. This verse reads,

Your remembrances shall be proverbs of ashes,
Your defences defences of dust.

The term "remembrances" means their traditional sayings, remembered from antiquity, their maxims, such as Bildad adduced, ch. viii., and Eliphaz with his *Remember now!* ch. iv. 7; these shall be found to be but ashes, easily dissipated, and not able to resist. The word "defences" is used of the boss of the buckler, ch. xv. 26, and may refer to some sort of breastwork or cover from which men assailed the enemy. These shall turn out defences of dust, lit. *clay*, i.e. dried clay, which crumbles into dust. "Defences" here are not works for defence strictly but for offence, they are the arguments of the friends; cf. Is. xli. 21, "strong reasons." These great arguments which the friends used in defence of God against Job shall be found by them, when God searches them out, to be mere ashes and crumbling clay. So it turned out, cf. ch. xlii. 7 *seq*.

13—22. Job now turns from his friends, whom he commands to be silent, to his great plea with God, resuming the intention expressed in *v.* 3. The passage has two parts, one preliminary, *vv.* 13—16, exhibiting a singular picture of the conflict between resolution and fear in Job's mind. He will go before God come upon him what will (*v.* 13). Yet he cannot hide from himself that it may be at the hazard of his life. Yet he will not be deterred; he will defend his ways to God's face (*vv.* 14, 15). And yet again, this very courage which he has, arising from his sense of innocence, is a token to him that he shall be

> Hold your peace, let me alone, that I may speak, 13
> And let come on me what *will*.
> Wherefore do I take my flesh in my teeth, 14
> And put my life in mine hand?
> Though he slay me, *yet* will I trust in him: 15
> But I will maintain mine own ways before him.

victorious (*v.* 16). The second part, *vv.* 17—22. Feeling that the victory is already his he commands his friends to mark his pleading of his cause. He knows he shall be found in the right. Nay, no one will even plead against him (*vv.* 17—19). Only he begs two conditions of God, That He would lift His afflicting hand from him, and, That He would not affright him with His terror (*vv.* 20—22).

13. *that I may speak*] Emphasis on *I,—that I now* may speak. The last clause intimates his resolve to speak at all risks.

14. *Wherefore do I take*] Or, **should I take**. This and the following verse are surrounded with difficulties. The meaning of the second clause of *v.* 14 is well ascertained from usage, it is: to expose one's life to jeopardy, Judg. xii. 3, 1 Sam. xix. 5, xxviii. 21, Ps. cxix. 109. The meaning of the first clause is doubtful, as the expression does not occur again. It is held by many that the figure is borrowed from the action of a wild beast, which seizes its prey in its teeth and carries it off to a place of security; in which case the meaning would be, Why should I seek anxiously to preserve my life? If this be assumed to be the meaning the interrogation must end with the first clause, *Why should I take my flesh in my teeth? nay, I will put my life in mine hand*. This is not quite satisfactory. Hence an endeavour is made by many to extract a sense from the second clause different from that sanctioned by usage, a sense indeed to appearance the opposite of it, and corresponding to the first clause. It is assumed that the phrase properly means to commit one's life to his hand to carry it through, to fight one's way through; in other words, to make strenuous efforts to save one's life. This is rather a hazardous mode of dealing with language the meaning of which is established by usage. The obscurity of the first clause makes it impossible to be certain of the construction of the verse.

15. The general meaning of *v.* 14 must be the same however the verse is construed, though it may be expressed in two ways, viz. either, Why should I painfully strive to preserve my life? or, I am ready to risk my life (or in both ways). Verse 15 reads most naturally,

> Behold he will slay me: I will not wait:
> Yet will I defend my ways to his face.

The words "he will slay me" refer to what Job anticipates may be the result of his daring to maintain the rectitude of his life to God's face, as the second clause intimates. These two clauses are in close connexion, and the words "I will not wait" are almost parenthetical—behold he will slay me (I will not wait for a more distant death), notwithstanding

16 He also *shall be* my salvation:
For a hypocrite shall not come before him.
17 Hear diligently my speech,
And my declaration with your ears.
18 Behold now, I have ordered *my* cause;
I know that I shall be justified.
19 Who *is* he *that* will plead with me?
For now, if I hold my tongue, I shall give up the ghost.

I will defend, &c. Others refer the words "behold he will slay me" to Job's certainty of speedy death from his disease. And again, some render the words "I will not wait," *I have no hope;* and thus a variety of meanings all more or less suitable arises. The word *to wait* hardly has the sense of *to hope*, at least in this Book, cf. ch. vi. 11, xiv. 14, xxix. 21, xxx. 26, and in another form in the mouth of Elihu, ch. xxxii. 11, 16.

Instead of the word *not* before *wait* another reading gives *for him*, or *for it*. This is the reading of many ancient versions; and the rendering of the Vulgate, *etiamsi occiderit me in ipso sperabo*, has been followed by most modern translations, as by our own. Such a sense, however, does not suit the connexion. If this *reading* be adopted, some such sense must be given to the clause as that preferred by Delitzsch: Behold he will slay me—I wait for him: only I will defend, &c.; that is, I wait for His final stroke.

16. *He also shall be*] Rather, **this also**.

for a hypocrite shall not] Rather, **that a godless man will not**; see on ch. viii. 13. A godless man will not dare to go before God; but Job dares and desires; and this courage, sweet evidence to himself of his innocence, he says will be his salvation, that is, will secure him victory in his plea with God. He hardly distinguishes between his own consciousness of innocence and his innocence itself and the proof of it. He is so conscious of it that he is sure it will appear before God, cf. *v.* 18 and the passage ch. xxvii. 8 foll.

17—22. Assured of victory, he commands his friends to mark his pleading of his cause.

18. *I know that I shall be justified*] i.e. be found in the right, ch. xi. 2.

19. *Who is he that will plead with me*] i.e. plead against me, enter to oppose me with good reasons—who will bring a valid argument against me? The words are a triumphant expression of the feeling that no one will or can, cf. Is. l. 8.

for now if I hold my tongue, &c.] Rather, **for then would I hold my peace, and give up the ghost**; that is, in case any one should appear against him with proof of his sin. The words form a splendid climax to the declaration of his consciousness of innocence. He is sure he shall be found in the right, nay, none will be found to contend with him; if he thought any one could he would be silent and die.

Only do not two *things* unto me:	20
Then will I not hide myself from thee.	
Withdraw thine hand far from me:	21
And let not thy dread make me afraid.	
Then call thou, and I will answer:	22
Or let me speak, and answer thou me.	

20, 21. Yet the thought recurs before whom he is to appear and against whom he has to maintain his plea, and he begs God to grant two conditions, cf. ch. ix. 34, 35.

22. With these conditions he is ready to appear either as respondent or as appellant.

CH. XIII. 22—XIV. JOB PLEADS HIS CAUSE BEFORE GOD.

Having ordered his cause and challenged his friends to observe how he will plead, Job now enters, with the boldness and proud bearing of one assured of victory, upon his plea itself. There is strictly no break between the passage which follows and the foregoing; the division is only made here for convenience' sake. It would scarcely be according to the author's intention to make *v.* 23 the plea, and assume that, as God did not answer the demand there made, Job's plea took another turn. The question whether Job actually did expect that he would be replied to out of heaven can hardly be answered. We must, however, take into account the extreme excitation of his mind, and the vividness with which men in that age realized the nearness of God and looked for His direct interference in their affairs and life. According to the modes of conception which appear everywhere in the Poem, there was nothing extravagant in Job's expecting a direct reply to his appeal; for that such an answer might be given is evidently the meaning of Zophar's words, ch. xi. 6; and in point of fact the Lord does at last answer Job by a voice from heaven, ch. xxxviii. *seq.*

The plea itself has a certain resemblance to that in chaps. vii. and x., but is more subdued and calm. The crisis is now really over in Job's mind. Though he has not convinced his friends, he has fought his way through any doubts which their suspicions and his afflictions might have raised in his own thoughts. The courage with which he is ready to go before God he feels to be but the reflection of his innocence; and this feeling throws a general peace over his spirit, which regrets over the brevity of his life, and perplexity at beholding God treat so severely so feeble a being as himself, are able only partially to disturb. After the few direct demands at the beginning to know what his sins are (*v.* 23), his plea becomes a pitiful appeal unto God, from which the irony of former appeals is wholly absent. As before, he contrasts the littleness of man and the greatness of God, but his conception both of God and man is not any more, so to speak, merely physical, but moral. He speaks of the sins of his youth (ch. xiii. 26), and of the universal sinfulness of man (ch. xiv. 4), and appeals to the forbearance of God in dealing with a creature so imperfect and shortlived.

23 How many *are* mine iniquities and sins?
    Make me to know my transgression and my sin.
24 Wherefore hidest thou thy face,
    And holdest me for thine enemy?

First, Job demands to know what his sins are, and wonders that God who is so great would pursue a withered leaf like him, and bring up now after so long the sins of his youth—one who wastes away like a garment that is moth-eaten (ch. xiii. 23—28).

Second, this reference to his own natural feebleness widens his view to the condition of the race of man to which he belongs, whose two characteristics are: that it is of few days, and filled with trouble. And he wonders that God would bring such a being into judgment with *Him*; when the race of man is universally imperfect and a clean one cannot be found in it. And he founds an appeal on the fated shortness of man's life that God would not afflict him with strange and uncommon troubles, but leave him to take what comfort he can, oppressed with only the natural hardships of his short and evil "day" (ch. xiv. 1—6).

Third, this appeal is supported by the remembrance of the inexorable "nevermore" which death writes on man's life. Sadder is the fate of man even than that of the tree. The tree if cut down will bud again, but man dieth and is gone without return as wholly as the water which the sun sucks up from the pool; his sleep of death is eternal (*vv.* 7—12).

Fourth, step after step Job has gone down deeper into the waters of despair—the universal sinfulness of mankind and the inexorable severity of God; the troubles of life of which one must sate himself to the full; its brevity; and last of all its complete extinction in death. The waters here reach his heart; and human nature driven back upon itself becomes prophetic: the vision rises before Job's mind of another life after this one, and he pursues with excited eagerness the glorious phantom (*vv.* 13—15).

Finally, the prayer that such another life might be is supported by a new and dark picture which he draws of his present condition (*vv.* 16—22).

23. Job begins his plea with the demand to know the number of his sins—how many iniquities and sins have I?—and in general to be made aware of them. He means what great sins he is guilty of, sins that account for his present afflictions. He does not deny sinfulness, even *sins* of his youth (*v.* 26); what he denies is special sins of such magnitude as to account for his calamities. Job and his friends both agree in the theory that great afflictions are evidence that God holds those whom He afflicts guilty of great offences. The friends believe that Job is guilty of such offences; he knows he is not, and he here demands to know what the sins are of which God holds him guilty.

24. *Wherefore hidest thou thy face*] This does not mean, Wherefore dost thou refuse to answer me *now*? the reference is to God's severity

| vv. 25—28; 1.] | JOB, XIII. XIV. | 101 |

> Wilt thou break a leaf driven to and fro? 25
> And wilt thou pursue the dry stubble?
> For thou writest bitter *things* against me, 26
> And makest me to possess the iniquities of my youth.
> Thou puttest my feet also in the stocks, 27
> And lookest narrowly unto all my paths;
> Thou settest a print upon the heels of my feet.
> And he, as a rotten thing, consumeth, 28
> As a garment that is moth-eaten.
> Man *that is* born of a woman **14**

in afflicting him, as is shewn by the words "holdest me for thine enemy," cf. ch. xix. 5, xxxv. 2 *seq*.

25. *Wilt thou break*] Or, **wilt thou affright**, that is, chase. The "driven leaf" and the "dry stubble" are figures for that which is so light and unsubstantial that it is the sport of every wind of circumstance. So Job describes himself, in contrast with God, and asks, Is thy determination to assail this kind of foe the explanation of my afflictions?

26. *for thou writest*] Or, **that thou writest**. To "write" is to prescribe, or ordain, Is. x. 1; Hos. viii. 12.

makest me to possess] Or, *inherit*. Job acknowledges sins of his youth, not of his riper manhood, and he conceives that his present afflictions may be for his former sins, which in his past fellowship with God he had deemed long forgiven. It is not to be supposed that he looks back on gross youthful sins, but on such as youth is not free from, and as he feared in his own children, ch. i. 5. Cf. the prayer of the Psalmist, Ps. xxv. 7.

27. *Thou puttest*] Rather, **and puttest my feet in** &c. The verse describes his afflictions under three figures, all denoting arrest, impossibility of movement or escape, and chastisement. The first words are brought up by Elihu, ch. xxxiii. 11, cf. Jerem. xx. 2; Acts xvi. 24.

settest a print upon the heels] Rather, **and drawest thee a line around the soles** of my feet. The figure means that God rigidly prescribed his movements, drawing bounds, which he must not overstep, around his feet. He is a prisoner under rigid surveillance.

28. *And he as a rotten thing*] Or, **one who as a** rotten thing. Job no more speaks of himself in the first person, but in the third, because he thinks of himself as one of the human race in general, which is feeble and short-lived.

Ch. xiv. **1.** In the last verse of ch. xiii. Job thought of himself as one of the race of men, and now he speaks of the characteristics of this race.

born of a woman] The offspring of one herself weak and doomed to sorrow (Gen. iii. 16) must also be weak and doomed to trouble, cf. ch. xv. 14, xxv. 4.

Is of few days, and full of trouble.
2 He cometh forth like a flower, and is cut down:
He fleeth also as a shadow, and continueth not.
3 And dost thou open thine eyes upon such a one,
And bringest me into judgment with thee?
4 Who can bring a clean *thing* out of an unclean? Not one.
5 Seeing his days *are* determined,
The number of his months *are* with thee,
Thou hast appointed his bounds that he cannot pass;
6 Turn from him, that he may rest,
Till he shall accomplish, as a hireling, his day.

2. *and is cut down*] Rather, **and withereth**, cf. similar figures Is. xl. 6 *seq.*; Ps. xxxvii. 2, xc. 6, ciii. 15 *seq.*

3. A question of astonishment at the severity of God's dealing with a creature of such weakness as man. "To open the eyes" is to look narrowly to, to watch in order to punish.

4. The question of astonishment in *v.* 3 supported by reference to the universal sinfulness of man. The verse reads,

Oh that a clean might come out of an unclean!
There is not one.

The phrase *who will give* (as margin) is a mere optative expression. Job throws his idea of the universal uncleanness of man, and that there is not one without sin, into the form of a wish that it were otherwise. If the race of men were not universally infected with sin, which each individual inherits by belonging to the race, God's stringent treatment of the individuals would not be so hard to understand. For similar ideas of the universality of the sinfulness of mankind cf. Gen. vi. 5; Is. vi. 5; Ps. li. 5, also the words of Eliphaz ch. iv. 17 *seq.* Job urges the admitted fact as a plea for forbearance on the side of God.

5, 6. Man being of few days and full of trouble Job pleads that God would not load him with uncommon afflictions, but leave him oppressed with no more than those natural to his short and evil life.

6. *turn from him*] lit. *look away from him*, cf. ch. vii. 19, x. 20.
—turn thy keen scrutiny away from him.

may rest] i. e. *have peace*, from unwonted affliction.

till he shall accomplish] Or, *so that he may enjoy*—so that he may have such pleasure as is possible in his brief and evil life, which is of no higher kind than the joy of the labourer during his hot and toilsome "day," cf. ch. vii. 1 *seq.* The sense given by the A. V., "to pay off," is, however, possible (Is. xl. 2), and not unsuitable here.

7—12. The irreparable extinction of man's life in death. His destiny is sadder even than that of the tree. His sleep in death is eternal.

For there is hope of a tree, 7
If it be cut down, that it will sprout again,
And that the tender branch thereof will not cease.
Though the root thereof wax old in the earth, 8
And the stock thereof die in the ground;
Yet through the scent of water it will bud, 9
And bring forth boughs like a plant.
But man dieth, and wasteth away: 10
Yea, man giveth up the ghost, and where *is* he?
As the waters fail from the sea, 11
And the flood decayeth and drieth up:
So man lieth down, and riseth not: 12
Till the heavens *be* no more, they shall not awake,
Nor be raised out of their sleep.

7. *For there is hope of a tree, if*] lit. *for a tree hath hope; if it be cut down it will sprout again* &c.
9. *like a plant*] i.e. a fresh and new plant; it begins a new life again.
10. *wasteth away*] lit. *is laid prostrate*.
11. *fail from the sea*] i.e. the inland sea or pool, cf. Is. xix. 5; so in Arabic *baḥr*, sea, is any mass of water whether salt or fresh, and also a river.
the flood] the stream. A graphic figure for complete extinction.
12. *till the heavens be no more*] i.e. never; cf. Ps. lxxii. 7, Till there be no moon. The heavens are eternal, cf. Jer. xxxi. 35, 36; Ps. lxxxix. 29, 36, 37.
13—15. Having pursued the destiny of man through all its steps down to its lowest, its complete extinction in death, Job, with a revulsion created by the instinctive demands of the human spirit, rises to the thought that there might be another life after this one. This thought is expressed in the form of an impassioned desire.
To understand these verses the Hebrew conception of death must be remembered. Death was not an end of personal existence: the dead person subsisted, he did not live. He descended into Sheol, the abode of deceased persons. His existence was a dreamy shadow of his past life. He had no communion with the living, whether men or God; comp. iii. 12—19; x. 21, 22, xiv. 20—22. This idea of death is not strictly the teaching of revelation, it is the popular idea from which revelation starts, and revelation on the question rather consists in exhibiting to us how the pious soul struggled with this popular conception and sought to overcome it, and how faith demanded and realized, as faith does, its demand, that the communion with God enjoyed in this life should not be interrupted in death. This was in short a demand and a faith that the state of Sheol should be overleaped, and that the believing soul should be "taken" by God in death to Himself, cf.

13 O that thou wouldest hide me in the grave,
That thou wouldest keep me secret, until thy wrath be past,
That thou wouldest appoint me a set time, and remember me.
14 If a man die, shall he live *again?*
All the days of my appointed time will I wait,
Till my change come.
15 Thou shalt call, and I will answer thee:
Thou wilt have a desire to the work of thine hands.

Ps. xvi. 10, xlix. 15, lxxiii. 24. This was the solution that generally presented itself to the mind when death was contemplated. The present passage differs in two particulars. It does not exhibit such assured faith as these passages in the Psalms. The problem before the Psalmists was a much simpler one than that before Job. They were men who, when they wrote their words of faith, enjoyed God's fellowship, and their faith protested against this fellowship being interrupted in death. But Job has lost the sense of God's fellowship through his afflictions, which are to his mind proof of God's estrangement from him, hence he has so to speak a double obstacle to overcome, where the Psalmists had only one, and this makes him do no more here than utter a prayer, while the Psalmists expressed a firm assurance. In the following chapters, especially ch. xix., Job also rises to assurance. In another particular this passage differs from these Psalms. It contemplates a different and much more complete solution of the problem. In both the hope of immortality has a purely religious foundation. It springs from the irrepressible longing for communion with God. The Psalmists, in the actual enjoyment of this communion, either protest against death absolutely (Ps. xvi.), and demand a continuance in life that this fellowship may continue—that is, they rise to the idea of true immortality; or, contemplating death as a fact, they protest against the popular conception of it, and demand that the deceased person shall not sink into Sheol, but pass across its gulf to God. Job's conception is different from either of these, because his circumstances are different. He does not enjoy the fellowship of God, his afflictions are evidence of the contrary. His firm conviction is that his malady is mortal, in other words, that God's anger will pursue him to the grave. On this side of death he has no hope of a return to God's favour. Hence, contemplating that he shall die under God's anger, his thought is that he might remain in Sheol till God's wrath be past, for He keepeth not His anger for ever; that God would appoint him a period to remain in death and then remember him with returning mercy and call him back again to His fellowship. But to his mind this involves a complete return to life again of the whole man (*v.* 14), for in death there is no fellowship with God (Ps. vi. 5). Thus his solution, though it appears to his mind only as a momentary gleam of light, is broader than that of the Psalmists, and

For now thou numberest my steps:	16
Dost thou not watch over my sin?	
My transgression *is* sealed up in a bag,	17
And thou sewest up mine iniquity.	
And surely the mountain falling cometh to nought,	18
And the rock is removed out of his place.	

corresponds to that made known in subsequent revelation. It is probable that this conception, which the Author of the Poem allows Job to rise to out of the very extremity of his despair, was one not unfamiliar to himself (cf. Is. xxiv. 22). The verses read as a whole:—

13 Oh that thou wouldst hide me in Sheol,
   That thou wouldst keep me secret till thy wrath be past,
   That thou wouldst appoint me a set time and remember me—
14 If a man die shall he live again?—
   All the days of my appointed time would I wait
   Till my release came;
15 Thou wouldst call and I would answer thee,
   Thou wouldst have a desire to the work of thine hands.

As Job follows the fascinating thought, the feeling forces itself upon his mind how much is implied in it, nothing less than that a man when dead should live again (*v.* 14), but he will not allow himself to be arrested in his pursuit of the glorious vision—he describes how he would wait all the period appointed to him (his "warfare," cf. ch. vii. 1) till his release came, and dwells upon the joy and readiness with which he would answer the voice of his Creator calling him to His fellowship again when He longed after the work of His hands long estranged and hidden from Him (ch. x. 3). The words "call" and "answer," *v.* 15, have here naturally quite a different sense from the forensic or judicial one which belongs to them in ch. xiii. 22 and similar passages.

16—22. This prayer for a second life is supported by a picture of the severity with which God deals with man in this life and the mournful consequences of it.

16. Figures expressing the keen scrutiny with which God watches man's life in order to detect his false steps and observe his every sin, cf. ch. xiii. 27.

17. Figures expressing the carefulness with which God treasures up a man's sins lest any of them should be lost, in order to visit the full tale of them upon him.

18—22. Under this severe treatment man must perish. For even the greatest and the firmest things in nature, and those most capable of resistance, are worn down by the influence of constant forces, and how much more man's life under God's continued severity.

18. *And surely*] Rather, **but;** cf. ch. xiii. 3, 4.
The "mountain falling" is the mountain from which great forces detach pieces—as man is subjected to the shattering strokes of God. The second clause shews this to be the meaning.

19 The waters wear the stones:
　　Thou washest away the things which grow out of the dust of the earth;
　　And thou destroyest the hope of man.
20 Thou prevailest for ever against him, and he passeth:
　　Thou changest his countenance, and sendest him away.
21 His sons come to honour, and he knoweth *it* not;
　　And they are brought low, but he perceiveth *it* not of them.
22 But his flesh upon him shall have pain,
　　And his soul within him shall mourn.

19. The turbulent waters wear away the stones of the brook by their constant action.

thou washest away, &c.] Rather, **the floods thereof** (i.e. of the waters) **do wash away the soil of the earth**.

and thou destroyest] i.e. *so* thou destroyest. The "hope" of man which God destroys is not the specific hope of a renewed life (*v*. 7)—this idea is dismissed—but more general, the hope of life.

20. *thou changest his countenance*] A graphic and pathetic description of death. The word "prevailest against," i.e. overpowerest him, refers to the last conflict and the final stroke, cf. ch. xv. 24.

21. "The dead know not anything ... also their love ... is now perished," Eccles. ix. 5, 6.

22. *But his flesh*] Or, *only*. The prep. rendered here "upon him" is the same as that rendered "within him," it means *with* him or in connexion with him, and the verse differs little from this, *Only his flesh hath pain and his soul mourneth*. The dead knoweth nothing of the upper world, only this can be said of him that his flesh hath pain and his soul mourneth; but the Hebrew expresses the idea more distinctly that his flesh and soul do these things in connexion with him. There are two ideas expressed: (1) that the body in the grave, being that of a still existing person, feels the gnawing and the wasting of corruption, cf. Is. lxvi. 24, and that the soul in Sheol leads a mournful and dreary existence; and (2) that these elements of the person though separated still belong to the person.

The first circle of speeches, now completed, started from Job's complaints in ch. iii. Job did not there name God nor make any open imputation against Him, but his bitter maledictions of the day of his birth and his impatient cry, Why gives He life to him that is in misery, (iii. 20), shewed too well against whom it was that he "turned his spirit" (xv. 12.)

Hence the three friends conceive that the first thing to aim at is to bring Job back to just and reverent thoughts of God. Therefore they dwell upon the attributes of God and contrast Him with man, hoping by this great thought of God to still the tumult in Job's breast and bring him to take his right place before the Creator.

The friends all impress this thought of *God* upon Job, each, however, doing it in his own way. The oldest and most thoughtful of the three, Eliphaz, lays hold of the moral purity of God and His universal goodness. Bildad insists on the discriminating rectitude of God in His rule of the world. While Zophar magnifies the omniscience of the Divine insight, which guides God's dealings with men. Each of these views is designed to meet some side of Job's feeling as expressed in his complaints. Job answers these arguments for the most part indirectly. His own unmerited afflictions furnished the answer to them, and he mainly dwells on this. Only at last is he driven by the form in which Zophar puts the common argument of the friends directly to meet it. To their great argument of "God," with which they thought to terrify and silence him, he replies that he does need to be taught regarding God. He is not inferior to them in knowledge of God; but it is just God that he desires to meet. He will go before Him to maintain his rectitude. He challenges God to make known the sins of which he has been guilty (xiii. 23).

However irreligious Job's demeanour might seem to his friends (xv. 4), it is obvious that he has struck from their hands the weapon they have hitherto been using against him. Their argument of "God" is exhausted. Job's passionate proclamation that what he desires above all things is to meet God and maintain his ways to His face has convinced them that he is not to be vanquished with this weapon. Hence they are obliged to look about for others.

Ch. XV.—XXI. The Second Circle of Speeches.

The laudable attempts made by Job's friends to bring him to acknowledge his sins and humble himself before God have signally failed. The sublime truths they have sought to impress on him regarding God have been without effect. He has found means to turn the point of every one of their weapons. And his passionate declarations of his innocence, and challenge of the Divine omniscience itself, with which the three friends had thought to silence him, convince them that they have to do with a man on whom just and reverent thoughts of God make no impression. The argument from the attributes of God has, indeed, been exhausted; and even if it had not, Job's violent assault upon his friends for their use of it, and his charge that they were insincere and moved only by partizanship for God (xiii. 4 *seq.*), might have deterred them from arguing further in this direction. Hence the argument takes now a somewhat different form.

Job's protestations of his innocence did not convince his friends, nor yet his challenge of God and attempt to force an answer from Him (xiii. 23 *seq.*). The manner of the latter shocked them by its irreverence, and the former appeared to them nothing but a crafty attempt on Job's part to conceal his guilt. And of this guilt they were now more firmly convinced than ever (xv. 4—6). Job's demeanour under his sufferings only confirmed the conclusions which his sufferings themselves compelled them to draw. Perhaps his abortive appeal to heaven persuaded them that God was casting him finally off. At all events his behaviour explained to them with sufficient distinctness his afflictions, as well as made them dread a terrible issue to them, seeing Job under them could so tempt God and defy His righteousness (xv. 6). However unwillingly, they are forced to conclude that they see in Job a type both of the calamities that befall the wicked and of their rebellious impatience under them. In this way the thoughts of the friends are drawn away from heaven to earth. God is no more their theme, but man, especially *the wicked man as history and experience shew him to be dealt with in the providence of God.* The effect of this change is naturally to draw the arguments of the friends closer around Job, and bring the debate to a crisis. For though the object of the three friends in drawing their dark pictures of the heaven-daring sinner and his fate is to awaken Job's conscience and alarm him, that he may turn from his evil, their arguments are now of a kind that can be brought to the test of experience, and Job so soon as he can be induced to grapple with them has little difficulty in disposing of them.

When Job fully realizes this new turn that things are taking he is overwhelmed by it. He had anticipated that his sincere protestations of his innocence would carry conviction to the mind of his friends. But when he sees them regarding these protestations as nothing but a crafty cover of his guilt he realizes for the first time his true position. His isolation and misery come home to him in their full and bitter meaning. Men and God alike are against him and hold him guilty. For a long time Job is too much occupied with his new position to be able to turn his mind to the arguments of his friends. He is absorbed in the thought of his isolation, and dwells with affecting pathos on the thought how men hate him and flee from him. Only in his very last speech, after he has fought his way through to more composure of mind, does he seem to awaken to what the argument is which his friends are using against him, and then he deals it some crushing blows which effectually demolish it (ch. xxi.).

Ch. XV. The Second Speech of Eliphaz.

As before Eliphaz takes the lead in the debate, and his speech strikes the key in which all the friends conduct it. His discourse attaches itself to Job's last speech (ch. xii.—xiv.), two things in which Eliphaz lays hold of, first, Job's contemptuous deriding of the opinions of his friends and his claim to a higher wisdom (ch. xii. 3, 7 *seq.*, xiii. 2); and second, his irreverence and the impiety of his sentiments (ch. xiii. 23 *seq.*, xii. 6). By the first the *amour propre* of Eliphaz is deeply hurt; and this very aged (ch. xv. 10) and dignified counsellor, a man of pure and noble blood (ch. xv. 19), betrays by a number of allusions to himself and his former speech (ch. xv. 10 *seq.*) his sense of having been unworthily treated. Besides his irreverence in challenging God's omniscience and seeking to thrust himself into God's very presence, Job had spoken words destructive of all godliness, saying, that the tents of robbers were in peace, and that they that provoked God were secure (ch. xii. 6). In opposition to such sentiments Eliphaz will shew him the truth in

vv. 1—3.] JOB, XV. 109

Then answered Eliphaz the Temanite, and said, 15
Should a wise *man* utter vain knowledge, 2
And fill his belly *with* the east wind?
Should he reason *with* unprofitable talk? 3

regard to the feelings and the fate of the wicked man. The speech thus falls into two parts:—

First, *vv.* 2—16, Eliphaz's rebuke of Job's contemptuous treatment of his friends and assumption of superior wisdom, and his irreverence.

Second, *vv.* 17—35, the doctrine of Eliphaz regarding the wicked man's conscience and fate.

2—16. ELIPHAZ REBUKES JOB'S CONTEMPTUOUS TREATMENT OF THE OPINIONS OF HIS FRIENDS, AND HIS IRREVERENCE TOWARDS GOD.

First, starting with Job's claim to a wisdom beyond that of his friends (ch. xii. 3, 7 *seq.*, xiii. 2), Eliphaz asks if it be in the manner of a wise man to use loud and empty words as arguments (*vv.* 2—3). But in truth Job was more than unwise, he was impious. His demeanour and sentiments did away with all devoutness and religion. Such language as he uttered could be inspired only by deep evil in his heart; and was proof enough without anything more of his wickedness (*vv.* 4—6).

Second, then coming back upon these two points, Job's claim to wisdom and his irreverence, Eliphaz developes each of them separately.

(1) This claim to wisdom, which he puts forth, whence has he it? Was he the first man born? Did he come straight from God's hand? Did he sit in the council of heaven and appropriate wisdom to himself? And how came he, a man not yet old, to have such preeminence in wisdom over them, some of whom were old enough to be his father, that he thought himself entitled to put away from him admonitions which were consoling truths of God's revelation and spoken to him in gentleness and temperance? (*vv.* 7—11).

(2) And why did he allow his passion to carry him away into making charges of unrighteousness against God? For how can a man be pure in God's sight? In His eyes the heavens are not clean, much less man, whose avidity for evil is like that of a thirsty man for water (*vv.* 12—16).

2. *Should a wise man utter vain knowledge*] Or, *will a wise man answer with vain*, &c., lit., *knowledge of wind*, i.e. empty and loud, cf. ch. viii. 2, xvi. 2. The word *wise* refers back to Job's claims to superior wisdom, ch. xii. 3, xiii. 2. Eliphaz asks, Is this the manner of one possessed of wisdom?

fill his belly with the east wind] i.e. puff himself up and then bring out of his mouth violent blasts of mere barren words; cf. Hos. xii. 1.

3. *Should he reason*] Or, *will he reason*, or better, **reasoning with unprofitable talk**. The verse is subordinate to the last, carrying out its idea.

Or *with* speeches wherewith he can do no good?
4 Yea, thou castest off fear,
And restrainest prayer before God:
5 For thy mouth uttereth thine iniquity,
And thou choosest the tongue of the crafty.
6 Thine own mouth condemneth thee, and not I;
Yea, thine own lips testify against thee.
7 *Art* thou the first man *that* was born?
Or wast thou made before the hills?

4. Job was more than unwise, he was doing away with all fear of God.
castest off fear] Or, as margin, **makest void**, doest away with, **the fear of God**.
restrainest prayer] Rather, **impairest reverence** or **devotion**. The charge of Eliphaz is not merely that Job was irreligious himself, but that the tendency of his conduct and principles must be to diminish and do away devoutness and religion among men.
5. *for thy mouth uttereth thine iniquity*] Rather, **for thine iniquity** (or, guilt) **teacheth thy mouth**; the meaning being that his mouth was prompted by his iniquity, used as its instrument. His inquity taught his mouth what to say.
choosest the tongue of the crafty] i.e. choosest and makest use of,—speakest as the crafty do. The charge of Eliphaz is that Job's complaint of unrighteousness in God's treatment of him and his assertions of his own innocence, and such words as those in ch. xii. 6, were mere crafty pretences put forward to cover his own wickedness. If the first clause have precisely the same sense as the latter, the word "iniquity" must be translated "guilt."
6. But in truth such utterances of his mouth clearly suggested the source which inspired them, other proof of his guilt than they was not needed. Thus in *v.* 5 Job's language and sentiments are explained by his guilt, and in *v.* 6 his guilt is proved by his language; and both verses support the charge in *v.* 4 that he was doing away, breaking with, the fear of God.
7—11. But coming back to Job's assumption of superior wisdom, Eliphaz must ask on what it rests?
7. *Art thou the first man*] lit. *wast thou born a man first?* The first man that came from God's hand would naturally be endowed with preeminent wisdom and other attributes. Schlottmann (p. 303) quotes an ironical proverb current in India, "Yes, yes, he is the first man, no wonder that he is so wise." The second clause of the verse, however, as well as *v.* 8, seems to express the conception of a Being formed before the earth, either the Wisdom of Prov. viii. 22 *seq.*, or a Being similar, cf. especially Prov. viii. 25; and the query of Eliphaz is, Art thou the very Wisdom of God? or, Art thou such a Being as the Wisdom of God?

Hast thou heard the secret of God? 8
And dost thou restrain the wisdom to thyself?
What knowest thou, that we know not? 9
What understandest thou, which *is* not in us?
With us *are* both the grayheaded and very aged men, 10
Much elder than thy father.
Are the consolations of God small with thee? 11
Is there *any* secret thing with thee?

8. *Hast thou heard the secret*] Rather, **didst thou listen in the council of God?** Cf. Jer. xxiii. 22, Ps. lxxxix. 7 (assembly = council).

dost thou restrain the wisdom] Rather, **didst thou draw wisdom to thyself?** i.e. appropriate or absorb wisdom. The "wisdom" here is the highest, divine wisdom. The question put is, whether Job was a a member of the Divine council, so as to have full knowledge of the mysteries of God? The Mohammedan conception of evil spirits (satans) listening and overhearing the Divine secrets is quite different from the idea here. Such spirits have no access to heaven, and seek only to filch fragments of God's counsels. The shooting stars are bolts which God hurls at these intruding eavesdroppers; Kor. xxxvii. 6—10.

9. Abandoning irony Eliphaz comes to the facts, which hardly bear out Job's pretensions. His words recall those of Job, ch. xii. 3, xiii. 2.

10. This verse should probably read,

Among us is one both grayheaded and very aged,
One older in days than thy father.

Eliphaz with a dignified indirectness in which, however, a certain personal feeling is displayed, alludes to himself. Others take the words "grayheaded" and "very aged" as collectives—among us are both the grayheaded and the very aged; in which case "among us" must mean "belonging to our tribes." But in reproving Job's demeanour a reference to persons absent seems out of place.

11. *small with thee*] Rather, **are the consolations of God too small for thee?** do they seem to thee beneath thy deserts and notice? Numb. xvi. 9; Is. vii. 13.

is there any secret thing with thee] Rather, **and a word that dealt gently with thee?** The consolations or comforts of God are such as proceed from God and are authorized by Him. Eliphaz so describes his own teaching, e.g. the oracle, ch. iv. 12 *seq.*, which came directly from God; but also, no doubt, such consoling views of God's providence as he shewed ch. v. 8 *seq.* In the phrase "a word that dealt gently with thee" he describes the gentle and conciliatory manner of his own first speech. He may include his friends with him in all this, but there runs throughout this discourse an under-current of references to himself.

12—16. Turning from Job's arrogant claims to superior wisdom Eliphaz must rebuke his violent and irreverent behaviour towards God: What is man that he should be clean?

12 Why doth thine heart carry thee away?
And what do thine eyes wink at,
13 That thou turnest thy spirit against God,
And lettest *such* words go out of thy mouth?
14 What *is* man, that he should be clean?
And *he which is* born of a woman, that he should be righteous?
15 Behold, he putteth no trust in his saints;
Yea, the heavens are not clean in his sight.
16 How much more abominable and filthy
Is man, which drinketh iniquity like water?

12. *what do thine eyes wink at*] Rather, **wherefore do thine eyes wink?** i.e., flash or roll, sign of violent passion. In the first clause "heart" is the excited mind under strong feeling.

13. *turnest thy spirit*] "Spirit" may be breath, i.e., anger, fury, ch. iv. 9 "blast"; cf. Prov. xvi. 32; Is. xxv. 4. The words *against God* are emphatic.

lettest such words go out] lit. *bringest forth words* out of thy mouth. The reference is less to the kind of words spoken than to the passionate manner in which they are uttered.

14. What is there to justify such passion—thy pretended innocence? What is man that he should be clean? cf. ch. xiv. 1. Eliphaz recurs again to his principles formerly enunciated, ch. iv. 17 *seq.*, for his former speech is in his mind throughout.

15. *his saints*] **his holy ones**, i.e. His angels, cf. on ch. v. 1.

the heavens] These are here the material heavens, not the celestial inhabitants, cf. ch. xxv. 5. So Ex. xxiv. 10, "And they saw the God of Israel, and there was under his feet as it were a paved work of a sapphire stone, and as it were the very heaven in its clearness"; see also Ezek. i. 22.

16. According to the Hebrew punctuation the verse runs,

How much less the abominable and corrupt,
Man, which drinketh in iniquity like water.

The word "corrupt," only here and Ps. xiv. 3 (liii. 3), occurs in Arab. in the sense of "turned," sour, of milk; it is used in Heb. only in a moral sense (A. V. filthy). "Man" here is said, of course, of mankind, not specially of Job, and Eliphaz declares that his greedy avidity for evil is like that of a thirsty man for water. The words strongly indicate to Job the view which Eliphaz takes of him and his sufferings, and thus naturally form the transition to the second half of his speech.

17—35. ELIPHAZ INSTRUCTS JOB REGARDING THE TROUBLED CONSCIENCE AND THE DISASTROUS FATE OF THE WICKED MAN.

Having sufficiently rebuked Job's presumption and irreverence Eliphaz proceeds to take up his principles, which "did away with the fear of

I will shew thee, hear me;	17
And that which I have seen I will declare;	
Which wise *men* have told	18
From their fathers, and have not hid *it:*	
Unto whom alone the earth was given,	19
And no stranger passed among them.	
The wicked *man* travaileth with pain all his days,	20
And the number of years is hidden to the oppressor.	
A dreadful sound *is* in his ears:	21

God," *v.* 4. They are such principles as Job gave forth ch. ix. 22 *seq.*, xii. 6. The passage has two parts:—

First, *vv.* 17—19, a brief preface, in which Eliphaz states that his doctrine is that of the wise of all times among the pure-blooded races of men, who have never been contaminated by mixture with foreign tribes, and whose traditions are uncorrupted.

Second, *vv.* 20—35, the doctrine regarding the wicked man itself, in which there are three points: (1) the troubled conscience and presentiments of coming evil that continually haunt the evil man, *vv.* 20—24; (2) the cause of this, his defiance of God and sensual life, *vv.* 25—28; and (3) finally, a picture of his punishment and disastrous end, *vv.* 29—35.

17. *I will shew thee*] Eliphaz assumes a high tone with Job; one is entitled to do so with a man in his unfortunate condition.

18. The doctrine of Eliphaz is no novelty,—it is his (*v.* 17), but it is the consistent moral tradition of the wise from generation to generation. The phrase "have told...and have not hid" means, have told openly, it is matter of public consent and teaching among them; cf. Is. iii. 9, where the same words occur.

19. And it is a tradition pure and uncorrupted by admixture of foreign elements, for it is the moral wisdom of races to whom alone the land has been given, who have dwelt always in the same seats, and never been displaced, and among whom foreign and inferior races have never penetrated.

20—35. This doctrine itself. The passage gives a picture of the conscience of the wicked man filled with presentiments of evil, in opposition to such statements as that of Job, ch. xii. 6, and to his whole claims regarding himself.

20. The sense is,

All the days of the wicked man he is in pain,
And the number of years that are laid up for the oppressor,

i.e., constantly and throughout his whole life, as long as it endures, the wicked man is in pain (or, torments himself). The word "laid up" means appointed, reserved, for the oppressor. This is said against Job's statement, xii. 6, that the tents of robbers were in peace.

21. *A dreadful sound*] *A sound of terrors;* he continually thinks he hears the sound of coming destruction.

In prosperity the destroyer shall come *upon* him.
22 He believeth not that *he* shall return out of darkness,
    And he *is* waited for of the sword.
23 He wandereth abroad for bread, *saying*, Where *is it?*
    He knoweth that the day of darkness is ready at his hand.
24 Trouble and anguish shall make him afraid;
    They shall prevail against him, as a king ready to the battle.
25 For he stretcheth out his hand against God,
    And strengtheneth himself against the Almighty.
26 He runneth upon him, *even* on *his* neck,
    Upon the thick bosses of his bucklers:
27 Because he covereth his face with his fatness,

in prosperity the destroyer shall come] A picture of the wicked man's anticipations.

22. *return out of darkness*] "Darkness" is calamity, and the words mean that the wicked man anticipates a calamity which shall be final, and from which, when it befals him, there shall be no escape.

he is waited for of the sword] So he feels in regard to himself; he is marked out for the sword, i.e., the hostile sword or the avenging sword of God, ch. xix. 29; Is. xxxi. 8.

23. He anticipates the time when he shall be a hungry wanderer, roving in search of bread and crying, Where is it? The picture of the rich oppressor tormented by visions of famine is very graphic.

ready at hand] Or, *at his side;* the dark day of calamity stands constantly beside him ready to envelop him in its shadows. Such is his own foreboding ("he knows").

24. *shall make him afraid*] Rather, **make him afraid.**

ready to the battle] Fully prepared and therefore irresistible.

25—28. Reason of these terrors of conscience and presentiments of evil—his defiance of heaven and sensual life.

25. *he stretcheth out*] Rather, **stretched.** The tenses in the following verses would all be better put in the past, as they describe either distinct or continued past actions. So **strengthened**, or **emboldened himself**, lit. behaved himself mightily (Is. xlii. 13 margin), or, proudly.

26. The whole verse means,

He ran upon him with stiff neck,
With the thick bosses of his bucklers.

The words describe the wicked man's demeanour towards God. The figure is that of a warrior making an assault. The Heb. is "he ran upon him with neck," Vulg., *erecto collo,* cf. Ps. lxxv. 5. The "bosses" are the convex sides of the bucklers, the sides turned to the foe, who here is God.

27. *he covereth*] Rather, **he covered**; and similarly, **he made** collops. The words express the idea of falling into a brutish fleshliness, which

And maketh collops of fat on *his* flanks.
And he dwelleth in desolate cities, 28
And in houses which no man inhabiteth,
Which are ready to become heaps.
He shall not be rich, neither shall his substance continue, 29
Neither shall he prolong the perfection thereof upon the earth.
He shall not depart out of darkness; 30
The flame shall dry up his branches,
And by the breath of his mouth shall he go away.
Let not him that is deceived trust in vanity: 31
For vanity shall be his recompence.
It shall be accomplished before his time, 32

causes insensibility to all that is spiritual and resistance of it, cf. Deut. xxxii. 15; Ps. lxxiii. 7.

28. *and he dwelleth*] **and he dwelt.**
which no man inhabiteth] **which should not be inhabited.**
are ready to become] **which were destined to be heaps.** The idea seems to be that the wicked man settled in and rebuilt places that were under the curse of God, and destined by Him for perpetual desolation. Such places in the East are those on which God's judgment has fallen because of some great wickedness perpetrated there. To settle in and rebuild such ruins indicates the extreme of impiety, cf. Deut. xiii. 13 *seq.*; Josh. vi. 26; 1 K. xvi. 34.

29—35. The disastrous end of the wicked man.

29. *neither shall he prolong the perfection*] Perhaps, *neither shall their produce bend down to the ground;* the figure being that of heavy grain, or branches thickly laden with fruit, bending down to the earth. The word rendered *produce* or *gain* is not found again and is of somewhat uncertain meaning.

30. Advance on *v.* 29, describing the sinner's actual destruction. The figures are common; on *darkness*, cf. *vv.* 22—23; the *flame* is the scorching sun or glowing wind; *breath* of his mouth, i.e., God's mouth, cf. ch. iv. 9.

31. The verse reads,
Let him not trust in vanity: he is deceived:
For vanity shall be his recompence.

Similarly, "they that plow iniquity reap the same," ch. iv. 8; v. 13. Eliphaz returns as in other passages to his former speech. "Vanity" or evil means both wickedness (first clause) and calamity or trouble (second clause). The word "recompence" means *exchange*, that received in barter or return.

32. *Before his time*] lit. *before his day*, that is, the natural day of his death, cf. ch. xxii. 16; and the clause means, in the midst of his years (Ps. lv. 23) his recompence, or exchange, is fulfilled and goes into

8—2

And his branch shall not be green.
33 He shall shake off his unripe grape as the vine,
And shall cast off his flower as the olive.
34 For the congregation of hypocrites *shall be* desolate,
And fire shall consume the tabernacles of bribery.
35 They conceive mischief, and bring forth vanity,
And their belly prepareth deceit.

accomplishment—he is cut off. The words might also mean that his recompence accrues to him in its fulness. In the second clause "branch" is the palm-branch, or crowning tuft (Is. ix. 14), and the figure is that of such a tree withered and dead.

33. It is doubtful if the A. V. expresses a meaning which is true to nature; the vine does not shake off its unripe grapes. The words must rather express the meaning that the grapes are not brought to maturity. The word "shake off" means to "wrong" Prov. viii. 36, and probably the idea is that the vine fails to nourish its grapes and leaves them to dry and wither. This carries out the conception of *v*. 32. The general idea of these verses is that the wicked man is "subject to vanity," his branch prematurely withers (*v*. 32), he puts forth grapes but cannot ripen them, he flowers but he fails of fruit. His endeavours in all directions come short.

34. The same truth as that expressed in *vv*. 31—32 now taught without figure, and reduced to a general principle.

congregation of hypocrites] Or, *company of the ungodly*, ch. viii. 13; xiii. 16. "Desolate" is *barren* (ch. iii. 7), unfruitful. The households of the godless are unfruitful, under God's curse they come to nought; but it is puerile to make the grapes and flowers of *v*. 33 figures for *children*.

tabernacles of bribery] *Bribery*, a common method of perverting justice in the East, is here a general name for wrong and injustice.

35. Finally Eliphaz condenses into an expressive figure the general doctrine both of this and his former discourse, namely, that suffering and disaster follow, as by a law of nature, doing evil and wrong. In iv. 8, "They that sow wickedness reap the same"; in this verse, "They that conceive mischief bring forth trouble". The word rendered "vanity" here is "affliction" in v. 6; see notes there and on iv. 8. Comp. Ps. vii. 14; Is. xxxiii. 11; lix. 4.

CH. XVI.—XVII. JOB'S REPLY TO ELIPHAZ.

Job's appeal to God (ch. xiii. 23 *seq.*) remained unanswered. God is resolved to hide His face from him. His friends, instead of seeing in his appeal to Heaven and his protestations of innocence proof that he is innocent, regard these as but a crafty attempt to hide his guilt, and as the most convincing evidence of it (ch. xv. 5, 6). Thus Job beholds God and men alike turned against him and holding him guilty. God of the world and of the present inexorably turns away from him; and

God's turning away from him causes men to avert their faces too. His isolation is complete. And to him who had once stood so high in the estimation of men, and as a man of deep human feelings yearned for men's sympathy (cf. the picture in ch. xxix), the thought comes home with a crushing effect. This is the new thought in Job's mind, and it is this thought that gives such a tragic pathos to his speeches in the second cycle of debate. In the first circle of speeches it is God's enmity alone of which Job complains (ch. vi. 4, &c.), but now there is added to this the universal alienation (ch. xvi. 7) and abhorrence of mankind. This feeling gives tone to all his speeches, and in ch. xix., which forms the climax of this division, finds its fullest expression in the words, Pity me, pity me, O ye my friends, why do ye persecute me like God? (*vv.* 21, 22, cf. *v.* 13 *seq.*). And this overmastering feeling forces its way to expression almost in spite of him (xvi. 6) in the first part of the present speech (*vv.* 7—17).

Nothing now remains to him but his own sense of his innocence; and to this he clings all the more tenaciously. He shall never be acknowledged in this life; he shall die under God's hand and go down to the grave numbered with the transgressors, for the hopes which the friends held out of restoration were but the veriest folly (xvi. 22 *seq.*, xvii. 10 *seq.*). But it is a martyr's death that he shall die. And so strong is his sense of his innocence that he rises to the assurance that it cannot remain unrecognised for ever. His innocent blood will appeal unto heaven with an unceasing cry till it finds a response (xvi. 18). And even now he has a Witness who will testify for him, even God as He is in Himself in heaven. And to this Witness he makes his appeal. Men mock him, but he lifts his tearful face (xvi. 20) to God, God as He is in truth and as He must reveal himself in the future, begging that He would uphold his right with God, who now is unjustly bringing him to death, and do justice between him and his fellows, whose suspicions so cruelly wrong him (xvi. 21, xix. 3). And if he may not ask or expect (xiii. 18 *seq.*) that God would appear for him in this life, yet he will beseech God to give him some pledge even here, that afterwards, when he shall have gone the way whence he shall not return, He will make his innocence to appear (xvi. 22, xvii. 3).

The Discourse consists of four somewhat unequal sections :—

First, *vv.* 1—5, Job expresses his weariness of his friends' monotonous speeches, which contained nothing; and justifies against the complaint of Eliphaz (xv. 11) his rejection of them.

Second, *vv.* 6—17, he gives a touching picture of his sorrowful isolation, and of the enmity with which God and men pursued him, though he was innocent of all wrong.

Third, *vv.* 18—xvii. 9, but this cruel fate, which both brings him to death and affixes to him the stigma of wickedness, cannot for ever prevail over him. He shall die under the imputation of guilt, but his blood will cry for reparation, filling earth and heaven with its voice, until he be vindicated. He has a Witness in heaven who will testify for him, even God as He is in heart; and he appeals unto God that He would do justice to him with God and between him and men —and even

16 Then Job answered and said,

2 I have heard many such *things:*
   Miserable comforters *are* ye all.
3 Shall vain words have an end?
   Or what emboldeneth thee that thou answerest?
4 I also could speak as ye *do:*
   If your soul were in my soul's stead,
   I could heap up words against you,
   And shake mine head at you.

that He would not let him die without some token to this effect (xvi. 21, xvii. 3).

Fourth, *vv.* 10—16, coming back to what is the ground tone of this speech, his certainty of a speedy death under God's hand, Job repudiates as mere folly the glowing hopes of restoration in this life which his friends held out to him. He knows better; he shall die, his hope is in the grave.

Ch. xvi. **1—5.** Job expresses his weariness of the monotony of his friends' speeches, and rejects their consolation, which is only that of the lip.

2. *many such things*] Job cannot help expressing his impatience of the sameness and the amount of his friends' talk, and its uselessness or even worse.

miserable comforters] The margin is, *troublesome comforters*, lit. comforters of trouble, whose comfort brings no ease but only more trouble. The words are a reply to the query of Eliphaz, Are the comforts of God too small for thee? xv. 11. Their comforts were all founded on a false assumption of his guilt, and contained the condition of his repentance. Such words only increased his perplexity and misery.

3. *Shall vain words have an end*] lit. *is there any end to words of wind?* To retort their charge of "windy knowledge" (ch. xv. 2), Job cannot help fearing that there is no end to such empty harangues on their side, though he cannot imagine what provokes them to reply instead of letting the controversy drop, as he had long ago besought them (ch. xiii. 5). For *emboldeneth* **provoketh** is better.

4, 5. Job then, with the supercilious contempt peculiar to him and in justification of his rejection of their "comfort," holds up a picture of it before them: their method is not a difficult one, he also could adopt it, if his case were theirs; he could shake his head over them and give them lip-comfort enough.

4. *I could heap up words*] Rather, **I could compose words.** By "composing" or joining together words Job means making formal, artificial and heartless speeches; cf. the string of traditional sayings put together by Eliphaz, ch. xv. 20 *seq.*

shake mine head at you] "A gesture of astonishment, as much as to say 'Eh! I would not have thought that the pious man, as it appears

> *But* I would strengthen you with my mouth,
> And the moving of my lips should asswage *your grief.* 5

from his misfortunes, had been so great a sinner'" (Hitzig), cf. Ps. xxii. 7, Is. xxxvii. 22.

5. The verse no doubt carries on the idea of the preceding:

> I could strengthen you with my mouth,
> And the condolence of my lips could assuage your grief.

The emphasis falls on *mouth* and *lips*. Job could give them lip-comfort enough, pour out abundance of words in which lay no power to uphold the heart as they did not proceed from the heart. "Condolence" as ch. ii. 11.

6—17. JOB REALIZES TO HIMSELF HIS NEW CONDITION: GOD AND MEN COMBINE TO PURSUE HIM WITH THEIR ENMITY, THOUGH HE IS INNOCENT OF ALL WRONG.

In *v.* 5 Job flung back with scorn the "comforts of God" which the friends proffered him. And now there seems to occur a pause, and the excited sufferer looks about him and realizes both the extremity of the evil in which he is held, and the new and unexpected trial, added to all others, of the judgment of men being against him. And he hardly knows whether he shall speak or be silent, so overcome is he and so unavailing to help him or make men judge truly of him are both speech and silence—*if I speak my grief is not assuaged, and if I forbear what am I eased?* v. 6.

Yet this new condition in which he realizes that he is, which makes speech useless, forces him to speak, and he sets before himself in an excited soliloquy the combined enmity to him of men and God.

First, *vv.* 7—11, he realizes to himself the complete estrangement from him of all familiar friends; God's enmity to him has turned men also into foes (*vv.* 7, 8). This combined enmity of God and men is represented under what seems the figure of a creature hunted by one great lion-like assailant, leading on a host of minor, ignobler foes. The chief adversary is first described, his rending anger, and gnashing teeth, and flashing eyes (*v.* 9); and then the pell-mell rout of baser foes that howled behind him, their open mouth and shameless gestures, and full cry after the prey, which is flung over into their hands (*vv.* 10, 11).

Second, *vv.* 12—17, then the hostility of God Himself is particularly dwelt upon in graphic figures, which express its unexpected suddenness, its violence and destructiveness. One figure is that of a man suddenly grasped by another of overwhelming strength and tossed about and dashed to pieces (*v.* 12). Then the figure changes, and this shattered frame is set up as a mark, and God's arrows hiss around him and split his reins and pour out his life to the ground (*v.* 13). Again the figure changes, and this body seems some fair edifice or fort which God dismantles by breach upon breach till it lies a sorrowful ruin (*v.* 14). And finally the condition of humiliation to which the sufferer

6   Though I speak, my grief is not asswaged:
    And *though* I forbear, what am I eased?
7   But now he hath made me weary:
    Thou hast made desolate all my company.
8   And thou hast filled me with wrinkles, *which* is a witness *against me*:
    And my leanness rising up in me
    Beareth witness to my face.
9   He teareth *me in* his wrath, who hateth me;
    He gnasheth upon me with his teeth;
    Mine enemy sharpeneth his eyes upon me.
10 They have gaped upon me with their mouth;

is brought is described; and all this befell him though he had done no wrong (*vv.* 15—17).

6. *my grief*] i.e. *my pain*; see on ch. ii. 13.

what am I eased] lit. as margin, *what* (of my pain or trouble) *goeth from me?*

7. *made me weary*] i.e. *exhausted* me; and *now* describes the new situation which he realizes. The second clause indicates in what way he had been wearied or exhausted, all his "company," his familiar friends, all on whom he could rely, or hope in, had been removed from him, and turned into his enemies and haters, cf. ch. xix. 13—19; every resource was taken from him, cf. ch. xv. 34. In the first clause *he* is God, to whom as his emotion rises the speaker turns directly in the second clause—thou hast made desolate.

8. The verse reads,

   Thou hast laid hold of me, and it is become a witness against me;
   And my leanness riseth up against me; it beareth witness to my face.

By God's seizing or laying hold of him Job means his afflictions. These afflictions sent by God were assumed by all to be witnesses of his guilt; his emaciation from disease rose up and testified to his face that he was a sinner. Such was the construction all men put on his calamities, and under this impression they all turned away from him, thinking him one stricken of God and afflicted (Is. liii. 4). See on ch. i. 11, and cf. Is. iii. 9.

9. Picture of God's hostility to him. The figure is that of a beast of prey.

who hateth me] lit. *and hateth me*, or, and is hostile to me, i.e. *assaileth me*. The picture of the lion-like assailant, his rending fury, and gnashing teeth, and flashing eyes, is graphic.

10. Picture of the hostility of men—the pack of petty foes that howl at the heels of his greater enemy.

have gaped] Rather, **they gape.** Similarly, **they smite.** The figure of wild beasts is not strictly maintained, but passes in the second clause

They have smitten me upon the cheek reproachfully;
They have gathered themselves together against me.
God hath delivered me to the ungodly,   11
And turned me over into the hands of the wicked.
I was at ease, but he hath broken me asunder: 12
He hath also taken *me* by my neck, and shaken me to pieces,
And set me up for his mark.
His archers compass me round about,   13
He cleaveth my reins asunder, and doth not spare;
He poureth out my gall upon the ground.
He breaketh me *with* breach upon breach,   14
He runneth upon me like a giant.
I have sewed sackcloth upon my skin,   15

into the reality. The gestures described are those of contempt and destructive hatred, see Ps. xxii. 13, Is. lvii. 4, Mic. v. 1, Lam. iii. 30; cf. John xviii. 22, xix. 3, Acts xxiii. 2.

they have gathered themselves] **they gather.** The phrase means probably that they fling themselves in one body upon him, they combine in their attack against him.

11. *hath delivered*] **delivereth.** Similarly, *turneth* or **casteth** me into. By the "ungodly" Job does not mean his friends, but the low rabble of men, such as are described in ch. xxx.

12—14. More particular description of the hostile attack of God, its unexpectedness and destructiveness.

12. The figure of a man seized by another of overwhelming strength and dashed to pieces. This attack was sudden and unexpected, when Job was at ease and in security cf. ch. xxix. 2 *seq.* This meets what Eliphaz said of the forebodings of conscience, ch. xv. 20 *seq.*

13. The second figure—Job has been set up by God as a mark for His arrows.

his archers] Rather, **his arrows**, cf. ch. vi. 4. These arrows fly about him and cleave his vital parts and pour out his life to the ground. The Oriental speaks of the gall and gall-bladder where we might refer to the blood and the heart.

14. Another figure, that of an edifice or fort overthrown by repeated breaches, and stormed by warriors. *Giant* is a mighty man, or warrior, Is. xlii. 13.

15—17. Condition to which the sufferer was brought by these destructive attacks of God in His hostility.

15. Putting on sackcloth was the sign of mourning; it was worn next the skin, 2 Kings vi. 30. By *sewing* it on Job indicates that it is his habitual garment, which he never puts off; though the word may also suggest the closeness with which it adheres to his shrunk and emaciated frame.

And defiled my horn in the dust.
16 My face is foul with weeping,
And on mine eyelids *is* the shadow of death;
17 Not for *any* injustice in mine hands:
Also my prayer is pure.

defiled my horn] The word "defiled" or fouled may also mean, *thrust my horn* into the dust; the sense remains the same. To lift up the horn is to increase in power or eminence, or to shew a proud sense of greatness (Ps. lxxxix. 17, 24, xcii. 10, lxxv. 4, 5); to thrust it into the dust, or to foul it in the dust, is to feel the sense of deepest humiliation. Job's once honoured head which he held erect was brought down low in shame.

16. *My face is foul*] The word may mean *inflamed*, from a root signifying to be red; or the root of the word may mean to ferment, and the reference be to the swollen and blurred appearance of the face from excessive weeping. Involuntary weeping is said to be a symptom of Elephantiasis. The second clause expresses another effect of this weeping, his eyes became dim (ch. xvii. 7, Ps. vi. 7, lxix. 3), and there lay thick darkness upon them—though this was also a sign of diminishing vitality; comp. Goethe's dying cry, More light!

17. *Not for any injustice*] i.e. *though there is no wrong in my hands*, cf. Is. liii. 9. The first clause denies that he had done anything amiss in action; and the second affirms that his "prayer," i.e. his whole religious walk with God, was pure. The last words give a reply to the insinuations of Eliphaz, ch. xv. 4, and the former to his allusion ch. xv. 34.

CH. XVI. 18—XVII. 9. JOB, DYING A MARTYR'S DEATH, BESEECHES GOD THAT HE WOULD UPHOLD HIS RIGHT WITH GOD AND AGAINST MEN, AND GIVE HIM A PLEDGE THAT HE WILL MAKE HIS INNOCENCE APPEAR.

In *vv.* 12—14 Job described the terrible hostility of God, who dashed him to pieces, laid him in ruins and poured out his soul to the ground—brought him unto death. Then the other thought rose in his mind that all this befell him though he was innocent both in life and in spirit. Here he comes to the point at which he always loses self-control—when he realizes that in spite of his innocence he is held guilty. This is an overwhelming feeling, and under it Job either wildly challenges the rectitude of God, as in the first cycle of speeches; or he flings off from him altogether the form of things in the present world, and forces his way into another region, where such perversions cannot prevail and where the face of God, clouded here, must be clear and propitious. This second direction, entered upon first in ch. xiv., is pursued in the present passage, and reaches its highest point in ch. xix. Already in ch. x. Job had drawn a distinction between God of the present, who persecuted him as guilty though he was innocent, and God of the past, whose gracious care of him had been wonderful; though there he

> O earth, cover not thou my blood,
> And let my cry have no place. 18

grasped at a frightful reconciliation of the contradiction: God of the present, who destroyed him, seemed the real God, and His past mercies were no true expression of His nature (see on x. 13 *seq.*). In ch. xiv. Job reached out his hand into the darkness and clutched at another idea, a distinction between God of the present who would pursue him unto death, and God of the future—God when His anger should be overpast and He would yearn again towards His creature, the work of His hands (see on xiv. 13 *seq.*). This God of the future was God as He is in truth, true to His own past dealing and to man's conceptions of Him. It is on this line of thought that the present passage moves.

The two great ideas which fill Job's mind in all this discourse are, first, the certainty of his speedy death under God's afflicting hand; and second, the moral infamy and the inexplicable contradiction to his conscience which death in such circumstances carries with it. The first, his speedy death, Job accepts as inevitable, and he cannot restrain his contemptuous indignation at the foolishness of his friends, who talk as if something else were possible (xvii. 2—4, 10—16). But such a death under the hand of God meant to Job the reprobation of God and the scorn and abhorrence of men. And it is against this idea, not his mere death, that Job wrestles with all his might. This is the meaning of such a death; but it cannot be that God will allow this obloquy and injustice to overwhelm His innocent creature for ever. His blood will utter a ceaseless cry for reparation. And even now he has in heaven one who will witness to his innocence. And he prays to God that He would maintain his right with God and against men.

It is impossible to escape the conclusion that Job prays or hopes for this vindication not before but after death. For he contemplates dying an unjust death—his blood will cry for vengeance. His present unjust afflictions will bring him to the grave. But these fatal afflictions are just God's witness to his guilt. Any interference of God, therefore, to declare his innocence cannot take place in this life, for an intervention of God to declare his innocence, all the while that He continued to declare him guilty by His afflictions, could not occur to Job's mind.

The passage xvi. 18—xvii. 9 embraces two sections similar to one another, each of which contains a fervent appeal to God, followed by words which support it, xvi. 18—xvii. 2, and xvii. 3—9.

18. God's destructive enmity will bring Job to death, though there is no wrong in his hands and his prayer is pure (xvi. 17). This feeling makes him appeal to the earth not to cover his innocent blood. He shall die, but it is an unjust death, and his blood shall lie on the bosom of the earth open, appealing to heaven for vindication, and uttering an unceasing cry for justice.

let my cry have no place] i.e. no resting place, where it should cease and be dumb and penetrate no further. His "cry" is his cry for reparation, as in Gen. iv. 10 "The voice of thy brother's blood crieth unto me from the ground." His "blood" is, of course, a figure; it does

19 Also now, behold my witness *is* in heaven,
  And my record *is* on high.
20 My friends scorn me:
  But mine eye poureth out *tears* unto God.
21 O that *one* might plead for a man with God,
  As a man *pleadeth* for his neighbour.

not imply actual bloodshed, but merely a wrongful death; but it cannot mean anything short of death, because the figure is taken from a violent death. The word is used in a similar way, Ps. xxx. 9, "What profit is there in my blood, in my going down to the pit"? where death at God's hand from sickness seems referred to. On the idea that uncovered blood is blood calling for reparation see the remarkable passage Ezek. xxiv. 7, 8; cf. Is. xxvi. 21.

19. If his blood is to cry with an unceasing voice for reparation until it find it, there must be some one to take up the cry and see reparation made. Job is assured that already he has such a Witness and sponsor in heaven. The verse reads,

  Even now, behold my witness is in heaven,
  And he that voucheth for me is on high.

my record] This is inexact; the word describes a person and means precisely the same as Witness, being the Aramean equivalent to the Heb. in the first clause. The word occurs again in the expression Jegar *Sahad*utha, *heap of witness*, Gen. xxxi. 47, as the Hebrew word does in the corresponding phrase, Gal-'*Ed*. It is difficult to find a corresponding noun in English; perhaps advocate or sponsor comes pretty near, as there was no difference between advocate and witness in the Hebrew courts, the part of a witness being to testify in behalf of one and see justice done to him, as *v.* 21 describes what part Job desires his witness to play for him. "Witness" does not mean merely one who *knows* Job's innocence, but one who will testify to it and see it recognised, just as in xvii. 3 *surety* is one who undertakes to see right maintained.

20, 21. Job now names his Witness and states what he hopes for from Him.

  20. My friends scorn me:
    Mine eye poureth out tears unto God,
  21. That he would maintain the right of a man with God,
    And of a son of man against his neighbour.

20. *scorn me*] lit. *are my scorners*, or, mockers—instead of being my witnesses, cf. xii. 4, xvi. 4, 5. Because his friends mock him and no sympathy or insight is to be looked for from them (xvi. 7, xvii. 4), his eye *droppeth*—he appeals with tears to God; cf. Is. xxxviii. 14. What Job desires of his Witness is that he would see right done him both with God and with men—with God who wrongly held him guilty, and against men, his fellows, who founding on God's dealing with him held him guilty also and were his mockers. On first clause of *v.* 21 cf.

When a few years are come,
Then I shall go the way *whence* I shall not return.
My breath is corrupt,
My days are extinct,
The graves *are ready* for me.
Are there not mockers with me?
And *doth not* mine eye continue in their provocation?

xiii. 15, xxiii. 7. The "man" and "son of man" to whom Job refers is himself; there is nothing mystical in the phrase "son of man," which means merely "man," Hebrew poetry requiring for its parallelism such variety of expression.

22—xvii. 2. What Job sought with tears was that God would cause his innocence to be acknowledged by God, and made manifest against men. Now he adds words in support of his prayer, or gives the reason for it. He so prays, for here in this life he has no hope of restoration. God's anger will pursue him to the grave, which is already his portion.

22.   For a few years shall come,
      And I shall go the way whence I shall not return!
xvii. 1. My spirit is spent,
      My days are extinct.
      The grave is ready for me!
   2. Surely mockeries encompass me,
      And mine eye must dwell on their provocation!

22. It is doubtful whether Job means by "a few years" his whole life, or the years that are still to run of it. The last sense is fairest to the language. His disease though mortal was not immediately fatal; but at least his days were consumed "without hope."

1. *my breath*] Rather as margin, **my spirit is spent**, i.e. consumed. The "spirit" is the principle of life.

the graves are ready for me] lit. *graves are mine;* the meaning being: the grave is my portion; cf. *v.* 13 *seq.* Coverdale: I am harde at deathes dore.

2. *Are there not mockers with me*] lit. *mockery.* The interrogative form is possible, but more likely the verse is a strong asseveration, uttered in a tone of indignant impatience. The connexion indicates that the reference is to the illusory hopes and promises of restoration in this life which the friends held out to Job. He complains that he is beset with such mockeries. This seems also the meaning of the "provocation" on which his eye has to dwell, though in this their offensive exhortations to repentance may also be included. This provocation of theirs his friends were always inflicting upon him, troublesome comforters as they were (xvi. 2). The true state of things Job knows very well (*vv.* 1, 10—16); their delusive hopes are not things *he* can hope for; and he turns in impatience from them with a greater importunity unto God, and appeals to Him for that which may yet be attained, and which above all things he longs for (*v.* 3).

3   Lay down now, put me in a surety with thee;
    Who *is* he *that* will strike hands with me?
4   For thou hast hid their heart from understanding:

3—9. New appeal to God that He would undertake for Job or give him a pledge that he would cause his innocence to be acknowledged by God, *v.* 3; with the grounds for this prayer as before, *vv.* 4—9.

3. The verse reads,

> Give a pledge now! be surety for me with thee!
> Who is there (else) that will strike hands with me?

Lay down now] i.e. lay or put in a pledge. *Now* is not temporal, but a particle of importunate entreaty.

put me in a surety] As above, **be surety for me with thee**. The first expression, give a pledge, is more fully expressed by the second, be surety for me with thee; and the question, Who (else) will *strike hands* with me? refers to the gesture or action by which suretyship was undertaken, viz. by striking hands; cf. Prov. vi. 1, xi. 15 (margin), xvii. 18, xxii. 26. First, Job beseeches God to become surety for him; that is something to be done in the present. But second, a suretyship necessarily refers to the future; though undertaken in the present it is to be fulfilled later. This is expressed by the words *with thee*, i.e. with God. Job beseeches God to undertake now that He will cause his innocence to be yet acknowledged with God. The same division of God into two parties, God who persecutes Job and wrongs him and God who becomes surety for Job and undertakes to see his cause righted with God, appears here as before in xvi. 21; see something similar Heb. vii. 22. The phrase *be surety for me* is translated *undertake for me*, Is. xxxviii. 14, cf. Ps. cxix. 122; and it might be made a question whether the suppliant went so far as to expect any visible or audible sign from heaven.

4—9. These verses support the petition in *v.* 3. If God will not undertake for Job none else will, for the hearts of his friends have been blinded. This thought of the perverse obstinacy and cruelty of his friends leads Job again to a gloomy survey of his whole condition (cf. xvi. 22—xvii. 2). He is become a public contempt to mankind and brought to the lowest ebb of mortal weakness and humiliation (*vv.* 6, 7). Such moral perversions on the earth astonish the righteous and rouse them to indignation against the wicked in their prosperity (*v.* 8). Yet they will not permit themselves to be misled by such things to err from the paths of rectitude. Full of moral terror as these perversions are the righteous will in spite of them cleave to his righteousness. He will feel that he is in possession of the only true good, and even because of them and though he sees the world under the rule of God given over to wrong, he will wax stronger and stronger in well doing (*v.* 9)—an astonishing passage.

4. This verse answers the question in *v.* 3, Who (else) will strike hands with me? None else will, for the hearts of the three friends and all others have been blinded, and can take no true view of the sufferer's cause.

Therefore shalt thou not exalt *them*.
He *that* speaketh flattery to *his* friends, 5
Even the eyes of his children shall fail.
He hath made me also a byword of the people; 6

exalt them] i.e. give them the upper hand or victory; cf. xlii. 7, 8. To give the friends the upper hand would be to give an issue to Job's cause such as answered their expectations. The connexion may be: give a pledge now, none else will, for thou hast blinded them, and having blinded them thou wilt not give an issue that meets their expectations.

5. This verse is very obscure. In some way or other it must carry on Job's severe reflection on the conduct of his friends (*v.* 4), and express it in a stronger way. The word rendered in A. V. *flattery* usually means a *portion* or share, that which falls to one on a division of land, booty, and the like, or that which is one's possession. This must be the meaning here. The sense may be,

> They give over (their) fellow for a prey,
> While the eyes of his children fail.

The expression seems to be of the nature of a proverb, which illustrates the cruel treatment to which men are subjected—they are given over, lit. *assigned* or *declared*, as a prey or possession to others (to whom, as debtors and the like, they are sold), while no pity is had for their perishing children. The language is general, though the conduct of Job's friends towards him furnishes an illustration of the truth. The word "fellow" is plur., "fellows" or friends, the plur. being used to express the general idea; the sing., referring to each individual, appears in *his* children. Job regards his own treatment as an instance of similar ruthlessness, and his friends and those around him as shewing a similar cruelty. The passage expresses a sentiment similar to that in ch. vi. 27. Others render, *he that betrayeth* (or, denounceth) *friends for a prey, may the eyes of his children fail*, or, *the eyes of his children shall fail*. But a malediction or a threat on Job's part does not suit his tone at this moment, nor the general scope of the passage, in which he is drawing a gloomy picture of his own treatment at the hands of men and God.

6. This verse reads,

> I am made also a byeword of the peoples,
> And am become one to be spit on in the face.

The words, *I am made* might mean, as A. V., *He hath made me*, the reference being to God. Undoubtedly Job turns away here from men and refers to a broader evil, the inexplicable course of the world in God's hand. But probably the allusion to God is made in this indirect way. By the "peoples" Job means mankind in its various tribes, for his calamity and the wickedness that was inferred from it would be widely known. Comp. what is said by Job of his treatment by the debased races of men about him, ch. xxx. 9 *seq.*; and see a similar statement in Bildad's reply, ch. xviii. 20.

And aforetime I was *as* a tabret.
7 Mine eye also is dim by reason of sorrow,
And all my members *are* as a shadow.
8 Upright *men* shall be astonied at this,
And the innocent shall stir up himself against the hypocrite.
9 The righteous also shall hold on his way,
And he that hath clean hands shall be stronger and stronger.

aforetime I was as a tabret] Rather as above; lit. *I am* (must be) *a spitting-in-the-face*. A *tabret* is a timbrel or tambourine (comp. *tabering*, i.e. beating, upon their breasts, Nah. ii. 7); the Heb. word *topheth* (spitting) has been wrongly assumed by the A.V. to be of the same meaning as *toph* (timbrel).

7. The sorrowful condition to which Job was reduced by his afflictions.

8, 9. Effect produced on religious minds by the sight of such sufferings inflicted on the godly. Such moral perversions in the rule of the world "confound" religious men, and rouse their moral indignation against the wicked, who are prosperous; cf. similar thoughts Ps. xxxvii. 1 *seq.*, lxxiii. 2 *seq.* The word *this* refers to Job's case as an instance of the moral wrong that is observed in the rule of the world. On "hypocrite," i.e. *godless*, see ch. viii. 13.

9. *The righteous also shall hold on*] Or, **But the righteous shall hold on**. The righteous will not allow themselves to be misled from the path of rectitude by these moral wrongs which they see prevail in God's rule of the world, they will cling in spite of them to their righteous life. Nay such obscurities and wrongs will but make the joy which they possess in righteousness the dearer and deeper, and instead of faltering they will be (rather, **will wax**) stronger and stronger. Though Job speaks here in the name of the "righteous" and "clean of hands" it is his own sentiments and resolution that he gives expression to, and the passage is perhaps the most surprising and lofty in the Book. In ch. xix. 25 Job, conscious of his innocence and assured by his heart that he is a God-fearing man, is enabled to reach out his hand to grasp what must yet in the future be the solution of the riddle of his present life. And, no doubt, a similar thought precedes the present passage (ch. xvi. 18 *seq.*). It does not appear, however, that this thought is present to his mind here. Rather he is again completely enveloped in the darkness of his present life, the awful problem of which confounds him and all religious men. But no mysteries or wrongs shall make him falter in the way of righteousness. And the human spirit rises to the height of moral grandeur, when it proclaims its resolution to hold on the way of righteousness independently both of men and God.

10—16. Final repudiation by Job of the false hopes of recovery which the friends held out to him. He knows better, *his* hope is in the grave.

But *as for* you all, do you return, and come now: 10
For I cannot find *one* wise *man* among you.
My days are past, 11
My purposes are broken off,
Even the thoughts of my heart.
They change the night into day: 12
The light *is* short, because of darkness.

Turning with a last word to his friends Job bids them renew as often as they chose their attempts to explain his condition, they should only shew themselves ignorant and incapable (*v.* 10). The hopes they held out were vain; his days were at an end and all the enterprises and dearest purposes of his life for ever broken off (*vv.* 11, 12). His hope was in the grave, where alone he would find rest (*vv.* 13—16).

10. *do ye return, and come*] Job bids them renew, if they please, their attempts to solve his problem or deal with his case; as often as they did so they only revealed their incapacity and foolishness.

for I cannot find one wise man] Rather, **I shall not find.** Their renewed attempts would have no better success than their former ones, they would be found by Job as foolish as before.

11. Very different from their delusive anticipations was the truth in regard to Job's condition. His days were past, and his life with all its cherished purposes cut off. The *thoughts* of his heart is lit. as margin, *the possessions*, i.e. the enterprises and purposes which he cherished and clung to as that dearest to him.

12. This verse appears to be a description by Job of the delusive and foolish proceeding of his friends.

They change the night into day] The night of calamity and death in which Job is enveloped and into which he is entering more deeply they change into the day of life and renewed prosperity. While in truth the shadows of the final night encompass Job the friends are for ever pretending that the bright day of restoration is going to dawn (cf. ch. v. 17 *seq.*, viii. 20 *seq.* &c.). The second clause of the verse is obscure.

the light is short because of darkness] The meaning of the A. V. is not easy to perceive. The words most naturally continue Job's account of the representations of his friends, and express what they hold out. The fair literal rendering is either, *the light is near the face of darkness;* or, *the light is nearer than the face of darkness.* The *light*, the same as the "day" of the first clause, is life and prosperity; this the friends make out to be near, close upon, the face of darkness—Job's present condition of affliction. The other translation, "nearer than the face of darkness," gives a fuller sense to the phrase *face of darkness.* By this expression Job means the darkness of death, whose face was visible and manifest, so close was it upon him.

13—15. The natural sense and connexion of these verses is as follows:

13.   If I wait for the grave as mine house;
       If I have spread my bed in the darkness;

13 If I wait, the grave *is* mine house:
    I have made my bed in the darkness.
14 I have said to corruption, Thou *art* my father:
    To the worm, *Thou art* my mother, and my sister.
15 And where *is* now my hope?
    As for my hope, who shall see it?
16 They shall go down *to* the bars of the pit,
    When *our* rest together *is* in the dust.

  14. If I have said to the pit, thou art my father,
    To the worm, thou art my mother, and my sister:
  15. Where then is my hope?
    And as for my hope, who shall see it?

 13. *If I wait, the grave*] Rather as above. The *grave* is in Heb. *Sheol*, the place of the departed. The word *wait* is the same as *hope*, *v.* 15.

 14. *to corruption*] Rather as above, **the pit**, or grave, Ps. xvi. 10. The words father, mother and sister, expressing the nearest relationship, indicate how closely Job now feels himself connected with the grave, he wholly belongs to it, and he greets it as taking the place of all related to him on earth.

 15. If in fact and in his own feeling Job so surely belongs to death, where is the brilliant hope which his friends hold out, and who shall ever see such a hope realized? or, who can perceive a trace of it? His hope in truth is another (*v.* 13).

 16. The truth in regard to his hope is this, something different from the tale of his friends,

    It shall go down to the bars of the pit,
    When once there is rest in the dust.

The *pit* is in Heb. *Sheol*. As a great subterranean prison-house it has bars or bolts, for it has also gates, ch. xxxviii. 17; cf. Is. xxxviii. 10, Ps. ix. 13. In the New Test. its "keys" are spoken of, Rev. i. 18. The word *together* means perhaps, "at the same time"; his hope shall go down to the grave, when at the same time, or, "when once" he himself finds rest in the dust.

See the Additional Note to ch. xix. in the Appendix.

CH. XVIII. THE SECOND SPEECH OF BILDAD.

 Eliphaz with more inwardness than his fellows had made the punishment of the sinner to come greatly from his own conscience (ch. xv. 20 *seq.*, cf. Job's reply as to himself ch. xvi. 12); Bildad attributes it to the order of nature and the moral instinct of mankind, both of which rise up against the sinner (ch. xviii.); while Zophar, with a certain variation on both views, explains it from the retributive operation of sin itself (ch. xx). Interesting points of contact may be observed between these views and the first speeches of the three friends.

Then answered Bildad the Shuhite, and said, 18
How long *will it be ere* you make an end of words? 2
Mark, and afterwards we will speak.

Several things in Job's last discourse deeply offended Bildad :—
1. Job had used very hard words regarding his friends; he had called them annoying comforters (ch. xvi. 2) and scorners (ch. xvi. 20), and complained of being beset by their illusory mockeries (ch. xvii. 2); and said that God had sent blindness and want of understanding upon them, and that there was not one wise man among them (ch. xvii. 4—10).

But he had gone further. He had appeared to regard himself and them in their treatment of him as types of two classes—himself as the type of the "upright" and "innocent" and "clean of hands" (ch. xvii. 8, 9), exposed to the contumely and spitting of the "peoples," the "godless" (ch. xvii. 6—8) and the ruthless (ch. xvii. 5).

2. Then he spoke impiously of God, saying that He tore him in His anger (ch. xvi. 9), and appealed to the earth and nature to rise up on his side (ch. xvi. 18).

Such things provoke the personal and moral indignation of Bildad alike. It seems to him that Job holds his brethren and him little higher than the beasts (although it was Job himself that was destitute of understanding), and that in his extravagant self-righteousness he flings them away from him as belonging to the class of the "unclean" (*vv.* 2—3).

And it is not God that tears him in His anger; rather in his outrageous fury he is tearing himself. And does he suppose, as his appeal to the earth might suggest, that the eternal flow of law and order in the universe is to be interrupted for his sake—that he may be reputed innocent, or that being guilty he may not suffer the penalty of his evil, and that his principles may prevail? (*v.* 4).

This question naturally leads over to the principal theme of the discourse, the certainty of the destruction of the wicked through the operation of the fixed order of the world and the moral instincts of mankind (*v.* 5—21).

ere you make an end of words] Rather, **how long will ye hunt for words**, lit. *set snares for words*. Bildad begins with the same exclamation of impatient astonishment that he used on a former occasion, ch. viii. 2, *how long? quousque tandem abutere patientia nostra?* By "hunting for words" he means making subtle and artificial attempts at finding arguments—which were only words. He probably refers to the distinctions which Job, in wrestling with his great problem, drew between God and God, and his appeals to the one against the other. Such things seem subtleties to Bildad and but the theme of speakers; man's destiny in the world of God is a thing of more solid stuff, and its principles not so intangible.

mark, and afterwards] Rather, **understand**. Bildad gives back Job's words, 'Thou hast hid their heart from understanding, ch. xvii. 4. It was not they but he that was without wisdom, and until he came to some admission of first principles talking was of little avail. In

> Wherefore are we counted as beasts,
> *And* reputed vile in your sight?
> He teareth himself in his anger:
> Shall the earth be forsaken for thee?
> And shall the rock be removed out of his place?

answering Job Bildad uses here the plur. *ye,* with reference no doubt to Job's identifying himself with the class of righteous sufferers persecuted by the wicked, ch. xvii. 6 *seq.*

The circumstances of the Author's time perhaps shine out through these allusions—the collision of classes, the conflicting claims of parties to represent the true people of God, and the diverse solutions which various minds sought for the hard problem of the national affliction, which turned the servant of the Lord over into the hands of the wicked (ch. xvi. 11) and made him the servant of rulers (Is. xlix. 7).

3. *and reputed vile*] lit. *and are unclean.* Bildad describes what Job's treatment of his friends suggests to him as Job's idea of them. The reference is to the passages, ch. xvii. 4, 10, and the words "clean of hands" ch. xvii. 9, which Job had used of himself and other unjustly persecuted men, cf. Ps. lxxiii. 22.

4. The first clause must be rendered in English,

> Thou who tearest thyself in thine anger.

The Heb. uses in preference the objective form, *One who teareth himself in his anger,* shall the earth be forsaken for thee? See on ch. xii. 4. The words refer to ch. xvi. 9—it is not God who tears him, it is Job who tears himself in his insensate passion, cf. ch. v. 2.

shall the earth be forsaken] i.e. depopulated and made a wilderness, where no man dwells; Lev. xxvi. 43; Is. vi. 12, vii. 16. The desolation of the earth, which God has not created a waste but made to be inhabited (Is. xlv. 18), and the removal of the fixed rock from its place, are figures which mean, overturning the fixed moral order of the universe established by God. Bildad asks if the current of the moral order of the world is to be interrupted or turned back for Job's sake, that he may escape the imputation of wickedness, or the penalty of it, and that his principles may be accepted? cf. ch. xvi. 18.

5—21. The disastrous end of the wicked, in the moral order of the world, is certain.

The last verse naturally led over to this idea, which is the theme of the speech. The idea is set out in a great variety of graphic figures, and the speech is studded with sententious and proverbial sayings in the manner of the speaker's first discourse (ch. viii). The history of the wicked man's downfall is followed through all its stages:—

vv. 5—7. The principle—the sinner's light goes out.
vv. 8—11. The progress of his downfall.
vv. 12—14. The final scenes.
vv. 15—17. The extinction of his race and name.
vv. 18—21. Men's horror of his fate and memory.

Yea, the light of the wicked shall be put out, 5
And the spark of his fire shall not shine.
The light shall be dark in his tabernacle, 6
And his candle shall be put out with him.
The steps of his strength shall be straitened, 7
And his own counsel shall cast him down.
For he is cast into a net by his own feet, 8
And he walketh upon a snare.
The grin shall take *him* by the heel, 9
And the robber shall prevail against him.

5—7. The principle—the sinner's light goes out. The word *yea* means "notwithstanding"—in spite of Job's struggling against the law, the law remains and verifies itself universally. The bright beacon light on the sinner's tent goes out, and the cheerful flame on his hearth shines no more. His home is desolate. The word "light" lends itself in all languages for such general use, as the Arab proverb says, Fate has put out my light—extinguished my prosperity. The picture here however is scarcely to be so generalized.

6. *his candle shall be put out with him*] The meaning is either: his lamp shall be put out over him, the idea being that it was hung in his dwelling above him or shone upon him, cf. ch. xxix. 3, "when God's lamp shined upon my head"; or, his lamp shall be put out to him, the prep. being the same reflexive, untranslateable word referred to on ch. xiv. 22.

7. Another figure for the same thought. His firm, wide steps of prosperity and security, when he walked in a wide place (Ps. iv. 1), become narrowed and hampered. Widening of the steps is a usual Oriental figure for the bold and free movements of one in prosperity, as straitening of them is for the constrained and timid action of one in adversity, cf. Prov. iv. 12 and Ps. xviii. 36. The figure hardly describes the consequences of the sinner's light going out, it is rather independent and parallel to that figure. Cf. ch. xiii. 27.

his own counsel] The evil principles that guide his conduct, ch. x. 3, Ps. i. 1. These inevitably lead him into calamity, cf. ch. iv. 8.

8—11. All things hasten on his ruin; the moral order of the world is such that wherever he moves or touches upon it it becomes a snare to seize him. "Snares" do not mean temptations, they are hidden instruments of destruction that seize and hold the hunted creature. His "counsel," and his own feet (*v.* 8), his evil nature and its outcome, his evil conduct, carry him into these snares—laid for wickedness in the constitution of things.

9. *the robber shall prevail*] Rather, **the trap layeth hold of him**, as all the verbs in this passage should be put in the present tense. The word is that occurring ch. v. 5. The world of God is one network of snares for the wicked man, he walks upon snares, in the field and in the way alike. The idea that the world is a moral constitution

10   The snare *is* laid for him in the ground,
     And a trap for him in the way.
11   Terrors shall make him afraid on every side,
     And shall drive him to his feet.
12   His strength shall be hunger-bitten,
     And destruction *shall be* ready at his side.
13   It shall devour the strength of his skin:
     Even the firstborn of death shall devour his strength.
14   His confidence shall be rooted out of his tabernacle,
     And it shall bring him to the king of terrors.

is very prominent in the Old Testament, a mere physical constitution of things is an idea unknown to it.

11. This verse does not seem to give a picture of the sinner's conscience, but rather of his consciousness at last. The preceding verses described how he walked on snares unwitting that they were there; now he awakens to the perception of his condition, he feels the complications that surround him, and would flee from the terrors that he has come to realize.

and shall drive him to his feet] Rather, **and drive him away at his heels.** A spectral host of terrors pursue close behind him.

12—14. The closing scenes in three steps: his strength is weakened; his body consumed by a terrible disease; he is led away to the dark king.

12. *hunger-bitten*] A word formed like "frost-bitten," "canker-bit" (Lear, v. 3). The word literally means "hungry," and the figure expresses the idea that his strength shall diminish and become feeble, as one does that is famished; cf. a similar strong figure, Joel i. 12, "Joy is withered away from the sons of men." On the figure in the second clause cf. ch. xv. 23.

13. The verse reads,
    It shall devour the members of his body,
    Even the firstborn of death shall devour his members.

The subject *it* in clause one is the "firstborn of death" in clause two; cf. a similar construction, Judg. v. 20, "they fought from heaven, the stars in their courses fought against Sisera". "Members of his body" is literally the *pieces* ("parts" ch. xli. 12) *of his skin.* The firstborn of death is the strongest child of death (Gen. xlix. 3); or else, less naturally, the "deadliest death," cf. firstborn of the poor (=the very poorest) Is. xiv. 30; in any case the phrase means the most terrible and fatal disease. The Arabs call deadly diseases "daughters of destiny"—destiny, as the bacchanal fatalist sings,
    Ordained for us and we ordained for it.

14. The meaning is,
    He shall be plucked out of his tent wherein he trusted,
    And he shall be brought to the king of terrors.

It shall dwell in his tabernacle, because *it is* none of his: 5
Brimstone shall be scattered upon his habitation.
His roots shall be dried up beneath, 16
And above shall his branch be cut off.
His remembrance shall perish from the earth, 17
And he shall have no name in the street.
He shall be driven from light into darkness, 18
And chased out of the world.

In the phrase "his tent wherein he trusted" Bildad goes back to his former figure of the sinner's house which he grasps to maintain himself, ch. viii. 15. The "king of terrors" is death. In Ps. xlix. 14 a somewhat different figure is employed, that of a shepherd: The wicked "like sheep are put in Sheol, Death herds them," cf. Is. xxviii. 15. Death is personified as *rex tremendus*, Virg. *Geo.* IV. 469 (Hitzig); there is no reference to Satan, who has rule in the realm of death, Heb. ii. 14, nor to any mythical personage like the Pluto of classical antiquity. The last scenes of the sinner's fate have been described: he sought to flee from terrors, he is brought at last to the king of them. Then the fate of those belonging to him is stated.

15—17. The extinction of his name and race.
15. The sense probably is,

> There shall dwell in his tent they that are not his,
> Brimstone shall be showered upon his habitation.

So Conant excellently. The two clauses of the verse are not to be taken logically together, they describe the destiny awaiting the sinner's possessions and dwelling under different conceptions—in the one case they pass into the hands of strangers, in the other they are accursed of God, like Sodom, (Gen. xix. 24) and Edom (Is. xxxiv. 9 *seq.*), and overwhelmed with a rain of brimstone from heaven.

16. *shall his branch be cut off*] Rather, **his branches shall wither**, see on ch. xiv. 2. The tree is not a figure for the sinner as a single person, but as the centre of a family, widely ramified and firmly established (his roots), and numerous (his branches). These all perish with him, cf. Bildad's former plant-life lore, ch. viii. 11 *seq.*, 16 *seq.*

17. *perish from the earth*] Rather, **from the land**.
in the street] Rather, **on the face of the earth**. The word means the outlying places (marg. to ch. v. 10), as opposed to the cultivated land, and "earth" as a word expressing wideness and distance seems nearest here.

18—20. Men's horror of his fate and memory.
Bildad now introduces the moral instinct of mankind and the part it takes in the sinner's downfall. The words go back somewhat on the ideas of the previous verses.

18 *He shall be driven*] lit. *they shall drive* (or, they drive) *him*. The subject is mankind, men; and the sinner himself is referred to, hardly, his name (*v.* 17).

19 He shall neither have son nor nephew among his people,
   Nor *any* remaining in his dwellings.
20 They that come after *him* shall be astonied at his day,
   As they that went before were affrighted.
21 Surely such *are* the dwellings of the wicked,
   And this *is* the place *of him that* knoweth not God.

19. *son nor nephew*] i.e. son nor *grandson*. So the word *nephew* (Lat *nepos*, through Fr. *neveu*) means in the English of the time—

> O thou most aunceint grandmother of all,
> Why suffredst thou thy nephews dear to fall.
>   Spens. *Fa. Q.* 1. 5. 22,

(Michie, *Bible Words and Phrases*). In Gen. xxi. 23 the word is rendered *son's son*. The Heb. expression is more general, he shall neither have *offspring nor descendant*.

20. *They that come after him*] The word "him" must be omitted; the expression refers to the later generations of men, as *they that went before* does to the earlier, those nearer the sinner's day, but, of course, both expressions describe generations living *after* the wicked man. Others take the two phrases to mean, *they of the West*, and *they of the East*. In the one case the idea is that men's horror of his memory and fate is eternal, lasting through all generations; in the other that it is universal,—both in the West and in the East. His *day* is the day of his downfall, Ps. xxxvii. 13; Jer. l. 27. Job had complained that he was made a "byword of the peoples" ch. xvii. 6; Bildad, with a singular hardness, rejoins, It is true, the deep moral instinct of mankind rises up against such a man.

Ch. XIX. Job's Reply to Bildad.

Bildad wrote under the picture which he had drawn, *these are the habitations of the wicked*, and held it up before Job. It was meant for him, for all that is specific in it is borrowed from the circumstances of his case. The terrible distemper, the "firstborn of death," that consumes the sinner's limbs, is too plain an allusion to his leprosy to be misunderstood by him (*v.* 13). The brimstone that burns up the sinner's habitation (*v.* 15), though there may lie in it a distant reference to the cities of the plain, is also the fire of God that fell on Job's cattle and their keepers (ch. i. 16). The tree dried up at the roots and withered in the branches (*v.* 16) reminds Job easily enough of his own wasted state and of the sad calamities that had blighted his home. The horror and detestation of men (*v.* 20) is but a picture of what was passing before the eyes of the disputants, and is a touch of ruthless severity, which brings Job utterly to the dust; for while in his former speech (ch. xvi.—xvii.) he is able in the strong sense of his innocence to resent the treatment of men he is here wholly broken by it (ch. xix. 21). Every sentence of Bildad's speech carries with it the charge, Thou art the man.

Then Job answered and said, 19
  How long will ye vex my soul, 2
  And break me in pieces with words?

Against this application Job's whole soul protests. Yet he realizes from Bildad's words, more clearly than ever he had done before, his dreary isolation, God and men being alike estranged from him, which he laments in most pathetic words. But so profound and unalterable is his consciousness of his innocence, that at the moment when he has entered step after step into the thickest darkness he makes a sudden leap out into the light, and rises by an inspiration, whether from above or from the depths of the human spirit, to the assurance that his innocence shall yet be revealed, that God will yet publicly appear for him, and that he shall see God—and he melts away, overcome by the joyful anticipation.

The order of thought is well marked:—

First, *vv.* 2—6, some preliminary words, as usual, of a personal kind, though these are here fewer, the speaker's mind being filled with greater things. He gives brief expression to his impatience of his friends' diatribes, and repudiates the inferences they drew from his calamities: his calamities were due to God, who had perverted his right.

Second, *vv.* 7—27. This reference to God leads over to the theme of the whole chapter, which is nothing but God. The sufferer's mind wrestles with his thought of God—the thought of Him as the author of his present terrible fate, from which he rises by a sudden revulsion to the thought of Him as One who must yet appear as his vindicator and joy. This part has three steps:—

1. *vv.* 7—12. A dark picture of the desertion of God and His terrible hostility to him.

2. *vv.* 13—22. Then even a more touching complaint of the alienation of men from him—which God has caused.

3. *vv.* 23—27. Hopeless in the present he turns his eye to the future. He desires that his protest of innocence might find indelible record in the rock, that the generations to come might read it. Yet how small a thing that would be to *him*, whose chief sorrow lay in the alienation of God from his spirit. He shall have more. He *knows* that God shall yet appear to vindicate him, and that he shall see Him with his eyes—in peace.

Third, *vv.* 28—29. Finally he adds a brief threat to his friends.

JOB, FORSAKEN OF GOD AND MEN, AND WITHOUT HOPE IN THIS LIFE, RISES TO THE ASSURANCE THAT GOD WILL YET APPEAR TO VINDICATE HIM, AND THAT HIS EYES SHALL SEE HIM ON HIS SIDE IN JOY.

2—5. Job expresses his impatience of his friends' words; and repudiates the inferences of his guilt which they draw from his calamities, declaring that his calamities are due to the unjust dealing of God.

2. There is more than impatience expressed in the words *vex* (afflict) and "break in pieces"; the words suggest the crushing effect which the friends' insinuations of wickedness had on Job's spirit.

3   These ten times have ye reproached me:
    You are not ashamed *that* you make yourselves strange
      to me.
4   And be it indeed *that* I have erred,
    Mine error remaineth with myself.
5   If indeed ye will magnify *yourselves* against me,
    And plead against me my reproach:
6   Know now that God hath overthrown me,
    And hath compassed me with his net.
7   Behold, I cry out *of* wrong, but I am not heard:
    I cry aloud, but *there is* no judgment.
8   He hath fenced up my way that I cannot pass,

3. *Ten* times is a round number for *often*, Gen. xxxi. 7; Numb. xiv. 22.

make yourselves strange to me] An expression of uncertain meaning, as the word does not occur again, unless, as some suppose, it be found in Is. iii. 9. The meaning may be, *ye wrong me*, the root having some resemblance to an Arabic verb rendered by Lane "to wrong," also "to be persistent in contention." Ew., *ye are unfeeling towards me*.

4. In this verse Job must mean to repudiate the offences insinuated against him. The precise force of the second clause, however, is obscure. It might mean, "my error is my own and no matter for your intermeddling"; or, "I alone am conscious of it and you can know nothing regarding it,"—in either case a mere passing rejection of the charges of his friends. Or, "had I indeed sinned my error would remain with myself, I should be conscious of it," cf. ch. ix. 36. Ewald's idea that the "error" which Job alludes to is his mistaken hope of judgment and righteousness on God's part is less suitable to the connexion.

5. If his friends mean in earnest to found inferences on his calamities then he will tell them that it is *God* who hath brought these on him unjustly (*v.* 6).

6. *Know now*] Or, as we say, *know then*. The word *God* is emphatic.

overthrown me] More probably, **perverted my right** (*v.* 7); this, not his guilt, is the explanation of his afflictions. By his reference to the "net" of God Job repudiates the statements of Bildad, ch. xviii. 8 *seq.*; it was not his own feet that led him into the net, God had thrown it about him.

7—12. God's hostility to him and destructive persecution of him.

In *v.* 6 the transition is already made to the account of God's hostility. The picture is sufficiently graphic. First there was the general feeling of being entangled, as a creature snared.

7. This drew from him in his helplessness cries of wrong, which were unheeded.

8. No outgo or escape was possible, for there rose a wall before

And he hath set darkness in my paths.
He hath stript me of my glory, 9
And taken the crown *from* my head.
He hath destroyed me on every side, and I am gone: 10
And mine hope hath he removed like a tree.
He hath also kindled his wrath against me, 11
And he counteth me unto him as *one of* his enemies.
His troops come together, 12
And raise up their way against me,
And encamp round about my tabernacle.
He hath put my brethren far from me, 13
And mine acquaintance are verily estranged from me.
My kinsfolk have failed, 14

him if he would move; neither was there any outlook, for thick darkness fell close about him. These images are common to express the extremest perplexity.

9. Then came the consciousness of the meaning of his calamities—they were evidence that he was a transgressor. God took thus his crown of righteousness from his head, and stripped the glory of godliness from him, cf. ch. xxix. 14.

10. *He hath destroyed*] Rather, **he breaketh me down**; the figure of a building. In the second clause the image is that of a great tree torn up by the roots, whose fall is pitiful. The words, *and I am gone*, refer to his inevitable death from his disease, which he regards as already virtually come, as is expressed in the next clause—his hope (of life or recovery) is removed like a tree.

11—12. Figures of hostile assault; God directs charge after charge of His army against Him. The reference is to his afflictions, cf. ch. x. 17.

12. *raise up their way*] i.e. cast up a way or high bank on which to advance againt the beleaguered fort or city.

13—19. The estrangement and abhorrence of men.

Job's complaint now is even more touching than before: God not only afflicted him with trouble but removed far from him all human sympathy. And there is something more breaking to the heart in the turning away of men from us than in the severest sufferings. It crushes us quite. We steel ourselves against it for a time and rise to it in bitterness and resentment, but gradually it breaks us and we are crushed at last. And this seems the way whether men frown on us with justice or no. And there came on Job when he contemplated his complete casting off by men, by his friends and his household and even by the little children, a complete break-down, and he cries, Pity me, O ye my friends (*v.* 21). This alienation of men was universal:—

13—14. First, his relations outside his own immediate circle and his acquaintances stood aloof from him.

And my familiar friends have forgotten me.
15 They that dwell in mine house, and my maidens,
Count me for a stranger:
I am an alien in their sight.
16 I called my servant, and he gave *me* no answer;
I intreated him with my mouth.
17 My breath is strange to my wife,
Though I intreated for the children's *sake* of mine *own* body.

15—16. Then those unrelated to him within his house, the menials and slaves. Those who, as Oriental servants, used to be subservient and observant of the slightest sign from their master (Ps. cxxiii. 2)—these "ducking observants" now refuse to answer when he calls, and must be besought for their service. Very soon the reflection of one's fall is thrown from the countenances of those higher in rank down upon the faces of the servants, where it shows itself without any delicacy or reserve. Verse 16 reads, *I call my servant and he giveth me no answer: I must entreat him with my mouth.*

17. Once more, if possible an acuter misery—he is become intolerable to those most dear to him.

though I intreated] Perhaps, **and I am loathsome to the children of**—. The word as known in Heb. means *to be gracious to, to pity* (*v.* 21), in the simple form (here), and *to seek favour to oneself*, or *beseech*, in the reflexive (*v.* 16), but the simple form has nowhere the meaning of "beseech" or entreat. The Arab. has a root of the same spelling, which means to smell badly, *to stink*,—a sense parallel to the meaning of the first clause, where "strange" means *offensive*.

The last words of the verse "children of mine own body" are difficult; they mean literally, *children of my womb*. The word usually rendered *womb* is used occasionally of the father, Ps. cxxxii. 11; Mic. vi. 7. The Prologue narrates the death of Job's children, and the same assumption is made in the Poem, ch. viii. 4, xxix. 5, and it is not to be thought that another mode of representation appears here. In *vv.* 15—16, however, Job has still maids and servants, though his servants are represented in the Prologue as having perished. As he has other servants he might have other children. These might be children of concubines, as Job lived in the patriarchal age, though no allusion is made to such connexions, and the references to his wife are of such a kind as to suggest that Job lived in a state of strict monogamy. Or the expression "children of my body" might be used somewhat loosely to mean grandchildren—children of his sons. The impression conveyed by the Prologue is that the seven sons were unmarried, though this is left uncertain. Others consider the phrase "children of my womb" to mean, children of my mother—children of the same womb with myself.

18. Another affecting touch—the little children mock his ineffectual attempts to rise from the ground.

Yea, young children despised me; 18
I arose, and they spake against me.
All my inward friends abhorred me: 19
And they whom I loved are turned against me.
My bone cleaveth to my skin and to my flesh, 20
And I am escaped with the skin of my teeth.
Have pity upon me, have pity upon me, O ye my friends; 21
For the hand of God hath touched me.
Why do ye persecute me as God, 22
And are not satisfied with my flesh?

children despised] Better, **despise**.

I arose, and they spake] Better, **if I would arise they speak**—they jeer at his painful efforts to rise.

19. *my inward friends*] A fine expression, lit. *the men of my council.* "Inward" means intimate:

"Who is most inward with the royal duke?" *Rich. III.*

The reference is to such as his three friends, men whose high converse and fellowship seemed to Job, as a thoughtful godly man, something almost better than relationship, Ps. lv. 14. See Prelim. Remarks to ch. iii.

abhorred] Better, **abhor**.

20. The desertion and loathing of mankind is universal, and to this is added his exhausted state from disease.

My bone cleaveth to my skin] The words describe his emaciated condition, cf. Lam. iv. 8; Ps. cii. 5, My bones cleave to my skin (marg. *flesh*); Ps. xxii. 17, I may tell (count) all my bones.

escaped with the skin of my teeth] i.e. with nothing else. The "skin of my teeth" is usually held to mean the gums, which Job represents as still sound, otherwise he would be unable to speak; the last stage of his disease has not yet been reached. In *v.* 17 however he referred to his fetid breath, and in such distempers the mouth and throat are usually rapidly affected. Besides, such a sense is prosaic and flat. The phrase is probably proverbial; the meaning of Job being that he is wholly fallen a prey to his disease, cf. Am. iii. 12.

21, 22. Overcome by his sense of the terrible enmity of God, Job piteously cries out for the compassion of men. There is a strong antithesis between "ye my friends" and the "hand of God," "God" (*v.* 22). The whole speech, even when the enmity of men is referred to (*v.* 13 *seq.*), is occupied with the thought of God, He is regarded as the cause of men's abhorrence. Job for a moment seeks refuge with men from God's severity.

22. *satisfied with my flesh*] Why cannot ye be sated with devouring me? The figure is sufficiently plain. In Oriental phrase "to devour or eat the parts or pieces of one" is to calumniate him, to accuse him, Dan. iii. 8, vi. 34. Job asks why they will not cease to bring accusations against him?

23 O that my words were now written!
    O that they were printed in a book!
24 That they were graven with an iron pen and lead
    In the rock for ever!

23—27. Job turns to the future. He desires that his protestation of innocence could find indelible record in the rock, that it might stand a perpetual witness to all generations. But he shall have something greater: he knows that God will yet appear for his vindication, and that he shall see Him with joy.

The passage should probably be read something as follows:

23 Oh now that my words were written,
    Oh that they were inscribed in a book;
24 That with a pen of iron and lead
    They were graven in the rock for ever.
25 But I know that my redeemer liveth,
    And in after time he shall stand upon the dust,
26 And after this my skin is destroyed
    And without my flesh I shall see God:
27 Whom I shall see for myself,
    And mine eyes shall behold and not another—
    My reins consume within me!

In *vv.* 21, 22 Job in his terror of God appealed to his friends for pity, but probably he saw no signs of relenting there. They could not relent; their friend might be dear, but truth and religion were greater. Secure in their principles, their countenances shewed but austere reprobation of their wicked friend. They will be more austere because they are putting down humanity and sacrificing themselves in being austere. And turning from them the desire suddenly seizes Job to make his appeal to posterity, to record in writing his protestation of his innocence, or to grave it in the rock, that when he is gone men might read it to all time. Yet this thought satisfies him but for a moment. Even if the generations to come should pass a more gentle sentence upon him than his own time, being better able to estimate his circumstances and no more warped by the heats of controversy, and more inclined amidst the acknowledged mystery of his life to allow weight to the persistent testimony of his conscience, as that behind which it is impossible to go — even if they should not only mitigate but reverse the judgment of his contemporaries, how small a thing that would be to him. And his mind rebounds from this thought forward to a greater—he *knows* that his redeemer liveth and shall appear for his vindication and peace.

23. *in a book*] The Heb. says in *the book*, using the Art. to indicate the *kind* of record, Ex. xvii. 14; Numb. v. 23; 1 Sam. x. 25. The phrase means merely to "commit to writing." The "words" which Job desires written are not those in *v.* 25 *seq.*, but his general and oft repeated protestations of his innocence.

24. In *v.* 23 Job longed that his words were written. But ordinary writing is perishable. And now he desires that his words were hewn

For I know *that* my Redeemer liveth,   25
And *that* he shall stand *at* the latter *day* upon the earth:

in indelible characters upon the rock. The "lead" was probably run into the traces cut in the stone. It need not be said that "the rock" like "the book" means merely rock, and not any particular rock.

25. *For I know*] Rather, **but** I know. This is now something higher to which his mind rises. He desires no doubt to be vindicated before men, and would wish that all generations to come should know his claim to rectitude, when he no more lived himself to make it (*vv.* 23, 24); but what he desires above all things is that he might see God who now hides His face from him, and meet Him, for the meeting could not but be with joy (cf. ch. xxiii. 6 *seq.*). Job's problem is first of all a problem of religious life, and only in the second place a speculative one. And the speculative elements in it have no further meaning than as they aggravate the practical religious trouble. A solution of his problem, therefore, was possible in only one way, viz. by his seeing God (cf. ch. xlii. 5)—for to see God is to see Him in peace and reconciliation. And it is to grasp the assurance of this that Job's heart now reaches forth its hand.

my Redeemer liveth] "Liveth" means more than *is, exists*. Job uses the word in opposition to himself—he dies but his redeemer lives after him. The term *redeemer* (Heb. *gō'ēl*) is frequently used of God as the deliverer of His people out of captivity, e.g. very often in Is. xl. *seq.* (ch. xlix. 7, 26, liv. 5, 8), and also as the deliverer of individuals from distress, Gen. xlviii. 16; Ps. xix. 14, ciii. 4. Among men the *Goel* was the nearest blood-relation, on whom it lay to perform certain offices in connexion with the deceased whose Goel he was, particularly to avenge his blood, if he had been unjustly slain (Ruth ii. 20, &c.; Numb. xxxv. 19). Job here names God his Goel. The passage stands in close relation with ch. xvi. 18, 19, where he names God his "witness" and "sponsor" or representative. It is probable, therefore, that there is an allusion to the Goel among men—Job has in God a Goel who liveth. This Goel will vindicate his rights against the wrong both of men and God (*vv.* 3, 7). At the same time this vindication is regarded less as an avenging of him, at least on others (though cf. *vv.* 28, 29), than as a manifestation of his innocence. This manifestation can only be made by God's appearing and shewing the true relation in which Job stands to Him, and by Job's seeing God. For his distress lay in God's hiding His face from him, and his redemption must come through his again beholding God in peace. Thus the ideas of Goel and redeemer virtually coincide.

he shall stand at the latter day] To *stand* means to arise and appear, to *come forward* (as a witness, Deut. xix. 15; Ps. xxxvii. 12), or to *interpose* (as a judge, Ps. xii. 5). The word *day* has no place here. The expression "the latter" means either *last* or *later*. It is used of God as the first and the *last* (Is. xliv. 6, xlviii. 12), but also otherwise in a comparative sense, *later, to come, following* (Ps. xlviii. 13, lxxviii. 4; Ecc. iv. 16; Job xviii. 20). Here the word is an epithet of God and

26 And *though* after my skin *worms* destroy this *body*,
Yet in my flesh shall I see God:

can hardly describe Him as the *last*, for Job certainly does not contemplate his vindication being put off till the end of all things. The expression is parallel to "my Goel" in the first clause, and literally rendered, means: and he who cometh after (me) shall stand; or, and as one who cometh after (me) he shall stand. The trans., *in after time he shall stand*, is nearly equivalent. Ewald and other high authorities render, *an afterman*, i.e. a vindicator.

upon the earth] Better, *the dust*. The word does not mean earth in opposition to heaven; such an antithesis did not need to be expressed; if God came forward or interposed in Job's behalf He must do so upon the earth. The word "dust" carries rather an allusion to the earth as that wherein Job shall have been laid before God shall appear for him —the same allusion as is carried in the words "Goel" and "he who cometh after me;" cf. ch. vii. 21, xvii. 16, xx. 11, xxi. 26, &c.

26. *and* though *after my skin* worms *destroy*] See trans. above. The word *destroy* means *to break off*, strike down or off, as branches from a tree (Is. x. 34). The words literally run, *and after my skin which they have destroyed* even *this* (probably pointing to himself). The indeterminate construction *which they have destroyed* is equivalent to our passive, *which has been destroyed*. The Heb. construction must be given somewhat freely in English, as above. The words "worms" and "body" have nothing corresponding in the original.

yet in my flesh] Better, as above, **and without my flesh.** The margin, *out of* (or, *from*) *my flesh*, suggests the explanation how such opposite senses may be arrived at. The Heb. prep. *from* has the same ambiguity as *from* in English. When Regan in *Lear* II. 1 says,

"Our father he hath writ, so hath our sister,
Of differences, which I best thought it fit
To answer from our home,"

her words most naturally perhaps suggest the meaning that she thought it best to answer *at* home, her home being the place from which the answer was sent. Her meaning, however, is that she thought it best to answer when she was *away from* home. Similarly when Job says, from (or, out of) my flesh shall I see God, the meaning may be, that (looking) from his flesh he shall see God, i.e. as A. V. *in* his flesh; or that he shall see God, (when) away from his flesh, i.e. *without* his flesh. The context and general scope of the passage decides for the latter sense. For a similar use of the Heb. prep. see ch. xi. 15, *away from* (=without) *spot*; xxi. 9, margin; xxviii. 4, they hang (far) *away from men*, they swing; cf. Gen. xxvii. 39, away from (without) the fatness; Numb. xv. 24, marg. The whole expression "after this my skin has been destroyed and without my flesh" means "when I have died under the ravages of my disease." The words do not express *in* what condition precisely, but *after* what events Job shall see God.

shall I see God] The connexion is, But I know that my Redeemer liveth, and he who shall be after me shall stand upon the dust, and...

Whom I shall see for myself, 27
And mine eyes shall behold, and not another;
Though my reins be consumed within me.
But ye should say, Why persecute we him? 28
Seeing the root of the matter is found in me;
Be ye afraid of the sword: 29

I shall see God. The last words explain who Job's Redeemer or Goel is, and who He is who remaineth or shall come after him, viz. God. After his skin is destroyed and without his flesh he shall see God. Before death he shall not see Him, for he shall die under His afflicting hand (cf. ch. xxiii. 14), but he shall yet behold Him. To *see* God is to see Him reconciled and in peace, for this is implied in seeing Him at all, because now He hides His face (ch. xxiii. 3 *seq.*, 8 *seq.*, ch. xxiv. 1 *seq.*).

27. *Whom I shall see for myself*] These words might mean merely, whom I myself shall see; or, *for myself* may mean, favourable to me, on my side and to my joy.

and not another] i. e. I and not another (shall see). Job heaps up phrases to express his assurance that *he* shall see God, "I shall see for myself," "mine eyes shall behold," "I and not another." The whole of his misery might be expressed in saying that God hid Himself from him, and the whole of his redemption and joy will consist in seeing God. Others take the words "not another," lit. *not a stranger*, to refer to God—whom I shall see not as a stranger, i. e. no more estranged or hostile. The position of the words, however, close beside the phrase "mine eyes," is rather in favour of the other view.

though my reins be consumed] Rather, **my reins consume within me**, lit. *in my bosom* (marg.). The words are an exclamation, meaning *I faint*, cf. Ps. lxxiii. 26, lxxxiv. 2, cxix. 81, 123. The reins are the seat of the deepest feelings and experiences, especially of those toward God. Job began with expressing his assurance that he should see God, but as he proceeds so vivid is his hope that it becomes almost reality, the intensity of his thought creates an ecstatic condition of mind in which the vision of God seems almost realized, and he faints in the presence of it. See Additional Note on ch. xix. 23—27 at the end of the Volume.

28, 29. Brief threat to his three friends. God's appearance, which will bring joy to Job, will carry terror to those who persecute him and fasten false charges of guilt upon him. The language in these verses is in some parts obscure, and there may be faults in the text. Verse 28 reads in connexion with *v.* 29,

> If ye say, How we will pursue him!
> And the root of the matter is found in me:
> Be ye afraid of the sword, &c.

Verse 28 forms the supposition and *v.* 29 states the consequence, the penalty of the conduct referred to on the part of Job's friends. If they shall continue their unjust persecution of him, asserting that the "root

For wrath *bringeth* the punishments of the sword,
That ye may know *there is* a judgment.

of the matter," i.e. the real cause of his afflictions, is found in himself, in his transgressions, then Job warns them that they will bring on themselves the "sword" of Divine vengeance.

29. *for wrath bringeth the punishments of the sword*] This translation seems to assume that "wrath" here is that of men, such wrath as Job's friends shewed towards him. But the word is too strong to be taken in this sense. The Divine "wrath" or fury is meant. The phrase "punishments of the sword" means most naturally, the punishments inflicted by the sword. The whole expression would thus mean, *for wrath* (i.e. in wrath, or, wrathful) *are the punishments of the sword* —the "sword" being as before God's judicial sword. Others render, "*transgressions* of the sword," i.e. such transgressions as bring down the Divine sword; but the phrase "transgressions of the sword are wrath," i.e. have to bear wrath as their reward or chastisement, (Delitzsch) is exceedingly cumbrous.

that...there is a judgment] The reference is not to any final or general judgment, but to the fact that God does in truth judge and punish injustice, such as the friends were guilty of; cf. xiii. 10 *seq*. The translation assumes a form of the relative conjunction *that* which nowhere else occurs in the Book of Job, and there may be some fault in the text. Ewald and others by a slight change of spelling obtain the meaning, *that ye may know the Almighty.*

Ch. XX. Zophar's Second Speech.

Zophar breaks in upon the close of Job's speech with a fiery haste and passionateness not quite easy to account for. No doubt Job had spoken of his friends as persecuting him and devouring his flesh. Then he had turned away from them and appealed to posterity against them (ch. xix. 23 *seq*.). And finally he had threatened them with the sword and judgment of God (ch. xix. 29). These and former reproaches (ch. xvii. 4) may rankle in Zophar's breast, and he may not have forgotten the sarcastic treatment which Job gave his first speech. Perhaps, however, his irritation is due less to personal than to moral reasons. Job's last speech was certainly ill to understand, as it has been found ever since. He had accused God of "wronging" him and being his enemy and with bringing him though innocent to the grave. And yet he had affirmed that he knew that God would vindicate his right after his death, and that he should see Him with his eyes in peace. In all this there seems to Zophar a lack of common understanding. Hence he draws an answer to it out of the "spirit" and "understanding" within himself (*v*. 3). Cf. Elihu's references to his "spirit," ch. xxxii. 8.

Bildad (ch. xviii.) had enlarged upon the certainty of the sinner's downfall from the moral order in the world and the moral sense in men, which rose up against wickedness. Zophar's point is slightly different, it is the brevity of the wicked man's prosperity, which arises from the

Then answered Zophar the Naamathite, and said, 20
  Therefore do my thoughts cause me to answer, 2
  And for *this* I make haste.
  I have heard the check of my reproach, 3
  And the spirit of my understanding causeth me to answer.

fact that wickedness brings about its own retribution—sin, sweet in the mouth, turns into the poison of asps in the belly.

> The Gods are just, and of our pleasant vices
> Make instruments to scourge us.

He illustrates this theme by drawing the picture of a rapacious, oppressive man of power suddenly brought to destruction and destitution in the midst of his days, with the hand of every one that is wretched against him, and forced to disgorge that which he had greedily swallowed. Job may understand that the fable is narrated of him. Zophar is too much of the "plain blunt man"; his meaning is so transparent that he commits himself and his friends into his adversary's hands.

One general idea pervades the speech, the brevity of the wicked man's prosperity.

vv. 2, 3. Zophar, in a brief preface, acknowledges that he is roused.

vv. 4—11. This is because of Job's reproaches, and because he seems unaware of the acknowledged principle that the triumphing of the wicked is brief.

vv. 12—22. Sin brings its own retribution—after the manner of a man's evil doings so is his chastisement.

vv. 23—29. God sates at last with his judgments the sinner's insatiable greed for wrong-doing.

CH. XX. THE PROSPERITY OF THE WICKED IS BRIEF; SIN, SWEET IN THE MOUTH, BECOMES THE POISON OF ASPS IN THE BELLY.

2, 3. Zophar is roused to indignation by Job's perverse blindness to unalterable principles experienced since the world was. The verses should perhaps read,

2. Therefore do my thoughts make answer to me,
  And because of this have I haste within me:
3. I hear the rebuke that putteth me to shame—
  But the spirit out of my understanding answereth me.

The words "therefore" and "because of this" refer to the first clause of *v.* 3.—I hear the rebuke that puts me to shame (i.e. Job's last words), therefore do my thoughts make answer to me, and because of this have I inward haste, i.e. strong feeling. The speaker means that he feels driven to answer Job by the exasperating words of the latter, but he distinguishes between himself and his thoughts and speaks of them answering him. So (*v.* 3) his "spirit" answers him, drawing the answer out of his "understanding." The *answer* furnished to Zophar by his spirit follows *v.* 4 *seq.* The last words of *v.* 2 are lit. "is my

4   Knowest thou *not* this of old,
    Since man was placed upon earth,
5   That the triumphing of the wicked *is* short,
    And the joy of the hypocrite *but* for a moment?
6   Though his excellency mount up to the heavens,
    And his head reach unto the clouds;
7   *Yet* he shall perish for ever like his own dung:
    They which have seen him shall say, Where *is* he?
8   He shall fly away as a dream, and shall not be found:
    Yea, he shall be chased away as a vision of the night.
9   The eye also *which* saw him shall *see him* no more;
    Neither shall his place any more behold him.
10 His children shall *seek to* please the poor,
    And his hands shall restore their goods.

haste within me;" cf. their cord·in them, iv. 21, my help within me, vi. 13. The word "check" in A. V. *v.* 3 means *reproof;*

"Now, by my life,
Old fools are babes again; and must be used
With checks, as flatteries."   *Lear*, I. 3.
"Check'd like a bondman; all his faults observed."
                                    J. Caesar, IV. 3.

4—10. The prosperity of the wicked is brief.

4. *Knowest thou not this of old*] i.e. knowest thou not this to be or to have been of old, lit. *from for ever*. "This" which is from of old and from the time man has been upon the earth is the fact that the felicity of the wicked is brief (*v.* 5). On "hypocrite" see ch. viii. 13.

6. *his excellency*] Or, *his height*, or rising up (Ps. lxxxix. 9); cf. Is. xiv. 13—15, Obad. *v.* 4.

7. *like his own dung*] Zophar is not the most refined of the three, cf. 2 Kings ix. 37. On the last words of the verse cf. ch. xiv. 10.

8. *as a dream*] Comp. Ps. lxxiii. 20, "As a dream when one awaketh; so, O Lord, when thou awakest thou shalt despise their image"; Is. xxix. 8, of the enemies of Israel.

9. See ch. vii. 8—10; viii. 18; Ps. ciii. 16.

10. *His children shall seek to please*] Or, *seek the favour of.* The margin is possible, The poor shall oppress his children, but less suitable.

restore their goods] Rather, **his goods**. He shall give back his wealth which he has gotten by unlawful and violent means. The first clause of *v.* 10 is closely connected with *v.* 9, and paints the abject condition of the sinner's children after his death; the second clause of *v.* 10 and *v.* 11 return to the idea of the sinner's destruction and assume that he is in life.

His bones are full *of the sin of* his youth, 11
Which shall lie down with him in the dust.
Though wickedness be sweet in his mouth, 12
Though he hide it under his tongue;
Though he spare it, and forsake it not; 13
But keep it still within his mouth:
Yet his meat in his bowels is turned, 14
It is the gall of asps within him.
He hath swallowed down riches, and he shall vomit them 15
   up again:
God shall cast them out of his belly.
He shall suck the poison of asps: 16
The viper's tongue shall slay him.
He shall not see the rivers, 17
The floods, the brooks of honey and butter.
That which he laboured for shall he restore, and shall not 18
   swallow *it* down:

11. *full of the sin of his youth*] Rather, **his bones are full of his youth, but it shall lie down,** &c.; in the midst of his years, when his bones are full of his youthful strength, like a vigorous marrow, he shall be cut off, and his youth go down to the grave with him.

12—22. His sin changes into his punishment.

12. Sin is spoken of under the figure of a dainty which tickles the palate, and which one retains and turns in his mouth with delight.

13. *forsake it not*] i.e. *do not let it go*—do not swallow it.

14. *is turned*] i.e. is changed,—it becomes the poison of asps in his belly.

15. The same general figure of a delightful food particularized. The ill-gotten riches which he amassed do not abide with him; the wealth that he swallowed up he must disgorge. The figure is perhaps that of a food which the stomach cannot retain.

16. A slight change of the figure. The meaning is: that which he sucks shall prove the poison of asps.

17—22. That long time of enjoyment which he promised himself shall never come; according to his insatiable lust and greed shall be his utter destitution at last.

17. *the floods, the brooks of honey*] The marg. *the streaming brooks* is unnecessary. The words "honey and butter" apply both to "floods" (streams) and brooks. The figure is common for fulness of blessings. Cf. Ex. iii. 8, "A land flowing with milk and honey."

18. *That which he laboured for*] i.e. that which he has acquired—the fruit of his labour; this he shall restore and shall not swallow down, or enjoy.

According to *his* substance *shall* the restitution *be*, and he shall not rejoice *therein*.
19 Because he hath oppressed *and* hath forsaken the poor;
Because he hath violently taken away a house which he builded not;
20 Surely he shall not feel quietness in his belly,
He shall not save of that which he desired.
21 *There shall* none of his meat *be* left;
Therefore shall no *man* look for his goods.
22 In the fulness of his sufficiency he shall be in straits:
Every hand of the wicked shall come *upon* him.
23 *When* he is about to fill his belly,

according to his substance] This half verse reads: according to the wealth which he has gotten he shall not rejoice, lit. *according to the wealth of his exchange* (cf. ch. xv. 31). The meaning is, however great the substance be which by his evil he has acquired he shall not have the joy of it he promised himself.
The following verses read most naturally,
19. Because he hath oppressed and forsaken the poor,
The house which he hath violently taken away he shall not build up;
20. Because he hath known no rest in his belly,
He shall not deliver himself with that wherein he delighteth;
21. There was nothing left that he devoured not,
Therefore his good shall not abide.

19. *and hath forsaken*] Abandoned them, after oppressing them, to their destitution. Thus, though joining house to house (Is. v. 8) and dispossessing the poor, the houses which he robs he shall not build up—as Is. says, Many houses shall be desolate, even great and fair without inhabitant (ch. v. 9).

20. *quietness in his belly*] Rather as above. The belly is the seat of appetite; the words mean, because he felt and displayed a restless insatiable greediness.

21. *his goods*] This may mean his prosperity. In all these verses the retribution corresponds to the sin—the insatiable greediness is recompensed by utter loss and want.

22. In the moment of his great abundance his straitness comes suddenly upon him.

every hand of the wicked] Rather, **of the wretched** (ch. iii. 20, him that is in misery). All those in destitution, and the lawless, both those whom he has oppressed and those perhaps who make common cause with them, shall rise up against him and make him their prey. The picture is similar to that drawn by Eliphaz, ch. v. 5.

23—29. His insatiable greed shall be satisfied at last. God shall fill him full of his judgments.

God shall cast the fury of his wrath upon him,
And shall rain *it* upon him while he is eating.
He shall flee from the iron weapon, 24
And the bow of steel shall strike him through.
It is drawn, and cometh out of the body; 25
Yea, the glistering sword cometh out of his gall:
Terrors *are* upon him.
All darkness *shall be* hid in his secret places: 26
A fire not blown shall consume him;
It shall go ill with him that is left in his tabernacle.
The heaven shall reveal his iniquity; 27
And the earth shall rise up against him.

23. His belly shall be filled!
God shall cast the fury of his wrath upon him,
And shall rain upon him his food.

The food which the sinner shall be sated with is the terrible rain of judgments which God shall shower upon him; cf. Ps. xi. 6, Upon the wicked he shall rain snares, fire and brimstone and a burning tempest: this shall be the portion of their cup.

24. His inevitable destruction: seeking to escape one form of death he shall flee into another. The figure changes. The judgment of God is no more a rain from heaven, it is an attack on all hands of armed inexorable foes; cf. the same idea of inevitable destruction set forth under different figures, Am. v. 19. For bow of *steel* read bow of **brass**.

25. *It is drawn*] Rather, **he draweth it forth**—that is, the arrow (*v.* 24).

the glistering sword] Rather, the glittering **shaft** (Is. xlix. 2), or, more generally, the glittering steel; what is meant is the arrow that strikes the sinner through (*v.* 24). He draws it out hoping to save himself, not knowing that he is mortally stricken, but with the drawing of it out there fall on him the terrors of death. The picture, particularly the last isolated sentence "terrors are upon him," is graphic.

26. All darkness is laid up for his treasures;
A fire not blown shall consume him,
It shall devour him that is left in his tent.

"Darkness" is a figure for calamity; cf. ch. xv. 22, 23. "Laid up," i.e. reserved, destined, for. "Him that is left" may also mean "that which is left," *v.* 21. A fire "not blown" by mortal breath or man's mouth, but the fire of God, consumes him; or, it may be a fire which kindles itself,—an allusion to the self-avenging nature of sin; cf. ch. xv. 34.

27. Heaven and earth conspire together against the sinner. There may be allusion to Job's appeal to the earth, ch. xvi. 18, and his pretended assurance of having a witness in heaven, ch. xvi. 19, xix. 25. Heaven "reveals" his iniquity in the chastisements, e.g. the fire of

28   The increase of his house shall depart,
     And his goods shall flow away in the day of his wrath.
29   This *is* the portion of a wicked man from God,
     And the heritage appointed unto him by God.

heaven, ch. i. 16, that fall on him; and earth rises up against him in the hostility of men, ch. i. 15, 17, cf. ch. xvii. 6.

28.   *The increase*] i.e. the gain, possessions.

his goods shall flow away] lit. *things washed away;* his possessions shall be swept away with a flood in the day of God's wrath.

29.   Like all the speakers in this second round of debate Zophar concludes by pointing with an impressive gesture to the picture he has drawn. Job should see himself there. He finishes by saying "from God." This forces Job into the arena; he has no help, however unwilling he may be, but face this argument (ch. xxi. 27), and he shews that that which comes "from God" (ch. xxi. 22) is something very different.

CH. XXI. JOB'S REPLY TO ZOPHAR.

It is part of the Poet's art no doubt to make Job wait till all the three have spoken and fully developed their case before he replies to it. But his art is also nature. Job at the beginning of each round of speeches is too much occupied with himself, with the broad general impressions which his condition and the conduct of his friends make on him, to be able for a time to attend to their special arguments. In the earlier part of the first colloquy he is overpowered by the thought that God has become his enemy. In the beginning of the second the thought that men also have turned against him crushes him to the ground. And under the weight of these feelings he seems unable to fix his mind on mere points of argument, he only knows that his friends are arguing against him. There is much humanity in Job, and his mind moves by preference in the region of human feelings, the rights of the wretched, the claims of sentient life, the mysteries of human existence and the riddles of the world, and it is unwillingly that he descends from this region into the arena of disputation. It is only the corrosive language of Zophar that awakens him on each occasion to the particular meaning of his friends' addresses. Both times his challenge brings Job into the field, the first time with all the bitterness of sarcasm (ch. xii.), and now with the trenchant force of an argument from facts.

Zophar began his speech with the astonished query, Dost thou know this to have been from of old that the triumphing of the wicked is short? (ch. xx. 4, 5), and closed his history of the wicked man suddenly cut down in the vigour of his life (*v.* 11) with the words, Lo! this is the portion of the wicked man from God (*v.* 29). These words *from God* call up before Job's soul the great mystery with which he is struggling. According to his own former faith as well as that of his friends this should have been a true account of God's rule of the world. But Job's vision had been sharpened as well as widened by his own history, and

But Job answered and said,	21
Hear diligently my speech,	2
And let this be your consolations.	

he now observed much in the world which had formerly escaped him. He saw that this was no true statement of God's dealing with wickedness. God dealt with it quite otherwise; and the mystery overwhelms him, and instead of chiding his friends he can only appeal to them to contemplate the awful riddle of providence, at the thought of which he himself trembles (*v.* 6). This riddle, the prosperity of the wicked in God's hand (*v.* 16), their peaceful death (*v.* 13), and even the renown of their memory (*v.* 33), he then proceeds to unfold. The passage has these parts:

First, *vv.* 2—6, some words of introduction, in which Job bids his friends be silent till he unfolds before them the mystery which weighs down his own soul and the thought of which makes him tremble—then they may mock if they have a mind.

Second, *vv.* 7—34, the mystery itself, the prosperity of the wicked, in four turns :—

vv. 6—16. The wicked are prosperous, themselves, their children, their possessions, and they die in peace. This is an undeniable fact of experience.

vv. 16—21. On the other side, How often is it that they are seen overwhelmed by calamity? There is no such invariable principle. They do not die sudden and violent deaths as the friends represented.

vv. 22—26. Why then should men—the friends—be wiser than God? Why should they impose their petty principles on God's providence, and prescribe methods to Him which He does not follow?

vv. 27—34. Finally Job turns to the insinuations of his friends—he knows the meaning of their indirect allusions, when they say, Where is the house of the prince (*v.* 28)? but they only shew their ignorance of the testimony of those who have travelled (*v.* 30), and their little sense of the unfathomableness of God's ways, and even if possible less sense of the ways of men, who have no such horror of the wicked as the friends pretend, but who press forward in their footsteps, admiring their prosperity and forgetting their wickedness (*v.* 34).

CH. XXI. THE GREAT MYSTERY OF PROVIDENCE, THE PROSPERITY OF THE WICKED.

vv. 2—6. Job begs his friends to give audience till he speak. This is the consolation he seeks from them meantime; when he has spoken they may mock, if they are able (*vv.* 2, 3). It is not of men that he complains, it is a deeper divine mystery, at which his flesh trembles when he thinks of it, and which will fill them with astonishment when he discloses it (*vv.* 4—6).

2. *your consolations*] They believed they were offering him the consolations of God (ch. xv. 11); the consolation he seeks from them is that they listen to him.

3   Suffer me that I may speak;
    And after that I have spoken, mock on.
4   *As for* me, *is* my complaint to man?
    And if *it were so*, why should not my spirit be troubled?
5   Mark me, and be astonished,
    And lay *your* hand upon *your* mouth.
6   Even when I remember I am afraid,
    And trembling taketh hold on my flesh.
7   Wherefore do the wicked live,
    Become old, yea, are mighty *in* power?
8   Their seed is established in their sight with them,

3. *mock on*] This last word is sing. and seems addressed to Zophar the last speaker, whose pictures of the fate of the wicked deeply wounded Job. Having heard his account of the prosperity of the wicked, they shall have leave then to proceed with their bitter taunts and insinuations if they have a mind.

4. *is my complaint to man*] Rather, **of**, or, **concerning** man. The whole first clause means, Is *my* complaint about man? *my* emphatic. The words may express a reason for their listening to him, it is not of them nor of men at all that *he* complains; it is of another, and of a moral riddle and evil that may well excuse his impatience.

And if it were so...troubled] Rather, **or wherefore should I not be impatient?** lit. *should not my spirit be short?*

5. The mystery which he will lay before them if they will mark it will strike them dumb. To "lay the hand upon the mouth" is a gesture of awe-struck silence, cf. ch. xl. 4.

6. When Job himself reflects on it he trembles. When I *remember* means, When I think of it.

7—21. This great mystery of the prosperity of the wicked in God's providence Job now unfolds on both its sides: first, they and all belonging to them prosper, and they die in peace, although in conscious godlessness they bade the Almighty depart from them, *vv.* 7—16; and second, negatively, examples of calamity befalling them are few, *vv.* 17—21.

7—16. The mystery is, Why do the wicked prosper? They live long, they see their children grow up, and their homes are peaceful (*vv.* 7—9). Their cattle thrives (*v.* 10). Their children and they pass a mirthful life with music and dance (*vv.* 11, 12). And with no pain at last they die, though they had openly renounced God (*vv.* 13—15). Yet it is God who bestows this prosperity upon them (*v.* 16).

7. *Wherefore do the wicked live*] The question scarcely means, How is it, if your principles be true, that the wicked live? Job's mind is engrossed with the great problem itself, and he asks, Why in the government of a righteous God do the wicked live? They not only live, they live to old age, and wax mighty in the earth.

8. They have the additional felicity of seeing their children grow up

And their offspring before their eyes.
Their houses *are* safe from fear, 9
Neither *is* the rod of God upon them.
Their bull gendereth, and faileth not; 10
Their cow calveth, and casteth not her calf.
They send forth their little ones like a flock, 11
And their children dance.
They take the timbrel and harp, 12
And rejoice at the sound of the organ.
They spend their days in wealth, 13
And in a moment go down *to* the grave.
Therefore they say unto God, Depart from us; 14
For we desire not the knowledge of thy ways.
What *is* the Almighty, that we should serve him? 15
And what profit should we have, if we pray unto him?

beside them—a pathetic touch from the hand of the man whose sons had been taken from him.

9. Not merely themselves and their children but their homes and all in them are full of peace—another allusion to the rod of God which had fallen on all belonging to Job.

10. Their cattle thrives—no failure or barrenness assails them.

11. Their children, numerous like the flock and happy like the lambs, skip in their glee and sport.

12. And they themselves pass their days in gladness, surrounded with all the charms of life.

They take the timbrel] Rather, **they sing to**, i.e. to the accompaniment of, **the timbrel and the lute**; lit. *they lift up* the voice, cf. Ps. xlix. 4. The timbrel is the tambourine.

the sound of the organ] Rather, of the **pipe**, Gen. iv. 21, cf. Is. v. 12.

13. *in wealth*] i.e. *weal*, prosperity. The word has not here its modern meaning of riches, but its older, more general sense:—"in all time of our tribulation, in all time of our wealth...good Lord deliver us." *The Litany*.

to the grave] Heb., *to Sheol*. They die in a moment without pain— there are no bands in their death, Ps. lxxiii. 4. This idyllic picture of a joyous untroubled life, rich in possessions and filled with all that gives a charm to existence, and having a peaceful close, forms the counterpart to the picture drawn by the friends of the troubled conscience, xv. 20, the early death, xx. 11, the childless solitariness, xviii. 19, and the disastrous end, xx. 24, of the wicked man.

14, 15. All this joy and prosperity they enjoyed though they had bidden God depart from them and renounced His service.

Therefore they say] Rather, **though** (lit. and) **they said**. Their godlessness was not merely that of passion, it was almost formal and reasoned.

16 Lo, their good *is* not in their hand:
The counsel of the wicked is far from me.
17 How oft is the candle of the wicked put out!
And *how oft* cometh their destruction upon them!
God distributeth sorrows in his anger.
18 They are as stubble before the wind,
And as chaff that the storm carrieth away.

Coverdale's rendering of the words, Who is the Almighty? is quaint and vigorous, "What maner of felowe is the Almightie that we shulde serve him?"

16. Finally Job adverts to the mystery: this prosperity of theirs does not depend upon themselves, it is not of their own making; it comes from another, from God. God prospers the wicked, and Job had elsewhere said that He mocked at the despair of the innocent, ix. 23.

the counsel of the wicked is far] Or, perhaps, the counsel of the wicked **be** far from me! Having drawn in such attractive colours the prosperity of the wicked, a prosperity given from the hand of God, Job, even in the midst of his own misery, which is also from God, cannot refrain from repudiating their principles—far be from me the counsel (see ch. x. 3, xviii. 7) of the wicked, cf. ch. xxii. 18. The above seems the most simple and effective way of understanding this verse. Others take it as an objection of the three friends, which Job anticipates and answers; *Lo!* say ye, *their good is not in their own hand;* the meaning being that they cannot retain it, they have no certainty of tenure of it, it will speedily desert them (Hitzig). To this Job is then supposed to reply in the following verses: *How often, then, is it seen to desert them?* This gives a very good sense.

17—21. The negative side of his theme is now illustrated by Job. In *vv.* 7—16 he shewed that the wicked enjoy great, life-long prosperity; now he shews that they are free from calamity; such sudden and disastrous visitations of God do not come upon them as the friends incessantly insisted on. The interrogation, How often? means, What examples can be produced of such a thing? and goes to the end of *v.* 18.

17. How often is the lamp of the wicked put out?
And how often doth their destruction come upon them,
And God distribute sorrows in his anger?
18. How often are they as stubble before the wind
And as chaff that the storm carrieth away?

The A. V., by making *How oft!* an exclamation, gives a sense the opposite of that expressed by the speaker. The question in the first clause of *v.* 17 runs athwart Bildad's assertions ch. xviii. 5, 6, The light of the wicked shall be put out; the second clause contradicts ch. xviii. 12; with the third clause compare ch. xx. 23.

The images in *v.* 18 are familiar for utter destruction. They are taken from the threshing-floor, which was high and open that the force of the wind might be caught in winnowing, cf. Ps. i. 4; Is. xvii. 13.

God layeth up his iniquity for his children: 19
He rewardeth him, and he shall know *it*.
His eyes shall see his destruction, 20
And he shall drink of the wrath of the Almighty.
For what pleasure hath he in his house after him, 21
When the number of his months is cut off in the midst?

19—21. A conceivable objection, and its answer by Job. The verses read,

19. God (say ye) layeth up his iniquity for his children.—
    Let him recompense it unto himself, that he may know it;
20. Let his own eyes see his destruction,
    And let him drink of the wrath of the Almighty;
21. For what concern hath he in his house after him,
    When the number of his months is cut off?

To his argument that the wicked suffer no calamities Job supposes that his friends may object, founding on the old doctrine of retribution, that if the man himself do not suffer, his children shall be visited for his iniquity (Ex. xx. 5); and his answer is, Let the man himself suffer. The expression "that he may know it" means "that he may feel it."

The word "concern" means "pleasure" as A. V., but also, *interest in, care for;* so Coverdale, For what careth he what become of his houshold after his death? The phrase "when the number of his months is cut off" means, when his life is ended. The words might also mean, when the (full) number of his months is dealt out, distributed to himself—when his own life is prolonged to its full measure. But it is not necessary to regard the wicked man as so abandoned as to be destitute of interest in his children even in his life-time, and indifferent to their fate provided his own days be prolonged. Job's objection to the doctrine that a man's iniquity is visited on his children is that this is no punishment of the wicked man himself, for he hath no concern in or knowledge of his children's fate after his death (ch. xiv. 21). From the Prophetic Books of this age it appears that the ancient doctrine of retribution, the doctrine that the fathers have eaten sour grapes and the children's teeth are set on edge (Ezek. xviii. 2), had begun to awaken questionings, cf. Jerem. xxxi. 29 *seq.*, and in this book such doubts are, naturally, brought to a point.

22—26. By insisting on a doctrine of providence which did not correspond to God's providence as actually seen in facts, Job's friends were making themselves wiser than God and becoming His teachers—Will any teach knowledge unto God? Shall we insist on His method of government being what it plainly is not? This is what it is: One man dieth in his full prosperity,—wholly at ease and quiet. Another man dieth in the bitterness of his soul and has not tasted pleasure. They lie down alike in the dust and the worm covers them. Their different fortune is not determined by their different character. The one is not good and the other wicked. But God distributes to them as He chooses.

22. The emphasis falls on *God*—Shall any teach knowledge unto

22 Shall *any* teach God knowledge?
   Seeing he judgeth those that are high.
23 One dieth in his full strength,
   Being wholly at ease and quiet.
24 His breasts are full *of* milk,
   And his bones are moistened with marrow.
25 And another dieth in the bitterness of his soul,
   And never eateth with pleasure.
26 They shall lie down alike in the dust,
   And the worms shall cover them.

God? The principles of providence insisted on by the friends were not those according to which God's actual providence was administered. They were substituting their principles for His.

seeing he judgeth] The clause emphasises the word God: Shall any teach knowledge unto God—God who judges those that are high? "Those that are high" are the inhabitants of the heavens; and to "judge" means to decide in regard to, to bring His judicial power to bear upon; the word does not mean to *condemn*. God judges the heavens, and shall one teach Him how to rule the affairs of earth? Cf. ch. xxii. 13.

23. *in his full strength*] lit. *in his very perfection*, or completeness, meaning, in the full enjoyment of all that made his lot *complete*, wanting nothing—as the second clause explains.

24. *His breasts are full of milk*] Perhaps, **his vessels** are full of milk; but the meaning is uncertain, the word rendered "breasts" not occurring again. The word however has analogies in the cognate languages, and may mean *vessels*, or *troughs*, marg. *milk-pails*, the reference being to the plenty and richness of the man's herds and possessions, though this is a figure for plenty in general. By a slight alteration in spelling the word "milk" means *fat*, and the ancient versions so read, translating, *his inwards*, or *sides*, *are full of fat*.

his bones are moistened with marrow] Rather, **and the marrow of his bones is moistened**, lit. *watered*, i.e. made fresh and strong. If the first clause be translated with the ancient Versions this clause is parallel in sense; otherwise, it describes the effect of his plenty on the man himself.

25. A different history; cf. Job's words of himself, ch. iii. 20, vii. 11.

never eateth with pleasure] Rather, **and hath not tasted** (lit. eaten) **of good**.

26. Wholly different in life the two are alike in death; cf. Eccles. ii. 15 *seq.*

They shall lie down] **They lie down**. Similarly, **the worms cover**.

27—34. Finally, still pursuing his argument, Job turns to the insinuations of his friends against himself, which lie under their descriptions of the fate of the wicked. He knows what they mean when they

Behold, I know your thoughts, 27
And the devices *which* ye wrongfully imagine against me.
For ye say, Where *is* the house of the prince? 28
And where *are* the dwelling places of the wicked?
Have ye not asked them that go by the way? 29
And do ye not know their tokens,
That the wicked is reserved to the day of destruction? 30
They shall be brought forth to the day of wrath.
Who shall declare his way to his face? 31
And who shall repay him *what* he hath done?

say, Where is the house of the prince? But their conclusions were against the testimony of those who had travelled far and seen much. These testified that the wicked man was preserved in the day of destruction; that he came to an honoured grave, and the clods of the valley lay softly on him; and that his example, so far from being shunned, was followed by the mass of men, as there were multitudes that preceded him in the way he walked.

27. Job knows the covert meaning that lies under his friends' talk of the fate of the wicked man.

28. *house of the prince*] "Prince" here perhaps in a bad sense like the classical "tyrant," cf. Is. xiii. 2.

the dwelling places of the wicked] Or, **the tents in which the wicked dwelt**, lit. *the tent of the dwellings of the wicked*. The question, Where is the house of the prince? implies that it has been swept away and has disappeared.

29, 30. Travellers give a different account of the fate of the wicked; they tell that he is spared in the day of destruction:

29 Have ye not asked them that go by the way,
    And do ye not regard their tokens,
30 That the wicked is spared in the day of destruction,
    That they are led forth in the day of wrath?

29. *them that go by the way*] The travellers; here those who have travelled far, or come from a distance, and are full of experience.

do ye not know their tokens] Or, **regard**. Their "tokens" are no doubt the proofs, or examples which they bring forward. The word "regard," or have respect to, is so used ch. xxxiv. 19. In other places it means "not to acknowledge," to repudiate; with this sense the meaning would be, *and ye will not* (surely) *reject their tokens*.

30. *they shall be brought forth to*] Rather, **they are led forth in**, i.e. led away in safety from the destroying wrath, parallel to "spared" or withholden, in the first clause; cf. Is. lv. 12 (*led forth*), or "conducted," Ps. xlv. 14.

31. The person spoken of in this verse seems most naturally the wicked man. It is doubtful however whether the testimony of the travellers is here still carried on, or whether the present words are not those of Job himself. The history of the evil man is proceeded with:

32   Yet shall he be brought to the grave,
     And shall remain in the tomb.
33   The clods of the valley shall be sweet unto him,

his power makes him irresponsible and extorts the homage of men, who do him honour in death (*v.* 32). Others suppose the verse to be spoken of God, in which case the words are almost parenthetical, the history of the sinner being resumed in *v.* 32. If said of God the verse refers to the inscrutable dealings of His omnipotent power (*v.* 30), dealings against which the moral sense of mankind reclaims indeed, but of what avail are the reclamations of the moral sense against omnipotence? cf. ch. ix. 12, xxiii. 13. The language, however, seems less appropriate if spoken of God.

32, 33. The wicked man is buried in honour; and his example followed.

>   32 And he is carried to the grave,
>   And they keep watch over his tomb;
>   33 The clods of the valley are sweet unto him;
>   And all men draw after him,
>   As there were innumerable before him.

32. *Yet shall he be brought*] Rather, **and he is carried**, as above. Comp. ch. x. 19, where Job uses the same language of his own burial. The word is that used in *v.* 30 (led forth, cf. reff.), and suggests the pomp and slow solemnity of his interment.

shall remain in the tomb] Rather, as above, **keep watch over his tomb**, lit. *his heap* (ch. v. 26 of a heap of sheaves), meaning the monument raised over him. This may have been first a heap of stones, but naturally the word might be used in a wider sense of any sepulchral monument. This is watched against desecration. In the Sidonian inscription on the tomb of Eshmun'azar that monarch utters deep curses against any who shall violate his grave. Instead of "they keep watch" others render "he watches," considering the reference to be to the effigy of the deceased graven upon his sarcophagus. The practice of making such an effigy was common in Egypt, and the Author of the Book might be familiar with it. But the practice was not unknown elsewhere. The sarcophagus of Eshmun'azar has such an effigy, the inscription of 22 lines being cut upon the breast and body of the figure, and again in part around the head. The Author of the Book is fond of alluding to customs and things not specifically Hebrew. At the same time, whether we render "they watch over," or "he watches upon," the words might be used in a less precise sense, meaning in the one case that they looked with respect or reverence to his place of sepulture, and in the other that his memory and life were perpetuated in the monument upon his tomb.

33. After life's fever he sleeps well. Eurip. Alces. 462,

>   κούφα σοι
>   χθὼν ἐπάνω πέσειε γύναι.

Sit tibi terra levis, Light fall the dust upon thee.

And every man shall draw after him,
As *there are* innumerable before him.
How then comfort ye me in vain, 31
Seeing *in* your answers there remaineth falsehood?

draw after him] The prosperous wicked man has innumerable successors and imitators, just as he was preceded by countless others whom he resembled, Eccles. iv. 15, 16.

34. Job feels he has refuted the theories of his friends in regard to the pretended calamities and misery of the wicked man, whether in life or death. Hence their attempts to comfort him by this line of thinking are vain.

there remaineth falsehood] i.e. *there is left* (only) *falsehood*. When Job's proofs to the contrary are subtracted from the answers of his friends, there is left in them only the wrongful, false disposition they shew towards him.

CH. XXII.—XXXI. THE THIRD CIRCLE OF SPEECHES.

In the first round of speeches the three friends exhausted the argument from the general conception of God. In the second they exhausted the argument from the operation of His providence in the world, as observed in the fate of the wicked. To the last Job had replied by a direct contradiction, adducing facts and testimony in proof that the fate of the wicked man in God's providence was in no way so uniformly miserable as the three friends had represented (ch. xxi.) There is, manifestly, now left but one weapon in the hands of the three friends, namely, to express openly what they had hinted at formerly in a veiled manner, and charge Job directly with great sins. This charge is made by Eliphaz in the opening speech of the third round of debate (ch. xxii.)

As in the two preceding circles of debate, Job's mind is too much absorbed in the contemplation of the great mystery of providence, which he had set before himself in ch. xxi., to be able for a time to give heed to the shameful charges of Eliphaz against him. He dwells in his reply still, continuing the thought of ch. xxi., upon the riddle of God's rule of the world. He misses rectitude in this rule, and can observe no principle of moral government as he understands it. This is true not only in his own instance (ch. xxiii.), but also on the broad field of the world in general (ch. xxiv.). God, though He knows his innocence, has resolved to destroy him (ch. xxiii. 13). It is this feeling about God that terrifies and paralyses him, not his mere calamities in themselves (ch. xxiii. 15—17). But the same absence of righteousness in the rule of the world is observed everywhere. Men cannot perceive God doing judgment and dispensing righteousness among them (ch. xxiv. 1).

Bildad in his reply (ch. xxv.) passes by the facts adduced by Job, and touches only his arrogance in assuming to be innocent before God: How should man, who is a worm, be pure before the omnipotent ruler of the world? Such words in no way help Job. He knows God's power and greatness not less than Bildad, and he replies by rivalling this speaker in extolling the greatness of God (ch. xxvi.).

Then he comes to what he had not yet directly touched upon, the charges of wickedness made against him. These he denies under a solemn oath (ch. xxvii. 1—6). Here follow in ch. xxvii. 7 *seq.* and ch. xxviii. two passages which are difficult to fit into this part of the Book.

Finally Job takes a comprehensive survey of his mysterious history as a whole, ch. xxix.—xxxi :—

First, looking back with pathetic regret upon his former days, when his children were about him and he was prosperous and honoured among men, ch. xxix.;

Second, contrasting with this happier past his present abasement, the contempt in which he is held by the lowest of mankind, and the mysterious afflictions of God upon him, ch. xxx.;

And third, protesting that this affliction had come upon him for no sin of which he had been guilty; and ending with the impassioned cry that God would make known to him the charge which He has against him, ch. xxxi.

CH. XXII. ELIPHAZ DIRECTLY CHARGES JOB WITH GREAT WICKEDNESS.

Nothing now remains for the Friends but to make against Job openly the charge of great wickedness which they had hitherto only covertly insinuated. Eliphaz makes this charge in the present chapter. The charge, however, arises naturally out of Job's last speech. He had there spoken as if no moral principle could be detected in God's treatment of men (xxi. 23—26). He had said the like of this, indeed, before, but only in the heat of debate (ix. 22): now he propounded the theory as part of a settled conviction, and sustained it by arguments. Moreover, his fascinating pictures of the felicity and joyous existence of the wicked, who bade God depart from them, were painful to a righteous mind, and naturally suggested that, in spite of his professed repudiation of them (xxi. 16), he was in secret sympathy with the principles of such men (xxii. 15). To these two points in Job's speech Eliphaz attaches his rejoinder.

First, to Job's statement that he missed all principle of righteousness in God's providential rule of men Eliphaz replies that there must be some principle in it. The cause of God's afflicting a man is not to be sought for in God Himself, as if it arose out of any self-seeking on His part, or any respect He had to Himself, for a man's righteousness is no profit to God, neither is his wickedness any loss to Him. The reason of God's treatment of men is therefore to be sought in themselves. But it is inconceivable that He should chastise a man for his piety. It must therefore be for his sins (*vv.* 2—5).

Having by means of this syllogism confirmed his conviction of Job's guiltiness, Eliphaz proceeds to suggest what sins Job must have committed, which are those that a powerful, irresponsible, rich ruler of his time might most naturally be guilty of (*vv.* 6—10).

Then Eliphaz the Temanite answered and said,   22
  Can a man be profitable unto God,   2
  As he that is wise may be profitable unto himself?
  Is it any pleasure to the Almighty, that thou art righteous?   3
  Or *is it* gain *to him*, that thou makest thy ways perfect?
  Will he reprove thee for fear of thee?   4
  Will he enter with thee into judgment?

Then Job's pictures of the joyous life of the wicked man suggest to Eliphaz the kind of feeling under which, no doubt, Job committed the sins which he must be guilty of. It was under the feeling that God was enthroned on high in heaven and took no note of the affairs of earth— How doth God know? This was the state of mind of the ancient sinners who were carried away by a flood, and Eliphaz earnestly warns Job against such a feeling (*vv.* 12—20).

Finally he exhorts Job to reconcile himself with God, making Him his treasure and casting away earthly treasures. Then shall he have peace and great prosperity (*vv.* 21—30).

2—5. God's treatment of men cannot be due to any respect which He has to Himself, for He is too lofty to be affected by anything human. He deals with men according to their ways, and Job's afflictions can be due only to his sin.

2. This verse reads,

> Can a man be profitable unto God?
> Nay, he that is wise is profitable unto himself.

A man's actions cannot affect God; the advantage of wisdom, that is, prudent and right conduct, can only accrue to a man himself.

3. *Is it any pleasure*] Or, **advantage**, concern; see on ch. xxi. 21. The idea that men's actions cannot affect God is common in the Book, see ch. vii. 20, xxxv. 5—8. Verses 2, 3 go together, and express this single conception that God's treatment of men is not due to any respect He has to Himself, but is strictly according to the character of men.

4. God's treatment of men being for their sakes and according to what they are, it is inconceivable that He should chastise them for their piety.

for fear of thee] Rather, **for thy** (godly) **fear**, thy piety; comp. ch. iv. 6, xv. 4 for this use of the word *fear* by Eliphaz. The words scarcely contain the idea that if God derived advantage from men's piety He might be supposed to afflict them in order to increase their godliness (Ew.). The simple thought is that man's conduct does not affect God. If God deals with man it is on account of man himself. Can it be supposed then that God would afflict a man because he is pious? (*v.* 4). This is too extravagant a suggestion, therefore if Job is afflicted it is for his sins (*v.* 5). *V.* 4 forms a mere foreground to *v.* 5 *seq.*, in order to suggest by contrast the real cause of Job's calamities.

5—9. Job's afflictions are because of his sins—sins which Eliphaz

5 *Is* not thy wickedness great?
   And thine iniquities infinite?
6 For thou hast taken a pledge from thy brother for nought,
   And stripped the naked of their clothing.
7 Thou hast not given water to the weary to drink,
   And thou hast withholden bread from the hungry.
8 But *as for* the mighty man, he had the earth;
   And the honourable *man* dwelt in it.
9 Thou hast sent widows away empty,
   And the arms of the fatherless have been broken.
10 Therefore snares *are* round about thee,
   And sudden fear troubleth thee;
11 Or darkness, *that* thou canst not see;
   And abundance of waters cover thee.

now suggests and enumerates. They are such sins as a powerful Oriental ruler naturally falls into, inhumanity, avarice, and abuse of power.

6. Compare the laws, Ex. xxii. 26; Deut. xxiv. 10. The "naked" are those poorly clad. See Job's reply to this, ch. xxxi. 19.

7. Compare Job's answer, ch. xxxi. 16, 17.

8. The "mighty man," lit. *man of arm*, i.e. the powerful (Ps. x. 15), and the "honourable," lit. *man of respect*, i.e. high in rank (Is. iii. 5), is of course Job himself.

he had the earth] Or, *his is the land*.

dwelt in it] Or, *shall dwell in it*.

These words describe the feeling that, according to the supposition of Eliphaz, pervaded Job's conduct—his idea was that the land or earth belonged to him, and under this feeling he oppressed the poor and drove them from it.

9. His treatment of widows—he ejected them empty; or when they came seeking redress, or pleading their rights, he let them go unheard. Comp. Job's own language as to himself, ch. xxix. 13, xxxi. 16.

The "arms" of the fatherless are their helps or rights, on which they relied, and by which they were supported.

10, 11. The consequence of this inhumanity and injustice is seen in the snares and terrors from God that surround Job.

11. This verse should probably be read,

   Or seest thou not the darkness,
   And the floods of waters that cover thee?

i.e. dost thou not perceive the true meaning of the darkness and the overwhelming calamities that have come on thee? On the figures comp. ch. xviii. 18; xi. 16; xxvii. 20. See Job's reply, ch. xxiii. 16, 17.

12—20. Eliphaz, having in *vv.* 6—10 suggested what Job's offences must have been, now suggests under what feeling in regard to God he

Is not God *in* the height of heaven? 12
And behold the height of the stars, how high they are.
And thou sayest, How doth God know? 13
Can he judge through the dark *cloud?*
Thick clouds *are* a covering to him, that he seeth not; 14
And he walketh *in* the circuit of heaven.
Hast thou marked the old way 15
Which wicked men have trodden?
Which were cut down out of time, 16
Whose foundation was overflown *with* a flood:
Which said unto God, Depart from us: 17
And what can the Almighty do for them?
Yet he filled their houses *with* good *things:* 18
But the counsel of the wicked is far from me.

must have committed them. He thought God so far removed from the world that He did not observe men's conduct.

12, 13. Eliphaz points to God's place of abode in the lofty heavens (*v.* 12); and under this feeling of His infinite distance from the earth Job said, How doth God know? Men's conduct was not observed by Him; the thick clouds obscured His vision.

And thou sayest] Rather, **and thou saidst.** On this mode of thought comp. Ps. xciv. 7; Is. xxix. 15; Ezek. viii. 12.

14. *in the circuit of heaven*] Rather, **on the circle,** i.e. the arch of heaven that overspans the earth, Is. xl. 22.

15. It was under a similar feeling in regard to God that the great sinners before the Flood filled the earth with violence, and Eliphaz asks Job whether he will go the length of accepting the principles and following the conduct of such men? Compare the words of Elihu, ch. xxxiv. 8.

Hast thou marked the old way] Rather, **wilt thou keep...?** i.e. follow the path they walked in.

16. *out of time*] i.e. before their time, prematurely, by the judgment of God for their sin. Comp. xv. 32.

whose foundation was overthrown] lit. *whose foundation was poured away* and became *a flood*—that on which they stood became a flood in which they sank. The reference is probably to the Deluge, though others, e.g. Ewald, think of the Cities of the Plain.

17. *do for them*] Rather, do **unto** them.

18. Eliphaz expresses his abhorrence of the ingratitude and evil principles of such men, repeating the words employed by Job, ch. xxi. 16 (far be from me the counsel of the wicked); but while Job referred to the worldly prosperity of such persons, in spite of their ungodliness, Eliphaz lays stress upon their sure destruction, and how the righteous see in their downfall an illustration of God's righteous rule of the world (*vv.* 19, 20).

166 JOB, XXII. [vv. 19—23.

19 The righteous see *it*, and are glad:
And the innocent laugh them to scorn.
20 Whereas our substance is not cut down,
But the remnant of them the fire consumeth.
21 Acquaint now thyself with him, and be at peace:
Thereby good shall come *unto* thee.
22 Receive, I pray thee, the law from his mouth,
And lay up his words in thine heart.
23 If thou return to the Almighty, thou shalt be built *up*,
Thou shalt put away iniquity far from thy tabernacles.

19, 20. These two verses are connected together,

19. The righteous see it and are glad,
And the innocent laugh them to scorn,
20. *Saying*, Surely our adversaries are cut off,
And that which they have left the fire hath consumed.

The "remnant" of the wicked, or "that which they leave," is their substance and possessions.

21—30. Eliphaz exhorts Job to reconcile himself with God; assuring him of restoration and great felicity if he will do so.

The passage consists of two parts, first, a series of exhortations, each of which is accompanied by a promise (*vv.* 21—25); and second, a series of great promises simply (*vv.* 26—30). The exhortations are: (1) that Job should reconcile himself with God and receive His words into his heart—thus should he be in peace and good would come to him (*vv.* 21, 22); (2) that he should put away his evil—then should he be restored (*v.* 23); (3) that he should set his heart no more on earthly treasure, but fling it to the dust and among the pebbles of the brooks—then should the Almighty be his treasure (*vv.* 24, 25). The promises are: (1) that, delighting himself in the Almighty, he would be able to lift up his face to God in confidence, unashamed by afflictions (*v.* 26); (2) he would pray unto God with the assurance of being heard, and the vows which he made to God when presenting his request he would have cause to pay, his request being fulfilled (*v.* 27); (3) his purposes in regard to the future would stand and be realized, for the light of God would be on his ways (*v.* 28); (4) any casting down that might happen to him would speedily be turned by God into up-raising, because of his meekness and humility (*v.* 29); and finally, even others who had incurred guilt would be saved through his availing prayer (*v.* 30).

21. *and be at peace*] i.e. thus shalt thou have peace, or, safety.

22. *the law*] Or, **instruction**. The word is a general expression for "every word that proceedeth out of the mouth of God," as the parallel "his words" in the next clause indicates. Comp. Job's reply to this advice, ch. xxiii. 11, 12.

23. *built up*] i.e. probably *rebuilt*, or, restored.

thou shalt put away] Or, **if thou put away**. The words take up "if thou return" of the first clause

Then shalt thou lay up gold as dust, 24
And *the gold of* Ophir as the stones of the brooks.
Yea, the Almighty shall be thy defence, 25
And thou shalt have plenty of silver.
For then shalt thou have thy delight in the Almighty, 26
And shalt lift up thy face unto God.
Thou shalt make thy prayer unto him, and he shall hear 27
thee,
And thou shalt pay thy vows.
Thou shalt also decree a thing, and it shall be established 28
unto thee:
And the light shall shine upon thy ways.
When *men* are cast down, then thou shalt say, *There is* 29
lifting up;
And he shall save the humble person.

24, 25. These verses read,

24. And lay thou thy treasure in the dust,
    And gold of Ophir among the stones of the brooks;
25. Then shall the Almighty be thy treasure,
    And silver in plenty unto thee.

The word rendered "treasure" means properly *ore*. The expression "silver in plenty" is obscure, meaning perhaps "silver in bars," a phrase which may signify "precious" rather than plentiful silver. The word occurs again, Numb. xxiii. 22, xxiv. 8, of the "horns" of the "unicorn" (wild-ox), and in Ps. xcv. 4, of something pertaining to mountains, probably the "towering heights." The Arabic poets compare the glittering peaks of distant mountains suddenly appearing to gleaming swords brandished upright. The word seems to express the idea of rising up in great length. Most interpreters think of *bars* of silver; the A. V. has uniformly *strength*, as here in marg.

Eliphaz exhorts Job to fling earthly treasures away from him, making God his treasure. Comp. the reply of Job, ch. xxxi. 24, 25.

26. *lift up thy face unto God*] i.e. in confidence, and no more ashamed by God's afflictions. Cf. x. 15 and xi. 15.

27. *pay thy vows*] In making requests in prayer it was customary to make a vow to sacrifice or offer unto the Lord if the prayer was granted. Job shall have cause to fulfil his vows, his prayers being heard.

29. *When men are cast down*] The words must mean either : *when they* (i.e. thy ways, *v.* 28) *go downwards*, when decline or misfortune befalls thee; or, *when men cast thee down*.

there is lifting up] The word "lifting up" or simply, "Up !" is that which Job shall utter in prayer. The "humble person," lit. *him that is lowly of eyes*, is of course Job himself.

30   He shall deliver the island of the innocent:
And it is delivered by the pureness of thine hands.

30. *the island of the innocent*] Rather, **him that is not innocent.** Even others who are blameworthy shall be saved through Job's intercession, because of the cleanness of his hands, for the effectual fervent prayer of a righteous man availeth much. The curious translation "island of the innocent" arose from confounding *'I*, an unusual form of the privative particle "not," with *'I*, an island. This form of the privative appears occasionally in proper names as, *I*-chabod, "not glory" (inglorious). For *and it is*, better, **yea, he shall be.**

The charges of unrighteousness (*vv.* 5—11) and ungodliness (*vv.* 12—17), which Eliphaz allows himself to make against Job, furnish a singular illustration of the length to which good men will suffer their theoretical opinions in religion to carry them. His concluding words, however (*vv.* 21—30), are conciliatory and humane, and not unworthy of the very aged and very devout speaker.

CH. XXIII.—XXIV. JOB'S REPLY TO THE THIRD SPEECH OF ELIPHAZ. JOB CONTINUES TO MISS ANY MORAL GOVERNMENT OF THE WORLD BY GOD.

As before, in the two preceding cycles of debate, Job's mind is too much absorbed in contemplation of the painful mystery of God's providence, which he had set before his view in ch. xxi., to be able yet to turn away from it and give attention to the direct charges of wickedness which Eliphaz made against him (ch. xxii. 1—10). The riddle of the painful earth still fascinates him, the injustice and cruel wrong that goes unpunished, the misery of the poor and innocent, and the peaceful end of flagrant transgressors, who are "of those who rebel against the light" (ch. xxiv. 13). What he misses in the world is any true retributive rule of God (ch. xxiv. 1), who "gives no heed to wrong" (ch. xxiv. 12). The two chapters give broad expression to this thought, first, in reference to Job himself, ch. xxiii.; and second, in regard to the world of mankind in general, ch. xxiv.

CH. XXIII. THE MYSTERIOUS INJUSTICE SUFFERED BY JOB AT THE HAND OF GOD.

First, *vv.* 2—7, with his mind full of the sense of his own innocence, and of the mysterious wrong which he suffers from God, Job gives new and importunate expression to the wish that he knew where to find God, and that he could come to His tribunal and judgment-seat. Then he would set his cause fully before Him, and hear from the Almighty His plea against him, sure that his innocence would appear and that he would be delivered for ever from his judge.

Second, *vv.* 8—12, from this dream of a judgment-seat of God such as the judgment-seat of a human judge who would "give heed" to him, Job suddenly awakens to the feeling of what his actual position is. He cannot find God, whose presence he feels: He everywhere eludes

Then Job answered and said, 23
  Even to day *is* my complaint bitter: 2
  My stroke is heavier than my groaning.
  O that I knew where I might find him! 3
  That I might come *even* to his seat!

him. Nay, He does this of purpose, knowing Job's innocence and that if He tried him he would come forth as gold, for all his life long he has kept His way and not departed from the commandments of His lips.

Third, *vv.* 13—17. But He is unchangeable in His purpose. He has resolved to destroy Job, and who can turn Him from that on which He has set His mind? It is this arbitrary, mysterious way of God that confounds and paralyses Job's mind, not his calamities or his death in itself.

2. The A. V. is almost certainly wrong in its rendering of this verse, though a more satisfactory rendering is hard to give. The text is probably faulty. Literally rendered according to the usual meaning of the words the verse reads, *even to-day is my complaint rebellion, my hand is heavy upon my groaning.* The A. V. has assumed, after the Vulgate, that the word usually meaning "rebellion" (*mri*) is a form of the word "bitter" (*mar*), or that the latter word should be read. It has also assumed that "my hand" may mean *the hand* (of God) *upon me,* i.e. "my stroke." But this is scarcely possible; "my arrow," ch. xxxiv. 6, being no true parallel. Further, it has assumed that the well-known phrase "to be heavy upon," e.g. Ps. xxxii. 4, may mean "to be heavy above," i.e. *heavier than* my groaning. This also is scarcely to be believed. On the other hand it is difficult to extract sense from the literal rendering given above. The expression "my complaint is rebellion" may be used from the point of view of the three friends: *even to-day* (still) *is my complaint* accounted *rebellion*, though *my hand lies heavy upon my groaning*, i.e. represses it; the meaning being, that Job was accounted rebellious by his friends, while in fact his complaint and groaning in no way came up to the terrible weight of his calamities—the same idea as in ch. vi. 2. Then the following verses proceed to describe the cause he has for complaint. Or the words "my complaint is rebellion" may express Job's own feeling: "I refuse to submit to my afflictions, or acknowledge that they are just." In this case the next words: "my hand lies heavy on my groaning" must mean "my hand presses out my groaning in a continual stream." But this is an extraordinary sense to put on the phrase "to lie heavy upon." Others, assuming that the text is corrupt, make alterations more or less serious in words, as "*His* hand" for "*my* hand" in the second clause. So already the Sept.

3—7. Job ardently desires that he could come to God's judgment-seat to plead his cause before Him; and that God would give heed to him and answer him. Then assuredly his innocence would be established.

3. *his seat*] i.e. His judgment-seat, or tribunal.

4 I would order *my* cause before him,
   And fill my mouth *with* arguments.
5 I would know the words *which* he would answer me,
   And understand what he would say unto me.
6 Will he plead against me with *his* great power?
   No; but he would put *strength* in me.
7 There the righteous *might* dispute with him;
   So should I be delivered for ever from my judge.
8 Behold, I go forward, but he *is* not *there;*
   And backward, but I cannot perceive him:
9 *On* the left hand, where he doth work, but I cannot behold *him:*
   He hideth *himself on* the right hand, that I cannot see *him:*
10 But he knoweth the way that I take:

 5. Job would not only plead his own cause, but he would hear from the Almighty what charges He had to make against him; comp. ch. x. 2, xiii. 23. and especially ch. xxxi. 35—37.
 6. This verse runs:
  Would he plead against me in the greatness of his power?
  Nay, but he would give heed unto me.
The words express the thought which the idea of appearing before God's judgment-seat immediately suggests to Job—"Do I mean that God should exhibit His almighty power against me? far from that, but that He would listen to me." His wish is that God would hear his arguments and answer him as a human judge who gives heed to the plea of the accused, laying aside His omnipotent power with which He now crushes him; comp. ch. ix. 32, xiii. 20.
 7. This verse, as rendered in the A.V., seems to mean that in such circumstances (*vv.* 3—6) a righteous man might plead his cause before God. Rather the words run literally, *then a righteous man would be pleading with him*, i.e. then it would appear that the man who pleads with Him (i.e. Job) is righteous. This sense fits into the parallelism of the second clause.
 8—9. From this fascinating dream of a Divine tribunal after the manner of that of a human judge, Job awakens to realise the actual circumstances in which he is placed. God, everywhere present, everywhere eludes him; he feels His omnipotent power, but in vain seeks to see His face.
 10. The reason of God's thus hiding Himself and refusing to allow Himself to be approached is that He knows Job's innocence, but is resolved to treat him as guilty and bring him to death (*v.* 13).
 But he knoweth the way that I take] Rather, **for** He knoweth, &c.; lit. *the way that is with me,* i.e. the conduct I pursue, and the thoughts I cherish. Job refers in these words to his innocency (*vv.* 11, 12).

When he hath tried me, I shall come forth as gold.
My foot hath held his steps,   11
His way have I kept, and not declined.
Neither have I gone back from the commandment of his   12
   lips;
I have esteemed the words of his mouth more than my
   necessary *food*.
But he *is* in one *mind*, and who can turn him?   13
And *what* his soul desireth, even *that* he doeth.
For he performeth the thing that is appointed for me: 14
And many such *things are* with him.
Therefore am I troubled at his presence: 15
When I consider, I am afraid of him.
For God maketh my heart soft,   16

when he hath tried me I shall] Rather, **if He tried me I should
come forth as gold**. God refuses to permit Job access to Him, or to
plead his cause before Him, because He knows his innocence, and that
if He tried him he would come forth as pure gold.

11—12. Fuller particulars given by Job of "the way that is with
him"—his innocent, upright life.

11. *hath held his steps*] Or, **held fast to** His steps, i.e. followed
closely His footsteps; comp. Is. ii. 3.

12. *more than my necessary food*] Lit. *more than* (or, above) *my
own* law; i.e. perhaps, more than the law of my own mind or inclina-
tion. The words recall the exhortation of Eliphaz, ch. xxii. 22. Any
reference to *food* seems out of place.

13—17. Job's innocency though known to God is disregarded by
Him. He is unchangeable in His resolution, and He has resolved to
destroy him.

14. *For he performeth*] Or, **Yea He will perform**, or, accomplish.
The "thing appointed" for Job is his death through his malady, which
the Almighty has resolved upon. This is the profound enigma to Job;
but it is far from being a solitary one: "many such things are with
Him"—the instance is but one out of many similar ones that happen
under God's rule of the world of mankind; comp. ch. xxi. 23 *seq.*

15. It is this thought of the moral riddle which his history presents, and of the moral iniquity that characterizes God's government,
that perplexes and paralyses Job.

at his presence] Or, **before him**, i.e. because of Him, or, at the
thought of Him; comp. "when I consider" in next clause. The
thought that God acts in such a manner confounds Job.

16. *For God maketh*] Or, **and** God. The emphasis is on *God;* it
is God,—the thought that God should act in this unrighteous manner—
that makes his heart "soft," i.e. makes him faint-hearted and terror-
stricken.

And the Almighty troubleth me:

17 Because I was not cut off before the darkness,
Neither hath he covered the darkness from my face.

17. This verse reads,
> For I am not dismayed because of the darkness,
> Nor because of myself whom thick darkness covereth.

The words refer back to the language of Eliphaz, ch. xxii. 11, "or seest thou not the darkness?" The "darkness" is the fatal calamity that has overtaken Job, a frequent use of the word. What dismays Job, or strikes him dumb with moral awe, is not his calamity in itself, nor himself (or, *his face*) marred and distorted by disease, but this, that it is *God* who has inflicted the calamity upon him, not because he is guilty, but in the arbitrary and unjust exercise of His almighty power. This is the point in this whole speech, both in ch. xxiii. and ch. xxiv.; Job misses any true moral rule in the world. The A. V. seems to make the enigma consist in this, that Job was not removed by death before such afflictions overtook him. But this would at best have substituted one enigma for another.

Cii. XXIV. The Divine Rectitude which Job misses in his own instance he equally misses on the broad field of the World.

The same thought of the absence of any righteous rule of the world is carried through this chapter and illustrated by many examples. Job turns from his own history and surveys that of the people around him, and as his own instance illustrated the misery of the just, the instances about him illustrate the felicity, the long-continued power, the freedom from visitation by God, and the natural death of the wicked. Thus both sides of his thesis are supported, that God's rule of the world is not retributive, and that the principles insisted on by his friends find no justification in the world as it is.

Job begins by asking, Why are not times (of assize) appointed by the Almighty? and, Why do they that know Him not see His days (of judgment)? This is Job's complaint, that God the judge and ruler of the world fails to judge and rule it in righteousness. Men do not behold Him appointing times and holding days for doing judgment on wrong, and righting the oppressed. On the contrary, the powerful tyrants oppress and the miserable poor are oppressed (*vv.* 3—11), and God regards not the wrong (*v.* 12).

Besides these public wrongdoers, there are other transgressors who shun the light. The murderer, the adulterer, and the robber ply their unhallowed trade in the darkness (*vv.* 13—17). And all of them, instead of being visited by God with sudden judgments, as the Friends insisted and as the popular literature described (*vv.* 18—21), are upheld in power by God, made to dwell in safety, and at last brought in peace to a natural death " like all others " (*vv.* 22—24).

Why, seeing times are not hidden from the Almighty, 24
Do they that know him not see his days?
Some remove the landmarks; 2
They violently take away flocks, and feed *thereof.*
They drive away the ass of the fatherless, 3
They take the widow's ox for a pledge.
They turn the needy out of the way: 4
The poor of the earth hide themselves together.

Finally Job, too sure of his facts, exclaims, Who will make me a liar? Who will disprove the things now advanced? (*v.* 25).

1. This verse reads,
Why are not times appointed by the Almighty?
And why do they that know him not see his days?

By "times" and "days" Job means diets of assize for sitting in judgment and dispensing right among men. The speaker complains that such times and days are not appointed by the ruler and judge of the world; He fails to exercise a righteous rule; they that know Him (the godly) and look for the manifestation of His righteousness are disappointed. The A. V. *why, seeing times are not hidden,* &c., appears to mean, Why, seeing God *has* appointed judgment-days known to Himself, are the godly not permitted to perceive them? The complaint in this case does not touch the Divine rectitude itself, but only laments that it does not manifest itself to men. But the distinction is one not drawn by Job. When he complains that God does not make visible His righteous rule, his meaning is that God does not exercise such a rule. This is the thought about God that alarms him, and makes his heart soft (ch. xxiii. 16).

2—4. Job now proceeds to illustrate his complaint of the absence of righteousness in God's rule of the world. The instances are in the first place general.

2. *Some remove*] Or, **there are who remove.** In the absence of hedgerows or walls, the landmark defined the boundary of a man's field or estate. Its removal was equivalent to violent appropriation of the property of another; see Deut. xix. 14; Hos. v. 10.

and feed thereof] Rather, **and feed them.** They are open and defiant in their violent wrong, they seize a flock and publicly graze it as their own.

3. By "the ass" and "the ox" is meant the single ass and ox which the fatherless and widow possess, needful for working their small field or affording them scanty nourishment. When deprived of these they are brought to complete destitution, and removed from the land.

4. "Turning the needy out of the way" is a general expression for doing them wrong, hindering them of their just rights; comp. Am. v. 12. The last clause "the poor hide themselves together" seems to sum up the general effect of the preceding wrongs. The poor, violently dispossessed of what belonged to them, or stripped through forms of law

5   Behold, *as* wild asses in the desert,
    Go they forth to their work; rising betimes for a prey:
    The wilderness *yieldeth* food for them *and* for *their* children.
6   They reap *every one* his corn in the field:
    And they gather the vintage of the wicked.
7   They cause the naked to lodge without clothing,
    That *they have* no covering in the cold.
8   They are wet with the showers of the mountains,

little different from violence ("for a pledge," *v.* 3), and deprived of their fields, are forced to hide themselves away from men, among whom they had formerly lived in respect, and huddle together in obscure haunts.

5—8. Job now directs his attention to a particular class of outcasts, giving a pathetic description of their flight from the abodes of men and their herding together like wild asses in the wilderness; their destitution, and the miseries they endure from cold and want, having only the rocks and caves to cover them, and only the roots and garbage of the desert to sustain them. The class of miserables here referred to are, no doubt, as Ewald first pointed out, the aboriginal races of the regions east of the Jordan, whose land and homes had been seized by more powerful tribes, and who had fled from the bitter oppressions to which they were subjected by their conquerors. Another detailed reference is made to them in ch. xxx.

5. The comparison to wild asses expresses their herding together, their flight far from the dwellings of men, and that they find their home and sustenance in the wilderness.

go forth to their work; rising betimes for a prey] Rather, **they go forth to their work, seeking diligently for food.** Their "work" is explained by "seeking for food."

for them and *for their children*] Rather, **food unto them for their children.** The roots and herbage of the desert are the only nourishment they can find for their children; comp. ch. xxx. 3—4.

6. The verse reads,

They reap their fodder in the field,
And glean the vineyard of the wicked.

The coarse food which they can possess themselves of is called by the poet "their fodder"; it is scarcely grain; and for fruit they have only the forgotten or neglected late gleanings of the vineyard of the wicked. The term "wicked" seems to mean here the rich, inhumane lords of the soil; comp. the converse use of "rich" for "wicked," Is. liii. 9.

7. The verse means,

They lie all night naked, without clothing,
They have no covering in the cold.

8. The mountain rains, more violent than even those in the plain,

And embrace the rock for want of a shelter.
They pluck the fatherless from the breast, 9
And take a pledge of the poor.
They cause *him* to go naked without clothing, 10
And they take away the sheaf *from* the hungry;
Which make oil within their walls, 11
And tread *their* winepresses, and suffer thirst.
Men groan from out of the city, 12
And the soul of the wounded crieth out:
Yet God layeth not folly *to them*.

drench these thinly-clad outcasts; and they "embrace the rock," i.e. huddle in closely under its ledge.

9—12. These verses describe the miseries of another class, those who have allowed themselves to be subjected, and become serfs and bondmen attached to the estates of the rich. Probably they are but a portion of the same aboriginal tribes mentioned in *vv.* 5—7.

9. *They pluck*] Or, **there are who pluck**. The reference is to the ruling class who, for some debt perhaps of the dependent, seize the infant of the debtor, in order by selling it or bringing it up as a slave to repay themselves.

take a pledge of the poor] The words might mean "take in pledge that which is on the poor," i.e. their scanty clothing. Others refer the words to the preceding inhuman act of plucking the child from the breast and render: "and take this pledge of the poor" (Ew.).

10. The verse carries on the idea expressed by "the poor" (*v.* 9)—the poor
Which go naked without clothing;
And hungry they carry sheaves.

The point lies in the antithesis between "hungry" and "carry sheaves"; though labouring amidst the abundant harvest of their masters they are faint with hunger themselves.

11. A similar contrast between "tread the winepresses" and "suffer thirst." The expression "within their walls" refers to the walled, well-protected vineyards of the rich nobility, within which these miserable serfs tread out abundant wine all the while that they themselves pant with thirst.

12. *Men groan from out of the city*] Rather, according to the pointing, *from out of the populous city they groan*. In this, however, there is no parallelism to the "soul of the wounded" in next clause. By a slight change of pointing, and as read by the Syriac, the sense is obtained: **from out the city the dying groan**. The phrase "from out" means merely "in connexion with" or *in* the cities, comp. Ps. lxxii. 16. Reference is made to the cities in order to indicate that this injustice and cruel oppression suffered by men is *universal*, in city and country alike.

layeth not folly to them] Rather, **regardeth not the folly**, or, **wrong**.

13   They are of those that rebel against the light;
     They know not the ways thereof,
     Nor abide in the paths thereof.
14   The murderer rising with the light
     Killeth the poor and needy,
     And in the night is as a thief.
15   The eye also of the adulterer waiteth for the twilight,
     Saying, No eye shall see me:
     And disguiseth *his* face.
16   In the dark *they* dig *through* houses,
     Which they had marked for themselves in the daytime:
     They know not the light.
17   For the morning *is* to them even as the shadow of death:
     If *one* know *them, they are in* the terrors of the shadow of death.

The same word occurred in ch. i. 22, see note. All this oppression is manifest on the face of the earth among men, but God giveth no heed to the wrong—He appointeth no days (*v.* 1) for doing judgment and staying the injustice.

13—17. The outrages perpetrated by a different class of wrong-doers, the murderer (*v.* 14), the adulterer (*v.* 15), and the robber (*v.* 16). Those described in former verses pursued their violent course openly, they had law or at least custom on their side, and their cruelties did no more than illustrate the rights of property; those now mentioned are "rebels against the light" and operate under cover of the darkness.

13.   *They are of those*] Rather, **these are of them that rebel**. The speaker introduces a new class of malefactors. The "light" here is of course the light of day, with the implication, however, that he that is righteous "cometh to the light."

14.   *with the light*] i.e. toward day-break, while it is still partially dark. At such an hour the murderer waylays the solitary traveller.

is as a thief] i.e. acts the thief, becomes a thief.

15.   The adulterer waits for the "twilight," i.e. of even. Then he disguises himself, or puts a cover on his face, that he may enter undetected the house of his neighbour.

16.   *which they had marked*] Rather, **they shut** (lit. *seal*) **themselves up in the daytime**. In the dark the housebreaker digs through the wall, which in many Eastern houses is of clay or soft brick; in the daytime he abides close in his own retreat; he is unacquainted with the light.

17.   This verse expands the last clause of *v.* 16 :—

For the morning is to them as the shadow of death,
For they know the terrors of the shadow of death.

The "shadow of death" is equivalent almost to "midnight;" see

He *is* swift as the waters; 18
Their portion is cursed in the earth:
He beholdeth not the way of the vineyards.

note ch. iii. 5. These malefactors know not the light (*v.* 16), the morning seems to them midnight, so much do they fear and shun it; but they know, they are familiar with, the terrors of midnight, for this is their day. Others make " morning " predicate, *for midnight is to them* (like) *the morning*. This, however, does not connect so closely with *v.* 16. "Shakespeare has the same thought—as indeed what thought has he not?—and tells us that 'when the searching eye of heaven, that lights this lower world, is hid behind the globe,'

> ' Then thieves and robbers range abroad unseen,
> In murders and in outrage...
> But when from under this terrestrial ball
> He fires the proud tops of the eastern pines,
> And darts his light through every guilty hole,
> Then murders, treason, and detested sins,
> The cloak of night being plucked from off their backs,
> Stand bare and naked, trembling at themselves.' "

(Cox, *Commentary on Job*, p. 317.)

18—24. This detailed and graphic picture of the enormities of wicked men (*vv.* 2—17) suggests the question, What then is the fate of such men? Are they seized by the sudden judgments of God and delivered into the hand of their own transgression (ch. viii. 4)? or, are they prolonged in the possession of their power, protected in their wickedness, and brought to a natural and peaceful end at last like men in general? The following passage gives both answers, one in *vv.* 18—21, and the other in *vv.* 22—24. The former answer is that of Job's friends, and perhaps of the common mind, a passage or fragment from a poetical expression of whose creed Job seems to cite. This answer is only introduced ironically and in order to supply the background to the true picture which Job himself draws of the history of these violent and wicked men. And this picture is a very different one.

18—21. The popular creed regarding the fate of the wicked in God's government of the world.

18. *He is swift as the waters*] Rather, **he is swift upon the face of the waters.** The person spoken of is the wicked man, especially such a tyrannical, proud oppressor as is alluded to in *vv.* 2—4 ; and what is said of him is, that he is like a waif or spray on the surface of the water, swept rapidly away, and disappearing in a moment from the eyes of men in destruction; comp. ch. xx. 28, Hos. x. 7, "As for Samaria, her king is cut off like foam (or, a twig) upon the face of the waters."

their portion] i.e. their fields and possessions. A curse is pronounced over the estates of such men by those who behold their downfall; comp. ch. v. 3.

he beholdeth not] Or, *he turneth not unto the way* of the vineyards—

19 Drought and heat consume the snow waters:
    So doth the grave *those which* have sinned.
20 The womb shall forget him; the worm shall feed sweetly
    on him;
    He shall be no more remembered;
    And wickedness shall be broken as a tree.
21 He evil entreateth the barren *that* beareth not:
    And doeth not good to the widow.

he shall no more return unto the smiling vineyards in which he delighted. The joys of his luxurious life shall no more be his, misery and destruction have overtaken him. The general meaning of the phrase is the converse of that expressed by "sitting under his vine and figtree," 1 Kings iv. 25; Mic. iv. 4.

19. As the fierce heat and drought evaporate the abundant waters of the dissolving winter snow, leaving no trace of them, so doth Sheol engulf the sinners, that they disappear without a remnant from the world; comp. ch. vi. 15 *seq.*, xiv. 11; Is. v. 14.

20. Even she whose womb bore the sinner shall forget him; none shall find pleasure in him but the worm, to whose taste he shall be sweet.

21. This verse is closely connected with the last clause of the preceding.

   And wickedness shall be broken like a tree—
   Even he that devoureth the barren that beareth not,
   And doeth not good unto the widow.

The "tree" is a frequent object of comparison, e.g. ch. xix. 10, "removed or plucked up like a tree," here "broken" like a tree. The "barren that beareth not" is she that is lonely, having no sons to uphold her right, Ps. cxxvii. 3, cf. Is. li. 18. Pleading for, or upholding the cause of the widow is often enjoined, as in Is. i. 17, and the Lord Himself is said to be her "judge," Ps. lxviii. 5.

The broad and somewhat exaggerated colours of the preceding picture (*vv.* 18—21) indicate that it is either actually in part the work of a popular hand, or that it is a parody after the popular manner by Job himself.

22—24. The other picture drawn by Job's own hand to exhibit the actual truth. Such (*vv.* 18—21), according to the popular imagination, is the fate and history of the wicked; the following (*vv.* 22—24) is their history according to facts:

22. Nay, he continueth the mighty by his power,
     They rise up, though they believed not that they should live.
23. He giveth them to be in safety, and they are upheld,
     And his eyes are upon their ways.
24. They are exalted: in a moment they are not;
     They are brought low, and gathered in as all others,
     And are cut off as the tops of the ears of corn.

He draweth also the mighty with his power: 22
He riseth up, and no *man* is sure of life.
Though it be given him *to be* in safety, whereon he resteth; 23
Yet his eyes *are* upon their ways.
They are exalted for a little while, but are gone 24
And brought low, they are taken out of the way as all *other*,
And cut off as the tops of the ears of corn.
And if *it be* not *so* now, who will make me a liar, 25
And make my speech nothing worth?

22. *he draweth also the mighty*] Rather as above, **he continueth the mighty**, i.e. He (God) prolongeth their life and continueth them in their place. The "mighty" are the oppressive lords of the soil, *v.* 2 *seq.* And it is God that upholds them by His power; comp. ch. ix. 24.
he riseth up, and no man is sure of life] Rather as above. Even when they fall under calamity or sickness and "believe not that they shall live," i.e. despair of recovery or of regaining their former prosperity, they are raised up again, their life and power being prolonged.
23. *though it be given*] Rather, **he giveth them to be in safety**. God makes the tents of the violent men to be secure, ch. xii. 6; He watches over them, His eyes being upon their ways; comp. ch. x. 3, "He shines upon the counsel of the wicked."
24. To be translated as above. The wicked are exalted, rise high in life, and suddenly, with no pain, they die; comp. ch. xxi. 13, Ps. lxxiii. 4. And when they are brought low at last in death, it is a natural death that overtakes them, like that of all others,—men in general; and they are cut off (or, wither) like the tops of the ears of corn, not prematurely, but having attained to full ripeness; comp. v. 26.
25. Job alas! is only too sure of his facts, and conscious that he has history and experience at his back he victoriously exclaims, Who will make me a liar?

Job has gained his victory over his friends, but he has received, or rather inflicted on himself, an almost mortal wound in achieving it. He has shewn that God's rule of the world is not just, in the sense in which the friends insisted that it was just, and in the sense in which his own moral feeling demanded that it should be just. God is not righteous, in the sense that he punishes wickedness with outward calamity and rewards the righteous with outward good. So far the three friends are defeated, and with their defeat on the general question their inferences from Job's calamities as to his guilt fall to the ground. To this extent Job has gained a victory. But his victory, if it secures the possibility of his own innocence, leaves to his mind a God whom he believes to be unrighteous. For his view of what could be called "righteousness" in the Ruler of the world coincides entirely with the view of his friends.

12—2

25 Then answered Bildad the Shuhite, and said,
2   Dominion and fear *are* with him,
    He maketh peace in his high places.
3   Is there *any* number of his armies?

CH. XXV. BILDAD'S THIRD SPEECH.

HOW SHOULD MAN, WHO IS A WORM, BE PURE BEFORE THE OMNIPOTENT RULER OF THE UNIVERSE?

Bildad perhaps feels himself unable to reply to the facts of experience adduced by his opponent, and he will not continue the dispute. Yet he will not retire without at least uttering a protest against the spirit of his adversary and in behalf of reverential thought concerning God. Let the facts of history brought forward by Job be as they may, the spirit in which they are brought forward, and the conclusions in regard to God founded on them, must be for ever false.

Bildad does not appear to touch Job's argument as to God's rule of the world. He only seeks to subdue the immeasurable arrogance of Job in thinking that he would be found guiltless if placed before the judgment-seat of God (ch. xxiii. 3—7), and in challenging the rectitude of God's rule of the world. With this view he contrasts the exalted Majesty of God and His universal power, which the countless hosts on high obey, and the purity of God in whose eyes the moon is dark and the stars are not pure, with the littleness and the earthly nature of man—who is a worm.

These thoughts had already been expressed by other speakers in the controversy, as by Eliphaz, ch. iv. 17 *seq.*, and ch. xv. 14 *seq.*, and the brief and simple repetition of them by Bildad indicates that the controversy has exhausted itself.

2. *dominion and fear*]   To God belongs rule, and His majesty inspires terror; He is the Omnipotent ruler over all.

his high places] i.e. the heavens where He dwells. There He "maketh peace" through the dominion and fear belonging to Him. The idea of "making peace in his high places" is suggested first perhaps by the atmospheric phenomenon, the stilling of the warring elements in the tempest on high. When God intervenes the storm becomes a calm. But probably the idea was extended, and the words may include a reference to traditional discords among the heavenly hosts, comp. ch. xxi. 22, xl. 10 *seq.*; Is. xxiv. 21; Rev. xii. 7.

3. *his armies*] The words still amplify the idea of the "dominion" and omnipotence of God. The armies that obey Him are innumerable. The reference is probably to the phenomena of the heavens by night; comp. Is. xl. 26, "He bringeth out their host by number, he calleth them all by their names; by the greatness of his might, for that he is strong in power, not one faileth." There was a tendency in Oriental thought to identify the angels with the stars, or at least to regard the stars as animated.

And upon whom doth not his light arise?
How then can man be justified with God? 4
Or how can he be clean *that is* born of a woman?
Behold *even* to the moon, and it shineth not; 5
Yea, the stars are not pure in his sight.
How much less man, *that is* a worm? 6
And the son of man, *which is* a worm?

his light arise] The reference is probably to the heavens or world by day; and the words express the pervading universality of God's influence and rule. The sun as a body is not directly alluded to, for the word "arise" is not that which ordinarily expresses rising or coming above the horizon; the meaning is rather " on whom doth not his light shine?" By "his light" is not meant the nature of God as essential light; the meaning rather is that by His light which He sends forth God reaches all (Ps. xix. 6) and brings all under His sway, though there may be in "*his* light" a reference to the light of day as symbolizing what He is. It is out of the question to limit the words "upon whom" to the "armies" of the first clause, making the query of Bildad to mean, Which of the bright heavenly hosts does not His light outshine? or, Which of them does not shine with a light which falls on it from Him and reflect not its own but His light? The reference in the words "on whom" is not limited to the heavenly host, but is universal.

4—5. Such is the Majesty and the universal power of God. How then should a man be righteous before Him?

be justified with God] i.e. be just or righteous before God; comp. iv. 17 *seq.*, xiv. 1, xv. 14.

5. The thought of *v.* 4 amplified. Even the moon, the brightest star, does not shine, is dark, when He looks upon it, and the stars are not pure, how much less man, which is a worm? The contrast drawn by Eliphaz between man and the angels is drawn here between man and the heavenly bodies; comp. ch. xv. 15. The Hebrew has two words for "worm" here, the one the worm of decay and corruption (ch. vii. 5, xvii. 14, xxi. 26, xxiv. 20; Ex. xvi. 24; Is. xiv. 11), the other in the second clause, used to express the utmost abasement and abjectness, "Fear not thou worm Jacob," Is. xli. 14, "But I am a worm and no man," Ps. xxii. 6, though occasionally occurring also in the sense of the other word. We have only one word in English, for though Shakespeare speaks of "Grubs and eyeless skulls," such a term can hardly be used now in language of any elevation.

CH. XXVI. JOB RIVALS BILDAD IN MAGNIFYING THE
GREATNESS OF GOD.

Bildad in his short speech magnified the greatness of God, and His purity, before which even the heavens are not clean. Job had heard all this before, it did not touch the enigma of his life and of providence.

26 But Job answered and said,

2 How hast thou helped *him that is* without power?
How savest thou the arm *that hath* no strength?

3 How hast thou counselled *him that hath* no wisdom?
And *how* hast thou plentifully declared the thing as it is?

4 To whom hast thou uttered words?

Hence, *first*, he pours out the full vials of his sarcasm on Bildad's irrelevant statements, ch. xxvi. 2—4. He knows God's greatness not less than Bildad, if knowledge of it only helped him in any way or had any bearing on the dispute, which was not concerning the Greatness of God, but concerning His Justice.

And *second*, to shew that he does not need to be taught concerning God's greatness, he proceeds to give a far more brilliant picture of it than Bildad had attempted, shewing how it manifests itself,

(1) in the underworld of the Shades, *vv.* 5—6;

(2) in the world above, the earth and heavens, *vv.* 7—13; ending with the sublime thought that, mighty and majestic as the operations of God are which are seen in these parts of the universe, they are but the fringes or outskirts of His ways, only a whisper in comparison to the full thunder of His power.

2—4. Job sarcastically expresses his admiration of Bildad's speech, and gratitude for the help it has been to him.

2. *how savest thou?*] Rather, how **hast thou saved?** i.e. succoured.

3. *plentifully declared the thing as it is*] Rather, **plentifully**, or, abundantly, **declared knowledge**, or, wisdom. The word is that which occurs in ch. v. 12; see notes. "Him that is without power," "that hath no wisdom" &c., is of course Job himself; and he expresses his admiration of the contribution made by Bildad to the clearing up of his perplexities and the solution of the riddle of his life. It is not quite clear whether Job means to say: "I *am* weak and unnerved, perplexed and ignorant, and how mightily in all this thou hast helped me!" or, whether he is not thinking with Bildad's mind and giving bitter expression to the thoughts which that speaker doubtless entertained of his own performance, and of the effect it should have on the person whom he addressed: "Doubtless thou hast abundantly instructed and strengthened the weak and ignorant man before thee!" The former sense is the more natural, the other fits better into connexion with *v.* 4.

4. *to whom hast thou uttered words?*] Job refers to himself and asks, Who is it that thou hast spoken such things to? The same feeling of conscious superiority to his friends and disdain of the instructions they were giving him reappears here, which came out already in ch. xii. 4. It is the same feeling as was expressed by the magnates of Jerusalem in reference to the continual harping of Isaiah: "Whom will he teach knowledge, and whom will he make to understand doctrine? them that are weaned from the milk and drawn from the breast?" Has he children before him that he gives precept upon precept, line upon line, &c.? Is. xxviii. 9.

And whose spirit came from thee?
Dead *things* are formed
From under the waters, and the inhabitants thereof.
Hell *is* naked before him,
And destruction hath no covering.
He stretcheth out the north over the empty place,

and whose spirit came from thee?] Or, **came forth** from thee. Job asks, Under what lofty inspiration hast thou spoken? Is it, indeed, the very spirit of God that has found expression through thy mouth? The words carry a sarcastic reference to the poverty of Bildad's speech, possibly also to the oracular air with which it was uttered.

5—13. That Job has no need to be instructed regarding the greatness of God he now shews, by entering upon an exhibition of its operations in every sphere of that which exists, Hades, the Earth and Heaven, in which he far outstrips the feeble effort of Bildad.

5, 6. God's presence and power in the underworld. Verse 5 reads according to the pointing,

> The Shades tremble
> Underneath the waters and their inhabitants.

The "Shades" (Heb. *Refáim*, the flaccid) are the departed persons, whose place of concourse is Sheol. Comp. Is. xiv. 9, where "the dead" are the shades, so Is. xxvi. 14 (the deceased). This abode of deceased persons lies deep down under the waters of the sea and all the inhabitants of these waters, for the sea belongs to the upper world. Yet the power of God is felt even at this immeasurable distance from His abode on high. Bildad had referred to the power of God as "making peace" on high; Job points to what is a more wonderful illustration of His power, it pervades the underworld, and the dead tremble under its influence. Whether the statement is general, or whether perhaps there may not be allusion to great convulsions in nature, shaking the earth, and rousing up out of their lethargy even the drowsy, nerveless, shades with terror, may be doubtful.

6. *Hell*] is in Heb. *Sheol*, the place where deceased persons congregate, the world beneath. It is not a place of pain, though a dark and dreary abode, ch. x. 21, 22. Those there are the dead, who still subsist, though they do not live. "Destruction," Heb. *abaddon*, is a synonym for Sheol, ch. xxviii. 22. This as well as all things is naked to the eyes of Jehovah. Comp. Am. ix. 2; Ps. cxxxix. 8.

7—13. God's power and greatness in heaven and earth.

7. It may be doubtful whether "the north" refers to the northern part of the earth or to the northern heavens. In favour of the latter reference is the fact that the expression "stretch out," often said in regard to the heavens (e. g. ch. ix. 8), is not elsewhere used with reference to the earth, and it is scarcely probable that "the earth" would be used as a parallel to "the north," a part of the earth. The northern region of the heavens also, with its brilliant constellations clustering round the pole, would naturally attract the eye, and

And hangeth the earth upon nothing.
8 He bindeth up the waters in his thick clouds;
And the cloud is not rent under them.
9 He holdeth back the face of *his* throne,
And spreadeth his cloud upon it.

seem to the beholder, who looked up to it through the transparent atmosphere, to be stretched out over the "empty place," that is, the vast void between earth and heaven. That a different mode of representation is found elsewhere, the arch of the heavens being spoken of as reposing on the earth (Is. xl. 22), is of little consequence. Where religious wonder and poetical feeling, not scientific thought, dictate the language in which nature and its phenomena are described, uniformity of conception or expression is not to be looked for. And the words seem to refer to the appearance of the heavens by night, when the horizon is not so visible, and the dark "void" between earth and heaven more impressive. Others think of the northern region of the earth, the region where lofty mountains rise, and whose stability without support seems most wonderful. It is difficult in this case, however, to conjecture what the void is over which the "north" is stretched; the opinion of Ewald that it is the abyss of Sheol is too adventurous.

hangeth the earth upon nothing] To hang "upon" is to hang *from*; the representation, therefore, is that the earth is suspended, attached to nothing *above* it which sustains its weight, not that it hangs with no support *under* it. The representation obviously is the other side of that in reference to "the north" in the first clause. The eye was impressed by the great void between earth and the starry heavens. The latter were stretched over this abyss, upheld by nothing under them, a striking instance of the power of God; while the broad face of the earth lay firm below this void though hung from no support that upheld it. The idea of modern astronomy that the earth is a ball, poised free on all sides in space, is of course not found here.

8. The wonder of the clouds, floating reservoirs of water, which do not burst under the weight of waters which they contain. Men bind up water in skins or bottles, God binds up the rain floods in the thin, gauzy texture of the changing cloud, which yet by His power does not rend under its burden of waters. Comp. Prov. xxx. 4; Job xxxviii. 37.

9. *he holdeth back*] Or, **he shutteth up**, or, enshrouds. The "face of his throne" is perhaps the outside of it, or that view which it would present if seen; and the meaning is that He enshrouds His throne so that it is not seen by those below. The idea cannot be that this is an occasional phenomenon, as if sometimes His throne could be seen, for though He has set His glory on the heavens, Ps. viii. 2 (comp. Ex. xxiv. 10; Ps. xviii. 12), this is but a reflection of the inner glory. The conception rather is that clouds are ever about Him, in His lofty abode, and even accompany and enshroud Him in all His movements; ch. xxxviii. 1; Am. ix. 6; Ps. civ. 3—13.

He hath compassed the waters with bounds,   10
Until the day and night come to an end.
The pillars of heaven tremble   11
And are astonished at his reproof.
He divideth the sea with his power,   12
And by his understanding he smiteth through the proud.
By his spirit he hath garnished the heavens;   13
His hand hath formed the crooked serpent.

10. The verse reads,
   He hath drawn as a circle a bound upon the face of the waters,
   At the confines of light and darkness.

The second clause is literally, *even to the confines of light with* (or, by) *darkness*, i. e. as far as where the utmost bound of light borders with darkness. The idea seems to be this: around the surface of the earth flows the ocean ("the face of the waters"); upon this like a circle all around the earth the arch of heaven comes down; all within this bound is light, for the sun rises on one side of it and goes down at the other; beyond this circle lies the utter darkness. Comp. ch. xxxviii. 19 *seq*.

11. The "pillars" of the heavens, if the conception be not wholly ideal, may be the lofty mountains on which the heavens seem to rest, and which, as they are lost in the clouds, are spoken of as belonging to heaven. At God's rebuke, when His voice of thunder rolls, or when earthquakes shake the earth, they tremble with terror of His majesty.

12, 13. These verses probably read,
   12. He quelleth the sea with his power,
      And by his understanding he smiteth through Rahab.
   13. By his breath the heavens are bright,
      His hand pierceth the fleeing serpent.

Others for "quelleth" or stilleth, prefer the meaning "stirreth up." Comp. Is. li. 15; Jerem. xxxi. 35. The word means "to terrify," and the parallelism of the second clause "smiteth through Rahab," which refers to the subduing of a raging monster, suggests that the sea when "terrified" or rebuked is in a state of fury, and is quelled by the power of God. So already the Sept. κατέπαυσεν. This sense is also more suitable to the words "by his power." On Rahab see notes, ch. ix. 13.

13. *by his spirit he hath garnished*] Rather as above. The reference is to the clearing away of storm clouds, that darken the heavens, by the breath of God.

hath formed] Rather as above, **pierceth**. The words express the half poetical, half mythological conception that the darkening in storm or in eclipse of the heavenly bodies was caused by the Dragon swallowing them up. See on ch. iii. 8, vii. 12. There is no reason to identify the swift or fleeing serpent with the *constellation* of the Dragon. Comp. Is. xxvii. 1, with Mr Cheyne's excellent note.

14 Lo, these *are* parts of his ways:
But how little a portion is heard of him?
But the thunder of his power who can understand?

14. The verse reads,
Lo these are the outskirts of his ways;
And how small a whisper is that which we hear of him!
But the thunder of his power who can understand?

The power of God is illustrated in the mighty works described in *vv.* 5—13. Yet what we see of Him in these is but the ends, the outskirts of His real operations. And what we hear of Him is but as a faint whisper; the thunder of the full unfolding of His power who can understand? The nervous brevity and sublimity of these words are unsurpassable.

CH. XXVII. JOB PROTESTS HIS INNOCENCE.

The third speaker, Zophar, fails to come forward; and Job, after a pause, resumes his discourse. This discourse is necessary in order to give this third cycle of speeches the same form as the previous two had. In each case Job in his third speech directly attacks the previous arguments of his opponents. In ch. xxii. Eliphaz had made against him plain charges of great wickedness. Job now meets these by a solemn protestation before God of his innocence (ch. xxvii. 1—6).

As the chapters are at present arranged Job's final discourse consists of two parts, one occupying chap. xxvii.—xxviii., and the other ch. xxix.—xxxi., at the close of which stands the formula, *The words of Job are ended*. The exposition of ch. xxvii.—xxviii. is beset with difficulty, partly because the line of thought is hard to trace, and partly because the sentiments expressed by Job seem to be in contradiction to the position he has hitherto maintained and which he again resumes in the following chapters. Hence doubts have been entertained by very many writers whether these two chapters ought really to be ascribed to Job, some considering that the discourses in this part of the Book have fallen into disorder and been attributed to the wrong speakers, and others that the main part of the passage ch. xxvii.—xxviii. is an altogether foreign element, which has been introduced into the Book after it left the hand of the original writer. See the Introduction.

Chap. xxvii. consists of two main parts,

First, *vv.* 1—6, a solemn protestation before God by Job of his innocence;

And second, *vv.* 7—23, a picture of the condition of the wicked man, in two divisions, (1) his dreary and desolate condition of mind, having no hope in God, when death or afflictions overtake him, *vv.* 7—10; and (2) the terrible external destruction that befalls him at the hand of God, *vv.* 11—23.

2—6. Job with the solemnity of an oath by God declares that he speaks in sincerity when affirming his innocence. Till he die he will

Moreover Job continued his parable, and said, 27
As God liveth, *who* hath taken away my judgment; 2
And the Almighty, *who* hath vexed my soul;
All the while my breath *is* in me, 3
And the spirit of God *is* in my nostrils;
My lips shall not speak wickedness, 4
Nor my tongue utter deceit.
God forbid that I should justify you: 5
Till I die I will not remove my integrity from me.
My righteousness I hold fast, and will not let it go: 6
My heart shall not reproach *me* so long as I live.

not admit his guilt; his conscience reproaches him for no part of his life.
Verses 2—4 read,
2. As God liveth who hath taken away my right,
And the Almighty who hath made bitter my soul,
3. (For my life is yet whole in me,
And the breath of God is in my nostrils),
4. My lips do not speak unjustly,
Neither doth my tongue utter deceit.

2. *my judgment*] As above, **my right.** God has taken this away by afflicting Job unjustly. The state of Job's mind here is altogether the same as before. He still cleaves to God and swears by His name, and still charges Him with iniquity in His treatment of himself.

vexed my soul] lit. *embittered*, i.e. by his mysterious afflictions; comp. Ruth i. 20 ("dealt bitterly").

3. *all the while*] The sense is rather as given above, according to the parallel passage, 2 Sam. i. 9. The phrase "my life" in the first clause is lit. *my breath*. The words are parenthetical, and are thrown in to add weight to the affirmation of his rectitude which Job is about to make (*v.* 4); they imply that, though reduced by disease, he is in possession of all his powers, and flings the whole force of his being into his affirmation.

4. *my lips shall not*] Rather, **do not.** These words contain Job's oath. He swears that he is sincere and speaks truly; comp. ch. vi. 28. The words refer to his utterances in general, especially in regard to himself, but naturally in the main, as the connexion requires, to his assertions in regard to his innocence of wrong-doing (*vv.* 5, 6).

5. *should justify you*] i.e. concede that you are in the right, viz. in charging me with evil.

remove my integrity] i.e. give up my blamelessness—refrain from asserting my innocence.

6. The second clause of *v.* 6 reads,
My heart reproacheth not one of my days,
or, *my heart reproaches* (*me*) *not since I was alive*, i.e. during all my life.

7 Let mine enemy be as the wicked,
   And he that riseth up against me as the unrighteous.
8 For what *is* the hope of the hypocrite, though he hath gained,
   When God taketh away his soul?

Of course the words have reference to the kind of charges laid against Job by his friends (e.g. ch. xxii. 6—9), and not to the sinfulness of nature common to all men, ch. xiv. 2. The "heart" in Heb. is the *conscience* or consciousness. Luther expresses the meaning vigorously when he translates: "My conscience bites me not in respect of my whole life." Comp. the whole of ch. xxxi., which is but an expansion of these words.

7—10. The dreary and desolate condition of the mind of the wicked man in affliction.

7. In *vv.* 2—6 Job protested his sincerity in affirming his innocence. With *v.* 7 commences a description of the misery of mind, and the outward destruction at the hand of God, which are the portion of the unrighteous. The "wicked" is the subject throughout to the end of the chapter; therefore in the words "let mine enemy be as the wicked" the emphasis falls on "wicked." The words express the speaker's abhorrence of the "wicked," they do not imprecate evil on his "enemy." It it understood that he wishes his "enemy" ill, and he can wish him nothing worse than that he should be as the "wicked"—so much does he himself shrink from the thought of being as the wicked are. Others (e.g. Delitzsch) put the emphasis on "enemy," taking that expression to mean "him who accuses me of iniquity"—mine enemy must appear an evil-doer, inasmuch as he charges me falsely. This makes the verse a mere parenthetical imprecation by Job on his friends, for the words taken in this sense have no connexion with *vv.* 8—10. The speaker, rather, repudiates the idea of his being one of the wicked, and he does so because he shudders to think that the condition of the mind of the wicked man, who has no hope in God, should be his—his condition of mind is very different (*vv.* 8—10). Still even when taken in this, their only natural sense, the words of *v.* 7 have no strict logical connexion with *vv.* 2—6. The connexion is: "I will never cease to maintain that I am a righteous man, for how comfortless in calamity is the condition of the wicked!" while strictly it should be: "I will never cease holding on to the way of righteousness, for how comfortless in affliction is the wicked man, having no hope in God!" So far as the mere language of *vv.* 5, 6 is concerned, the expressions "I will not remove mine integrity from me," "and my righteousness I hold fast," might have the meaning "I will continue to live a righteous life" (comp. ch. ii. 9), but such a meaning is absolutely excluded here by the connexion and general scope of *vv.* 2—6.

8. The verse most probably means,

For what is the hope of the godless man when God cutteth off,
When he taketh away his soul?

Will God hear his cry 9
When trouble cometh upon him?
Will he delight himself in the Almighty? 10
Will he always call upon God?

lit. *when He cutteth off, when God draweth out his soul.* The comfortless state of the ungodly man (A. V. hypocrite, see on ch. viii. 13), who has no trust in God, is described in three conditions of his history, first, when he is at the moment of death, when God "cutteth (him) off" and "draweth out his soul" (v. 8); second, when calamity overtakes him (v. 9); and in general, in his whole life (v. 10).

10. *will he delight himself?*] Or, **doth** he delight himself? The wicked man has no consolation, no resource, in the manifold conditions of life when men need higher help than their own; he has no pleasure in God nor fellowship with Him, and cannot appeal to Him.

It is manifest that in these verses the speaker means to contrast his own condition of mind with that of the godless man. He has hope in God, in death and in trouble, for he delighteth himself in God at all times. Such words as those in vv. 8, 10, are not out of place in the mouth of Job, comp. ch. xvi. 19 *seq.*, xix. 25 *seq.*, xxiii. 10 *seq.*, xxxi. 2—6. It is less easy, however, to combine what is implied in the words of v. 9, " Will God hear his cry when trouble cometh upon him?" with Job's repeated complaints that God refused to hear him, e. g. ch. xiii. 24, xix. 7, and many other passages. The only solution would be to consider that he had fought his way through to an assured trust in God, such as he had cherished during his past life (ch. xii. 4 *seq.*), or rather, that such a trust here suddenly broke upon him and filled his mind, and enabled him to look now for release from his calamities and restoration—in a word to anticipate that issue of his afflictions which actually ensued. And such is the construction which some of the ablest commentators (e. g. Ewald) put upon the language. Such a change of view in regard to the issue of his afflictions implies a complete revolution in Job's mind, for he had hitherto consistently and even pertinaciously (ch. xvii. 1—2, 10—16) contended that his malady was mortal, and continued to do this even so late as ch. xxiii. 14, "For he will perform the thing appointed for me." Such a revolution, however, may be conceived and admitted, provided Job's subsequent utterances are in harmony with it. Unfortunately, however, they are not; for in ch. xxx. 20 he exclaims, "I cry unto thee and thou dost not hear me, I stand up and thou gazest at me"; and in v. 23 of the same chapter he says, "For I know that thou wilt bring me unto death" (i.e. through his present afflictions). Here he is found again occupying the same position in regard to his malady under the hand of God as he had consistently maintained throughout. It is very hard to reconcile such expressions with ch. xxvii. 7—10, on the assumption that the last-named passage really belongs to Job.

11—23. The disastrous fate of the wicked man at the hand of God.

Verses 7—10 drew a contrast between the internal state of the mind of the speaker and that of the sinner; in these verses the contrast is

11   I will teach you by the hand of God:
     That which *is* with the Almighty will I not conceal.
12   Behold, all ye yourselves have seen *it;*
     Why then are ye thus altogether vain?

pursued in a terrible picture of the external history and fate of the sinner at the hand of God. From Job's hand such a picture can have no meaning, unless *either* he now anticipates for himself a happy issue out of his afflictions, and restoration to prosperity, while the calamities that befall the wicked are final; *or* regards his own afflictions, even though they should bring him unto death, as altogether different in their character and marks from those that bring the wicked man to destruction. Either side of the alternative sets Job in complete contradiction to his position in the chapters that precede and follow this one. On the former side see on *v.* 10. The latter side supposes Job now to take a view of his afflictions entirely opposed to that which he has hitherto taken and continues to take, namely that they are due to the enmity and hostility of God (ch. xiii. 24, xvi. 9, xix. 11, 22, but also ch. xxx. 21, and even the present chap. *vv.* 2—6)—a view which Elihu severely animadverts upon, ch. xxxiii. 10 *seq.* And the idea that to become the prey of pestilence and sword (*vv.* 14—15) is a sure mark of a wicked man, while to be the victim of a fatal and loathsome malady is no such proof of wickedness (Delitzsch), is one which it is difficult to treat with seriousness.

11. *by the hand of God*] Rather, **concerning** the hand of God. In a brief preface Job intimates that he will instruct his friends regarding the hand of God, that is, His operation, His method of dealing with the wicked.

with the Almighty] There is no just ground for restricting the phrase *with* the Almighty to the meaning, the plans or purposes of the Almighty, the general principles of His government, which continue to be His principles though they may not for a time appear in actual operation. Such a limitation is interpolated into the text, and is contrary to the parallelism of the first clause. In *v.* 13 the same phrase occurs, "the portion of the wicked man *with* God," which is interpreted in the next clause as "the heritage which they receive *from* the Almighty." The words refer to no *ideal* of moral government, such as always exists and *may* always manifest itself; they describe God's actual treatment of the wicked man, apart from all limitation. This is the doctrine of the three friends; that of Job in ch. xxi., and even ch. xxiv. was very different.

12. *are ye thus altogether vain?*] i.e. wherefore do ye cherish and express opinions regarding me so foolish? "Two things are surprising here," says Dillmann, "first, that Job should undertake to teach the three friends what they had always affirmed; and second, that he should say the opposite of what he had maintained in ch. xxi. and xxiv. of the prosperity of the wicked even to their death." A third thing might also seem surprising, namely that Job, while now coinciding with his friends in opinion, should reproach them with folly. To appropriate their

This *is* the portion of a wicked man with God,   13
And the heritage of oppressors, *which* they shall receive
  of the Almighty.
If his children be multiplied, *it is* for the sword: 14
And his offspring shall not be satisfied *with* bread.
Those that remain of him shall be buried in death: 15
And his widows shall not weep.
Though he heap up silver as the dust,   16
And prepare raiment as the clay;
He may prepare *it*, but the just shall put *it* on,   17

sentiments and cover the operation by calling them foolish persons was not generous. The connexion, however, of the two clauses in this verse implies that what the three friends had seen of the fate of the wicked (as now to be described by Job, *vv.* 13—23) ought to have prevented them from coming to such conclusions regarding Job's character as they had expressed or insinuated. Obviously to make such a reproach appropriate there must have been a difference clear to the eye between Job's case and the fate of the wicked. But wherein lay the difference, in Job's present condition? The three friends might be excused if they did not perceive it. The words do not seem to fit the condition in which Job still remains at the stage of development which the Poem has up to the present reached.

13—23. The utter destruction of the wicked man is exhibited in three turns: his children and descendants are destined for the sword, and become the prey of famine and pestilence (*vv.* 13—15); his wealth and possessions pass into the hands of the righteous, and his home perishes (*vv.* 16—18); and he himself is cut off suddenly by awful calamities at the hand of God, and amidst the execrations of men (*vv.* 19—23).

14. With the sentiment of this verse compare Job's former words in regard to the wicked, "Their seed is established in their sight with them, and their offspring before their eyes. They send forth their little ones like a flock, and their children dance. They spend their days in wealth," ch. xxi. 8 *seq.*

15. *buried in death*] "Death" is here, as often (Jer. xv. 2, xviii. 21, xliii. 11) *pestilence*. Those that sword and famine spare (*v.* 14) become the prey of the pestilence, and their burial shall be such as those so dying receive, without funeral rites and with no accompaniment of lamenting women. This idea is more distinctly expressed in the next clause, "his widows shall not weep"; comp. Ps. lxxviii. 64. Comp. Job's previous words as to the "burial" of the wicked, ch. xxi. 32.

16. The "dust" and "clay" or *mire* are images that express extreme abundance, Zech. ix. 3, 1 Kings x. 27. Great wardrobes of costly garments are a usual element of Oriental wealth, Gen. xxiv. 53, Josh. vii. 21, 2 Kings vii. 8, Matth. vi. 19.

17. When the ungodly are swept away the righteous remain and

And the innocent shall divide the silver.
13 He buildeth his house as a moth,
And as a booth *that* the keeper maketh.
19 The rich *man* shall lie down, but he shall not be gathered:
He openeth his eyes, and he *is* not.
20 Terrors take hold on him as waters,
A tempest stealeth him away in the night.
21 The east wind carrieth him away, and he departeth:
And as a storm hurleth him out of his place.

enter into their possessions, and the meek inherit the earth, Ps. xxxvii. 29, 34.

18. The "booth" of the "keeper" referred to is the flimsy hut erected in the vineyard or other gardens as a post for the watchman, who protects the fruit from theft or destruction by wild beasts. As described by Wetzstein (Del. *Comm. on Job,* Trans. ii. p. 74, 2nd ed. p. 348), it is built of four poles struck into the ground in the form of a square. About eight feet from the ground cross sticks are tied to these poles, over which boards are laid, and thus a couch is formed for the keeper. Some feet higher up other cross pieces of wood are fixed, and over these boughs or matting is thrown to form a roof. Such a booth is called a "lodge" Is. i. 8, and its unsubstantial character is indicated when it is said to "swing to and fro," Is. xxiv. 20.

19. *the rich man shall lie down*] " Rich " is equivalent to " wicked," Is. liii. 9. The words might be rendered, *he lieth down rich.*

shall not be gathered] The parallel in the next clause, *he is not,* suggests the general sense, *he shall rise no more.* Perhaps the most probable sense is that he shall not "be gathered and buried," according to the passages, Jer. viii. 2, xxv. 33, Ezek. xxix. 5 ; he shall have no funeral solemnities but shall be carried away by a sudden destruction. Others assume (after the Sept.) a different vocalization, *he shall do it* (lie down) *no more.* This is rather flat.

he openeth his eyes, and he is not] The words describe the suddenness of his destruction. The phrase is no more remarkable than that in 2 Kings xix. 35, "When they arose early in the morning behold they were all dead corpses." It is hardly necessary to circumscribe the words, "Hardly shall the sinner open his eyes, to view his destruction, when he is swept away."

20. The figure of overwhelming waters is a natural one in the East and common in Scripture, Ps. xviii. 16, Nah. i. 8. Comp. the language of Eliphaz to Job, ch. xxii. 11.

21. The east wind is gusty and tempestuous, ch. xxxviii. 24, Ps. xlviii. 7. See Wetzstein's note in Del.

and as a storm hurleth] Or, **and in storm hurleth.** With this which Job says of the sinner compare what he says of himself, ch. ix. 17, xxx. 22, "Thou liftest me up to the wind : thou causest me to ride upon it,

For *God* shall cast upon him, and not spare: 22
He would fain flee out of his hand.
Men shall clap their hands at him, 23
And shall hiss him out of his place.
Surely there is a vein for the silver, 28
And a place for gold *where* they fine *it*.

and dissolvest me in the tempest"; and see his former query regarding the wicked, ch. xxi. 18.

22. *shall cast upon him*] i.e. shall shoot down upon him His destroying arrows, Numb. xxxv. 20. Comp. again what Job says of himself, ch. vi. 4, xvi. 13, "His arrows compass me round about, he cleaveth my reins *and doth not spare*."

23. *men shall clap their hands*] Clapping the hands is a token of malignant gladness, Lam. ii. 15, and "hissing" a token of scorn and dislike, Jer. xlix. 17. See ch. xviii. 18, xx. 27. Comp. what Job says of his own treatment by men, ch. xvii. 6, xxx. 9—14.

CH. XXVIII. WISDOM CAN NOWHERE BE FOUND BY MAN; GOD ALONE IS IN POSSESSION OF IT; THE WISDOM OF MAN IS TO FEAR THE LORD.

The chapter contains a single thought, viz. that Wisdom cannot be reached by man. The thought, however, is set forth and illustrated in many ways and with much poetical adornment.

First, *v.* 1—14, the precious ores and stones *have* a place where they may be found, to which men penetrate and from which they bring them forth to the light; but Wisdom has no place where it can be found in all the land of the living.

Second, *vv.* 15—22, Wisdom is not to be seen in the marts of mankind; it cannot be purchased though gold and all precious things were offered for it. It is not found even in the world below, the realm of the dead.

Third, *vv.* 23—28, God alone knoweth the way to it and is in possession of it, for He is the Creator of the World. The Wisdom of man is the Fear of the Lord.

1. *surely there is*] Rather, **for** there is. The connexion, however, with the preceding is difficult to perceive (see at the end of the chapter).

there is a vein] lit. an *issue* or *source*. The emphasis falls on *is*—there *is* a place from which silver comes forth, it *has* a source out of which it may be gotten.

where they fine it] Rather, **which they** (men) **refine.** The most precious ores, both silver and gold, have a place where they may be found; however distant and dark and deep in the earth their place be, such a place is known, men penetrate to it, and bring them forth. The antithesis is presented in *v.* 12, But whence shall Wisdom be found? and where is the place of understanding? It hath no place known to man.

Iron is taken out of the earth,
And brass *is* molten *out of* the stone.
He setteth an end to darkness,
And searcheth out all perfection,
The stones of darkness, and the shadow of death.
The flood breaketh out from the inhabitant;
Even the waters forgotten of the foot:
They are dried up, they are gone away from men.
As for the earth, out of it cometh bread:
And under it is turned up as it were fire.

2. *brass is molten out of the stone*] lit. *they* (men) *melt the stone into brass*, i.e. copper. Men know how to possess themselves of the metals.
3—11. Description of mining operations.

he setteth] To prevent ambiguity it is better to translate, **man** setteth, or, **men** set. The phrase "setteth an end to darkness" hardly refers to the light shed by the miner's lamp; the expression is more general, meaning that men penetrate into what is dark and deep in the earth as if it were light and above ground—as the next clause explains.

searcheth out all perfection] Rather, **searcheth out to the very end**, or, utmost limit, **the stones of darkness and the shadow of death**, that is, the darkest recesses in the bowels of the earth. The word, very *end* or utmost *limit* is that occurring, ch. xxvi. 10 (see notes) and ch. xi. 7. On "shadow of death" see on ch. xxiv. 17.

4. This verse reads as a whole,
> They break a shaft away from man's abode;
> They are forgotten of the foot;
> Far away from men they hang, and swing.

The first clause, lit. *away from the dweller* or *inhabitant*, describes how the miners sink their shaft deep down below and away from the abode of men above. There they are forgotten by the foot of those overhead, who walk oblivious of them. And the last clause describes how they "hang and swing," i.e. swing suspended in cages or from ropes as they pursue their unnatural operations—
> half way down
> Hangs one that gathers samphire—dreadful trade.

5. The same idea of the distance from the life of men and the unnaturalness of the miner's work is pursued in the fine contrast between the peaceful, cultivated and fruitful face of the earth above and the destructive operations carried on in her bowels, which leave a confusion and devastation like that caused by fire. The second clause must be rendered,
> And underneath it is overturned as if by fire.

The reference is hardly to actual blasting; rather to the overthrow and confused ruin that follows the miner's operations.

The stones of it *are* the place of sapphires: 6
And it hath dust of gold.
There is a path which no fowl knoweth, 7
And which the vulture's eye hath not seen:
The lion's whelps have not trodden it, 8
Nor the fierce lion passed by it.
He putteth forth his hand upon the rock; 9
He overturneth the mountains by the roots.
He cutteth out rivers among the rocks; 10
And his eye seeth every precious thing.
He bindeth the floods from overflowing; 11
And the thing that is hid bringeth he forth *to* light.

6. Through these operations which carry ruin into the bowels of the earth men, however, find the richest reward. The stones of the heart of the earth are the place of sapphires, and of auriferous dust.

it hath dust of gold] "It" refers to the "place" in the first clause, hardly to the sapphire, although a particular kind of sapphire is described as being grained or striated with gold. This, however, can hardly be what is meant by "dust of gold." Instead of *it* hath dust we might render *he* hath—i.e. man; he finds his way to the place of sapphires and possesses himself of the auriferous earth.

7. *there is a path*] Rather, **that path no eagle knoweth**, lit.—*a path which no eagle* &c., the words taking up what is said in *v.* 6,—the way to the place of sapphires. The sharp-sighted birds of prey have not seen that path.

8. Neither have the proud wild beasts, which fearlessly penetrate into the darkest places, ever trodden that path.

the lion's whelps] Rather, **the proud beasts**, lit. *sons of pride*, ch. xli. 34.

passed by it] i.e. passed **over** it, walked it.

9—11. Some further touches regarding the irresistible force and the skilful ingenuity with which man conducts his operations, with the result at last of bringing that which is hidden forth to light.

9. *upon the rock*] Or, the **flinty rock**; man puts forth his hand upon the rock either to break it or pierce a way through it. His force makes the hardest obstacle give way before him.

10. *cutteth out rivers*] The word "rivers" is that commonly used to denote the canals into which the Nile was divided, and might be translated *canals* or channels. Such canals might be intended for drawing off the water accumulating in the mine. The second clause suggests, however, that the word rather means *passages* or galleries, cut in order to pursue the vein, for it is said, "his eye seeth every precious thing."

11. *he bindeth the floods from overflowing*] Rather, **he bindeth up the streams that they drip not**, lit. *that they weep not*. The reference is to the use of lime or clay to prevent water percolating into the mine.

12   But where shall wisdom be found?
     And where *is* the place of understanding?
13   Man knoweth not the price thereof;
     Neither is it found in the land of the living.
14   The depth saith, It *is* not in me:
     And the sea saith, *It is* not with me.

"The picturesque phrase ('that they weep not') may have been a technical term among miners in ancient times, just as our colliers name the action of the water that percolates through and into their workings *weeping*, and our navvies call the fine sand which percolates through the sides of a tunnel *crying* sand" (Cox, *Comm. on Job*, p. 360).

These references to mining operations shew that the Writer was familiar with them. The frequent allusions to Egypt indicate that the Author of the Book was well acquainted with that country, and possibly the mines that were extensively worked in the peninsula of Sinai would be an object of interest to travellers from Palestine to Egypt. It appears, however, that mining was in ancient times carried on in the Hauran and even in the Lebanon; and in Deut. viii. 9 Palestine is described as "a land whose stones are iron, and out of whose hills thou mayest dig brass."

12—14. The precious ores and costly stones though hidden have a place where they may be found, and man knows how to reach it and bring that which is hid to light, but where can Wisdom be found? and where is the place of understanding? It has no place and is unattainable by man; it is not to be found in the land of the living, in the deep nor in the sea.

13. *the price thereof*] For "price" the Sept. read *way*—man knoweth not the way thereof (cf. *v*. 23), i.e. the *way to it*, and very many commentators adopt this reading, which gives a more direct answer to the question in *v*. 12. If *price* be read, the phrase "man knoweth not the price thereof" does not mean that "it is too precious to be bought with money," but that it is no article of merchandise in the markets of mankind, in other words, it has never been found and is unknown among men. This meaning is clearly expressed in the second clause, "neither is it found in the land of the living."

14. Three great regions are mentioned, none of which is the "place" of Wisdom, the land of the living, the deep, and the sea. These three exhaust the extent of the upper world. The "land of the living" is the earth as the abode of living beings, more especially of men, Ps. lii. 5. The "deep" is the primeval abyss, out of which perhaps the sea is fed, lying under the earth, Gen. i. 2, Ps. xxiv. 2—an almost mythological conception. Down under all these, however, lies the underworld of the dead, ch. xxvi. 5.

15—19. As the preceding verses (1—14) expressed the idea that there was no "place" of Wisdom where men could find it and from which they could bring it forth, these verses express the idea that it can be acquired by no price which men can offer for it. It is alto-

It cannot be gotten for gold, 15
Neither shall silver be weighed *for* the price thereof.
It cannot be valued with the gold of Ophir, 16
With the precious onyx, or the sapphire.
The gold and the crystal cannot equal it: 17
And the exchange of it *shall not be for* jewels of fine gold.
No mention shall be made of coral, or of pearls: 18
For the price of wisdom *is* above rubies.
The topaz of Ethiopia shall not equal it, 19
Neither shall it be valued with pure gold.
Whence then cometh wisdom? 20
And where *is* the place of understanding?

gether unattainable. The passage may contain the additional idea of the preciousness or desirableness of Wisdom (see *v.* 18), but the purpose of these verses is not to set forth wisdom as a good or as the chief good, for which one might willingly give all that he holds most precious; the thought of the passage is that *though* one should offer gold and precious stones for Wisdom it cannot be procured, being nowhere to be found. That the Writer's purpose is to express this conception mainly is evident from the refrain which closes the passage, as a similar one closed the preceding passage: But Wisdom whence cometh it? and where is the place of understanding? (*v.* 20).

15. *for gold*] Probably, as margin, *fine gold*, i.e. purified gold; comp. 1 Kings vi. 20, where a word somewhat similar occurs.

be weighed] In ancient times money was weighed, not counted, Gen. xxiii. 16.

16. *it cannot be valued*] lit. *weighed for gold of Ophir.* Wisdom is conceived as put in the balance as other articles are that are sold, the price given for it being gold of Ophir. The meaning is, it cannot be purchased for gold of Ophir. The word *weighed* here differs from that in *v.* 15, though it has the same meaning.

17. *and the crystal*] Probably **glass**, which was rare and counted precious in ancient times.

cannot equal it] The word means to arrange, to set over against, to compare with. The idea here is that gold and glass cannot be *set against* Wisdom by way of *barter*, as the next clause distinctly states.

18. *or of pearls*] Rather, **of crystal**.

price of wisdom is above rubies] Or, **the possession of wisdom is above** (or, more than) **pearls**, i.e. pearls cannot acquire it or give possession of it. The meaning is scarcely that Wisdom is a more precious thing to possess than pearls.

19. *equal it*] See on *v.* 17.

be valued] See on *v.* 16.

20—22. The preceding verses indicated that Wisdom cannot be acquired by man though he should bid for it the most precious things

21   Seeing it is hid from the eyes of all living,
     And kept close from the fowls of the air.
22   Destruction and death say,
     We have heard the fame thereof with our ears.
23   God understandeth the way thereof,
     And he knoweth the place thereof.
24   For he looketh to the ends of the earth,

that he possesses, in other words that it is unattainable; these verses state that idea again explicitly. The question *v.* 20 implies a negative answer—nowhere by man.

21. *seeing it is hid*] Rather simply, **it is hidden**. *V.* 20 as summing up *vv.* 15—19 meant, *thus Wisdom is nowhere to be attained; v.* 21 proceeds, *it is hidden* &c.

kept close] i.e. it is concealed from, unknown to the fowls of the air (comp. *v.* 7)—no *creature* can attain to it.

22. *destruction and death*] Heb. *Abaddon* and *Death*. Abaddon is Sheol, the realm of the dead, here personified, as also is Death. Comp. Rev. i. 18, ix. 11, and see on ch. xxvi. 6.

the fame thereof] i.e. the *report* or rumour thereof. Destruction and Death have only *heard of* Wisdom, they have no knowledge of it, much less is it to be found with them. It is not true, alas! in this sense that
     There must be wisdom with great Death.

The words "we have heard the report thereof" ascribe neither a less nor a greater knowledge of Wisdom to Death than the living possess. Both are equally ignorant of it, and equally without it. As verses 13—14 told how Wisdom was nowhere to be found in the upper world so *v.* 22 states that it is not to be found in the under world. The process of exhaustion is complete: Wisdom is nowhere to be found, neither in the bowels of the earth nor in the markets of mankind, in the deep nor in the sea; neither in the land of the living nor in the place of the dead.

23—28. Wisdom can nowhere be found either by man or by any creature (*v.* 21), only by the Creator. *God* knoweth the place of it and is in possession of it, for He is the maker and upholder of the universe with all its agencies. And He has assigned to man as *his* wisdom the fear of the Lord.

23. *God understandeth the way thereof*] i.e. the way **thereto** (ch. xxiv. 18, Gen. iii. 24). The word *God* stands emphatically first in the sentence, in opposition to "all living" (*v.* 21); *He* is in possession of Wisdom. It need not be said that the words "place" and "way" are merely parts of the figure; the verse means, Wisdom is *with God* alone.

24. God is in possession of Wisdom for He is the upholder and creator of the world.

for he looketh to the ends of the earth] His glance as creator and ruler of all extends over all, to the ends of the earth and to all that lies under the whole heavens.

And seeth under the whole heaven;
To make the weight for the winds;   25
And he weigheth the waters by measure.
When he made a decree for the rain,   26
And a way for the lightning of the thunder:
Then did he see it, and declare it;   27

25. *to make the weight for the winds*] Or, **making** (when he made), appointing the winds their greater or less force. The idea is of course that God weighed the winds themselves, i. e. defined their bulk exactly, not that, in modern language, he gave to each its weight or pressure, though the sense is little different.

and he weigheth the waters by measure] Or, **and he meted out the waters by measure**. The "waters" are the rains, *v.* 26. The "winds" and "waters" are examples, taken to represent all, of the agencies and forces of creation. These were and continue all weighed and measured, adjusted and directed by God. The second half of the verse explains the first. In the first half it is not God's abstract omniscience that is referred to, but His universal oversight as Creator; and the sense of the whole verse, which supports the assertion that God has Wisdom (*v.* 23), is not that God *must be* in possession of Wisdom in order to be Creator, which without Wisdom He could not be, but rather that His being Creator enables us to understand how Wisdom is or comes to be in His possession.

Wisdom in this passage, as in other parts of Scripture where it is spoken of, is properly the *idea* or conception lying behind or under the fixed order of the universe, the world-plan. This fixed order itself with all its phenomena and occurrences is nothing but God fulfilling Himself in many ways, but these ways may be reduced to one conception, and this is Wisdom, which is thus conceived as a thing having an objective existence of its own. Naturally such an objective thing is apt to be personified and may be "seen," "established," "searched out" and the like. In the same way the question may be put, Where is Wisdom to be found? and the answer given that it can be found nowhere. This question and answer merely mean that man cannot attain to *intellectual* apprehension of the idea of the universe, nor understand the principle underlying the phenomena and events of the world and human life.

26—27. The idea of the preceding verse taken up anew and expanded—in creation God saw Wisdom and searched it out.

26. *a decree for the rain*] This "decree" comprises all the laws that regulate the rain, appointing its measure and its seasons as early and latter rain.

27. *then did he see it*] *then*, i. e. when He made a decree for the rain—in the act or at the time of creation, when He gave material agencies their laws. Then He "saw" Wisdom, she presented herself to His view.

and declare it] The margin *number* or count (ch. xxxviii. 37) gives a

He prepared it, yea, and searched it out.
28 And unto man he said, Behold, the fear of the Lord, that
is wisdom;

very good sense, the meaning being that God went over, enumerated or *surveyed* the parts and complex powers of Wisdom. The meaning will not be greatly different if the rendering "declare" be retained and taken in the sense of *uttered*. This might be done by pronouncing the name of Wisdom, as God presents before His own mind the meaning of any servant or agent of His by calling him by his name (Is. xliii. 1, xlv. 3). Others take "declare" in the sense that God gave expression to Wisdom in the varied works of creation. This is a very unnatural sense in which to take "declare." Besides, of the four expressions used, "saw," "declared," "established," "searched out," the first and last refer exclusively to acts of the Divine mind and it is improbable that the middle terms should refer to acts or operations of God's creative hand. Nor is there allusion to any to whom the declaration was made, God alone being referred to in the verse.

he prepared it] Or, **established it**. The sense appears to be the same as in Prov. viii. 22 "the Lord *formed* me," i.e. gave me existence. The Writer conceives Wisdom, if not as a person, at least as something that has being or existence of its own. According to Prov. viii. 23 *seq.* Wisdom received its existence prior to the creation of the world. In the present passage it is not quite easy to say whether the idea be that Wisdom received existence *in* creation or before it, at least it did so in connexion with creation ("then"). It is unnecessary, however, and contrary to the Poet's vivid conception of Wisdom as a real thing or being, to suppose that it was "established" when embodied in the stable, permanent order of created things, as if, being merely an idea before, with wavering outlines, it then became fixed. Neither can the meaning be that God "set up" Wisdom before Him merely as an object of contemplation; much less that He set it up as a "model" after which to work in creating the world, or constituted it "the conductor of the whole general order of the world." These are all additional ideas, hardly warranted by the expression employed.

yea, and searched it out] The word *yea* implies that this searching out of Wisdom was something higher than the preceding acts. God explored Wisdom, He saw through it, and brought before Himself the full idea of all that was in its nature and its powers. The word can hardly mean He *proved* it, e.g. to see whether it was suitable or able for its great function, the guidance of the course of things in the world. This again is an additional idea, which the word does not express.

28. *and unto man he said*] This ordinance in regard to man is also considered contemporary with creation; then God saw and searched out Wisdom, and at the same time, as suitable to man's place, He ordained for him *his* Wisdom, which is the fear of the Lord and to depart from evil.

The Wisdom spoken of throughout the chapter is a possession of God alone, it is His who is Creator; man has a wisdom also, which

And to depart from evil *is* understanding.

is that of the creature, to fear the Lord. There is not, however, in all the chapter the shadow of a complaint; there is no turning of the spirit against God (ch. xv. 13) under the feeling that the "envious" Creator has reserved the higher insight for Himself, and only bound on mankind the heavy burden of "fearing" Him. Such a thought is wholly at variance with the spirit of the passage. The speaker is calm and reflective and, to all appearance, satisfied that things are as we see them because they could not be otherwise.

Wisdom is the idea or principle lying under the order of the Universe, the world plan. This order of the world, however, is not a mere physical one, an order of "nature." Such an idea as "nature" was foreign to the Hebrew mind. Equally unknown was the idea of a mere physical constitution of things. The constitution of the world was moral, and hence the life and destinies of men, no less than the phenomena of the world, were comprised under Wisdom.

When it is said that Wisdom has no place where it can be found and can be purchased for no price, the language is based upon the conception of Wisdom as an objective thing; but the meaning is that intellectual apprehension of the scope of the phenomena of the world and the events of man's life is beyond the reach of man; such knowledge belongs only to God, who made the world.

To inculcate this truth and the other truth related to it, that man's wisdom is the fear of the Lord, is the object of the chapter.

It seems an entire misapprehension of the meaning of the passage when it is regarded as teaching that "Wisdom, unlike earthly treasures, is nowhere to be found in the visible, sensible world"; that "not in the world of sense, but only from and with God can it be acquired, through the fear of God." The distinctions introduced here are modern. The passage teaches that Wisdom cannot be found either in the visible or the invisible world (*v.* 22), neither by man nor by any creature (*v.* 21). It is a thing possible to God alone; and man does not attain to it through the fear of the Lord,—the fear of the Lord is the substitute ordained for man instead of it; for as the absolute Wisdom belongs to the Creator, so the fear of the Lord is the wisdom that befits the creature.

The connexion between chapters xxvii. and xxviii. is difficult to perceive. Very many suggestions have been offered, of which two may be noticed.

Chap. xxvii. ends with a dark picture of the fate of the wicked at "the hand of God," and ch. xxviii. begins, "*for* there is a vein for the silver...but where shall Wisdom be found?" As Job in ch. xxvii. is understood to be modifying his former statements he is supposed by some to speak thus: "I concede that such (ch. xxvii. 13—23) is the fate of the wicked [but all riddles of Providence are not thereby solved, for example the afflictions of just men like myself, nor can they be solved] *for*, though men may attain to much by their skill and insight, Wisdom is beyond them." This makes the whole of ch. xxviii., introduced by *for*, the support of a thought which is not expressed nor even hinted at, but merely interpolated from the mind of the commentator.

Others, assuming Job to be the speaker, connect thus: "such (ch. xxvii. 13—23) is the disastrous fate of the wicked [and it must be so] *for* Wisdom [which is the way to prosperity in life] can be reached only through the fear of the Lord [which such men have rejected"]. Apart from the strong interpolations needful to help out the thought, the extraordinary circumlocution, in the shape of the long disquisition on Wisdom, which the speaker is supposed to employ in order to express his idea, marks this attempt to construct a bridge between the two chapters as desperate. Besides, if the remarks made above in regard to the general meaning of ch. xxviii. have any worth, the attempt is based upon a reading of the sense of that chapter which is entirely wrong.

See further on these two chapters in the Introduction.

CH. XXIX.—XXXI. JOB'S FINAL SURVEY OF HIS WHOLE CIRCUMSTANCES AND CAUSE.

The passage falls into three parts, corresponding to the separate chapters:

First, ch. xxix., a sorrowful and regretful retrospect of his past happiness.

Second, ch. xxx., a contrasted picture of his present abject condition.

Third, ch. xxxi., a solemn repudiation of all offences that might account for such a change, and a new entreaty that God would reveal to him the cause of his afflictions.

CH. XXIX. A PATHETIC PICTURE OF JOB'S FORMER PROSPERITY AND RESPECT.

The passage has these parts:

First, *vv.* 2—10, a sorrowful review of the happiness of former days, in which the things that made up this happiness, now departed, are enumerated: (1) God's keeping of him (*v.* 2), His light upon his path (*v.* 3), and His intimacy and protection over his tent (*v.* 4); (2) the presence of his children about him (*v.* 5); (3) the prosperity, almost more than natural, that flowed in upon him in ways unsought (*v.* 6); and (4) above all the respect and reverence paid him by his fellow citizens, as he sat in their council and went among them (*vv.* 7—10). This last is the great thought that fills the chapter and forms the contrast to the wretchedness and the contempt from the meanest of mankind which he now endures (ch. xxx.).

Second, *vv.* 11—17, the reason of this universal reverence of men for him—his benevolence and impartial justice.

Third, *vv.* 18—20, an almost involuntary reference to his calm and sure outlook into the future amidst this universal respect.

Fourth, *vv.* 21—25, after which the great thought of the passage, his high place among men and the delight which his benevolent intercourse with them was to him, again rushes into his mind.

Moreover Job continued his parable, and said, 29
O that I were as *in* months past, 2
As *in* the days *when* God preserved me;
When his candle shined upon my head, 3
And *when* by his light I walked *through* darkness;
As I was in the days of my youth, 4
When the secret of God *was* upon my tabernacle;
When the Almighty *was* yet with me, 5
When my children *were* about me;
When *I* washed my steps with butter, 6
And the rock poured me out rivers of oil;
When I went out *to* the gate through the city, 7

2. Job begins with a pathetic expression of regret as he remembers happier times. His former happiness was due to God's preserving or *watching over* him, and the loss of it was due to God's forsaking him.
3. This verse expands "preserved" or "watched over" in *v.* 2.
his candle shined upon] Or, **his lamp shined over.** God's lamp shone above him, and lighted his path, so that the darkness before him was made to be light, Is. xlii. 16. God's "lamp" is a figure for His favour and enlightenment and prospering of him.
4. *days of my youth*] lit. *days of my autumn.* It is doubtful if Job means to describe by this expression any period of his own *age*, namely his manhood. He rather compares his former time of prosperity to the *season* of the year, the autumn, the time of fruit-gathering and plenty and joy, and also thankfulness to God (clause second).
the secret of God] i.e. the intimacy and friendship of God; comp. on ch. xix. 19. God's friendship or intimacy watched over his tent.
5. Naturally the first element in Job's happiness in those past days was the presence of his children.
6. The second, though a less, element of his happiness was his overflowing abundance.
when I washed my steps] Or, **when my steps were washed** in butter, i.e. bathed—a figure for the overflowing abundance amidst which he walked.
the rock poured me out] As marg., poured out *with me* or *beside me.* The unfruitful rock poured out rivers of oil beside him; his blessings were so abundant that they came unsought and seemed above nature.
7. The third and chiefest element of his past happiness was the respect of men, and the joy of intercourse with them. This is the main subject of the chapter.
the gate through the city] Or, the gate **by the city.** Job, a rich landowner, probably did not live in the city but on his estate that adjoined it. He took part, however, in all the life of the city, and sat in the council that guided its affairs. The "gate" is spoken of as the place where the Council or Assembly of the town met. Such a "gate" is

When I prepared my seat in the street;
8   The young men saw me, and hid themselves:
And the aged arose, *and* stood *up*.
9   The princes refrained talking,
And laid *their* hand on their mouth.
10   The nobles held their peace,
And their tongue cleaved to the roof of their mouth.
11   When the ear heard *me*, then it blessed me;
And when the eye saw *me*, it gave witness to me:
12   Because I delivered the poor that cried,
And the fatherless, and *him that had* none to help him.
13   The blessing of him that was ready to perish came upon me:
And I caused the widow's heart to sing for joy.
14   I put on righteousness, and it clothed me:

usually a building of considerable size, like an arcade, and hence it is spoken of here as an independent edifice *by* or *beside* the city. Others render *up to* the city, supposing that the city, as not unusual, was built on an eminence.

in the street] lit. *broad place*, i.e. market place, a synonym for "gate."

8. *hid themselves*] The young men withdrew out of reverence, not knowing perhaps how to meet and rightly salute one so great as Job was.

arose, and stood up] The aged are supposed already met in the gate and seated; on Job's approach they rise and remain standing till he has sat down.

9, 10. The meaning seems to be that Job's arrival put a stop to speech and discussion already going on, which was not resumed until he should be heard.

11—17. The ground of this universal reverence—Job's benevolent care of the poor and his strict justice to their cause.

11. This verse may read,

For the ear that heard of me blessed me,
And the eye that saw me gave witness to me.

Those who had only heard of him by report "blessed" him, that is, "called him happy," as one whom blessing and prosperity must follow because of his benevolence and mercy to the needy; and they who saw him as he lived among men bore testimony to his goodness—as *v.* 12 indicates.

12. *and him that had none to help him*] Perhaps, *the fatherless, that had none to help him*, only two classes being referred to, the "poor" and the "fatherless."

14. *and it clothed me*] Rather, and it **clothed itself in me**. Job clothed himself with righteousness, so that as a man he was lost in the

My judgment *was* as a robe and a diadem.
I was eyes to the blind, 15
And feet *was* I to the lame.
I *was* a father to the poor: 16
And the cause *which* I knew not I searched out.
And I brake the jaws of the wicked, 17
And pluckt the spoil out of his teeth.
Then I said, I shall die in my nest, 18
And I shall multiply *my* days as the sand.
My root *was* spread out by the waters, 19
And the dew lay all night upon my branch.

justice that clothed him; and justice clothed itself in him—he on the other hand was justice become a person.

15. The blind he enabled to see that which of themselves they could not perceive; the lame he enabled to attain to that which of themselves they were unable to reach.

16. *the cause which I knew not*] Rather, **the cause of him whom I knew not.** Not merely the poor about him, to whom he might feel that he owed help, but even strangers who had a cause that needed unravelling he aided by his wisdom and justice.

17. The figure is that of a beast of prey, who has its booty already in its teeth. The verse carries on v. 16; even when the unjust oppressor seemed already to have triumphed and carried off his prey, it was torn from his jaws.

18—20. Job's outlook on the future, amidst this benevolent and active life. He anticipated length of days and continued prosperity.

18. *in my nest*] i.e. surrounded by those belonging to him; he should die before them, not they before him, and in the midst of his possessions.

my days as the sand] *Sand* is the usual rendering of the word occurring here—an image of countless number. Most modern writers translate *as the Phœnix*, in accordance with Jewish tradition. The Sept. renders *as the branch of the palm* (φοίνικος). The Heb. word however can hardly have been translated *palm*, a meaning which does not belong to it, and the present Sept. text may have arisen from a misunderstanding of its original reading, *like the Phœnix*. The word "nest" in the first clause favours this translation. This bird was fabled to live 500 years, and to consume himself and his nest with fire, only to arise anew to life out of the ashes. Hence the name became a proverb, expressing the highest duration of life, φοίνικος ἔτη βιοῦν, to live as long as the Phœnix. The fable being current in Egypt the author of the Book might readily become acquainted with it.

19, 20. These verses continue the description of Job's outlook into the future in those happy days. They read better thus,

    19. My root shall be spread out to the waters,
       And the dew shall lie all night upon my branch;

20   My glory *was* fresh in me,
    And my bow was renewed in my hand.
21   Unto me *men* gave ear, and waited,
    And kept silence at my counsel.
22   After my words they spake not again;
    And my speech dropped upon them.
23   And they waited for me as for the rain;
    And they opened their mouth wide *as* for the latter rain.
24   *If* I laughed on them, they believed *it* not;
    And the light of my countenance they cast not down.
25   I chose out their way, and sat chief,
    And dwelt as a king in the army,
    As *one that* comforteth the mourners.

> 20.   My glory shall be fresh in me,
>   And my bow shall be renewed in my hand.

19. Comp. the image, ch. xiv. 8, 9. The dew lying all night upon his branch would keep it fresh and green.

20. His "glory," i.e. high respect and rank, would continue "fresh," lit. *new*, never be tarnished or diminished. His *bow*, symbol of strength and power, would like a tree renew its freshness and suppleness in his hand.

21—25. Return to the main thought of the passage, his place among men, his brothers.

22. *dropped upon them*] i.e. like a refreshing, quickening rain, when they were wearied and perplexed in counsel.

24. The verse means rather,

> I laughed on them, when they had no confidence,
> And the light of my countenance they cast not down.

Job, with his broader insight and more capable counsel, smiled on those who were perplexed and despondent; what seemed insurmountable difficulty or threatened disaster to them, seemed to him a thing easy to overcome and nothing to create alarm; while on the other hand the despondency of others was never able to cloud the cheerfulness of his countenance, so full was his mind of resource.

25. A concluding picture of the joy which he had in the fellowship of men, and how they recognised his worth and set him as a king among them, and yet how he with his high advantages and great wealth felt towards them, being among them as one that comforteth the mourning.

I chose out their way] The words probably mean that Job "chose" the way that led to the society of men, he gladly sought intercourse with them, and delighted himself in their fellowship. The other sense, *I chose out the way for them to go*, is less natural.

But now *they that are* younger than I have me in derision, 30
Whose fathers I would have disdained
To have set with the dogs of my flock.
Yea, whereto *might* the strength of their hands profit me, 2
In whom old age was perished?
For want and famine *they were* solitary; 3
Flying *into* the wilderness
In former time desolate and waste.

CH. XXX. THE CONTRASTED PICTURE OF JOB'S PRESENT ABJECT CONDITION.

The chapter forms a contrast to ch. xxix.; and as in that picture of Job's past felicity the brightest part was the high respect he enjoyed among men, sitting a prince in the midst of them, so in this the darkest part is the contumely and indignity he now suffers from the basest and most abject of mankind. Ch. xxix. ended with a reference to his former high place among men, and the present chapter starts with the antithesis to this, the contempt in which the base-born races now hold him. The subjects touched upon in the chapter are the same as those in ch. xxix., though they are pursued in the reverse order.

First, *vv.* 1—8, a picture of the base and miserable race of men who now hold him in contempt.

Second, *vv.* 9—15, description of the indignities to which he is subjected at their hands.

Third, *vv.* 16—23, account of the condition to which he is reduced; his despondency of mind, his gnawing pains, and the terrible severity of God under which he suffers.

Fourth, *vv.* 24—31, a final contrast between his present unpitied, joyless condition and former days, when he himself was full of compassion for them in trouble and when his life was filled with music and gladness.

1. *younger than I*] Comp. what was said of the demeanour of the youths in former days, ch. xxx. 8.

would have disdained to have set] Or, **I disdained to set.**

2. The verse refers to the *fathers* (*v.* 1), and gives the reason why Job did not employ them, or consider them worthy of a treatment equal to that of his dogs—they were enfeebled and fallen into premature decay. Yet the children of these miserable people now have him in derision. In the East the "dogs of the flock" have only one use, viz. to guard the flock and the encampment from attacks by night.

3—8. Description of this wretched class of outcasts. The *tenses* should all be put in the present. The race of people referred to appears to be the same as that in ch. xxiv.

3. The verse reads,

With want and hunger they are gaunt,
They gnaw the desert, in former time desolate and waste.

4   Who cut up mallows by the bushes,
    And juniper roots *for* their meat.
5   They were driven forth from among men,
    (They cried after them as *after* a thief;)
6   To dwell in the clifts of the valleys,
    In caves of the earth, and *in* the rocks.
7   Among the bushes they brayed;
    Under the nettles they were gathered together.
    They were children of fools, yea, children of base men:
    They were viler than the earth.
9   And now am I their song,
    Yea, I am their byword.
10 They abhor me, they flee far from me,
    And spare not to spit in my face.

The first clause refers to the "shrivelled" appearance of these outcasts from want; the second to their devouring the roots which they can gather in the steppe (*v.* 4), which has for long been desolate and unproductive. The word rendered "they gnaw" occurs again of Job's gnawing pains, *v.* 17. For "in former time," i.e. *for long*, others translate *darkness*: the darkness of desolation and waste—a description of the desert.

4. *by the bushes*] i.e. *beside* or among the bushes. The "mallows" or "salt-wort" which they pluck as food is found among the bushes, which cover it from the heat and drought, and under the shadow of which it thrives.

juniper roots] Or, **roots of the broom.**

5—6. Such creatures when they approach civilized dwellings are driven forth and pursued with cries as men do a thief.

   They are driven forth from among men,
   They cry after them as after a thief,
   And they must dwell in the clefts of the valleys, &c.

The word "clifts" in the ordinary texts here is either a misprint for "clifts" or clefts, or is used in that sense.

7. *they brayed*] Rather, **they bray.**

were gathered] Better, **are gathered**, or perhaps rather, *stretch themselves*, i.e. fling themselves down. Their cries are like those of the wild ass seeking for food (ch. vi. 5), and they throw themselves down like wild beasts under the bushes in the desert.

8. The verse reads in close connexion with *v.* 7,

   Children of fools, yea children of base men,
   They are scourged out of the land.

Children of "base men," lit. *of no name*, i.e. base born, they are beaten or "crushed" out of the land.

9—10. Job's treatment now at the hands of these outcasts.

Because he hath loosed my cord, and afflicted me, 11
They have also let loose the bridle before me.
Upon *my* right hand rise the youth; 12
They push away my feet,
And they raise up against me the ways of their destruction.
They mar my path, 13

With "spit in my face" comp. ch. xvii. 6. In ch. xxiv. Job referred to this miserable race with compassion; they had often no doubt excited his pity, and he saw in their lot and in the injustice and cruelties which they suffered at the hands of more prosperous men a strange mystery of providence. Now he speaks of their conduct to himself with resentment; for it was no requital of any injury he had ever done them. Yet though they might mistake Job's individual feeling to them, he was one of the class that had robbed them and that continued the robbery and oppression, and they avenged their wrongs on him with a malicious delight in the calamities that had overtaken him.

11—14. Further description of the outrageous insults of these base outcasts.

11. *V.* 11 is very variously understood; it may mean,

For they have loosed their rein and humbled me,
They have cast off the bridle before me.

So taken, the two clauses have much the same meaning, each being a figurative manner of saying that the low rabble have cast off all restraint, and subject the sufferer to painful humiliations. The verb in the first clause is *sing.*, but may distribute to each the conduct of the whole. Others, however, make the subject to be *God*, rendering: Because he has loosed his rein and humbled me, they also have cast off the bridle before me (A. V.). There is nothing, however, to indicate such an antithesis between two different subjects in the two clauses. Another reading gives *my* rein or cord (A. V.), but no help comes from adopting this.

12. This verse reads,

Upon the right hand riseth up a (low) brood,
They push away my feet,
And they cast up against me their ways of destruction.

By "pushing away" his feet, appears to be meant thrusting him away from place to place. The last clause refers to the practice of besiegers casting up a "mount" or raised way on which to approach the beleaguered town and carry destruction to it; such "mounts" are here called "their ways of destruction."

13. *They mar my path*] Or, **they break up** my path. The reference can hardly be to the path or way leading to the besieged place (*v.* 12), so that the approach of succour is cut off; if the figure be continued the path must rather be the way of *escape*. Perhaps the figure is departed from in this clause, and the words may be taken more generally as meaning the path *of his life*, which they make it impossible to go in.

They set forward my calamity,
They have no helper.
14 They came *upon me* as a wide breaking in *of waters:*
In the desolation they rolled themselves *upon me*
15 Terrors are turned upon me:
They pursue my soul as the wind:
And my welfare passeth away as a cloud.
16 And now my soul is poured out upon me;
The days of affliction have taken hold upon me.
17 My bones are pierced in me in the night season:
And my sinews take no rest.

set forward my calamity] i.e. help on my downfall—aggravate my afflictions and advance the issue of them.
they have no helper] Or, **they who have** no helper. The phrase "to have no helper" means to be one shunned and despised of all. Yet such persons now persecute him with injurious insult. The words are an involuntary exclamation. The phrase might mean: *against whom there is no helper;* i.e. none to rescue Job from them, or to interfere in his behalf against them.

14. The verse reads,
They come in as through a wide breach,
Amidst the crash they roll themselves upon me.
The figure is that of a stormed fastness. The "crash" is that of the falling walls.

15. Terrors are turned against me,
They chase away my honour like the wind;
And my welfare is passed away as a cloud.
He is assailed by terrors. The words "like the wind" mean, like as the wind chases away (the chaff, &c.). On the figure of the dissolving cloud comp. vii. 9. The expression "terrors" indicates that, though Job is here speaking of his injurious treatment at the hands of this rabble, it is not merely the external ignominy that fills his mind; it is the deeper moral problem which such abasement raises. Such expressions, however, have suggested to several writers that what Job describes in *vv.* 11—15 is not the outrageous insults of the base-born outcasts referred to in *vv.* 1—10, but his afflictions, under the figure of an assailing army sent against him from God, comp. ch. xvi. 12—14, xix. 12. The passage is difficult, but upon the whole this view is less natural.

16. The condition of despondency to which Job was reduced.
17. His tormenting pains.
In the night season my bones are pierced (and fall) off from me,
And my gnawing pains take no rest.
The first clause refers to his tormenting pains, severest in the night,

By the great force *of my disease* is my garment changed: 18
It bindeth me about as the collar of my coat.
He hath cast me into the mire, 19
And I am become like dust and ashes.
I cry unto thee, and thou dost not hear me: 20
I stand *up*, and thou regardest me *not*.
Thou art become cruel to me: 21
With thy strong hand thou opposest thyself against me.
Thou liftest me up to the wind; thou causest me to ride 22
 upon *it*,
And dissolvest my substance.
For I know *that* thou wilt bring me *to* death, 23
And *to* the house appointed for all living.

under which his bones seem pierced and his limbs to be wrenched from him. "My gnawing pains" is lit. *my gnawers*.

18. The verse is obscure.
the great force of my disease] Or, **by his great power**; i.e. God's power, put forth in Job's afflictions.
my garment changed] lit. *disguised* or *disfigured*.
it bindeth me] The meaning may be: *it clingeth to me like the neck of my inner garment*. The reference is supposed to be to his emaciated condition; his outer garment hangs on him disfigured, clinging to him like the neck or opening of the close-fitting inner tunic. The connexion and the phrase "by His great power," i.e. the power that causes intolerable agonies, might suggest that the reference in the verse is to Job's writhing under his pains till the clothes are twisted tightly about him.

19—23. God's great severity.

19. The verse probably refers to the appearance which Job's body presented in its leprous condition; this was due to God, who is represented as causing it by plunging Job as it were into the mire.

20. This verse reads,

 I cry unto thee and thou dost not hear me,
 I stand up, and thou lookest at me.

The second clause describes Job's importunity in his appeal, but the only reply is that God "looketh" at him, i.e. with silent indifference, or in stern severity.

22. *dissolvest my substance*] Rather, **dissolvest me in the tempest**; lit. *in the roar* of the storm. He is carried away and dissolved or dissipated, that is, destroyed in the whirlwind.

23. This verse explains *v.* 22 and supports it. Job knows that his afflictions can end in nothing but his death.
house appointed for] Or, **house of meeting** for all living, i.e. the grave, or Sheol, the place of the dead.

24 Howbeit *he* will not stretch out *his* hand to the grave,
Though *they* cry in his destruction.
25 Did not I weep for him that was in trouble?
Was *not* my soul grieved for the poor?
26 When I looked for good, then evil came *unto me:*
And when I waited for light, there came darkness.
27 My bowels boiled, and rested not:
The days of affliction prevented me.
28 I went mourning without the sun:
I stood up, *and* I cried in the congregation.
29 I am a brother to dragons,

24. This obscure verse may mean,
Yet doth not one stretch out the hand in his fall?
When he is destroyed doth he not because of this utter a cry?

The word *fall* is lit. *heap,* i. e. ruin. The verse, so interpreted means, Does not one stretch out his hand for help in his downfall? does he not when being destroyed, or, in his misfortune, utter a cry? Job explains how in his misery he cries unto God, it is the instinct of mankind. The following verse, referring to Job's compassion when he saw others in trouble, suggests that he naturally looked for the same compassion to himself. The word *cry* (second clause), if referred to a different root, might mean *riches* (so ch. xxxvi. 19), and the verse would mean, *surely one stretches not out his hand against a heap* (of ruins), *or, hath he riches from another's* (lit. *his,* or *its*) *destruction?* Job characterizes himself as a heap of ruins, and, appealing to the Almighty, argues that against such a thing one does not stretch out a hostile hand; neither does one derive advantage to himself from another's calamity. This sense fits into *v.* 25 very well—Job, so far from increasing misfortune which he saw, commiserated and helped it.

25. The compassion which Job seeks in his affliction it was his practice and nature to bestow.

26. This being his feeling towards those in trouble he looked that his own prosperity would continue; his afflictions were unexpected.

27—30. Further details of his sufferings in his time of affliction. The *tenses* should be put in the present.

27. *My bowels boiled*] Rather, **boil.**
prevented me] i.e. *are come before me,* have overtaken me. The bowels are the seat of feeling; and the words "my bowels boil" describe the tumult of feelings, griefs, regrets and pains, that worked within him.

28. *I went mourning*] Better perhaps, **I go blackened, not by the sun.** The reference is to his appearance from his disease: he is black, but his blackness is not due to the sun, comp. Song i. 6.

29. The verse expands the words "I cry" in *v.* 28,

And a companion to owls.
My skin is black upon me, 30
And my bones are burnt with heat.
My harp also is *turned* to mourning, 31
And my organ into the voice of them that weep.
I made a covenant with mine eyes; 31

> I am a brother to the jackals,
> And a companion to the ostriches.

The mournful howl of the jackals is elsewhere referred to, Mic. i. 8; the ostrich also sends forth a weird, melancholy cry, particularly by night; hence in ch. xxxix. 13 the female ostrich receives the name of "wailer."

30. *is black upon me*] Or, *is black* and falls *from me*. The "heat" in his bones refers to his burning pains.

31. The joyous music of his former life is turned into wailing. The "organ" is the *pipe*, ch. xxi. 12; comp. Lam. v. 15.

CH. XXXI. JOB SOLEMNLY CLEARS HIMSELF OF ALL OFFENCES.

The chapter consists of a series of protestations on the one hand, accompanied on the other by curses on himself if these protestations of innocence are not true. Occasionally appeals are made to God to judge him; and in some instances the considerations are stated which weighed with him and restrained him from the sins of which he protests his innocence. In Job's present condition, when he now speaks, some of these imprecations appear unsuitable. But we must consider that as he is reviewing his past life, his mind throws him back into the circumstances in which he was then living, and this brings before him the considerations and feelings which then weighed with him.

The chapter falls into three sections,

First, *vv.* 1—12, Job clears himself of all those secret sensual desires of the heart which seduce men into shameful conduct.

Second, *vv.* 13—23, he repudiates all abuse of his power in reference to those inferior in rank, and all selfish indifference to the sufferings and wants of the unfortunate.

Third, *vv.* 24—40, he clears himself of every secret feeling that would be accounted dishonourable, whether in regard to men or God.

1—12. Job clears himself of cherishing or yielding to sensuous desires. This idea is pursued through a series of instances; (1) simple desire, excited by the eye, *vv.* 1—4; (2) actual yielding to such desire in word or deed, *vv.* 5—8; (3) the grossest form of sensual sin, *vv.* 9—12.

1. The "eye," the lusts of which are frequently spoken of in scripture, is the great inlet through which that which is without affects the heart and stirs evil desire. Job made a "covenant" or agreement with his eyes, that they should obey his mind, or act always in harmony with his higher self.

Why then should I think upon a maid?
2 For what portion of God *is there* from above?
And *what* inheritance of the Almighty from on high?
3 *Is* not destruction to the wicked?
And a strange punishment to the workers of iniquity?
4 Doth not he see my ways,
And count all my steps?
5 If I have walked with vanity,
Or *if* my foot hath hasted to deceit;
6 Let me be weighed in an even balance,
That God may know mine integrity.

why then should I think] Or, **how then should I look?** Under his contract with his eyes such sinful looking upon a woman (Matt. v. 28) was impossible; comp. Rom. vi. 2, We that died to sin, how shall we live any longer therein?

2—4. The considerations that restrained him from such a sin. These are recited as they then influenced his mind.

2. And what is the portion from God above?
   And what the heritage from the Almighty on high?
3. Is it not destruction to the wicked,
   And calamity to the workers of iniquity?

4. Here "ways" and "steps" are said of things so slight as the glance of the eye. These are "seen" and "counted" by God. The thought of God in these verses is as lofty as the conception of morality is close and inward.

5—8. These verses continue to amplify the thought that Job refused to give way to any evil desire. The protestation lies in *v.* 5 and *v.* 7, the curse imprecated on himself in *v.* 8, while *v.* 6 is parenthetical, thrown in to confirm the denial implicitly contained in *v.* 5.

5. If I have walked with falsehood,
   And my foot hath hasted after deceit
6. (Let him weigh me in an even balance,
   And let God know mine integrity),
7. If my step hath turned out of the way, &c.

5. "Falsehood" or vanity, which is not merely in word but in thought, and "deceit" are here treated as persons; with the one Job denies that he has "walked," i.e. accompanied it, and the other he denies that he "hasted after," i.e. followed it. He has made no companion of falsity nor followed after deceit, to do aught that they would seduce him to. From the imprecation in *v.* 8, Let me sow and another eat! it is probable that what Job clears himself of is all false dealing prompted by cupidity.

6. A solemn assertion before God the judge that his denial in *v.* 5 is true. The words are parenthetical.

If my step hath turned out of the way, 7
And mine heart walked after mine eyes,
And *if any* blot hath cleaved to my hands;
Then let me sow, and let another eat; 8
Yea, let my offspring be rooted out.
If mine heart have been deceived by a woman, 9
Or *if* I have laid wait at my neighbour's door;
Then let my wife grind unto another, 10
And let others bow down upon her.
For this *is* a heinous crime; 11
Yea, it *is* an iniquity *to be punished by* the judges.
For it *is* a fire *that* consumeth to destruction, 12
And would root out all mine increase.

7. *out of the way*] i.e. the way of rectitude, set before him by God, ch. xxiii. 11. This going out of the way is amplified in the next words, *if mine heart walked after mine eyes*, i.e. if my mind consented and yielded to the lust of the eye. By such yielding he would have fallen into deeds that would have left a "blot" or stain upon his hands; comp. Ps. xxiv. 4.

8. The imprecation.
let my offspring be rooted out] Rather, let my **produce**, i.e. what springs out of that which I have planted or sown; comp. Lev. xxvi. 16; Deut. xxviii. 33.

9—12. The grossest sensual sin, adultery.
heart have been deceived] Or, *befooled, infatuated.*

10. To "grind unto another," i.e. at the mill, is to be the slave of another, Is. xlvii. 2. The slave was at the same time usually the concubine of her master, and the curse means, Let my wife be the slave (first clause) and the concubine (second clause) of others. It is probable, however, that in usage the language of the first clause carried the same sense as the second.

11. *a heinous crime*] Or, *an enormity*, Hos. vi. 9 marg.; cf. Lev. xviii. 17. Adultery was a capital crime in Israel, Deut. xxii. 22; John viii. 5.

12. *to destruction*] Heb. *abaddon*, i.e. Sheol or Death, as a place, ch. xxvi. 6, xxviii. 22. As to the complete ruin which this sin entailed comp. the passage Prov. vi. 24—35, particularly the last verses; see also Prov. v. 8—14, vii. 26, 27.

13—23. Job repudiates all misuse of the power which his rank gave him, denying (1) that he treated contemptuously his servants when they had a cause against him, *vv.* 13—15; (2) that he was indifferent to the wants of the unprotected, or refused to bestow on them of his own bread and raiment, *vv.* 16—20; (3) that he violently wronged any, even though he could have secured a judgment favourable to him before the tribunal, *v.* 21; after which follows the imprecation, *vv.* 22, 23.

13 If I did despise the cause of my manservant or of my maidservant,
   When they contended with me;
14 What then shall I do when God riseth up?
   And when he visiteth, what shall I answer him?
15 Did not he that made me in the womb make him?
   And did not one fashion us in the womb?
16 If I have withheld the poor from *their* desire,
   Or have caused the eyes of the widow to fail;
17 Or have eaten my morsel myself alone,
   And the fatherless hath not eaten thereof;
18 (For from my youth he was brought up *with* me, as *with* a father,
   And I have guided her from my mother's womb;)
19 If I have seen *any* perish for want of clothing,
   Or *any* poor without covering;
20 If his loins have not blessed me,
   And *if* he were *not* warmed with the fleece of my sheep;
21 If I have lift up my hand against the fatherless,
   When I saw my help in the gate:

13. Job refers to what he might have done in his high position; he might have "despised" or slighted the cause of his servants when they had ground of complaint against him. He treated them not as possessions but as persons, who had rights as well as himself, 14, 15. This treatment of them was forced on him by the feeling that all men, his servant and himself alike, are children of the same one God, who will avenge wrong done to any, whether slave or free; Ephes. vi. 9.

14. *when God riseth up*] i.e. to judge, as the expression "visiteth" in the next clause suggests.

16. *eyes of the widow to fail*] i.e. with looking in vain for help, Ps. lxix. 3.

18. *he was brought up with me*] Rather, **he** (the fatherless) **grew up with me**. Job probably did not achieve his greatness, he was born to it. And possibly he inherited the traditions of a great and benevolent house. And thus even from his youth he took the place toward the poor of a patron and father.

19. *seen any perish*] Rather, **perishing**, or ready to perish, ch. xxix. 13.

21. *if I have lift up my hand*] i.e. to strike him down. The expression is figurative, meaning to oppress violently.

I saw my help in the gate] i.e. because he saw that if the cause came before the judges (the gate) he could secure from them, by his influence, a verdict favourable to himself.

Then let mine arm fall from *my* shoulder blade, 22
And mine arm be broken from the bone.
For destruction from God *was* a terror to me, 23
And by reason of his highness I could not endure.
If I have made gold my hope, 24
Or have said to the fine gold, *Thou art* my confidence;
If I rejoiced because my wealth *was* great, 25
And because mine hand had gotten much;
If I beheld the sun when it shined, 26
Or the moon walking *in* brightness;
And my heart hath been secretly enticed, 27
Or my mouth hath kissed my hand:
This also *were* an iniquity *to be punished by* the judge: 28
For I should have denied the God *that is* above.

22. The imprecation is closely connected in form with the preceding verse—if I have lifted up mine hand, then let mine arm, &c.
mine arm fall] Or, **my shoulder** fall.
from the bone] Marg. *the chanel bone*, "an old term for the collar bone" (Wright, *Bible Word-Book*). The word is lit. *tube*, or *shaft*.
23. *highness I could not endure*] Or, **majesty I was powerless**, lit. *I was unable.* The verse closes the whole passage *vv.* 16—22, expressing the feeling by which Job's conduct was regulated; his awe before the majesty of God and fear of His judicial anger restrained him, so that he was "powerless" to commit any of the wrongs to which he has just made reference.
24—34. Repudiation of another class of secret sins, that would have dishonoured him: (1) secret joy in the possession of wealth—that love of gain which is idolatry (Col. iii. 5), *vv.* 24, 25; (2) a momentary impulse to salute the rising sun or the moon in her splendour and thus be false to the true spiritual God on high, *vv.* 26—28; (3) secret joy of heart at the misfortune of his enemy, *vv.* 29, 30; (4) narrowness of soul and niggardliness, *vv.* 31, 32; and finally, hypocrisy, *vv.* 33, 34.
27. *or my mouth hath kissed my hand*] lit. *and my hand hath kissed my mouth.* The meaning is, if his hand touched his mouth "in order to wave the homage of the lips towards the object of adoration" (Con.). Pliny (quoted in Del.) says, *Inter adorandum dexteram ad osculum referimus et totum corpus circumagimus.* The worship of the heavenly bodies was widely spread in the East and in Arabia. The remarkable passage, Jer. xliv. 17 *seq.*, shews that before the Exile worship of the "queen of heaven" had long been practised among all classes and in all the towns of Israel; comp. Ezek. viii. 16.
28. Comp. Deut. iv. 19, xvii. 3—7. Such adoration would have been a "denial" of, or a being false to, God, the one spiritual God, above. Much more than a thousand years later Mohammed has still to say to his Arabs, "Worship not the sun, neither the moon: but worship God

29 If I rejoiced at the destruction of him that hated me,
    Or lift up myself when evil found him:
30 (Neither have I suffered my mouth to sin
    By wishing a curse to his soul.)
31 If the men of my tabernacle said not,
    O that we had of his flesh! we cannot be satisfied.

who created them," Kor. ch. xli. A pretty fable is told also of Abraham—
"When night closed over him he saw a star, and said, This is my Lord; but when it set he said, I love not those that set. And when he saw the moon appearing he said, This is my Lord; but when it set he said, Surely if my Lord direct me not aright I shall be of the people that go astray. And when he saw the sun rising he said, This is my Lord, this is the greatest; but when it set he said, O my people, verily I am clear of what ye associate with God; verily I have turned my face towards Him who hath created heaven and earth," &c. Kor. ch. vi. 76.

29. *at the destruction*] Or, at the **misfortune**, ch. xii. 5. *lift up myself*] Or, **exulted**.

30. The verse, which is parenthetical, reads,
(Yea, I suffered not my mouth to sin,
To ask, with a curse, his life).

He was so far from rejoicing in the evil that befell his enemy that he had never permitted himself even in hasty anger to throw out an imprecation against him. On the obligation of love to enemies comp. Prov. xxiv. 17 *seq.*, xxv. 21 *seq.*

31. The verse appears to mean,
If the men of my tent have not said,
Would that we could find any not filled with his flesh!

The men of his tent are of course his servants. The verse describes Job's princely hospitality; his servants are represented as expressing the wish that they could find any one who has not yet (like others) been filled from Job's rich table—hence the particular word *flesh* is used instead of the more general "meat," flesh being served chiefly on occasions of entertainment in the East. The servants were well aware of their master's generosity, and did their best to give it effect. The language might appear exaggerated were it not a question of Oriental manners. In the story of the Banker of Bagdad in the Arabian Nights the servants are introduced speaking in the same way. The Caliph Elmo'taddid and his companion Ibn Hamdoon went out one day, disguised as merchants, to divert themselves among the people; and being overpowered by the heat of the sun they sat down to rest at the door of a large mansion. Out of this house there came a servant, accompanied by another, like a piece of the moon; and the one said to the other, Our master will be sad to-day, for it is already this time of day and no one has come to him, and he loves to have guests. The Caliph was surprised at his words and said, This is proof of the generosity of the owner of this mansion, we must go in, &c.

The stranger did not lodge in the street: 32
But I opened my doors to the traveller.
If I covered my transgressions as Adam, 33
By hiding mine iniquity in my bosom:
Did I fear a great multitude, 34
Or did the contempt of families terrify me,
That I kept silence, *and* went not out *of* the door?
O that one would hear me! 35

32. *to the traveller*] The word might mean *to the way*, the street; the general sense is the same. The verse confirms Job's universal hospitality and liberality.

33—34. The verses should probably be read,

33. If I have covered my transgressions like men,
    Hiding mine iniquity in my bosom,
34. Because I feared the great multitude,
    And the contempt of the families terrified me,
    So that I kept still and went not out of the door.

33. *as Adam*] This is possible, and so Hos. vi. 7; such a reference, however, seems without motive here. The words rather mean, *like common men, like the world* (Ew.), Ps. xvii. 4.

34. *a great multitude*] i.e. the general mass, or the assembly, of the people.

contempt of families] i.e. the great clans or tribes. The verse gives the reason why Job, if he had been conscious of sins, would have refrained from going forth at the door,—fear of the contempt of men would have deterred him. The passage ch. xxix. 7 *seq.* shews that he was deterred by no such fear, he constantly frequented the assembly and "sat as king" in the midst of the people.

What Job affirms in these verses is not of course that, *when* he was guilty of any transgressions, he did not conceal but openly acknowledged them. On the contrary he affirms that he had no sins which he needed to conceal. He lived in the broad day and without fear confronted all (ch. xxix. 7 *seq.*) because he had nothing to hide. Job repudiates all hypocritical conduct or secret transgression. This was the charge his friends made against him. And this consciousness of purity of heart, struggling with false accusations of hypocrisy, forces from him a new appeal to God to make known to him the sins laid to his charge, *vv.* 35—37. The verses are closely connected with *vv.* 33, 34.

35. Oh that I had one who would hear me!—
    Behold my signature! Let the Almighty answer me!—
    And that I had the charge which mine adversary had written!
36. Surely I would carry it upon my shoulder,
    I would bind it as a crown unto me;
37. I would declare unto him the number of my steps,
    As a prince would I go near unto him.

35. The words "one that would hear me," though spoken generally,

Behold, my desire *is, that* the Almighty would answer me,
And *that* mine adversary had written a book.
36 Surely I would take it upon my shoulder,
And bind it *as* a crown to me.
37 I would declare unto him the number of my steps;
As a prince would I go near unto him.
38 If my land cry against me,

refer of course to God. It is He that Job desires to hear him. In the third clause he names Him his adversary, i.e. opponent in the plea concerning his innocence. And he desires that he had the charge, Heb. *book*, i.e. the *libellus*, libel or indictment, which his accuser had written and handed in against him. The middle clause consists of two exclamations which force themselves in between the two parts of the wish which he expresses. By the first, *behold my signature*, Job means to say that he affixes his signature to all the protestations of his innocence just made in the preceding verses of the chapter, and attests them as his plea on his side. By the other, *let the Almighty answer me*, he challenges God, his accuser, to put in *His* plea in answer to his own. The language is evidently taken from the judicial practice of the time, according to which both charge and defence were laid before the court in writing. This is known to have been the practice in Egypt, though perhaps in many parts of the East the proceedings may have been oral. The word *signature* or *sign* (Ezek. ix. 4) is *tav* in Heb. This is the name of the letter T, the old form of which was a *cross*, but the inference that Job's signature, or that signatures in his time, had the form of a cross is scarcely warranted.

36. *upon my shoulder*] If Job but possessed the Almighty's indictment against him he would not hide it as a thing that caused him shame, he would bear it in triumph before the world as that which was his greatest honour. He would even wear it as a diadem upon his brows, as that which would give him kingly dignity and adornment. The language expresses the strongest assurance of innocence and that the indictment could in truth contain nothing against him.

37. *the number of my steps*] i.e. every act of my life.

as a prince] In the consciousness and pride of true nobility; with the confident step and erect bearing of one who knows that nothing dishonouring can be laid to his charge.

38—40. Job resumes his protestations, imprecating a curse upon his lands if he have acquired them unjustly, and wishing that they may bring forth weeds instead of grain.

38. If my land cry out against me,
And the furrows thereof weep together;
39. If I have eaten the fruits thereof without money,
And caused the soul of its owners to expire:
40. Let thistles, &c.

38. The literal meaning of the figurative expressions in this verse

Or that the furrows likewise thereof complain;
If I have eaten the fruits thereof without money, 39
Or have caused the owners thereof to lose their life:
Let thistles grow instead of wheat, 40
And cockle instead of barley.
The words of Job are ended.

is given in *v.* 39. The land, unjustly seized, is supposed to cry out to heaven against the cruelty and wrong done its true owner from whom it had been robbed ("without money," *v.* 39). The land and its rightful owner have a common cause, it feels and weeps over the injury he has suffered.

39. *to lose their life*] lit. *if I have caused the soul of the owners thereof to breathe out.* The reference may be either to oppressions which brought the owners to death, after which their land was seized without money, or to oppressive appropriation of the land so that the rightful owner was brought to death through penury and misery.

40. For "thistles" perhaps *thorns* is more accurate. The word translated "cockle" means perhaps any noisome weed. The concrete expressions, however, add to the vigour of the passage.

Some have thought that these last verses (38—40) have been misplaced, and ought to be introduced at some other point in the chapter, allowing Job's challenge *vv.* 35—37 to be the last words which he utters. To modern feeling the passage would thus gain in rhetorical effect; but it is not certain that the Author's taste would have coincided with modern feeling in this instance. And it is difficult to find in the chapter a suitable place where the verses could be inserted. If the verses belong to the passage at all, which there is no reason to doubt, they seem to stand in the only place suitable for them.

The concluding statement "the words of Job are ended" hardly belongs to the Author of the Book. It is the remark of some editor or copyist, who drew attention to the fact that Job's connected discourses here come to an end. It is rather hazardous to draw any critical conclusion from it in reference to the immediately following speeches of Elihu.

CH. XXXII.—XXXVII. THE SPEECHES OF ELIHU.

CH. XXXII. INTRODUCTION OF ELIHU, A NEW SPEAKER; WITH HIS REASONS FOR TAKING PART IN THE CONTROVERSY.

The Chapter contains three parts:
First, *v.* 1. The reason why Job's three friends refrained from speaking further—they failed to make any impression on Job: he was right in his own eyes.
Second, *vv.* 2—5. The Author in his own words introduces Elihu, stating the reasons which constrained this speaker to take part in the dispute. The anger of Elihu was kindled, *first*, against Job, because he justified himself as against God, held himself in the right at the ex-

32 So these three men ceased to answer Job, because he *was*
2 righteous in his own eyes. Then was kindled the wrath of
Elihu the son of Barachel the Buzite, of the kindred of
Ram: against Job was his wrath kindled, because he justi-
3 fied himself rather than God. Also against his three friends

pense of God's righteousness; and *second*, against the three friends because they failed to bring forward such arguments as effectively to condemn Job, that is, shew him to be in the wrong in his complaints of God. In other words, the sole point which Elihu has in view is justification of God, and towards this point all his reasoning is directed. Job is guilty of wrong against God, and the three friends are to blame because they have not been able to bring this wrong home to Job.

These five verses are in prose, though curiously enough they are pointed with the Poetical Accentuation.

Third, *vv*. 6—22. Elihu is then introduced speaking in his own person, and stating the reasons which hitherto have kept him from speaking, and those which induce him now to take part in the controversy. He would have spoken sooner had he not been a youth in the midst of aged and presumably wise men. But he reflects, and indeed present events shew it, that wisdom is not the prerogative of mere age; it is a gift of God, and therefore he will advance his opinion. It is intolerable to him (*v*. 19) that a man like Job, who utters such perverse and godless sentiments (ch. xxxiv. 7), should not be put to silence; and he is conscious of ability (*vv*. 8, 18) to answer him and all his class (ch. xxxv. 4).

1. *he was righteous*] i.e. would admit no guilt, or, was in the right in his plea against God. Job's friends abandoned further argument with him because they could not move him from his assertion that God afflicted him wrongly and unjustly; comp. ch. xxvii. 2—6.

2—5. Introduction of Elihu, a new speaker, who appears to have been a listener during the progress of the former debate. The descent of Elihu is given with fuller details than in the case of the other speakers. The name Elihu, meaning probably *my God is he*, occurs elsewhere, 1 Sam. i. 1; 1 Chron. xii. 20. He is named the Buzite. Buz was brother of Uz, Gen. xxii. 21, and son of Nahor. In Jerem. xxv. 23 Buz is mentioned along with Tema (cf. Job vi. 19), and reckoned among the Arab tribes. The name Ram, therefore, which does not occur elsewhere, is scarcely to be taken as a contraction for Aram or Syria (though comp. 2 Chr. xxii. 5, where Ramites=Aramites).

justified himself rather than God] The meaning appears to be, justified himself as against God, in his plea with God and at the expense of God's justice. The sense is given in ch. xl. 8, where the Lord says to Job, "Wilt thou condemn me that thou mayest be righteous"? There are two points to be attended to in these passages when the question of *right* is raised, the one a formal point and the other a material one. God had afflicted Job and thus, in Job's view and the view of his time, passed a verdict of wickedness on him. Against this verdict Job reclaims, God does him wrong in this. This is the formal

was his wrath kindled, because they had found no answer, and *yet* had condemned Job. Now Elihu had waited till Job had spoken, because they *were* elder than he. When Elihu saw that *there was* no answer in the mouth of *these* three men, then his wrath was kindled.

And Elihu the son of Barachel the Buzite answered and said,

I *am* young, and ye *are* very old;
Wherefore I was afraid, and durst not shew you mine opinion.
I said, Days should speak,
And multitude of years should teach wisdom.
But *there is* a spirit in man:
And the inspiration of the Almighty giveth them understanding.

question of right between Job and God. But this naturally goes back into the material question of Job's past life. Elihu, defending the righteousness of God, keeps before him chiefly the formal question. He touches little upon Job's life and history, differing in this entirely from the three friends. He makes a general, abstract question out of Job's complaints against God, which he argues on general lines with almost no reference to Job's particular case. Job's complaints do little more than suggest to him the question, Can God be justly complained of?

3. *had found no answer, and yet had condemned*] Rather, **had not found an answer and condemned**, i.e. found no answer wherewith to condemn Job. Elihu's anger was kindled against the three friends because they had not found such an answer as effectively to put Job in the wrong in his charges against God; comp. *vv.* 5, 12. Elihu is more deeply pained and offended by Job's charges against God than even the three friends were (ch. xxxiv. 7 *seq.*, *v.* 35 *seq.*); he is far from blaming them for condemning Job; neither does he hold the balance between Job and them and blame them for condemning him without good reasons; he blames them for not finding such good reasons as effectively to condemn him, as he deserves. Coverdale: *because they had found no reasonable answer to overcome him*.

4. *waited till Job had spoken*] Rather, **waited to speak unto Job**, lit. *waited for Job with words*. Elihu had waited (till the friends spoke) prepared to address Job, as he now does.

6—10. Elihu, being a youth, shrank from interfering in a dispute in which aged men were engaged; but he perceived that wisdom did not always accompany grey hairs; it is a gift of God, and, conscious of possessing it, he desires now to be heard.

8. *the inspiration of the Almighty*] lit. *the breath* of the Almighty, as ch. xxxiii. 4. Both "spirit" and "breath" refer to God's spirit of

9   Great men are not *always* wise:
    Neither do the aged understand judgment.
10 Therefore I said, Hearken to me;
    I also will shew mine opinion.
11 Behold, I waited for your words;
    I gave ear to your reasons,
    Whilst you searched out what to say.
12 Yea, I attended unto you,
    And behold, *there was* none of you that convinced Job,
    Or that answered his words:
13 Lest ye should say, We have found out wisdom:
    God thrusteth him down, not man.
14 Now he hath not directed *his* words against me:
    Neither will I answer him with your speeches.

life breathed into man when he is brought into existence (Gen. ii. 7), there is no allusion to any extraordinary illumination given to Elihu at the moment when he speaks. This spirit of God is a spirit of intelligence as well as of life (ch. xxxiii. 4), and under the impulse of the crowding thoughts which rush into his mind at this instant Elihu feels that this spirit has been given to himself in great fulness.

9. *Great men*] Or, **old** men—great in age, as the parallel in the second clause explains; cf. Gen. xxv. 23 (lit. the greater shall serve the less).

11—14. Elihu, directly addressing the three friends, states more clearly his reasons for taking upon him to speak: he had hoped to hear them confute Job, and was disappointed in their arguments; Job may be shewn to be in the wrong, though with different arguments from those they had employed. In Elihu's opinion the cause of the three friends was much better than their advocacy of it.

11. *I gave ear to your reasons*] Or, **I listened for your reasons, until ye should search out what to say.** The meaning seems to be that Elihu looked for further and different arguments from the three friends.

13—14. These verses mean,

13. Say not, We have found wisdom,
    God may thrust him down, not man;
14. For he hath not directed his words against me, &c.

Elihu refuses to let the three friends excuse themselves for their failure to answer Job by the plea that they had found an unexpected wisdom in him, against which human logic was of no avail, and which only God could overcome. Job's wisdom was not so invincible. It remained to be seen how it would come out of the encounter with another wisdom, different from that of the Friends:—Job had not yet replied to Elihu's arguments, *he has not directed his words against me* (v. 14, cf. ch.

They were amazed, they answered no more: 15
They left off speaking.
When I had waited, (for they spake not, 16
But stood still, *and* answered no more:)
I said, I will answer also my part, 17
I also will shew mine opinion.
For I am full *of* matter, 18
The spirit within me constraineth me.
Behold, my belly *is* as wine *which* hath no vent; 19
It is ready to burst like new bottles.
I will speak, that I may be refreshed: 20
I will open my lips and answer.
Let me not, I pray you, accept *any* man's person, 21
Neither let me give flattering titles unto man.

xxxiii. 5), and these arguments would be found of another kind from those of the three friends.

15—22. Turning from the three friends Elihu seems to speak in soliloquy and present to his own mind the singular situation: the three friends are discomfited before Job and reduced to silence; this should not be; therefore he will express his convictions. His breast is filled with thoughts and emotions that will not be repressed: he must speak, that he may find relief. And he will speak fearlessly and in sincerity, not regarding the person of any man.

15. *they left off speaking*] lit. *words have removed*, or, *are gone from them* (Gen. xii. 8)—they are reduced to silence.

16—17. *V.* 16 is most naturally to be taken as a question,
16. And shall I wait because they speak not,
Because they stand still and answer no more?
17. I will answer also my part, &c.
The discomfiture and silence of the three friends shall not have the effect of imposing silence on him.

18—19. Elihu feels a crowd of thoughts and arguments fermenting in his bosom and pressing for utterance with a force not to be resisted. The word "belly" corresponds to the English "breast" or bosom. What stirs the spirit of Elihu is not only his eagerness to express his convictions on the question, but also indignation at the retreat and silence of the three friends.

20. *be refreshed*] Rather, **find relief**; lit. *get air* or *vent*. The figure is still that of fermenting wine, *v.* 19.

21. *neither let me give*] Rather, **neither will I give flattery.** The words express the speaker's resolution to be sincere and fearless, to have regard to the question itself solely, and not to allow himself to be influenced by respect to the persons interested in it. Elihu does not refer here to impartiality between Job and the three friends. There is no allusion to the friends. He speaks generally, saying that he will

22 For I know not to give flattering titles;
In so doing my Maker would soon take me away.

have respect to truth only; comp. the language, ch. xxxiii. 3, xxxiv. 2—4. Coverdale goes far enough when he renders: "no man wil I spare." Hitzig oversteps the line when he says that Elihu "intimates his intention of being rude to Job."

22. Elihu is conscious of sincerity; it is not in his nature to flatter. His fear of God also and sense of His rectitude would deter him from such a thing; comp. Job's language, ch. xiii. 7 *seq.*

These last words and many other things which Elihu says enable us to judge rightly of the part which the author intends him to play. There are some things in his manner of introducing himself and in the way in which he speaks of his own arguments, which seem to offend against modesty and almost shock our sense of decorum. We must not, however, apply Western standards of taste to the East. There was nothing further from the intention of the author of these Chapters than to make Elihu play a ridiculous part. This speaker is meant to offer what the writer judged a weighty contribution to the discussion, and to the vindication of the ways of God to man. It is just this fact, however, that Elihu is a serious speaker and yet so characterized by mannerisms that raises the question whether the author of such a character possessed the severe taste and high dramatic genius which so conspicuously belong to the author of the other characters; in other words, the question whether these chapters are not the composition of a different writer (see the Introduction).

CHAP. XXXIII. ELIHU'S FIRST REPLY TO JOB. JOB'S COMPLAINT THAT GOD DISPLAYS AN ARBITRARY HOSTILITY TO HIM, AND REFUSES TO HEAR ANY APPEAL OF MEN IS UNFOUNDED. GOD SPEAKS TO MEN IN MANY WAYS.

The following may be taken as an outline of the chapter:

First, *vv.* 1—7, Elihu in some introductory words bespeaks Job's attention. He addresses Job by name, and, full of confidence in his ability to answer his complaints, invites him to attend to his words (*vv.* 1, 2), and assures him of his sincerity (*vv.* 3, 4). He desires Job to reply to him, for he is a man like himself, and has no imposing authority or presence to overpower Job, who had often complained that God's power overawed him and prevented him from justifying himself (*vv.* 5—7).

Second, *vv.* 8—13, Elihu then refers to Job's complaint against God, reproducing passages from his speeches in which he said that God afflicted him unjustly, though he was innocent; that He displayed an arbitrary hostility to him; and refused to hear any appeal. Elihu refutes these charges by the general consideration (a favourite one with him) that to act in such a way is unworthy of God, who is greater than men, and whose ways are unlike theirs.

Third, *vv.* 13—28, taking up more formally Job's complaint that God refuses to answer man, Elihu replies that God does speak to man in

Wherefore, Job, I pray thee, hear my speeches,	33
And hearken to all my words.	
Behold now I have opened my mouth,	2
My tongue hath spoken in my mouth.	
My words *shall be of* the uprightness of my heart:	3
And my lips shall utter knowledge clearly.	
The Spirit of God hath made me,	4
And the breath of the Almighty hath given me life.	
If thou canst, answer me,	5
Set *thy words* in order before me, stand up.	

many ways; *first* (*vv.* 14—18) in dreams, to instruct him and turn him away from pride and from sin that might end in death; and *second* (*vv.* 19—28) by angelic messengers in the midst of afflictions, who shew to man what is right. If the sinner thus warned takes his instruction to heart, he is restored to health and prosperity, and in his thankfulness shews publicly to men God's mercy, who hath not rewarded him according to his work.

Finally, *vv.* 29—33, Elihu sums up the general lesson of his teaching regarding God in the preceding verses and invites Job to reply to it, or if he cannot to listen in silence to further instruction.

1—7. Introductory appeal to Job to listen to Elihu, who will speak in all honesty, and who being a man like Job himself may be argued with.

1. Elihu, unlike the other speakers, addresses Job by name.

2. The somewhat formal and circumstantial way in which he intimates that he is going to speak indicates his feeling of the importance of what he is going to say, and bespeaks Job's attention.

3. Reiteration of the speaker's sincerity; he possesses what Job had desiderated on the part of his three friends, uprightness (ch. vi. 25).

my lips shall utter knowledge clearly] lit. *and the knowledge of my lips they shall utter purely*, with no mixture of falsehood; his lips will express truly the sincere convictions of his mind.

4. On the language of this verse see ch. xxxii. 8. The verse seems connected with *v.* 3. Elihu will utter his sincere conviction, and it is a conviction flowing from that spirit of God given him in his creation; this is a guarantee of its worth as well as its sincerity. The appeal is to common reason (ch. xxxiv. 2, 3), which is a divine illumination (the lamp of the Lord, Prov. xx. 27), but in his animated zeal for God against the charges of Job Elihu feels that this spirit of God is within him in a powerful degree and gives him a higher wisdom than ordinary.

5—7. Full of this feeling Elihu invites Job to measure himself with this wisdom (*v.* 4). Let the matter be reasoned out as it may be on equal terms, for in Elihu a man like himself Job will have no reason to complain of being overawed and hindered from pleading his cause.

6 Behold, I *am* according to thy wish in God's stead:
  I also am formed out of the clay.
7 Behold, my terror shall not make thee afraid,
  Neither shall my hand be heavy upon thee.
8 Surely thou hast spoken in mine hearing,
  And I have heard the voice of *thy* words, *saying*,
9 I am clean without transgression,
  I *am* innocent; neither *is there* iniquity in me.
10 Behold, he findeth occasions against me,
   He counteth me for his enemy,
11 He putteth my feet in the stocks,
   He marketh all my paths.
12 Behold, *in* this thou art not just: I will answer thee,
   That God is greater than man.

    6. *according to thy wish in God's stead*] Rather, as already Coverdale, **behold, before God I am even as thou**; that is, in relation to God in the same position as Job, a man like himself. The words *in God's stead* suggest the false conception that Elihu was in some extraordinary way the representative of God.

    7. Job had often complained that the terror and majesty of God overpowered him and made it impossible for him to plead his cause and shew his rectitude; comp. ch. ix. 34, xiii. 21.

    my hand be heavy] The term *hand* may be an uncommon form of the Heb. word having that sense, or it may perhaps mean *burden*, pressure; comp. ch. xiii. 21.

    8—12. To Job's complaint that God shewed a hostility to him which was arbitrary and without cause Elihu replies that such a thing was unbecoming God and not to be thought of, for God is greater than man.

    9. For the expressions cited in this verse comp. ch. ix. 21, x. 7, xvi. 17, xxiii. 10, xxvii. 5.

    10. See ch. x. 13 *seq.*, xiii. 24, xix. 11, xxx. 21.

    he findeth occasions] lit. *enmities*, i.e. grounds of enmity or hostility; he "findeth" is almost equivalent to He "invents." Coverdale quaintly, "he hath pyked a quarell agaynst me."

    11. See ch. xiii. 27.

    12. The verse probably reads,

        Behold in this thou art not in the right, I will answer thee,
        For God is greater than man.

The words *I will answer thee* are equivalent to, "Behold, *my answer is*, in this thou art not right," &c. The answer to Job's charges which Elihu contents himself with giving meantime is simply: "in this thou art not in the right, for God is greater than man." Elihu, as he does often, e.g. ch. xxxiv. 10, xxxvi. 3—5, 24—25, falls back on man's necessary thoughts of God. Job's charges are incompatible with just

Why dost thou strive against him? 13
For he giveth not account of any of his matters.
For God speaketh once, 14
Yea twice, *yet man* perceiveth it not.
In a dream, *in* a vision of the night, 15
When deep sleep falleth upon men,
In slumberings upon the bed;
Then he openeth the ears of men, 16
And sealeth their instruction.

conceptions of God. The three friends had argued in the same way, though they hardly gave the idea the same important place that Elihu does; comp. ch. viii. 3.

13—28. When Elihu gives the general answer to Job's charges against God that "God is greater than man" he means that the moral loftiness of God's nature made it impossible that He should act in the arbitrary, hostile manner charged against Him by Job (comp. ch. xxxvi. 5). It was but another form of the same charge of arbitrary hostility to man when Job affirmed that God was deaf to all appeal and refused to speak to man; comp. ch. xix. 7, xxx. 20, and often. To this general form of the charge Elihu directs his attention and replies that God speaks to man in many ways, though He may not answer when challenged as Job had challenged Him; comp. ch. xxxv. 14. He speaks to man in ways becoming His greatness, ways that shew that His goodness is over all His works. Verse 13 probably reads

> Why dost thou contend against him
> That he giveth not account of any of his matters?

that is, Job's contention or plea against God is that He deals arbitrarily and refuses all account of His dealing.

14—18. To Job's charge Elihu replies that God speaks to man in many ways, as in dreams and visions of the night, by which He instructs men and seeks to turn them away from doing evil that would destroy them.

14. *yet man perceiveth it not*] Or, **when man regardeth it not.**
15. The language recalls the vision of Eliphaz, ch. iv. 13 *seq.*
16. *sealeth their instruction*] The instruction is that communicated when the ear is opened, and a revelation given (comp. ch. xxxvi. 10, 15; 1 Sam. ix. 15; Ps. xl. 6); and "to seal" it is to confirm it and give it abiding efficacy. This is done partly by the impressive circumstances and manner of the dream; compare the impression produced on Eliphaz, after the model of whose vision the passage seems moulded. Perhaps the figure of "sealing" the instruction arises from the idea of closing up again the opened ear over the divine communication.

Others understand by "instruction" here the chastisement of affliction, assuming that the person to whom the vision was sent was one under trouble. "Instruction" is possibly used in this sense by Elihu,

17 That *he* may withdraw man *from his* purpose,
And hide pride from man.
18 He keepeth back his soul from the pit,
And his life from perishing by the sword.
19 He is chastened also with pain upon his bed,
And the multitude of his bones *with* strong *pain:*
20 So that his life abhorreth bread,
And his soul dainty meat.
21 His flesh is consumed away, that it cannot be seen;
And his bones *that* were not seen stick out.
22 Yea, his soul draweth near unto the grave,
And his life to the destroyers.
23 If there be a messenger with him, an interpreter,

ch. xxxvi. 10; but in this chap. the case of affliction seems introduced first in *v.* 19.

17, 18. The object of this intervention of God is the gracious one of anticipating the sinner in the evil which he meditates and hindering it, and withdrawing him from his sinful purpose, *v.* 17; and the effect of it is that man is preserved from committing deadly sin, which would have brought destruction upon him, *v.* 18.

The "sword" or *javelin*, *v.* 18, is a figure for God's destructive judgments; comp. ch. xxxvi. 12.

19—28. These verses may describe another instance of God's dealing with man, or a further discipline of the same person (*vv.* 15—18), the result stated in *v.* 18 not having been attained. The passage has four steps:

(1) The affliction, graphically presented, *vv.* 19—22.

(2) The intervention of the Divine messenger, who interprets to the sufferer what it becomes him to do; and God's gracious pardon of him, *vv.* 23, 24.

(3) The restoration to prosperity and righteousness of him who was afflicted, *vv.* 25, 26.

(4) His thankfulness, publicly shewn among men, *vv.* 27, 28.

19. *multitude of his bones with strong pain*] Rather, **and with a continual strife in his bones**—the word "strife" meaning "conflict of pain." This is the reading of the Heb. text. The A. V. has adopted the Heb. margin; but if this be taken the sense must be: *while the multitude of his bones is strong*, in his freshness and youth. Besides putting a doubtful meaning on some of the words, this sense is less to the purpose here.

20. *his life*] Or, **desire** (appetite, ch. xxxviii. 39). The words mean lit. *his desire maketh him abhor.*

22. *the destroyers*] that is, perhaps, the angels that bring death; 2 Sam. xxiv. 16; 1 Chron. xxi. 15; Ps. lxxviii. 49.

23, 24. The intervention of the heavenly messenger.

23. *a messenger*] Or, *angel.* Such an angel is called an *interpreter,*

One among a thousand,
To shew unto man his uprightness:
Then he is gracious unto him, and saith, 24
Deliver him from going down *to* the pit:
I have found a ransom.
His flesh shall be fresher than a child's: 25
He shall return to the days of his youth:
He shall pray unto God, and he will be favourable unto 26
him:
And he shall see his face with joy:
For he will render unto man his righteousness.
He looketh upon men, and *if any* say, 27
I have sinned, and perverted *that which was* right,
And it profited me not;

that is, as the last clause of the verse explains, one who interprets to man God's providential treatment of him, and shews him what is right for him to do—*his uprightness*, that is, wherein uprightness will consist, and what his duty is.

one among a thousand] lit. *one of a thousand*. The words do not ascribe any superlative position to this angel; he is one of the thousand (cf. Rev. v. 11) ministering spirits sent forth to do service on behalf of the heirs of salvation (Heb. i. 14).

24. *then he is gracious*] God is gracious; God, not the angel, is the speaker in the rest of the verse. It is assumed that when the sufferer is shewn what is right (*v.* 23) he follows it; then God is gracious unto him, and commands that he be delivered from his affliction and saved from death. It is hardly of consequence to enquire what the *ransom* is which God has found. It may be the sinner's repentance and return to rectitude; or it may be that the affliction is held sufficient (Is. xl. 2; Job xxxvi. 18); or possibly the words may mean nothing more than that God is pleased of His goodness to hold the sinner as ransomed and delivered from the consequences of his sin.

25, 26. The sufferer's restoration. For the future tenses of A. V. present tenses would be better in these two verses.

25. His restoration out of his affliction to health is like the freshness of a new childhood and the strength of a new youth.

26. His restoration to the fellowship of God with its joy.

for he will render] Rather, **and he restoreth unto man his righteousness.** God restores to him his righteous standing before Him with its joys, regards him again as righteous, and admits him to all the blessings of righteousness. The clause generalizes the ideas of the rest of the verse.

27, 28. The restored sinner's thankfulness:

27. He singeth before men and saith,
   I sinned and perverted that which was right,
   And it was not requited unto me;

28   He will deliver his soul from going into the pit,
     And his life shall see the light.
29   Lo, all these *things* worketh God
     Oftentimes with man,
30   To bring back his soul from the pit,
     To be enlightened with the light of the living.
31   Mark well, O Job, hearken unto me:
     Hold thy peace, and I will speak.
32   If *thou* hast any thing to say, answer me:
     Speak, for I desire to justify thee.
33   If not, hearken unto me:
     Hold thy peace, and I shall teach thee wisdom.

28. He hath redeemed my soul from going into the pit,
   And my life shall see the light.

On account of the construction the sense "singeth" is more probable than *looketh upon* of A. V., though the form of the word is unusual.

28. The *light* which the sinner sees is the light of life (*v.* 30), for he is redeemed from the darkness of the pit. The A. V. has followed the Heb. margin and read *his* soul, *his* life. If this reading were adopted the words would be a general statement by Elihu, but this unnaturally anticipates *vv.* 29, 30.

29, 30. Elihu sums up his doctrine regarding the gracious purpose and effect of God's methods of speaking unto man.

31—33. The speaker requests Job to hear his further arguments (*v.* 31); or if he can reply to what has been said, by all means let him do so, for Elihu desires that he should be in the right (*v.* 32); but if not let him listen and learn wisdom (*v.* 33).

31. *mark well*] These words do not mean, *weigh and apply*, but *listen*, namely, to that which Elihu will further say.

32. *to justify thee*] Elihu could not say that he desired to justify Job in his plea against God; the words must refer to the cause between Job and himself. Elihu would be glad if Job could give such a reply to his arguments that he could say he thought him in the right. The words seem to imply little more than the speaker's desire to be fair, and to conduct the argument on equal terms with Job; comp. *vv.* 6, 7.

CHAP. XXXIV. ELIHU'S SECOND REPLY TO JOB. JOB'S COMPLAINT THAT GOD AFFLICTS HIM UNJUSTLY IS WITHOUT REASON. A MOTIVE FOR INJUSTICE IN HIM WHO IS CREATOR OF ALL ALIKE CANNOT BE FOUND; AND INJUSTICE IN THE HIGHEST RULER IS INCONCEIVABLE.

Having in ch. xxxiii. replied to Job's charge that God's afflictions were examples of an arbitrary hostility to men, Elihu in this chapter replies to another charge, that God was unjust in the afflictions which He laid on him. His answer is, That a motive for injustice in Him

34 Furthermore Elihu answered and said,
2 Hear my words, O ye wise *men*;

who is Creator of all cannot be found; and, That injustice in the Ruler of all is inconceivable—shall not the Judge of all the earth do right?

The line of thought in the chapter is something as follows:

First, *vv.* 1—4, in a brief introduction Elihu invites his intelligent hearers to listen further to him, and to unite with him in seeking to discover what was the right, the just state of the case, in Job's cause with God and his charges against Him.

Second, *vv.* 5—9, these charges he then recites: Job had said that God perverted his right, and that he was incurably afflicted though he had done no wrong (*vv.* 5, 6). Elihu cannot mention such charges without expressing his detestation of them: Job has not his parallel for impiety (*vv.* 7, 8). He has even gone the length of saying that it was no advantage to a man to be religious (*v.* 9). This last sentiment Elihu does not deal with in the present chapter, its discussion follows in ch. xxxv.

Third, *vv.* 10—20, coming to his argument, Elihu, *first* expresses his reprobation of such sentiments as those of Job, they are contrary to right thoughts of God; such ways of acting are not to be thought of in connexion with the Almighty (*vv.* 10—12). *Second*, this reproof of Job's charges from God's nature in general Elihu then particularizes into two distinct thoughts: (1) a motive for injustice in Him who is the Creator of all cannot be discovered; on the contrary His calling all things into being and upholding them by sending forth His spirit is evidence of unselfish goodness, for were He to set His mind on Himself and withdraw His spirit all flesh would perish (*vv.* 13—15). (2) The foundation of government is justice, without which rule would come to an end. Injustice in the highest Ruler is inconceivable. And in truth His rule approves itself, by its impartiality, to be just (*vv.* 16—20).

Fourth, *vv.* 21—28, this justice is secured by God's omniscient insight into men, and by His goodness which is the spring and motive of His rule of mankind.

Fifth, *vv.* 29—33, shall any one then murmur at this absolute disposing of all things by the hand of God? To murmur is to usurp the rule of God, and to claim to dictate how He should dispense His recompences.

Finally *vv.* 34—37, Elihu, having shewn what is involved in Job's charges of injustice against God, draws the conclusion, in which he is confident all reflecting minds who listen to him will concur with him, that Job speaks without wisdom; to the sin of his life he has added a defiant and mocking impiety, which one must wish to see purified out of him in the furnace of severer afflictions.

2—4. Elihu invites the wise among those who listen to him to attend to what he further says, and to unite with him in seeking to discover the right in this cause between Job and God.

2. The *wise* men are not the three friends, but the bystanders who hear Elihu; cf. *v.* 34.

And give ear unto me, ye that have knowledge.
3 For the ear trieth words,
  As the mouth tasteth meat.
4 Let us choose to us judgment:
  Let us know among ourselves what *is* good.
5 For Job hath said, I am righteous:
  And God hath taken away my judgment.
6 Should I lie against my right?
  My wound *is* incurable without transgression.
7 What man *is* like Job,
  Who drinketh up scorning like water?
8 Which goeth in company with the workers of iniquity,
  And walketh with wicked men.
9 For he hath said, It profiteth a man nothing
  That he should delight himself with God.

3. Elihu makes his appeal to his hearers *for* the ear trieth words. His appeal is to the common reason, or to the common reverent and just thoughts of God in men. The "ear" is the inner ear, the understanding, which is a judge of sentiments as much as, or like as, the palate is a judge of meats, ch. xii. 11.

4. The word *judgment* means *right*, or, *the right*, the just decision in the cause under consideration, Job's plea with God.

5—9. Elihu recites Job's statement of his cause against God, expressing his abhorrence of Job's sentiments.

5. *I am righteous*] Or, *in the right*, I have right on my side.

my judgment] As before means *my right*, what is rightly due to me—God has dealt with me unjustly; comp. ix. 15, 20, xiii. 18, xxvii. 2, 6.

6. *should I lie against my right?*] This sense is possible, the meaning being, "shall I admit guilt when I am not guilty but wrongly afflicted"? Perhaps the sense is rather: *against* (or, notwithstanding) *my right I am made to lie:* when I affirm my rectitude God's treatment of me belies my affirmations by making me guilty, and this against my right; comp. ch. ix. 20, xvi. 8.

my wound] lit. *my arrow*, the arrow of divine affliction infixed in me, comp. ch. vi. 4, xvi. 13.

7. Elihu cannot restrain his abhorrence of Job's sentiments. By *scorning* is meant impiety and scepticism. On the figure comp. ch. xv. 16.

8. In expressing such opinions Job goes over to the camp of the professed ungodly; comp. xxii. 15; Ps. i. 1.

9. Job had nowhere used this precise language, though the idea is not an unnatural inference from much that he had said; comp. ch. ix. 22, xxi. 7, xxiv. 1, and ch. xxi. throughout. This charge that a man is nothing bettered by being religious Elihu refutes in ch. xxxv.,

Therefore hearken unto me, ye men of understanding: 10
Far be it from God, *that he should do* wickedness;
And *from* the Almighty, *that he should commit* iniquity.
For the work of a man shall he render unto him, 11
And cause every man to find according to *his* ways.
Yea, surely God will not do wickedly, 12
Neither will the Almighty pervert judgment.
Who hath given him a charge over the earth? 13
Or who hath disposed the whole world?

directing his attention in the meantime to the general charge of injustice so far as it bore on God Himself.

10—19. This charge of injustice Elihu rebuts, *first*, on the general ground of its impiety: God cannot be thought of as acting in the way Job asserted—He rewardeth every man according to his works (*vv.* 10—12); and *second*, he then resolves the general idea into two distinct thoughts, *vv.* 13—15, and *vv.* 16—19.

10—12. Elihu's argument in these verses is the truest answer that can be given: injustice on the part of God is inconsistent with the idea of God. The three friends had urged the same plea. And Job would have accepted the argument had his friends or himself been able to take it up as a general principle and keep it clear from complications with the events of actual providence. When, however, they combined it with their other theory that good and evil befell men solely according to the principle of retribution, and that this latter principle was that according to which God's actual providence was entirely administered, Job could not consent to their reasoning. And as he agreed with them that retributive righteousness was or ought to be the principle of God's rule of the world, he was obliged, as he entirely failed to perceive such a principle adhered to, to charge God with injustice. It is not easy to see how Elihu differs from the friends in the position which he takes up here and in *vv.* 20—33. He is concerned in the meantime, however, with a theoretical defence of God's justice.

13—15. The first thought of Elihu is that the earth, the world, is not entrusted to God by another; He himself arranged it all as it is; there is therefore no motive to injustice. This is one side of his idea; the other (*v.* 14) is that the fact of the creation and sustaining of all things and creatures by God is proof of unselfish benevolence, for if God thought of Himself and ceased to send forth His spirit, all flesh would perish.

The Oriental thinker was not a pessimist; to his mind life was not an evil but the highest good, and its continuance proof of goodness in God who gave it and continued it. Neither would it occur to such a thinker, when he argued that there was no temptation to injustice in the Creator, that a temptation might be found in His own malevolent nature. A first cause that was evil could not be supposed by any one in the position of the speakers in this Book. Even when Job touches

14 If he set his heart upon *man*,
    If he gather unto himself his spirit and his breath;
15 All flesh shall perish together,
    And man shall turn again unto dust.
16 If now *thou hast* understanding, hear this:
    Hearken to the voice of my words.
17 Shall even he that hateth right govern?
    And wilt thou condemn him that is most just?
18 *Is it fit* to say to a king, *Thou art* wicked?
    And to princes, *Ye are* ungodly?
19 *How much less to him* that accepteth not the persons of princes,
    Nor regardeth the rich more than the poor?
    For they all *are* the work of his hands.

upon such an idea, as in ch. vii. 17 *seq.*, x. 3 *seq.*, it is for the purpose of shewing the inconsistency of malevolence with God's necessary attributes. Comp. remarks at the end of ch. x.

14. *if he set his heart upon man*] lit. as marg. *upon him*. The interpretation of the A. V. is possible, the meaning being, if God should set His mind strictly on man, to mark iniquity and the like (ch. vii. 17). More probably the meaning is: set His mind *upon Himself;*—if He were the object of His own exclusive regard and consideration. If God thought alone of Himself and ceased to think of all creatures with a benevolent consideration, giving them life and upholding by His spirit, all flesh would perish.

16—19. The second thought: without justice rule is impossible; and therefore injustice in the supreme Ruler is inconceivable. The thought is one that finds repeated expression in Scripture, as in the words of Abraham, "Shall not the Judge of all the earth do right?" Gen. xviii. 25, and in those of St Paul, "Is God unrighteous...? God forbid; for then how shall God judge the world?" Rom. iii. 5; comp. Matt. xii. 25.

17. *condemn him that is most just*] Or, **condemn the just, the mighty One.**

18. The verse reads,
    Is it fit to say to a king, Thou wicked!
    Or to princes, Ye ungodly!

The word "wicked" means *worthless*, Heb. *belial*. No doubt many kings, whether in the past or the present, might be justly enough addressed as "wicked," and princes in abundance as "ungodly," but the speaker is thinking here less of persons than of the offices which they fill as rulers. If earthly rule implies righteousness, how much more the rule of the Supreme (*v.* 19).

19. Partiality or injustice is not to be thought of in God, for all men, rich and poor, are alike the work of His hands. In these words the

In a moment shall they die, 20
And the people shall be troubled at midnight, and pass
  away:
And the mighty shall be taken away without hand.
For his eyes *are* upon the ways of man, 21
And he seeth all his goings.
There is no darkness, nor shadow of death, 22
Where the workers of iniquity may hide themselves.
For he will not lay upon man more *than right;* 23
That *he* should enter into judgment with God.
He shall break in pieces mighty *men* without number, 24
And set others in their stead.
Therefore he knoweth their works, 25

disputant makes the transition from his principle to the illustration of it in God's actual rule of men, and this illustration he pursues at length.

20—28. God's strict justice may be seen in His government of the peoples and their princes alike. His justice is unerring, for it is guided by omniscient insight. Punishing oppression, it avenges the cause of the poor and afflicted.

20. Display of God's just rule over people and princes. According to the punctuation the verse is thus divided,

> In a moment they die and at midnight;
> The people are shaken and pass away,
> And the mighty are taken away without hand.

The phrase *at midnight* means suddenly and without anticipation, comp. *v.* 25; Ps. cxix. 62. *Without hand*, i.e. through no human agency, by an unseen power, the ruling hand of God; comp. ch. xx. 26; Dan. ii. 34, 35; Zech. iv. 6. The *mighty* are the princes, opposed to "the people" in the second clause.

21—24. This just rule of God operates unfailingly, being guided by infallible insight.

23. The verse reads probably,

> For he needeth not to consider a man further,
> That he should come before God in judgment.

The meaning is that no inquisition on God's part is needed of a man, beyond his evil deed, with the view of bringing him before God in judgment. God beholds all, and His insight and judgment operate simultaneously.

24. *he shall break...without number*] Rather, **he breaketh...without inquisition.** The verse amplifies the conception of the preceding verse.

25—27. Armed with such omniscient insight (*therefore, v.* 25) He knoweth men's works, and His judgment overtakes them without fail.

And he overturneth *them* in the night, so that they are destroyed.
26 He striketh them as wicked *men*
In the open sight of others;
27 Because they turned back from him,
And would not consider any of his ways:
28 So that *they* cause the cry of the poor to come unto him,
And he heareth the cry of the afflicted.
29 When he giveth quietness, who then can make trouble?
And when he hideth *his* face, who then can behold him?
Whether *it be done* against a nation,
Or against a man only:

28. *so that they cause the cry*] Rather, **thus he causeth the cry of the poor to come before Him**; lit. *to cause* (or, causing) *to come*. The words sum up the general purpose (or, effect) of God's destructive judgments on the oppressors; He thus brings before Him and hears the cry of the afflicted.

29—33. The connexion of the following verses is rather uncertain. The sense of *v.* 30 might suggest the connexion of *vv.* 29—30 with the preceding. In this case *v.* 31 would make a new start, and the connexion would be maintained to the end of the chapter. It is probable, however, that *vv.* 34—37 should be taken by themselves. In *v.* 29 the word *he* is emphatic; similarly in *v.* 31 an emphasis falls on *God.* This common emphasis, in *vv.* 29—30 on the absoluteness of God's operation and in *vv.* 31—33 on the presumption of any one who questions it, seems to bind these two groups of verses together. The verses read as a whole,

29. When he giveth quietness, who shall condemn him?
And when he hideth his face, who shall behold him?
Whether it be done to a nation or to a man alike:
30. That the godless man reign not,
That the people be not ensnared.
31. For hath any said unto God,
I have borne (chastisement) though I offend not,
32. That which I see not teach thou me,
If I have done iniquity I will do it no more?—
33. Shall God's recompense be according to thy mind
That thou dost reject it?
For thou must choose, and not I;
Therefore speak what thou knowest.

29. Here *he*, God, is emphatic. Elihu while upholding the rectitude of God conjoins with it His sovereignty. To *give quietness* or rest seems to mean to give peace and security from oppression, when the oppressed cry unto Him (Judg. v. 31; Is. xiv. 7). The antithesis to this is *He hides His face*, words which always mean, He withdraws His

> That the hypocrite reign not, 30
> Lest the people be ensnared.
> Surely it is *meet to be* said unto God, 31
> I have borne *chastisement*, I will not offend *any more:*
> *That which* I see not teach thou me: 32
> If I have done iniquity, I will do no more.
> *Should it be* according to thy mind? he will recompense it, 33
> Whether thou refuse, or whether thou choose; and not I:
> Therefore speak what thou knowest.

favour or help in anger, ch. xiii. 24; and to *behold Him* has of course a sense the opposite of this, viz. to obtain His favour, to make Him gracious. God acts in both ways in His sovereign rule, and when He acts in the one way who shall condemn Him, and in the other who shall compel Him to alter His aspect? And thus He acts on the widest stage and in the most particular instance, with nations and men alike.

30. His operations are directed by the great purpose of the good of men, that the nations be righteously and mercifully ruled.

31—33. Elihu gradually approaches the conduct of Job. He supposes the case of one animadverting on the Divine procedure and complaining of unjust affliction. This is presumption and implies that one usurps the government of the Most High.

31, 32. A supposition is put: Has any one said unto God? where *God* is emphatic, the emphasis implying the unseemliness and presumption of the act. The case is put generally, but the case is that of Job, as *v.* 33 reveals. The meaning of the passage is that the complainer under affliction protests his innocence (*v.* 31); disclaims knowledge of any offence; desires, as Job frequently expressed his desire, to know what his sin was; and professes his readiness to desist from it, when it is made clear to him (*v.* 32).

33. Elihu's answer to this complaint is that it is a claim to regulate the government of God, to give laws to Him how He shall act, and to decide how He shall recompense. Such a position the complainer takes—but for himself Elihu repudiates it: *Thou must choose, not I.* In the concluding words, *speak that which thou knowest,* Elihu invites Job to state that method of "recompense" which shall be "according to his mind" and better than that observed in God's rule of the world.

The above seems the most natural interpretation to put on this difficult passage. The A.V., in rendering *surely it is meet to be said* (*v.* 31), assumes an irregularity of punctuation which is very improbable. And to regard *vv.* 31, 32 as a serious confession and example of how a right-minded man would speak greatly impairs the vigour of the passage, and gives a much looser connexion with *v.* 33.

34—37. The verdict regarding Job's demeanour which all men of understanding and those who listen to Elihu will give,

4 Let men of understanding tell me,
And let a wise man hearken unto me.
35 Job hath spoken without knowledge,
And his words *were* without wisdom.
36 My desire *is that* Job may be tried unto the end
Because of *his* answers for wicked men.
37 For he addeth rebellion unto his sin,
He clappeth *his hands* amongst us,
And multiplieth his words against God.

> 34. Men of understanding will say unto me,
> And the wise man who heareth me:
> 35. Job speaketh without knowledge,
> And his words are without wisdom.
> 36. Would that Job were tried unto the end,
> Because of his answers in the manner of wicked men.

36. It is not certain whether *v.* 36 be a continuation of the judgment of Elihu's hearers or be his own words. The sentiment is excessively harsh, and probably Elihu, though of course concurring in it, puts it forth indirectly as the judgment of others. The wish is expressed that Job might be *tried unto the end*, constantly—that his afflictions might be continued till he should give over answering in the manner of wicked men. His "answers" are his speeches in reply to the three friends, which are characterized as such as only ungodly men would utter.

37. Job's *sin* is that of his former life, for which he has been cast into afflictions; his *rebellion* is his unsubmissive, defiant demeanour against God in his speeches. This "rebellion" is further described as *clapping of the hands*, a gesture of open mockery and contempt. The next clause, "multiplieth his words against God," that is, his rebellious speeches, indicates that it is against God that Job "claps his hands," not against his friends and counsellors—he shews his defiant scorn of God *among* them.

The passage is decisive as to the position taken by Elihu towards Job. His judgment of Job extends far beyond the mere bearing of the latter under his afflictions; it embraces Job's former life. And the language exceeds in harshness almost anything that the three friends had said.

CH. XXXV. ELIHU'S THIRD REPLY TO JOB. JOB'S COMPLAINT THAT A MAN IS IN NO WAY PROFITED BY HIS RIGHTEOUSNESS MORE THAN IF HE HAD SINNED IS MADE WITHOUT KNOWLEDGE. NEITHER RIGHTEOUSNESS NOR SIN AFFECTS GOD; THEIR INFLUENCE MUST BE FELT AMONG MEN. APPARENT EXCEPTIONS CAN BE EXPLAINED.

Job's complaint that under God's government of the world it availed

35

Elihu spake moreover, and said,
  Thinkest thou this to be right,
  That thou saidst, My righteousness *is* more than God's?
For thou saidst, What advantage will it be unto thee?
  And, What profit shall I have, *if I be cleansed* from my sin?

a man nothing to be righteous, to which Elihu had referred, ch. xxxiv. 9, is now taken up and disposed of.

  The passage has three parts:—

  First, *vv.* 1—4, Elihu states Job's complaint that godliness avails a man nothing, and undertakes to answer it.

  Second, *vv.* 5—8, his answer. Neither godliness nor irreligiousness can affect God, who is too exalted to be touched by anything human. Their influence therefore must be on men, to their advantage or hurt.

  Third, *vv.* 9—16, having made this philosophical retort, Elihu proceeds to dispose of some cases that might seem exceptions to his principle or anomalies. There are cases where apparently religious men are not heard when they cry to God: men cry out because of oppression and there is no answer. But why? Because they cry amiss. Their appeal to heaven is the mere instinctive cry of suffering like that of the lower creatures, without trust in God—they say not, Where is God my Maker?

  And the controversialist ends as in ch. xxxiv. with a charge of foolish talk against Job.

  2—4. Statement of Job's charge against God that under His rule of the world to be righteous is no advantage to a man. The verses read,

    2. Thinkest thou this to be thy right,
      And callest thou it, My just cause against God,
    3. That thou sayest, What advantage hast thou?
      And, What am I profited more than if I had sinned?

Throughout Elihu's speeches there runs the idea of a cause or plea between Job and God. Job is regarded by him as maintaining that he has a right or just cause against God. Elihu here asks if Job considers that the rectitude of his cause will appear in his maintaining that godliness profits a man nothing?—the word *this* in *v.* 2 refers to the questions in *v.* 3. If Job could successfully maintain this contention his cause against God would be good. Therefore Elihu controverts his assertion, contending that righteousness does avail a man, as it must. Both parties conduct the dispute in a somewhat external way, meaning by the "advantage" of religion the possession of outward goods and immunity from suffering. Job does this of necessity, because he is still entangled in the old theory of retribution, though he is breaking through its meshes on one side. And Elihu in his theoretical argument naturally follows him, without referring to the deeper comforts of religion, the joy in God, with which some of the Psalmists delight themselves in affliction, Ps. xvii. 15, lxxiii. 23 *seq.*

4   I will answer thee,
    And thy companions with thee.
5   Look unto the heavens, and see;
    And behold the clouds *which* are higher than thou.
6   If thou sinnest, what doest thou against him?
    Or *if* thy transgressions be multiplied, what doest thou unto him?
7   If thou be righteous, what givest thou him?
    Or what receiveth he of thine hand?
8   Thy wickedness *may hurt* a man as thou *art;*
    And thy righteousness *may profit* the son of man.
9   By reason of the multitude of oppressions they make *the oppressed* to cry:

4. The "companions" of Job referred to in this verse can hardly be the three friends, for Eliphaz (ch. xxii. 2) had advanced substantially the same answer to Job as is here given, which even Job himself had touched upon, ch. vii. 20, though with a different purpose. Most probably Job is considered here the centre of a circle of persons who cherished the same irreligious doubts in regard to God's providence as he did.

5—8. The reply of Elihu to Job's complaint. A glance at heaven, the infinitely exalted abode of God, must tell us that our conduct whether good or bad cannot affect Him. Our righteousness confers no profit on Him, neither does our wickedness entail any loss. It is men themselves that their conduct affects. It is in human life that the influence of righteousness or evil-doing is seen. And being so eternally unlike they cannot have the same effect.

Elihu does not contemplate any one going so far as to maintain that godliness and unrighteousness do not differ in themselves. Job assumes and most strongly asserts their difference. He even rises to the sublime height of resolving to adhere to righteousness though God and men should shew their indifference to it (ch. xvii. 9). And what he complains of is that God is indifferent to it, and that in His government the righteous is treated as the wicked. This is the point which Elihu touches.

8. The verse reads literally: *thy wickedness is to* (touches, affects) *a man as thou art, and thy righteousness is to one of mankind,* i.e. thyself who art a man; for it cannot touch God who is exalted above such influence.

9—15. Having laid down his principle Elihu now proceeds to clear away some anomalies which seem to support Job's contention. There are instances where godliness does not seem to advantage men, where oppressed innocence cries in vain for redress. The reason is that the cry is merely the natural voice of suffering; it is no true devout appeal to heaven—none saith, Where is God my maker?

9. *they make the oppressed to cry*] Rather, **men cry out because**

They cry out by reason of the arm of the mighty.
But none saith, Where *is* God my Maker, 10
Who giveth songs in the night;
Who teacheth us more than the beasts of the earth, 11
And maketh us wiser than the fowls of heaven?
There they cry, but none giveth answer, 12
Because of the pride of evil men.
Surely God will not hear vanity, 13
Neither will the Almighty regard it.
Although thou sayest thou shalt not see him, 14
Yet judgment *is* before him; therefore trust thou in him.

of the multitude of oppressions--which powerful and cruel men lay upon them (*v.* 12). This is the anomaly.
10. The explanation of the anomaly.
Where is God] The language of one devoutly seeking God.

songs in the night] They seek not God in truth, who by sudden deliverances (comp. ch. xxxiv. 20, 25) fills the mouth of the afflicted with singing, Ps. xxxii. 7.

11. God has given to men a higher wisdom than to the beasts, and communicates to them a continuous instruction through His fellowship and ways. Their appeal to heaven should not be the mere instinctive cry of suffering, but the voice of trust and submission.

12. The first and last words of the verse are in connexion: "they cry because of the pride of evil men, but none giveth answer." They remain unheard because their cry is "vanity" (*v.* 13).

14—16. The interpretation and connexion of these verses is difficult. *V.* 14 might carry on the idea of *v.* 13,

13. Surely God will not hear vanity,
Neither will the Almighty regard it;
14. Much less when thou sayest, Thou seest him not,
The cause is before him and thou waitest for him.

God refuses to answer the cry which is vanity, not the voice of true religious trust; much less will He hear one who like Job complains that he cannot see Him (ch. xxiii. 8 and often), who misses His righteous government in the world and charges Him with refusing to receive his just appeal (ch. xiii. 18 *seq.*, xxiii. 3, xxxi. 35 *seq.*). There are objections to this interpretation, such as that *much less when* is not a natural translation of the words in *v.* 14, though in the elliptical and rather strained style of Elihu this might not go for much. Or, *v.* 14 might stand apart from *v.* 13,

Yea, when thou sayest, Thou seest him not,
The cause is before him; therefore wait thou for him.

the meaning being that though God appears indifferent to the cry of the distressed (*vv.* 9, 12) He is not unaware of the evil, the cause has come before Him, or, His judgment upon it is determined, and therefore He

16—2

15   But now, because *it is* not *so,* he hath visited *in* his anger;
     Yet he knoweth *it* not in great extremity:
16   Therefore doth Job open his mouth in vain;
     He multiplieth words without knowledge.

is to be waited for till He manifest Himself by His just interposition. Though the second person *thou* be used, Job's own case does not appear to be referred to; Elihu speaks generally, and Job is merely addressed as an example of persons who complain of God's indifference to wrong-doing.

15. This verse is very obscure, and the A. V. competes worthily with the original in darkness. The word translated *extremity* does not occur again, and, if it be a word at all and not a mere error of copyists (the Sept. read "*transgression*"), its meaning can only be guessed at. The connexion, however, suggests what general meaning the expression must have. Perhaps the easiest way to construe the verse is to take it in connexion with *v.* 16,

15.   But now because his anger visiteth not,
      And he doth not strictly regard transgression,
16.   Therefore doth Job open his mouth in vanity,
      He multiplieth words without knowledge.

Because sentence against an evil work is not executed speedily (Eccles. viii. 11), and God seems as if He took no knowledge of wrong and oppression, therefore Job draws the futile conclusion (*vv.* 2, 3), that there is no advantage in being righteous more than in sinning. Elihu has already accounted for God's refusal to interpose on very different grounds (*vv.* 10—13), grounds which Job would do well to lay to heart. The word rendered "extremity" (*fash*) may have a correspondent in the Arab. *fashsha* of which Lane says, "*fashsha* is *syn.* with *fâsha* as meaning, *He gloried* or *boasted and magnified himself, imagining (in himself) what he did not possess.*" This would suggest such a meaning as *pride* or *arrogancy*.

Though this construction of *v.* 15 is simple it is doubtful if it be the true one. *V.* 16 certainly looks independent, and if so *v.* 15 is also complete in itself,

But now because his anger visiteth not,
Therefore he careth nothing for transgression!

the second clause expressing the conclusion which Job draws from God's inactivity and His refraining to punish (first clause), namely that God was indifferent to evil, or as expressed in *vv.* 2, 3, that righteousness was of no profit to a man more than sin. The sense remains the same as on the other construction. And *v.* 16, as before, expresses Elihu's verdict regarding Job,

Nay, Job openeth his mouth in vanity,
He multiplieth words without knowledge.

CHAP. XXXVI.—XXXVII. ELIHU'S FOURTH SPEECH.

In his former speeches Elihu was more theoretical, being intent upon correcting the false principles in regard to God enunciated by Job (see

Elihu also proceeded, and said, 36
  Suffer me a little, and I will shew thee
  That *I have* yet to speak on God's behalf.

headings to ch. xxxiii., xxxiv., xxxv.); in his present speech he is more practical and hortatory. He keeps still before him the same great object, namely to present just thoughts of God; but having in the former speeches corrected the false ideas of Job he proceeds now, more positively, to present his own elevated conceptions of the Creator.

The object of the passage is to extol the greatness of God in all His operations, both among men and in the world. Thus the passage falls into two parts,

First, ch. xxxvi. 1—25; in which the greatness of God in His providential treatment of men is extolled. Here the speaker gives a fuller statement of his theory of the meaning of the afflictions sent on men by God (*vv.* 1—15); and exhorts Job to recognise God's purpose in his sufferings, and to unite with all men in exalting Him.

Second, ch. xxxvi. 26—ch. xxxvii.; in which the greatness and wisdom and unsearchableness of God, as these are manifested in the phenomena of the heavens, are magnified (ch. xxxvi. 26—xxxvii. 13); and Job is exhorted to lay these great wonders to heart, and bow beneath the wisdom and power of God, who far transcends man's comprehension (ch. xxxvii. 14—24).

CHAP. XXXVI. 1—25. GOD'S GRACIOUS DESIGNS IN AFFLICTING MEN; AND EXHORTATION TO JOB TO UNITE WITH ALL MEN IN EXTOLLING HIS GREATNESS.

First, *vv.* 1—4. In some words of introduction Elihu beseeches Job to listen to him still further, for he has yet something to say on God's behalf; and he will speak what is true, for he has perfect knowledge.

Second, *vv.* 5—15. Then he proceeds to his theme, the greatness of God. This is a greatness of mind and understanding, which does not despise the weak, but rules all with goodness and wisdom. Afflictions are but instances of this gracious wisdom, for by them He opens the ear of men to instruction.

Third, *vv.* 16—25, application of this doctrine of the meaning of afflictions to Job—God is through them alluring him into a prosperous and happy life. And the speaker adds a warning against murmuring, and an exhortation to adore and magnify as all men do the great God.

1—4. Introductory: Elihu desires Job to hear him still further. He has still more to say in God's behalf; and it is not trivial or commonplace, either in its object—for he will ascribe right to his Maker; nor in itself, for he is one perfect in knowledge.

2. The verse reads,
  Suffer me a little and I will shew thee;
  For I have somewhat still to say on God's behalf.

The first words are lit. *wait for me* a little.

3 I will fetch my knowledge from afar,
And will ascribe righteousness to my Maker.
4 For truly my words *shall* not *be* false:
He that is perfect in knowledge *is* with thee.
5 Behold, God *is* mighty, and despiseth not *any:*
He is mighty in strength *and* wisdom.
6 He preserveth not the life of the wicked:
But giveth right to the poor.
7 He withdraweth not his eyes from the righteous:
But with kings *are they* on the throne;
Yea, he doth establish them for ever, and they are exalted.

3. *from afar*] He will speak comprehensively, embracing the distant parts of the subject in his survey, or throwing light upon it from far-off regions.

righteousness to my Maker] Elihu gives here in a word the ruling idea of his discourses: they are all meant to ascribe righteousness or right to God; they are a defence of God against the charges of Job. The expression rendered *my Maker* does not occur elsewhere in the Old Testament.

4. The speaker makes a higher claim than to sincerity here; he claims the character of absolute truth for his teaching—he is perfect in knowledge. In a slightly different form the phrase "perfect in knowledge" is applied to God, ch. xxxvii. 16; cf. 1 Sam. ii. 3.

5–25. Elihu's doctrine is in a word: God is great and despiseth not, He is great in strength of heart. His greatness is that of understanding, which enables Him to estimate all rightly, to see through all right and wrong, and to adapt His providence to the strong and to the weak, the evil and the good. This thought with the illustrations of it, *vv.* 6—15, and the application of it to Job, *vv.* 16—25, exhaust the first half of this concluding speech.

5. *and despiseth not*] Though God is mighty He despiseth or disdaineth not, He gives the weakest his rights as much as the most powerful, for they are all the work of His hand, ch. xxxiv. 19. The words express Elihu's conception of God, which He opposes to the conception of Job (e.g. ch. vii. and often).

in strength and wisdom] Rather, **in strength of understanding**; lit. *of heart*. It is this perfection of understanding, in which God's greatness consists, that makes it impossible that He should "despise" any. To know life, however mean, is to love it.

6. Illustration of the operation of God's understanding, giving to all conditions of men their due.

right to the poor] Rather, **his right**; *poor* may be, as marg., *afflicted*.

7. The second half of the verse reads,
But with kings upon the throne
He setteth them for ever, and they are exalted.

vv. 8—14.] JOB, XXXVI. 247

And if *they be* bound in fetters, 8
And be holden in cords of affliction;
Then he sheweth them their work, 9
And their transgressions that they have exceeded.
He openeth also their ear to discipline, 10
And commandeth that they return from iniquity.
If they obey and serve *him*, 11
They shall spend their days in prosperity,
And their years in pleasures.
But if they obey not, 12
They shall perish by the sword,
And they shall die without knowledge.
But the hypocrites in heart heap up wrath: 13
They cry not when he bindeth them.
They die in youth, 14
And their life *is* among the unclean.

God's careful providence especially keeps the righteous, whom He exalts to the loftiest stations, 1 Sam. ii. 8; Ps. cxiii. 7 *seq.*

8—10. If life often appears to present a different picture and men are seen in affliction, this affliction is a discipline, needful to warn them and bring their evil before them.

8. The expression "fetters" is rather to be taken figuratively, meaning affliction or adversity, as "cords of affliction" in the next clause suggests.

9—10. The meaning of afflictions—they are a divine warning and stimulus to rouse men out of a sinful lethargy and bring their sin to their remembrance.

9. *that they have exceeded*] Or, **have dealt proudly**, ch. xxxiii. 17.

11, 12. Such afflictions, though graciously meant, may have different issues according as men receive them. On the expression "the sword" in *v.* 12 see ch. xxxiii. 18.

13, 14. Such afflictions indeed are sometimes the means of revealing what character men are of, ch. v. 2.

13. *hypocrites in heart*] Rather, **godless in heart**; comp. ch. viii. 13.

heap up wrath] Rather, **lay up anger**, i.e. in their hearts, Ps. xiii. 2; Prov. xxvi. 24; they cherish anger at the Divine discipline (ch. v. 2). The "wrath" or anger referred to is their own, not that of God (Rom. ii. 5). The phrase does not occur elsewhere.

14. *They die*] lit. *their soul dieth.* They perish in the midst of their days.

is among the unclean] Or, **perisheth among the unclean**, i.e. *like* the unclean. They die prematurely or in debasement like the *hierodouloi* in the temples of Baal comp. 1 Kings xiv. 24, xv. 12.

JOB, XXXVI. [vv. 15—17.

15 He delivereth the poor in his affliction,
And openeth their ears in oppression.
16 Even so would he have removed thee out of the strait
Into a broad place, where *there is* no straitness;
And that which should be set on thy table *should be* full
of fatness.
17 But thou hast fulfilled the judgment of the wicked:
Judgment and justice take hold on *thee*.

15. The verse goes back to the great general principle of the use of affliction in God's hand (*v.* 8 *seq.*), in order to connect with it the case of Job, and to found an exhortation to him upon it (*v.* 16 *seq.*). The word *in* affliction, *in* oppression, might mean *through* affliction, &c.

16—25. Application to Job of the principles in regard to affliction just enunciated by Elihu.

Verses **16—19** are difficult and have been understood in a great variety of ways. The general sense expressed by the A. V. is probably correct, unless probability be considered too strong a term to employ of any rendering.

16. Even so doth he allure thee out of the mouth of distress
Into a broad place, where there is no straitness;
And that which is set on thy table shall be full of fatness.
17. But if thou art filled with the judgment of the wicked,
Judgment and justice shall keep hold on thee.
18. For beware lest wrath entice thee into scorning,
And let not the greatness of the ransom lead thee astray.
19. Will thy riches suffice, without stint?
Or all the forces of wealth?

Many objections may be urged against this rendering, as may be against any rendering that can be proposed.

16. The words *even so* connect Job's case with the general principles in regard to suffering just inculcated by Elihu. The figures of "straitness" and "broad place" are usual for affliction and prosperity, cf. ch. xviii. 7. The figure of a plenteous table is also common, Ps. xxiii. 5. The speaker does not say by what means God is alluring the sufferer out of the mouth or jaws of distress into a broad place. He means probably the disciplining effects of the distress itself, unless the "distress" here refer to a future, greater evil, from which Job's present affliction is designed to save him. Comp., however, ch. xxxiii. 14—28.

17. The A. V. takes this verse positively; it is more suitable to the connexion and purpose of the speaker to understand it conditionally— *if thou art filled with*, or as A. V. *fulfillest*. To be full of, or to fulfil, the judgment of the wicked, is to join the wicked in their judgment of God when He afflicts, to lay up wrath against God (*v.* 13), an idea immediately taken up in *v.* 18. If Job acts in this way, as he is too much inclined (*v.* 21), then judgment and justice shall keep hold on him. God's condemnation of him will reveal itself in the continuance

Because *there is* wrath, *beware* lest he take thee away 18
with *his* stroke:
Then a great ransom cannot deliver thee.
Will he esteem thy riches? *no*, not gold, 19
Nor all the forces of strength.
Desire not the night, 20
When people are cut off in their place.

and increase of his chastisement (cf. *vv.* 13, 14, ch. v. 2 *seq*.). The word "judgment" is used in the one clause of man's, and in the other of God's judgment, making a forcible antithesis.

18. In this verse *wrath* appears to be that of Job, as "anger," *v.* 13. Elihu warns him against allowing it to entice him into rebellion against God, comp. ch. xxxiv. 37. The A. V. takes "wrath" as that of God, visible in Job's afflictions. This gives a good parallel to the "greatness of the ransom" in the next clause. Elihu's doctrine, however, is that afflictions are not the expression of God's wrath but of His disciplinary mercy; and his great object is to warn Job against putting this false construction on God's dealing with him; cf. ch. xxxiii. throughout, ch. xxxvi. 5.

In the second clause he warns Job against being led astray by the greatness of the *ransom*, by which he means Job's severe afflictions; cf. ch. xxxiii. 24.

19. No other ransom will avail,—not riches nor all the power of wealth. Only the purification of suffering will cleanse him from his evil (cf. ch. xxxiv. 36), and deliver him. Elihu demands with emphasis whether all his riches will be accepted as a ransom? It need not be said that the question is put merely for the purpose of heightening the effect of the idea in *v*. 18, that suffering is the only ransom possible. A similar thought is expressed in Ps. xlix. 7: "None of them can by any means redeem his brother, nor give to God a ransom for him; for the redemption of their soul is too precious and it ceaseth for ever."

The word translated "without stint" (Conant) is lit. without *straitness*. The word is often used for *distress* (*v*. 16), and the clause might be rendered : *will thy riches suffice* (lit. *be equal to it*, ch. xxviii. 19), *without distress*, i.e. such afflictions as those now suffered? This is rather flat. The A. V. assumes that the expression is the word *ore* or gold, ch. xxii. 24, differently spelled. This assumption is both improbable in itself and contrary to the balance of the verse.

20—21. Elihu continues his warning to Job.

20. Desire not that night
When the peoples are cut off in their place;
21. Take heed, turn not unto iniquity,
For this thou choosest rather than affliction.

20. The "night" is as usual a figure for destruction and judgment. By this destroying judgment of God nations are "taken away" *in their place*, i.e. on the spot, suddenly and without power of escape;

21   Take heed, regard not iniquity:
     For this hast thou chosen rather than affliction.
22   Behold, God exalteth by his power:
     Who teacheth like him?
23   Who hath enjoined him his way?
     Or who can say, Thou hast wrought iniquity?
24   Remember that thou magnify his work,
     Which men behold.
25   Every man may see it;
     Man may behold *it* afar off.

and Job is warned against desiring, lit. *panting for*, such a judgment. Job had often desired to meet God in judgment, and there may be a reference to this in the words, but the passage contains a general warning against Job's rebellious words and demeanour towards God, and means "Act not as if thou soughtest to bring on thyself the dark and sudden judgment day of calamity when nations are swept away in their place."

21. The verse continues the warning against a rebellious mind under affliction, called here "turning unto iniquity"; for Job shews himself more inclined to this than to submission to God's chastening hand.

22—25. Instead of murmuring Job should bow under the mighty hand of God, who through the operations of His providence is a great teacher of men (*v.* 22); who is supreme (*v.* 23); and whose work all men celebrate (*v.* 24), looking to it with admiration and awe (*v.* 25).

22. *exalteth by his power*] Rather, **God doeth loftily in his power**. *who teacheth*] Or, **who is a teacher**.

23. The verse expresses the idea that God is supreme; none enjoins or appoints Him His way; He is "God over all;" and hence none can pass judgment upon His doings.

24. *which men behold*] Rather, **which men do sing**, that is, celebrate with praise.

25. The verse is better without the "may" of the A.V.
     All men look thereon,
     Man beholdeth it afar off.
Men look on God's work, His operations, with wonder and awe.

CHAP. XXXVI. 26—XXXVII. THE GREATNESS AND UNSEARCHABLENESS OF GOD, SEEN IN HIS MARVELLOUS OPERATIONS IN THE SKIES; AND EXHORTATION TO JOB TO ALLOW THESE WONDERS DULY TO IMPRESS HIM, AND TO BOW BENEATH THE GREATNESS OF GOD, WHO SURPASSES ALL COMPREHENSION.

The passage has two sections:
First, ch. xxxvi. 26—xxxvii. 13, the incomprehensible greatness of God, seen in the phenomena of the atmosphere: in the formation of

Behold, God *is* great, and we know *him* not,   26
Neither can the number of his years be searched out.
For he maketh small the drops of water: 27
They pour down rain according to the vapour thereof:
Which the clouds do drop   28
And distil upon man abundantly.

the rain-drops (ch. xxxvi. 26—28); in the thunder-storm (ch. xxxvi. 29—xxxvii. 5); in snow and ice, which seals up the hand of man and makes him powerless before the mighty power of God (*vv*. 6—10); in His lading the cloud with moisture, and guiding it to the fulfilment of His varied behests upon the whole earth (*vv*. 11—13).

Second, ch. xxxvii. 14—21, Elihu exhorts Job to consider these marvels of Him which is wonderful in counsel and excellent in working, and to let them duly impress him; bidding him behold the wonderful balancing of the summer cloud in the heavens, when the earth is still with the south wind (*vv*. 14—17), and the burnished sky is stretched out like a molten mirror (*v*. 18). With what words shall man come before the Omnipotent to contend with Him! Man, who is dazzled by the light of the sky, how should he behold the terrible glory around God! Therefore all men do fear Him; and He hath not respect to those that are wise in their own understanding (*vv*. 19—21).

Ch. xxxvi. 26—xxxvii. 13, The greatness of God and the wonderfulness of His operations in the phenomena of the atmosphere.

26. *we know him not*] He is so great as to transcend all knowledge of man. The Eternity of God is referred to in the second clause in order to fill the mind more completely with the sense of His greatness.

27, 28. The wonder of the rain-drops.

27. For he maketh small the rain-drops;
They distil the rain of his vapour;
28. Which the clouds pour down,
And drop upon the multitude of mankind.

27. *he maketh small*] lit. *he draweth away*, the reference being probably to the formation of the rain, which God draweth away *in drops* from the great mass of waters above. Others render, *he draweth up*, supposing the reference to be to the ascent of the rain in the form of vapour, as it then comes down in rain-drops. But this is rather scientific and complete; neither does the word mean to *draw up*.

28. *upon man abundantly*] This is possible, but the more natural meaning is as above, the reference being to the universal reach of the rain, and its fall on all mankind.

29—xxxvii. 5. The marvel of the thunder-storm.

29, 30. Verse 30 needs some modification—

29. Also can any understand the spreadings of the clouds,
And the crashings of his pavilion?
30. Behold, he spreadeth his light around him,
And covereth him over with the deeps of the sea.

29 Also can *any* understand the spreadings of the clouds,
Or the noise of his tabernacle?
30 Behold, he spreadeth his light upon it,
And covereth the bottom of the sea.
31 For by them judgeth he the people;
He giveth meat in abundance.
32 With clouds he covereth the light;
And commandeth it *not to shine* by *the cloud* that cometh betwixt.
33 The noise thereof sheweth concerning it,
The cattle also concerning the vapour.

29. The "spreadings" of the clouds refers probably to the accumulation and diffusion of the storm clouds over the heavens; and the second clause to the loud thundering within the dark cloud, where God is enshrouded, and which is therefore called His "pavilion." So the word is rendered Ps. xviii. 11, where the representation is similar.

30. Though God is enveloped in the dark cloud, He is there encircled with His light, which, though the masses of waters cover Him, manifests itself to men's eyes in the lightning that shoots from the cloud and illumines it.

the bottom of the sea] lit. *the roots* of the sea, a singular figure, which must mean *the deeps* or recesses of the sea. The reference is no doubt to the masses of water in the thunder clouds which enshroud the Almighty, but the precise idea of the poet is uncertain. Either he must call the heavenly waters the "sea" (cf. Ps. xxix. 3), and mean by its "roots" its densest recesses; or if he refer to the sea on earth, his idea must be that it has been, as it were, drawn up from its bottom in cloud and vapour to form the pavilion of the Lord. This second idea has a certain extravagance which makes it less probable.

31. *For by them judgeth he the people*] Rather, the **peoples**. He judges the peoples by the lightning and the rain cloud. By the one He "scatters" and "discomfits" His enemies (Ps. xviii. 14), and by the other He watereth the earth and makes it fruitful (Is. lv. 10).

32—33. The verses read,

32. He covereth over his hands with light,
And giveth it commandment against the adversary;
33. His thundering telleth concerning him;
Unto the cattle, even concerning him that cometh up;

32. The "light" here is the lightning, which grasped in His hands illuminates them. Hitzig refers to Hor. Od. I. 2,

et rubente
dextera sacras jaculatus arces
terruit urbem.

33. *the cattle also*] The A. V. makes "cattle" subject—they also tell of God; in which case the reference would be to their presentiments of

At this also my heart trembleth,	**37**
And is moved out of his place.	
Hear attentively the noise of his voice,	2
And the sound *that* goeth out of his mouth.	
He directeth it under the whole heaven,	3
And his lightning unto the ends of the earth.	
After it a voice roareth:	4
He thundereth with the voice of his excellency;	
And he will not stay them when his voice is heard.	
God thundereth marvellously with his voice;	5
Great *things* doeth he, which we cannot comprehend.	
For he saith to the snow, Be thou *on* the earth;	6
Likewise *to* the small rain,	
And *to* the great rain of his strength.	

a coming storm. The context, however, describes a storm actually present, and it is more natural to repeat the words "it telleth" from the first clause and render, (it telleth) *unto the cattle;* for the reference throughout appears to be to the impression produced on all creatures by God's mighty thunderings and how these reveal His majesty—even the cattle hearing with terror His awful voice; just as in ch. xxxvii. 1 Elihu describes the effect produced on himself.

concerning the vapour] Rather as above, *concerning Him that cometh up*, i.e. approaches or advances in the thunder cloud.

The above rendering assumes that the present Heb. text is correct. Others by alterations in the pointing elicit various senses.

xxxvii. **1.** This verse reads,

> Yea, at this my heart trembleth,
> And leapeth up out of its place.

2. *the sound that goeth*] Or, *the muttering.* The thunder is the voice of God, going forth out of His mouth.

3. *he directeth*] Rather, assuming another derivation of the word, **he sendeth it forth,** lets it loose.

4. *with the voice of his excellency*] Rather, **with his voice of majesty.**

he will not stay them] Rather, **he stayeth them not**; He restrains not His lightnings. The words describe the play of the lightning, rapidly succeeding the thunder. When God's presence is announced by His terrible voice, there also are His awful ministers, the lightnings, swift to do His commandments against His adversaries (ch. xxxvi. 32).

6—10. Another wonder of God's power, snow and frost.

6. The verse reads as a whole,

> For he saith to the snow, Fall thou on the earth;
> Likewise to the showers of rain,
> Even to the showers of his mighty rains.

7   He sealeth up the hand of every man;
    That all men may know his work.
8   Then the beasts go into dens,
    And remain in their places.
9   Out of the south cometh the whirlwind:
    And cold out of the north.
10 By the breath of God frost is given:
    And the breadth of the waters is straitened.
11 Also by watering he wearieth the thick cloud:
    He scattereth his bright cloud:

The reference in the second and third clauses is probably to the heavy rainfall of the winter season.

7. *He sealeth up the hand*] Effect of the winter rains and snow on men: all labour in the field is suspended; the hand of man is as it were "sealed up."

that all men may know his work] The Heb. must be rendered: **that all men whom he hath made may know**, lit. *all men of his workmanship*. The meaning is, that men by their enforced inactivity through His operations in nature may know His sovereign power and that they are subject to it. The sense given by the A.V. is that of some of the ancient Versions, but implies a different reading.

8. *their places*] Their coverts or lairs. The reference is to the hibernation of the animals, or to their retreat into their coverts for shelter from the snow and rains.

9—10. Frost and ice.

9. The rendering of this verse in the A.V. is free and in some measure conjectural.

the south] lit. *the chamber*. In ch. ix. 9 reference was made to the "chambers of the south," and it has been assumed that the same is the meaning here. There is no reason, however, why the southern heavens should be called "chamber" more than any other quarter of the sky; and the passage appears to refer to the season of winter, while the south wind brings heat, *v.* 17. The term "chamber" is most probably used in the sense of "treasury" (ch. xxxviii. 22), as Ps. cxxxv. 7, "He bringeth the wind out of his treasuries." The meaning probably is, *out of its* (or, *his*) *chamber cometh the whirlwind*.

the north] The word is of uncertain meaning. It may signify, *the scattering* (winds), that is, possibly the north winds that scatter the clouds and bring frost.

10. *By the breath of God frost*] Rather, **ice**. The wind is the breath of God as the thunder is His voice. This cold breath gives ice.

11—13. The wonderful movements of the clouds directed by the guidance of God, and fulfilling His several behests.

These verses read,

11. Also he ladeth the thick cloud with moisture,
    He spreadeth his lightning-cloud abroad;

And it is turned round about by his counsels: 12
That they may do whatsoever he commandeth them
Upon the face of the world in the earth.
He causeth it to come, whether for correction, 13
Or for his land, or for mercy.
Hearken unto this, O Job: 14
Stand still, and consider the wondrous works of God.
Dost thou know when God disposed them, 15
And caused the light of his cloud to shine?
Dost thou know the balancings of the clouds, 16
The wondrous works of *him which is* perfect in knowledge?
How thy garments *are* warm, 17
When he quieteth the earth by the south *wind*?

12. And it is turned round about by his guidance,
That it may do whatsoever he commandeth it
Upon the face of the whole earth;
13. Whether it be for correction, or for his earth,
Or for mercy that he causeth it to come.

12. In the second clause the words are lit. "that *they* may do," the *plur.* referring to "cloud" (*v.* 11) collectively. Others make the pronoun *they* refer to men, which is very unnatural. The expression "the whole earth" is lit. *the world of the earth*, Prov. viii. 31.

13. This is the natural rendering of the Heb. If right the words "correction" (rod, ch. xxi. 9) and "mercy" must refer to God's purposes in regard to *men*, while the words "for his earth" refer more to the inanimate world, as God "causeth it to rain on the earth, where no man is," ch. xxxviii. 26. Many have felt, however, that the balance of the verse requires only *two* objects to be stated, namely "correction" and "mercy," and would render the first line, *whether it be for correction, when* due *to his earth*.

14—23. Elihu's own imagination kindles at the thought of the wonders which he is unfolding, and he beseeches Job to observe them with a reverent awe, and learn from them the unsearchableness of Him who is their Author.

15. *when God disposed them*] Rather, **how God layeth his command upon them, and causeth,** &c.?

16. *the balancings*] That is, how the clouds are poised in the heavens (comp. ch. xxvi. 8), which Elihu regards as an unspeakable marvel.

17. *how thy garments are warm*] Rather perhaps, **thou whose garments are warm, when the earth is still because of the south wind.** Verse 15 referred to the storm cloud; *vv.* 16, 17 refer rather to the sultry summer cloud. The words express how feeble man has no part in causing these wonders, but only passively feels the effect of them. "This sensation of dry, hot clothes is only experienced during the

18 Hast thou with him spread out the sky,
    Which is strong, *and* as a molten looking glass?
19 Teach us what we shall say unto him;
    For we cannot order *our speech* by reason of darkness.
20 Shall it be told him that I speak?
    If a man speak, surely he shall be swallowed up.
21 And now *men* see not the bright light
    Which *is* in the clouds:
    But the wind passeth, and cleanseth them.

siroccos" (Thomson, *Land and the Book*). In reference to the *stillness* of the earth under such a wind, this writer says, "There is no living thing abroad to make a noise. The birds hide in thickest shades, the fowls pant under the walls with open mouth and drooping wings, the flocks and herds take shelter in caves and under great rocks, and the labourers retire from the fields and close the windows and doors of their houses.... The very air is too weak and languid to stir the pendent leaves even of the tall poplars."

18. The present tense is better in this verse,
> Canst thou with him spread out the skies,
> Strong, as a molten mirror?

"With Him" may mean "along with Him," or rather *like* Him. The comparison of the clear, dry, burnished summer skies of the East to "brass" is made in other parts of Scripture. The Eastern mirrors were plates of metal, Ex. xxxviii. 8.

19. This thought of the strong expanse of heaven stretched out by God suggests to Elihu His unspeakable greatness and unsearchableness, and he demands of Job with what words of man such a Being is to be addressed, if one sought to contend with Him.

by reason of darkness] That is, of understanding—in presence of the unsearchableness of God.

20. The verse means,
> Shall it be told him that I would speak?
> Or shall a man wish that he should be swallowed up?

Elihu recoils from the thought of going into God's presence to strive with Him; such daring presumption would be voluntarily to court destruction. The words "shall a man wish?" are lit. *has a man said* or commanded? i.e. has any one ever voluntarily ordered his own annihilation? Nothing other than this does the man do who ventures to contend with the Almighty.

21. The natural meaning of this verse is,
> And now men cannot look upon the light,
> When it is bright in the skies,
> And the wind hath passed and cleansed them.

The "light," here the sunlight, is too great to look upon, it dazzles the beholder, when the wind has passed over and cleared the heavens.

Fair weather cometh out of the north: 22
With God *is* terrible majesty.
Touching the Almighty, we cannot find him out: *he is* 23
    excellent in power,
And *in* judgment, and *in* plenty of justice: he will not
    afflict.

Others render, as A.V. in the main, *and now men see not the light*, though *it is bright in the clouds* (i.e. *behind* the clouds); *but the wind passeth over and cleareth them*. It is difficult to reconcile this translation of the third clause with grammar. The idea supposed to be suggested by this rendering is, that just as behind the clouds there is light, which will by and by appear, so the darkness around God's face and ways will speedily clear away. But such a thought remains altogether unexpressed; and besides, the whole passage refers to the unsearchableness of God and the terrible majesty that surrounds Him and makes Him unapproachable (*vv.* 22, 23). The verse is evidently incomplete in sense, expressing but half the idea; the other half is given in *v.* 22.

22. *fair weather*] lit. *gold*, that is, probably, **golden brightness** or splendour, the reference being to the *light* (*v.* 21). This is said to come from the North because the north wind (*v.* 21) clears away the clouds and reveals it. With this sense the verse carries on the thought of *v.* 21, and the antithesis is expressed in the second clause of *v.* 22, *with God is terrible glory*—if men cannot look upon the light when it shines in the cloudless heaven, how much less shall they bear to look upon the majesty of God, surrounded with terrible glory.

Others adhere to the literal sense of *gold*, considering the general meaning to be, that men may penetrate into the furthest and darkest regions of the earth and bring out to view whatever precious things they contain, but around God is a terrible majesty which exalts Him above all comprehension. However good this meaning be in itself, it leaves *v.* 21 isolated and incomplete in sense. And although to Classical Antiquity the North may have been the region of gold, no trace of such a conception appears in the Old Testament, for any identification of Havilah (Gen. ii. 11) with Colchis is more than adventurous. The comparison too of the light to gold is common in the poetry of all languages.

23, 24. Elihu sums up his teaching regarding the greatness of God, which is ever conjoined with righteousness. It is befitting men, therefore, not to judge Him, but to fear Him, for He regards not them that are wise in their own understanding.

23. According to the original the members of the verse stand thus:

The Almighty! we cannot find him out; who is great in power,
And in justice and fulness of righteousness: he will not afflict.

The connexion shews that *afflict* has the sense of afflict *unjustly*, or *oppress*. Taken thus the verse has a certain halting movement. Hence others take the word "afflict" in the sense of *wrest* or *do violence to*,

24 **Men do therefore fear him:
He respecteth not any** *that are* **wise of heart.**

rendering the second clause, *and justice and fulness of righteousness he will not pervert* (Ew.).

Elihu returns here at the end of his discourse to the thought of God with which he started, ch. xxxvi. 5, "Behold God is mighty, and despiseth not any." This is the thought of God that fills all his discourses; God's power is ever conjoined with righteousness, and He unjustly afflicts or oppresses none.

24. *wise of heart*] That is, wise in their own thoughts. God has respect unto the humble—a final exhortation to Job to abstain from presumptuous complaints of God, and to unite with mankind everywhere in fearing Him.

CH. XXXVIII.—XLII. 6. THE LORD ANSWERS JOB OUT OF THE STORM.

We are now to witness the last act of the drama. And to understand it we have to go back to the starting-point and recall the idea of the Poem. This idea is expressed in the question, *Doth Job serve God for nought?* Or, as otherwise put, the idea is, *The trial of the Righteous.* This trial has been observed proceeding throughout the whole Book. Now it approaches its conclusion. The Lord, who caused it or permitted it, and has watched it from afar, must now interpose to bring it to an end, and bestow on Job the fruits of it. The trial has been successfully borne: for though Job has sinned under it, his sin has not been of the kind predicted by the Adversary; he has continued to cleave to God, and even sounded deeps of faith profounder than ever he had reached before (ch. xix.), and tasted the sweets of righteousness with a keener delight than during his former godly life (ch. xvii. 9).

At the point at which we are now arrived the sole object of interest is Job's mind in its relations to God. The speculative question discussed between him and his friends concerning the meaning of his sufferings, or the meaning of evil in general in the providence of God, has no importance, except so far as the conclusions which Job has arrived at have left his mind in a condition of perplexity in regard to the ways of God. The Author's didactic purpose in raising the discussion between Job and his friends has been served (ch. xxi. xxiii.—xxiv.). Job himself now remains the problem.

Though the trial has been successfully borne upon the whole, Job has not come out of it scatheless. His demeanour towards God, especially in presuming to contend with Him, has been at many points profoundly blameworthy. And the thought, which he refuses to abandon (ch. xxvii. 2—6, xxxi. 35 *seq.*), that God is unjust in His rule of the world, even though he maintains it more as a theory and necessary construction of facts as he observes them, without allowing it much to influence his life, or destroy his larger faith in God, is a thought not only derogatory to God, but one that must cripple every religious movement of Job's heart. So long as such a feeling remains his trial cannot be said to be ended. But nothing that Job himself can do, nor anything that his friends can urge, is able to remove it. It was God, by His mysterious providence, who raised this dark doubt in His servant's mind, and He must interpose to drive it away.

It might be supposed at first that the simplest way of restoring Job to peace would have been to reveal to him that his afflictions were not due to his sin, but were the trial of his righteousness, and in this way solve the problem that perplexed him. But the elements of blameworthiness in Job's conduct forbade this simple treatment. The disease had spread in his mind, and developed moral symptoms, which required a broader remedy. Besides, it is God who now speaks to Job; and in His teaching of men He never moves in the region of the mere understanding, but always in that of the religious life. He may remove perplexities regarding His providence and ways from men's minds, but He does not do so by the immediate communication of intellectual light, but by flushing all the channels of thought and life with a deeper sense of Himself. Under the flow of this fuller sense of God perplexities disappear, just as rocks that raise an angry surf when the tide is low are covered and unknown when it is full. This is the meaning of God's manifestation to Job out of the storm. He brings Himself and His full glory near to Job, and fills his mind with such a sense of Him as he had never had before—"Now mine eye seeth thee" (ch. xlii. 5). At this sight of God his heart not only quivers with an unspeakable joy, but he abhors his past thoughts of Him, and his former words, and repents in dust and ashes.

The object of the Lord's answer to Job out of the storm is twofold, to rebuke Job, and to heal him—to bring home to his heart the blameworthiness of his words and demeanour towards God, and to lift him up out of his perplexities into peace. The two things hardly differ; at least both are effected by the same means, namely by God's causing all His glory to pass before Job.

The Lord's answer to Job out of the storm consists of two parts, or contains two questions:—

First, ch. xxxviii. 1—xl. 5, Shall mortal man contend with God?

Second, ch. xl. 6—xlii. 6, Shall man charge God with wrong in His rule of the world?

The two questions, however, are hardly kept apart, for the first implies the second, inasmuch as a man's contention with God will naturally be because of His unjust treatment of himself. And Job, in his final words of penitence (ch. xlii. 1—6), refers back to ch. xxxviii. 2.

In the beginning of His first address Jehovah invites Job to enter upon that contention with Him which he had so often sought, "Gird up thy loins like a man; and I will demand of thee, and answer thou me" (ch. xxxviii. 3). The point aimed at by the Divine Speaker is the presumption of Job in desiring to contend with the Almighty. Then the Lord causes a panorama of creation, both inanimate and living, to pass before Job (ch. xxxviii. 4—xxxix. 30). Having done so He demands, "Will he that reproveth the Almighty contend with Him"?

(ch. xl. 2.) Does Job, now that the glory of God has been made to pass before his eyes, continue to desire to contend with Him? To which Job replies, "Behold I am too mean; how shall I answer thee? I lay mine hand upon my mouth" (ch. xl. 4). The exhibition of the great panorama of creation was but a method of revealing God, not in one attribute but in all His manifoldness and resource of mind. It was designed to abase Job before God, and rebuke his presumption. And this was its effect: "Behold I am too mean"! But the revelation of God had another design besides abasing Job. It was given to Job that he might know God, and be at peace (ch. xxii. 21).

The process, however, is not yet complete. In a second address the Lord again commands Job to gird up his loins and answer Him. But now He is more specific: "Wilt thou condemn me that thou mayest be in the right"? (ch. xl. 8.) And He ironically invites Job to clothe himself with the attributes of the Supreme Ruler, and conduct the rule of the world himself. The invitation brings home to Job a still deeper feeling of that which the Almighty is, and he exclaims, "I had heard of thee with the hearing of the ear, but now mine eye seeth thee" (ch. xlii. 5). And in this light of God his own past thought of Him seems the darker: "I abhor it, and repent in dust and ashes."

Thus the solution to Job's problem given in God's answer from the storm is a religious solution, not a speculative one. It is a solution to the heart, not to the intellect. It is such a solution as only God could give; a solution which does not solve the perplexity but buries it under the tide of a fuller life and joy in God. It is a solution as broad as Job's life and not merely the measure of his understanding; the same solution as was given to the doubting Apostle, making him to exclaim, "My Lord and my God!" and teaching him that not through his sense of touch or his eyesight, but through a broader sense, God makes himself felt by man.

CH. XXXVIII. 1—XL. 5. THE LORD'S FIRST ANSWER TO JOB OUT OF THE STORM. SHALL MORTAL MAN CONTEND WITH GOD?

The passage has three general divisions:
First, ch. xxxviii. 1—38, a review of inanimate nature, the wonders of earth and sky, all revealing the manifoldness of the Divine mind, and suggesting by contrast the littleness of man.

Second, ch. xxxviii. 39—xxxix. 30, a review of the world of animal life, having the same object as the former division.

Third, ch. xl. 1—5, the impression produced on Job by this vision of the glory of God in creation—he is abased and brought to silence.

This first address to Job touches simply the presumption of a man seeking to contend with God. Hence it is taken up with presenting God and man in opposition to one another. The vivid pictures of the inanimate creation, with its wonders, and the world of animal life, with its instincts and properties—all of them originated and bestowed by God—are but the means used for displaying God. And the sharp, ironical questions put to Job, where he was when God laid the

Then the LORD answered Job out of the whirlwind, and said, 38
Who *is* this that darkeneth counsel 2
By words without knowledge?
Gird up now thy loins like a man; 3
For I will demand of thee, and answer thou me.
Where wast thou when I laid the foundations of the earth? 4
Declare, if thou hast understanding.

foundations of the earth; whether he hunts her prey for the lioness; or combined such contradictory qualities in the ostrich; or created that wonder of beauty and fierceness, the war-horse—these questions but serve to bring out by contrast with God the feebleness and meanness of man.

1. *out of the whirlwind*] Rather, **out of the storm**. Jehovah, even when condescending to speak with men, must veil Himself in the storm cloud, in which He descends and approaches the earth. Even when He is nearest us, clouds and darkness are round about Him. His revelation of Himself to Job, at least, was partly to rebuke him, for he had sinned against His majesty, and He veils Himself in terrors. *The* storm is not necessarily that which Elihu describes; the Art. is rather generic, the meaning being that *thus* Jehovah spoke, namely, *out of storm*.

2. *who is this that darkeneth counsel*] lit. *who then is darkening counsel?* The word *then* merely adds the emphasis of impatience or astonishment to the question, *who...?* The expression *counsel* suggests that the Lord had a plan or meaning in Job's afflictions, which the perverse and ignorant construction put on them by Job obscured. The word might have a wider sense and refer to sound wisdom in general in reference to man's life, which Job, by his particular utterances on God's providence, only darkened. The participle *darkening* is thought by many to imply that the Divine Speaker broke in upon Job when in the act of darkening, that is, when speaking. If so, the speeches of Elihu are an interpolation. It is rather to strain the argument from the use of the participle to say that this *must* be the meaning.

3. *for I will demand*] Rather, **and** I will. Jehovah now invites Job to prepare for that contention with Him which he had so often desired, ix. 35, xiii. 20 *seq.*; and as Job had said, "Then call thou and I will answer, or let me speak and answer thou me" (ch. xiii. 22), Jehovah, as becomes Him, chooses the former half of the alternative, it may be that when He has "called" Job will be less ready than he thought to "answer" (ch. xl. 3—5).

4—38. A SURVEY OF THE INANIMATE CREATION, THE WONDERS OF EARTH AND SKY—THE EARTH, *vv.* 4—18; THE HEAVENS, *vv.* 18 —38.

4—11. Earth and sea.

4. Was Job present, possibly taking part in the operation, when Jehovah laid the foundations of the earth? Let him then "declare"

5 Who hath laid the measures thereof, if thou knowest?
   Or who hath stretched the line upon it?
6 Whereupon are the foundations thereof fastened?
   Or who laid the corner stone thereof;
7 When the morning stars sang together,
   And all the sons of God shouted for joy?
8 Or *who* shut up the sea with doors,
   When it brake forth, *as if* it had issued out of the womb?
9 When I made the cloud the garment thereof,
   And thick darkness a swaddling band for it,
10 And brake up for it my decreed *place*,
   And set bars and doors,

how all was done. The word *declare* of course refers to the queries in *vv.* 5—7.

5. *if thou knowest*] Rather, **that thou shouldest know.** Job knew well who laid (rather, **fixed**) the measures of the earth, but the point of the question is, Was he present to see who fixed them and how they were fixed, so as to be able to speak with knowledge?

6. *are the foundations fastened*] Or, **were the foundations sunk?** All the *tenses* here should be put in the simple past.

The creation of the earth is likened to the rearing of a great edifice, whose extent was determined by line, whose pillars were sunk in their bases, and its corner-stone laid with shoutings and songs of rejoicing among the heavenly hosts (comp. Ezra iii. 10 *seq.*, Zech. iv. 7).

> Such music, as 'tis said,
> Before was never made,
>   But when of old the sons of morning sung,
> While the Creator great
> His constellations set,
>   And the well-balanced world on hinges hung;
> And cast the dark foundations deep,
> And bid the weltering waves their oozy channel keep.
>   *Hymn on the Nativity.*

The stars and the angels are here as usual conjoined, and the morning stars are named as the brightest and most glorious, as also because the earth rose into existence at the morning dawn.

8—10. The sea.

8. *as if it had issued*] Rather, **and issued** out of the womb.

9. *thick darkness*] Or, **and the thick cloud.**

10. *brake up for it my decreed place*] Rather, **and brake for it my bound,** i.e. set it my appointed boundary. The expression "brake" may refer to the deep and abrupt precipices which mark the coast line in many places.

The figures in these verses are very splendid. First, the ocean is represented as an infant giant, breaking forth from the womb. (It is

And said, Hitherto shalt thou come, but no further: 11
And here shall thy proud waves be stayed?
Hast thou commanded the morning since thy days; 12
And caused the dayspring to know his place;
That *it* might take hold of the ends of the earth, 13
That the wicked might be shaken out of it?
It is turned as clay *to* the seal; 14
And they stand as a garment.
And from the wicked their light is withholden, 15
And the high arm shall be broken.
Hast thou entered into the springs of the sea? 16

not necessary perhaps to ask whether the interior of the earth be thought of as the " womb " of the ocean, or whether " womb " merely belongs to the figure of the ocean's birth.) Then the infant ocean was swathed in clouds and thick clouds were its swaddling bands. Finally the new-born monster must be tamed by almighty power, and an impassable bound set to its proud fury.

12—15. The dawn that daily overspreads the earth.

12. *since thy days*] i.e. since thou wast born, all thy life. The question, naturally, implies the other query, whether Job be coeval with the dawn?

the dayspring] i.e. the dawn.

13. *ends of the earth*] lit. *skirts* or *wings* of the earth. The figure is beautiful; the dawn as it pours forth along the whole horizon, on both sides of the beholder, lays hold of the borders of the earth, over which night lay like a covering; and seizing this covering by its extremities it shakes the wicked out of it. The wicked flee from the light. The dawn is not a physical phenomenon merely, it is a moral agent.

14. Another charming figure. Under the light of morn the earth, which was formless in the darkness, takes shape like the clay under the seal.

It is changed as clay under the seal,
And they stand forth as a garment.

In the first clause the words are lit. *as seal-clay*. All things with clear-cut impression and vivid colouring stand forth under the light, and together form a various, many-coloured garment, in which the earth is robed.

15. *shall be broken*] Rather, **is broken**. The "light" of the wicked is the darkness, ch. xxiv. **17.** The "high arm" is the arm already uplifted to commit violence. Again the moral meaning of the dayspring is expressed.

16—17. The deep and the underworld.

16. *hast thou entered*] Perhaps, **didst thou enter?** The whole passage seems under the influence of the first question, *v.* 4, Where wast thou when I laid the foundations of the earth? Did Job then explore

Or hast thou walked in the search of the depth?
17 Have the gates of death been opened unto thee?
Or hast thou seen the doors of the shadow of death?
18 Hast thou perceived the breadth of the earth?
Declare if thou knowest it all.
19 Where *is* the way *where* light dwelleth?
And *as for* darkness, where *is* the place thereof,
20 That thou shouldest take it to the bound thereof,
And that thou shouldest know the paths to the house thereof?
21 Knowest thou *it*, because thou wast then born?
Or *because* the number of thy days *is* great?

the abysses of the deep, and enter the gates of the underworld? Did he then survey all parts of the new-born world?

walked in the search] Rather, **in the recesses.**

17. *have the gates of death*] Or, **were** the gates? Death is personified; it is Sheol, the place of the dead, ch. xxviii. 22. This is a lower deep than the recesses of the sea; Job, no doubt, went down there also.

hast thou seen] Or, **didst thou see?**

18. Final query, Whether Job surveyed the whole earth, and comprehended its breadth.

hast thou perceived] Rather perhaps, **didst thou comprehend?**

19—38. The wonders of the heavens.

19—21. Light and darkness.

19. The first clause reads,

What is the way to where light dwelleth?

Light and darkness are here regarded as things independent of one another; they are both real agents, each of which has its place or abode, from which it streams forth over the earth, and to which it is again taken back (*v.* 20).

20. *take it to the bound thereof*] The second clause, the path *to* its house, suggests that the *bound* or border of light is not the furthest limit *to* which it flows forth, but its own place of abode, the bound between it and darkness, *from* which it issues. Job is asked if he knows the way to the dwelling-place of light and darkness, so that he might take them back to the place of their abode.

21. The verse is ironical,

Thou knowest; for thou wast then born,
And the number of thy days is great.

The words "thou knowest" refer to the question, *v.* 19, Which is the way...? Job knows the way to the place of light, for he was born contemporary with it; he is as old as the dayspring which morning by morning has overspread the earth since creation's dawn.

Hast thou entered into the treasures of the snow? 22
Or hast thou seen the treasures of the hail,
Which I have reserved against the time of trouble, 23
Against the day of battle and war?
By what way is the light parted, 24
Which scattereth the east wind upon the earth?
Who hath divided a watercourse for the overflowing of 25
waters,

"Light is considered here, as in Gen. i., to be a natural force, with an independent existence, apart from the heavenly luminaries that transmit it. And in this, as is well known, modern investigation coincides with the direct perceptions of antiquity" (Schlottmann, *Comm. on Job*, p. 468). To this remark it has to be added that in the present passage "darkness" also, no less than light, is regarded as a natural force, with an independent existence, and a "place" where it abides, contiguous to light. Science, to which Scripture is taught to look so humbly for approval, will no doubt confirm this representation also.
22, 23. Snow and hail.
22. *the treasures*] That is, the treasuries, the magazines. Snow and hail are represented as having been created and laid up in great storehouses in the heavens or above them, from whence God draws them forth for the moral ends of His government (*v.* 23). The idea may be suggested by observation of the vast masses in which snow falls. Job, no doubt, has inspected these treasuries, or was present when at creation the Almighty filled them.
23. Compare such passages as Josh. x. 11; Ps. lxviii. 14; Is. xxx. 30; Ezek. xiii. 13.
24—27. The stormy wind, rain and lightning.
24. The verse seems to mean:
 Which is the way to where the light is parted,
 And the east wind spreadeth over the earth?
The phrase in clause first is the same as in *v.* 19. The words may mean *by which way*, or road, *is light parted?* The "light" was already referred to in *v.* 19, and some consider the word to mean *lightning* here. This, however, comes from above and is spoken of in *v.* 25. More probably the reference is to the wonderful diffusion of light over the whole earth, and the query concerns the way or path by which this takes place. Such a path appears to lie in the East, from whence also the stormy wind spreads over the earth; hence the two are brought into connexion. Job, of course, knows the way along which this diffusion of light and wind takes place.
25. *for the overflowing of waters*] Rather, **for the rain-flood**. The second clause indicates that by the "watercourse" is meant the conduit (Is. vii. 3) or channel cut through the arch of the heavens, down which the rain-flood pours to the earth. In like manner the lightning follows a track or path prepared for it through the heavens.

Or a way for the lightning of thunder;
26 To cause it to rain on the earth, *where* no man *is;*
On the wilderness, wherein *there is* no man;
27 To satisfy the desolate and waste *ground;*
And to cause the bud of the tender herb to spring forth?
28 Hath the rain a father?
Or who hath begotten the drops of dew?
29 Out of whose womb came the ice?
And the hoary frost of heaven, who hath gendered it?
30 The waters are hid as *with* a stone,
And the face of the deep is frozen.
31 Canst thou bind the sweet influences of Pleiades,
Or loose the bands of Orion?

26, 27. Man is not, as he might think, the only object of God's regard. God is great and His providence very wide. His goodness is over all His works. He satisfies with rain the thirsty wilderness where no man is, that the tender grass may be refreshed.

28—30. Rain, dew, frost and ice.

28. *the rain a father*] That is, a human father; does any man, Job perhaps, beget the rain or the drops of dew?—They are marvels of God's creative power.

29. *who hath gendered it*] Rather, **brought it forth,** or borne it (Is. xlix. 21), as the parallelism of the first clause requires.

30. *as with a stone*] lit. *the waters hide themselves like a stone*, that is, becoming like stone.

is frozen] lit. *cleaveth together*. The phenomenon of ice, rare in the East, naturally appeared wonderful.

31—38. The direction of the regular movements of the heavens, and their influence upon the earth.

31. *canst thou bind*] Rather, **dost** thou bind? The questions addressed to Job, throughout the chapter, mean in general, Is it he that effects what is observed to be done? not, Can he undo what is done, or do what is not done? Hence the questions here imply that the Pleiades *are* bound and that Orion is loosed, and Job is asked whether it be *he* that binds in the one case and looses in the other.

the sweet influences] The idea suggested by "influences" is that man's life on the earth is ruled by the stars, as Shakespeare calls the moon

the moist star,
Upon whose influence Neptune's empire hangs.

There is, however, no trace of this idea in the original word. Those who retain this translation suppose the reference to be to the genial influence of spring, of which this cluster of stars, when appearing before the sun in the east, was a joyful herald. Such a reference is too remote; neither does it allow any just meaning to "bind." Besides, the

Canst thou bring forth Mazzaroth in his season? 32
Or canst thou guide Arcturus with his sons?
Knowest thou the ordinances of heaven? 33
Canst thou set the dominion thereof in the earth?

exegetical tradition is that the word rendered "sweet influences" has the same sense as "bands" in the second clause (so Sept. δεσμόν), as the parallelism requires. The verse rather means,

> Dost thou bind the bands of the Pleiades,
> Or loose the cords of Orion?

It is not certain that these are the stars meant, and the allusions are obscure. As "loosing the cords" or bands of Orion cannot mean dissolving the constellation and separating its stars from one another, so, if the parallelism is exact, "binding the bands" of the Pleiades ought not to refer to the fact that the stars of this constellation always appear as a group in the same form, although this is the idea which most writers consider to be expressed. The word in the second clause, being from a root always meaning *to draw* (ch. xli. 1, Is. v. 18, Hos. xi. 4), ought to have some such sense as *cords*,—that by which anything is drawn, rather than that by which it is bound. The reference is probably to the motion of the constellation in the heavens. An Arabic poet, bewailing the slowness of the hours of a night of sorrow, says that, in their immobility and tardiness to turn towards their setting-place, "its stars seem bound by cords to a rock." The same poet, however, compares the Pleiades, including perhaps Orion under the name, when it appears upon the horizon, to a girdle studded with jewels; and some have supposed that the sense in the present passage is similar, rendering, *Dost thou bind into a band* (or fillet) *the Pleiades?* This is an improbable conceit. So far as the mere language is concerned, the first clause most naturally refers to some star or constellation which appears bound to one place, whether it be that it stands always high in the heavens or is unable to rise much above the horizon; and the second clause to some star or group whose motion in the heavens is free, whether it be that it is able to rise high or that it sets and disappears.

32. *canst thou bring forth*] Rather, **dost thou...?** and similarly, **dost thou guide?** The meaning of *Mazzaroth* is uncertain. The word has been supposed to be another form of *Mazzaloth*, 2 Kings xxiii. 5, which is thought to mean the signs of the Zodiac. The connexion as well as the parallelism of the next clause suggests that some single star or constellation is meant. Others would render *the bright stars;* the planets, perhaps, or some of them being referred to.

Arcturus with his sons] Or, *the bear with her young.* The reference is supposed to be to the constellation of the Great Bear. Her "young" are the stars that project from the square; or, taking the popular conception of the constellation as a "plough," they are the bright stars that form the "beam."

33. *canst thou set*] Rather, as before, **dost thou set?** The idea is

34 Canst thou lift up thy voice to the clouds,
    That abundance of waters may cover thee?
35 Canst thou send lightnings, that they may go,
    And say unto thee, Here we *are*?
36 Who hath put wisdom in the inward parts?
    Or who hath given understanding to the heart?
37 Who can number the clouds in wisdom?
    Or who can stay the bottles of heaven,
38 When the dust groweth into hardness,
    And the clods cleave fast together?

that the heavens and the stars exercise an influence over the earth and the destinies of man.

34, 35. For *canst thou* it is better, as before, to read, **dost thou**?

36. The verse is obscure, owing to the terms "inward parts" and "heart" being of uncertain meaning. The translation of the A.V. may be certainly set aside, (1) because the introduction of a reference to the "inward parts" and "heart" of man in the middle of a description of celestial phenomena is not to be thought of; and (2) any laudatory reference to man is out of keeping with the whole drift of the speech, the purpose of which is to abase man before the wonders of God's creation and His operations outside the sphere of man's life. The word rendered "inward parts" may be the same as that so rendered, Ps. li. 6. There the parallel word is "hidden part," and the reference may be to the dark and deep *cloud-masses*. The word "heart" does not occur again; it may mean, *form, figure*, and refer to the manifold cloud formations or phenomena. These fulfilling the purposes of God seem themselves endowed with wisdom. If this be the sense, the best commentary on the verse would be the words of Elihu, ch. xxxvii. 12, "And it (the cloud) turneth about every way by His guidance, that it may do whatsoever He commandeth it upon the face of the whole earth."

37. The verse carries on the thought of the preceding.

who can number] Or, **who numbereth in wisdom?** Who musters or counts off the clouds, that they be sufficient and not in excess for the purpose required of them?

The second clause means,

Or who poureth out the bottles of the heavens?

CH. XXXVIII. 39—CH. XXXIX. 30. THE MANIFOLDNESS OF THE DIVINE MIND AS DISPLAYED IN THE WORLD OF ANIMAL LIFE.

The instances chosen are the lion and the raven (*vv*. 39—41); the wild goats and the hinds (ch. xxxix. 1—4); the wild ass (*vv*. 5—8; the wild ox (*vv*. 9—12); the ostrich (*vv*. 13—18); the war horse (*vv*. 19—25); the hawk and the eagle (*vv*. 26—30).

These brilliant pictures from the animal world have the same purpose as those given before (*vv*. 4—38) from inanimate nature; they make

Wilt thou hunt the prey for the lion?	39
Or fill the appetite of the young lions,	
When they couch in *their* dens,	40
And abide in the covert to lie in wait?	
Who provideth for the raven his food?	41
When his young ones cry unto God,	
They wander for lack of meat.	

God to pass before the eye of Job. They exhibit the diversity of the animal creation, the strange dissimilarity of instinct and habit in creatures outwardly similar, the singular blending together of contradictory characteristics in the same creature, and the astonishing attributes and powers with which some of them are endowed; and all combines to illustrate the resources of mind and breadth of thought of Him who formed them and cares for them, the manifold play of an immeasurable intelligence and power in the world.

Yet though each of these pictures utters the name of *God* with an increasing emphasis, and though the Poet presents them in the first instance that we may hear this name from them, it is evident that his own eye follows each of the creatures which he describes with a delighted wonder and love. The Poet felt like a later poet,

He prayeth best who loveth best all things both great and small,
For the dear God who loveth us, He made and loveth all.

The words of Carlyle might be quoted, who says of the Book of Job and of these descriptions in particular, "so *true* every way; true eyesight and vision for all things; material things no less than spiritual" (*Heroes*, Lect. ii), were it not that this writer's raptures are so often founded on intellectual mistake and imperfect appreciation of facts, and are therefore, like all such ideal raptures, only nauseous.

39, 40. The lion.

wilt thou hunt] Rather, **dost thou hunt the prey for the lioness?** That the lioness is enabled to catch her prey is due to some power which brings it into her hand. Is it Job, perhaps, that finds it for her?

41. The raven. The question extends to the end of the verse,

Who provideth for the raven his food,
When his young ones cry unto God,
And wander without meat?

The raven is one of the commonest birds in Palestine; by its incessant croaking it presses itself upon the attention, and is often alluded to in Scripture. The cry of its young is an appeal unto God (Joel i. 20), and the feeding of it is proof of His universal providence, which does not overlook even the least of His creatures (Ps. cxlvii. 9, Luke xii. 24). The lion and the raven are here associated perhaps by way of contrast, the one being the most powerful and the other one of the least of God's creatures. Their natures too are most dissimilar,—the silent, subtle, self-reliance of the one, couching patiently in his lair, and the clamorous

39

1 Knowest thou the time when the wild goats of the rock bring forth?
 Or canst thou mark when the hinds do calve?
2 Canst thou number the months *that* they fulfil?
 Or knowest thou the time when they bring forth?
3 They bow themselves, they bring forth their young ones,
 They cast out their sorrows.
4 Their young ones are in good liking, they grow up with corn;
 They go forth, and return not unto them.
5 Who hath sent out the wild ass free?
 Or who hath loosed the bands of the wild ass?
6 Whose house I have made the wilderness,
 And the barren *land* his dwellings.

outcry and appeal of the other, wandering over the land in search of food. The raven, of course, is a general name, covering the whole Crow tribe.

Ch. xxxix. 1—4. The goats of the rock and the hinds.

1. *canst thou mark*] Rather, **dost** thou. The goats of the rock are the mountain goats, a species of chamois.

2. *canst thou number*] Rather, **dost** thou. The "months that they fulfil" is the time they go with young. The words "knowest thou", "dost thou mark", and the like, though no doubt referring partly to man's ignorance of the habits of these remote and timid creatures, carry also the question, Is it Job who presides over and determines all connected with the life and habits of these solitary creatures?

3. *cast out their sorrows*] That is, their *pains;* with the birth of their young they are rid of their pains also. Or "their pains" may mean "their young," by a figure common in all poetry.

4. *in good liking*] i.e. in good condition, strong.

grow up with corn] Rather, **they grow up in the open field.**

These shy, solitary creatures, inhabiting the rocks, are without the care and help in bearing their young which domesticated creatures enjoy; yet their bearing is light and speedy; their young are robust; they grow up in the desert and rapidly provide for themselves. The care of God suffices for them.

5—8. The wild ass. Who gave the wild ass his freedom and his indomitable love of liberty—who scorns the noise of cities and laughs at the shouts of the driver, which his tame brother obeys? The point of the questions lies not only in the striking peculiarities of the beautiful creature itself, but in the strange contrast between it and the tame ass, which in external appearance it resembles.

7. The verse reads,

> He scorneth the tumult of the city,
> And heareth not the shoutings of the driver.

He scorneth the multitude of the city, 7
Neither regardeth he the crying of the driver.
The range of the mountains *is* his pasture, 8
And he searcheth after every green thing.
Will the unicorn be willing to serve thee, 9
Or abide by thy crib?

The wild ass is frequently referred to in the poetry of the Arabs, who were passionately fond of hunting it. Prof. Ahlwardt has collected from his unequalled reading in the Poets a list of statements regarding the creature which is of great interest (*Chalef Elahmar*, pp. 341—360). The colour on the upper part of the body, the neck and higher part of the head is light bay, with a coffee-brown band running down the back to the tuft of the tail; between this band and the bay there is some white. The other parts are of a silver grey, tending to white on the under-side of the body. The animal is described as "thick," "thick-fleshed," but also "narrow-built," that is, behind and in front, and hence it is compared to the point of an arrow. The tail is long. Its pace is exceedingly quick, only the fleetest horses being able to overtake it; and when running it holds its head to the side in frolicsomeness and performs all manner of pranks and capers. A troop of wild asses is usually small, consisting of a male, one or two females, and the young. This is confirmed by Tristram, who says, "I have seen this ass wild in the desert of North Africa, in troops of four or five" (*Nat. Hist. of the Bible*, p. 43). Wetzstein on the contrary speaks of the herd as consisting of "several hundred" (*Del.* ii. p. 331). The abode of the wild ass is in deserts, untrodden by man (comp. *v.* 6), hence he is called "the solitary" (comp. Hosea viii. 9, "A wild ass alone by himself"). In spring he frequents the plains in which there are pools, and later the heights where grass is abundant (comp. *v.* 8). On these heights he passes the summer with the females; and there he stands and keeps watch, spying the approach of foes (comp. Jer. xiv. 6, "The wild asses did stand in the high places &c."). The poets compare a deep ravine or abyss to the "belly" of the wild ass, which is often lank and empty from want of food (Jerem. xiv. 6). He is said to live to a great age, over a hundred years. The flesh is delicious, and for this reason, as well as for the excitement of the chase, the creature was eagerly hunted by the Arabs. His vigour and hardiness are testified to in the proverb, "sounder than a wild ass."

9—12. The wild ox.

9. *will the unicorn*] Rather, **the wild ox** (Heb. *re'ēm*, or, *rêm*). From the allusions to this creature in Scripture two things may be inferred with some certainty, (1) that the animal had *two* horns: Deut. xxxiii. 17 "his horns are like the horns of an unicorn"; comp. Numb. xxiii. 22, xxiv. 8 (where for "strength" some such words as "towering horns" should be read, see on ch. xxii. 25), Ps. xxii. 21; and (2) that the animal was considered to belong to the ox tribe. This appears from the present passage, where it is contrasted with the

10 Canst thou bind the unicorn *with* his band in the furrow?
  Or will he harrow the valleys after thee?
11 Wilt thou trust him, because his strength *is* great?
  Or wilt thou leave thy labour to him?
12 Wilt thou believe him, that he will bring home thy seed,
  And gather *it into* thy barn?
13 *Gavest thou* the goodly wings unto the peacocks?
  Or wings and feathers *unto* the ostrich?

domestic ox, the labours of which it was fitted to perform if its disposition had not been untameable; and from two other passages, in both of which it is brought into connexion with the ox: Ps. xxix. 6, "He maketh them to skip like a *calf*, Lebanon and Sirion like a young unicorn", and Is. xxxiv. 7, "And the unicorns shall come down with them, and the bullocks with the bulls." The *reêm* was probably either the animal called by the Germans *Auerochs* (*Bos primigenius*) or "primitive ox," now extinct all over the world, or the bison, which still lingers in scanty numbers in one or two parts. The Arabs give the name *rī'm* to the white antelope. The translation "unicorn" came from the Sept. μονοκέρως. A one-horned animal, though abundantly testified to by travellers, probably exists only in the imagination. Jerome adheres to the general "unicorns" in Ps. xxii. 21 and Is. xxxiv. 7, but usually he renders "rhinoceros," the nearest approach to a "unicorn" that exists in the world of reality. "The Unicorne, as Lewes Vartinian testifieth, who saw two of them in the towne of Mecha, is of the height of a yoong horse or colt of 30 moneths old, hee hath the head of a Hart, and in his forehead he hath a sharpe pointed horne three cubites long...His horne is of a merueilous greate force and vertue against venome and poyson" (see Wright, *Bible Word-Book*).

The point of the passage lies not so much in the terrible attributes of the creature himself, as in the contrast between him and the tame ox, which he externally resembled. He was fitted for all the labour performed by the domestic animal, but was wild and untameable. Man uses the one, let him lay his hand upon the other and subdue him to his service! Who is the author of this strange diversity of disposition in creatures so like in outward form?

13—18. The ostrich.
13. The verse reads,
  The wing of the ostrich beats joyously,
  Is it a kindly pinion and feather?

The word rendered *ostrich* means lit. *crying* or *wailing*, that is, the cryer or wailer; the female ostrich is probably meant, see on ch. xxx. 29. The word "kindly," lit. *pious*, is the name given to the stork (Ps. civ. 17), whose affection for its young is proverbial, and there may be in the term an allusion to this bird, which the ostrich in some points resembles externally, but from which it differs so strangely in disposition.

Which leaveth her eggs in the earth, 14
And warmeth them in dust,
And forgetteth that the foot may crush them, 15
Or *that* the wild beast may break them.
She is hardened against her young ones, as though *they* 16
were not hers:
Her labour *is* in vain without fear;
Because God hath deprived her of wisdom, 17
Neither hath he imparted to her understanding.
What time she lifteth up herself on high, 18
She scorneth the horse and his rider.

15. *may break them*] lit. *trample them*.
16. *she is hardened against*] Or, **she treateth hardly**.
her young ones] The words refer here to her eggs, from which the young come forth, not to the young brood—as the second clause explains.
in vain without fear] The meaning is that she is without fear, has no apprehension of danger, and consequently her labour is often in vain—"she forgetteth that the foot may crush" her eggs.
The verses refer to the popular belief that the ostrich did not brood but left her eggs to be hatched in the sun; hence she is a type of unnatural cruelty, Lam. iv. 3, "Even the sea monsters (the *jackals*, Streane, *Jerem. and Lam.*) draw out the breast, they give suck to their young ones: the daughter of my people is become cruel, like the ostriches in the wilderness." The belief is not sustained by observation, except to this extent, that the bird does not brood till her complement of eggs (thirty in number) be laid, and that during the early period of incubation she often leaves the nest by day to go in search of food. It is also said that she lays a number of eggs outside the nest, which are not incubated but serve as food for the poults when they are hatched.
17. *God hath deprived her of wisdom*] The Arabs have a proverb, "more stupid than an ostrich." A poet suggests the reason of this charge of stupidity,

Like a bird that abandons her eggs in the desert,
And covers the eggs of another with her wings.

(Meidani, *Prov.* i. 405).
18. *lifteth up herself on high*] That is, in flight. The flying of the ostrich is properly a very swift running, in which she is helped by her outspread wings and tail. "Its speed has been calculated at twenty-six miles an hour by Dr Livingstone, and yet the South African ostrich is smaller than the northern species; and I have myself, in the Sahara, measured its stride, when bounding at full speed, from twenty-two to twenty-eight feet" (Tristram, p. 237).
The cruel disposition of the ostrich and her foolishness have been

19 Hast thou given the horse strength?
    Hast thou clothed his neck with thunder?
20 Canst thou make him afraid as a grasshopper?
    The glory of his nostrils *is* terrible.
21 He paweth in the valley, and rejoiceth in *his* strength.
    He goeth on to meet the armed men.
22 He mocketh at fear, and is not affrighted;
    Neither turneth he back from the sword.
23 The quiver rattleth against him,
    The glittering spear and the shield.
24 He swalloweth the ground with fierceness and rage:

implanted in her by God, yet in strange contradiction to these qualities are others which He has bestowed on her, such as her swiftness when pursued, which enables her to laugh at the horse and his rider. This singular union of dissimilar qualities, as if it were the work of creative power at play, shews both the inconceivable freedom and resource of the Mind that operates in creation.

19—25. The war horse.
19, 20. The verbs are better put in the present.

>   19. Dost thou give strength to the horse?
>   Dost thou clothe his neck with trembling?
>   20. Dost thou make him leap like the locust?
>   The glory of his snorting is terrible.

19. The word "trembling" hardly refers to the mane alone, but rather describes the quivering of the neck, when the animal is roused, which erects the mane.

20. The comparison of the horse to the locust is not uncommon, Joel ii. 4, Rev. ix. 7. The picture of the horse is taken at the moment immediately preceding the onset, and thus his "bounding" and "snorting" are brought into connexion.

21. *the armed men*] lit. *the weapons*.
22. *from the sword*] lit. *because of*, or, *before* the sword.
23. *rattleth against him*] Rather perhaps, **upon** him. The quiver is that of his rider, the clang of which excites him.

the shield] Rather, **the javelin**, or, **lance**. The Poet does not seek to describe the actual conflict; it is a picture of the horse that he gives, and the moment before the conflict is that at which the animal's extraordinary attributes are most strongly exhibited. "Although docile as a lamb, and requiring no other guide than the halter, when the Arab mare hears the war-cry of the tribe (cf. *v.* 25), and sees the quivering spear of her rider (cf. *v.* 23), her eyes glitter with fire, her blood-red nostrils open wide, her neck is nobly arched, and her tail and mane are raised and spread out to the wind (cf. *v.* 19). A Bedouin proverb says, that a high-bred mare when at full speed should hide her rider between her neck and her tail" (Layard, *Discoveries*, p. 330).

Neither believeth he that *it is* the sound of the trumpet.
He saith among the trumpets, Ha, ha; 25
And he smelleth the battle afar off,
The thunder of the captains, and the shouting.
Doth the hawk fly by thy wisdom, 26
And stretch her wings toward the south?
Doth the eagle mount up at thy command, 27
And make her nest on high?
She dwelleth and abideth on the rock, 28
Upon the crag of the rock, and the strong place.
From thence she seeketh the prey, 29
And her eyes behold afar off.
Her young ones also suck up blood: 30
And where the slain *are*, there *is* she.

24. *neither believeth he*] That is, most probably, he hardly trusts his ears for gladness.

25. *he saith among the trumpets*] Rather, **as oft as the trumpet soundeth he saith, Ha, ha!** The "thunder" of the captains is the roar of command; and the "shouting" is the battle-cry of the soldiery.

Has Job created this wonder of beauty and fierceness and endowed him with his extraordinary qualities, which make him mingle in the conflicts of men with a fury and lust of battle greater even than their own?

26. The hawk.

her wings toward the south] The allusion is to the migration of the bird southward when the cold season of the year begins. Is it Job's wisdom that directs her flight to the south?

27—30. The eagle.

Is it at Job's command that the eagle fixes her habitation fearlessly on the dizzy crag? Did he bestow on her her penetrating vision, which scans the wide expanse of country and pierces into the deep ravine? or did he endow her with her terrible instincts, that shew themselves at once in her young, which "suck up blood"?

CHAP. XL. 1—5. EFFECT OF THE DIVINE SPEECH ON JOB.

As if the purpose of the preceding survey of Creation might be lost in the brilliancy of the individual parts of it, the Divine Speaker gathers up its general effect and brings it to bear on Job directly, demanding whether he will persevere in his contention with Jehovah;—will the reprover contend with the Almighty? *vv.* 1, 2.

Job is abased by the glory of God which He has made to pass before him, and brought to silence—I am too mean, what shall I answer thee? I lay my hand upon my mouth; *vv.* 3—5.

40 Moreover the LORD answered Job, and said,
2 Shall he that contendeth with the Almighty instruct *him*?
He that reproveth God, let him answer it.
3 Then Job answered the LORD, and said,
4 Behold, I am vile; what shall I answer thee?
I will lay my hand upon my mouth.
5 Once have I spoken; but I will not answer:
Yea, twice; but I will proceed no further.

1. *answered Job*] That is, took up anew His words and directly appealed to Job.

2. The verse means,
Will the reprover contend with the Almighty?
He that disputeth with God let him answer it.

The "reprover" or blamer is of course Job; and so is "he that disputeth," or, "he that would dispute." The word *it* refers to the foregoing display of God's glory in creation, which Jehovah has set before Job. And the question means, Will Job now, having God in the manifoldness of His Being thus set before him, really enter on a contention with the Almighty?

3—5. Job's answer: he will no more contend; he is silent before God.

4. *behold, I am vile*] The word *vile* here is not a moral term, it signifies, *mean*, small. The verse may be read,

Behold I am too mean; what shall I answer thee?
I lay mine hand upon my mouth.

Job is abased before Jehovah; he feels his meanness and is silent, comp. ch. xxi. 5, xxix. 9.

5. *I will proceed no further*] Or, but I will not again. The words "once", "twice", that is, sundry times, refer to what Job had often said in his speeches concerning the Almighty.

The purpose of making these wonders of creation pass before Job's eyes was to display God before him, and to heal the presumption of his heart. Every one of these wonders utters the name of *God* with a louder emphasis in Job's ears. It is not any attribute of God that is dwelt upon, it is God in all the manifoldness of His being that passes before Job's mind. It is entirely to misinterpret the design of these visions of creation presented to Job when we suppose that what is aimed at is to impress on Job the incomprehensibility of the Creator's works, or the *mystery* that lies in them all; as if he was bidden consider that not in his own life alone, but everywhere, beneath his feet and around him, there lay unfathomable mysteries. The Lord does not reason with Job after the manner of the author of the *Analogy of Religion*. He does not say "you complain of darkness in your own history, look into the world and behold darkness everywhere". This would have been sorry reasoning on the part of the Father of lights. On the contrary, He bids Job look away from his own darkness to the world which is luminous with God; and the exceeding light about God there, breaking on Job, swallows up his own darkness.

It is scarcely just to say that what Jehovah demands of Job here is simple submission, that he should bow absolutely and unconditionally under God. If this had been the meaning of Jehovah's speeches out of the storm there was no reason for His speaking. Silence would have been more effective; or if He had spoken, it should have been with the voice of the thunder, terrifying Job into the dust. That the Lord speaks at all implies that He says something that may be understood by the creature of His hand. His speaking may be indirect, and in parables, but it will contain meaning. It is true that the object of the Divine speeches is, partly at least, to bring Job's heart to submission and cause him to assume his right place before the Creator. And this was necessary, for Job, as he acknowledges, had sinned against the majesty of God. But the Lord does not command Job to take this place; He induces him. And he does so by the only means that will ever induce any human spirit to put itself right with God, the revelation of Himself. This revelation given to Job was patient, broad, and manifold. It was anything but a categorical command. *We*, indeed, may feel now that the revelation might have been different, that it might have contained other traits. The traits which we desiderate could hardly, perhaps, have been exhibited on an Old Testament stage. It was not the design of the revelation, if it ever was the design of revelation, to communicate new truths to Job, but to make him feel the truth which he knew, and enable him to live aright before God.

CHAP. XL. 6—XLII. 6. THE LORD'S SECOND ANSWER TO JOB
OUT OF THE STORM.

SHALL MAN CHARGE GOD WITH UNRIGHTEOUSNESS IN HIS RULE
OF THE WORLD?

All that the first speech of the Lord touched upon was the presumption of a mortal man desiring to contend with the Almighty. The display from Creation of that which God is had the desired effect on Job's mind: he is abased, and will no more contend with the Almighty.

But Job had not only presumed to contend with God, he had charged Him with unrighteousness in His rule of the world and in His treatment of himself. This is the point to which the second speech from the storm is directed.

The passage has properly two parts.

First, *vv.* 6—14, as Job had challenged the rectitude of God's rule of the world, he is ironically invited to clothe himself with the Divine attributes and assume the rule of the world himself.

Then follows, ch. xl. 15—xli. 34, a lengthy description of two monsters, Behemoth and Leviathan.

Second, ch. xlii. 1—6, Job's reply to the Divine challenge. He confesses that he spoke things which he understood not. He had heard

6 Then answered the LORD unto Job out of the whirlwind, and said,
7 Gird up thy loins now like a man:
   I will demand of thee, and declare thou unto me.
8 Wilt thou also disannul my judgment?
   Wilt thou condemn me, that thou mayest be righteous?
9 Hast thou an arm like God?
   Or, canst thou thunder with a voice like him?
10 Deck thyself now with majesty and excellency;
   And array thyself with glory and beauty.

of God by the hearing of the ear, but now his eye saw Him, and he abhorred his former words and demeanour, and repented in dust and ashes.

6. *the whirlwind*] As before, **the storm.**

8. The verse reads,

Wilt thou even disannul my right?
Wilt thou condemn me that thou mayest be righteous?

To disannul Jehovah's "right" does not seem to mean, to depose Him from His place as Supreme, but rather to *break*, or *make void*, that is, *deny* His rectitude as Ruler of the world. The second clause suggests this meaning, and also adds the motive under which Job denied the rectitude of God, namely, that he himself might be righteous, or in the right. The word *even* suggests that this is an offence against God additional to the former one of daring to contend with Him (*v.* 2).

9—14. As Job questions the manner of the Almighty's rule of the world, God invites him to deck himself with the thunder and majesty of the supreme ruler, and himself undertake the government of the world; and in the execution of this government to bring low all that is proud (comp. Is. ii. 12 *seq.*), to subdue and keep down the forces of evil, and hide the faces of the wicked in darkness.

Under this ironical invitation to Job there lie two general thoughts, *first*, that omnipotence is necessary in the ruler of all; and *second*, that rule of the world consists in keeping in check the forces of evil. This is the idea under which rule of the world is conceived; in other words it is regarded as necessarily moral; and it is assumed that God's rule is in fact a rule of this kind. In his present frame of mind Job probably would not now contest this. But if God's rule be moral on the whole, it must be so in every particular; real exceptions are inconceivable, however like exceptions many things may appear.

10. This verse reads literally,

Deck thyself now with excellency and loftiness;
And array thyself with honour and majesty.

The two words in the second clause are so translated, Ps. xxi. 5, xcvi. 6, civ. 1.

Cast abroad the rage of thy wrath: 11
And behold every one *that is* proud, and abase him.
Look on every one *that is* proud, *and* bring him low; 12
And tread down the wicked in their place.
Hide them in the dust together; 13
And bind their faces in secret.
Then will I also confess unto thee 14
That thine own right hand can save thee.
Behold now behemoth, 15

11. *cast abroad the rage of thy wrath*] Or, **send forth the floods of thy wrath**; the figure is that of a raging, overflowing stream.

12. *in their place*] That is, where they stand; suddenly and on the spot, comp. ch. xxxiv. 26.

13. *bind their faces in secret*] lit. *bind up their faces in the hidden place*, that is, shut them up in the darkness of the prison-house of Death.

14. The verse reads,

Then will I also praise thee,
That thine own right hand can save thee.

If Job will shew himself worthy of that place to which he aspires when he reproves the rule of God in the universe, then even Jehovah Himself, who elsewhere says, "Is there a God beside me? yea there is no God; I know not any" (Is. xliv. 8), will admit his independent might, and laud him as one whose own right hand can save him, comp. Ps. xcviii. 1; Is. lix. 16, lxiii. 5.

15—ch. xli. 34. Description of two monsters, Behemoth and Leviathan.

Many writers consider the two passages, ch. xl. 15—24 and ch. xli., in which Behemoth and Leviathan are described, to be interpolations (see the Introduction). Whether the passages be interpolations or parts of the original poem, the meaning of their introduction in this place will be the same.

In ch. xl. 6—14 Jehovah invited Job to assume the rule of the world, and to bring low all opposing forces of evil. He is able to do this, seeing he challenges the rule of the Almighty. And to bring to his consciousness whether he is able or not two creatures, the work of God's hand like himself (*v.* 15), are brought before him and the question put, Is he able to enter into conflict with *them* and subdue them? Is he therefore able to assume the rule of the world or to enter into conflict with the Creator of these formidable monsters?—"Who then will stand before me?" ch. xli. 9—11.

15. *Behold now behemoth*] The word, *behemoth*, may be a Heb. *plur.* of intensity, signifying *the beast* or *ox, par excellence;* but probably it is an Egyptian name Hebraized. It has been supposed to be the Egyptian *p-ehe-mout*, i.e. *the water*, or *river ox*. At all events the animal referred to appears to be the hippopotamus, or river-horse, of the Greeks.

Which I made with thee;
He eateth grass as an ox.
16 Lo now, his strength *is* in his loins,
And his force *is* in the navel of his belly.
17 He moveth his tail like a cedar:
The sinews of his stones are wrapt together.
18 His bones *are as* strong pieces of brass;
His bones *are* like bars of iron.
19 He *is* the chief of the ways of God:
He that made him can make his sword to approach *unto him*.
20 Surely the mountains bring him forth food,
Where all the beasts of the field play.
21 He lieth under the shady trees,

I made with thee] Or, **have made with thee**; that is, have created, as well as thee. This strange animal, though fitted by his size and strength to prey upon other creatures, feeds upon grass like the cattle.
16—18. These verses read,
16. Lo now, his strength is in his loins,
And his force in the sinews of his belly.
17. He bendeth his tail like a cedar;
The muscles of his thighs are knit together.
18. His bones are pipes of brass;
His limbs are like bars of iron.

17. The "tail" of the hippopotamus is short, naked and muscular, resembling that of the hog. The great strength of the animal may be inferred from the muscular stiffness of the tail, which bends like the branch or young stem of a cedar.
18. *strong pieces of brass*] Rather literally, **are pipes of brass.**
19, 20. These verses are connected,
19. He is the chief of the ways of God;
He that made him provideth him with his sword;
20. For the mountains, &c.

By "chief," lit. *beginning*, is meant the first in magnitude and power, in whom the full, fresh creative force has embodied itself. The meaning of the second clause is less certain. The reference seems to be to the teeth or the eye-tusks of the hippopotamus, which are said to be two feet long, and with which he shears the vegetation as with a sword or sickle.
20. The verse seems to mean that in order to satisfy his hunger the animal depastures whole mountains, tracts where all the beasts of the field play. The hippopotamus is said to wander to the higher grounds, at a distance from the river, when food cannot be found in its vicinity.
21. *the shady trees*] Rather, **the lotus trees.** And so in *v.* 22.

In the covert of the reed, and fens.
The shady trees cover him *with* their shadow; 22
The willows of the brook compass him about.
Behold, he drinketh up a river, *and* hasteth not: 23
He trusteth that he can draw up Jordan into his mouth.
He taketh it with his eyes: 24
His nose pierceth through snares.
Canst thou draw out leviathan with a hook? 41
Or his tongue with a cord *which* thou lettest down?
Canst thou put a hook into his nose? 2
Or bore his jaw through with a thorn?
Will he make many supplications unto thee? 3

23. The verse means,
Behold the stream swelleth, he trembleth not;
He is careless, though Jordan break forth upon his mouth.

The word "swelleth" means lit. *oppresses*, that is, rushes violently against him. The term "Jordan," or "a Jordan," is used by way of example, meaning a violent outbreak of water. The term "break forth" is that used of the sea, ch. xxxviii. 8.

24. The meaning probably is,
Shall they take him before his eyes?
Or pierce through his nose with a snare?

"Before his eyes" or "in his sight" (Prov. i. 17), that is, openly, when the animal is aware. The words might be taken ironically: *Let them take him before his eyes!* &c. (comp. *v*. 32), but the interrogative form is more natural. Others consider the language to be a statement of fact: they take him before his eyes, &c. But with this sense the whole meaning of the introduction of the creature in this chapter disappears. Such a description might have found a place in the gallery of animal portraits in the previous chapter, but as a companion picture to that of Leviathan it is out of place.

Ch. xli. Leviathan, that is, the crocodile.
1—9. The impossibility of capturing the animal.
1. The second clause appears to mean,
Wilt thou press down his tongue with a cord?

The "cord" may be that of the hook; when the hook is swallowed and the cord drawn tightly, it presses down the tongue.
2. *a hook*] lit. **a cord of rush.**
a thorn] That is, a spike.
The reference in the first clause may be to the habit of passing a cord through the gills of fish when caught, and letting them down into the water again, to preserve them in freshness.
3. Ironical question whether Leviathan will beg to be spared or treated kindly.

Will he speak soft *words* unto thee?
4 Will he make a covenant with thee?
Wilt thou take him for a servant for ever?
5 Wilt thou play with him as *with* a bird?
Or wilt thou bind him for thy maidens.
6 Shall the companions make a banquet of him?
Shall they part him among the merchants?
7 Canst thou fill his skin with barbed irons?
Or his head with fish spears?
8 Lay thine hand upon him,
Remember the battle, do no more.
9 Behold, the hope of him is in vain:
Shall *not one* be cast down even at the sight of him?
10 None *is so* fierce that dare stir him up:
Who then is able to stand before me?
11 Who hath prevented me, that I should repay *him*?

4. Will he consent to be one of thy domesticated animals, and serve thee?

5. Wilt thou make a pet thing of him? The commentators quote Catullus, *passer, deliciæ meæ puellæ.*

6. The first clause reads,

Will the partners bargain over him?

This sense is sustained by the second clause; comp. ch. vi. 27. By "the partners" is meant the company of fishermen; comp. Luke v. 7, 10.

the merchants] lit. *the Canaanites.* The Phoenicians were the great merchants of antiquity; comp. Is. xxiii. 8; Zech. xiv. 21; Prov. xxxi. 24.

8. The verse is ironical,

Lay thine hand upon him!
Think of the battle: thou shalt do so no more.

The last words, *thou shalt do so no more* (so the Geneva), refer to the ironical advice given in the first clause, "lay thine hand upon him"! The thought of the "battle," that is, the conflict, will be sufficient to deter from any attempt to renew it.

9. *the hope of him is in vain*] Rather, **behold, one's hope is belied**; lit. *his hope.* The hope of the assailant to overcome Leviathan is disappointed.

10, 11. In these verses the speaker turns aside from describing the invincibility of Leviathan to impress the moral which he intends to teach by introducing the monster. If none dare stir up this creature, which God has made, who will stand before God who created him, or venture to contend with Him?

11. *who hath prevented me*] Rather, **who hath first given to me?**

Whatsoever is under the whole heaven *is* mine.
I will not conceal his parts,   12
Nor *his* power, nor his comely proportion.
Who can discover the face of his garment?   13
Or who can come *to him* with his double bridle?
Who can open the doors of his face?   14
His teeth *are* terrible round about.
His scales *are his* pride,   15
Shut up *together as with* a close seal.
One is so near to another,   16
That no air can come between them.
They are joined one to another,   17
They stick together, that they cannot be sundered.

So Tyndale, *Or who hathe geven me anye thinge afore hand, that I am bounde to reward him agayne?* As none dare contend with God (*v.* 10), so none have any *ground* of contention with Him. None hath given aught to God, so as to have a claim against Him, for all things under the heavens are His; comp. Ps. l. 10 *seq.*

12—34. Description of the parts of Leviathan.

13, 14. The terrible jaws of the animal.

13. The verse reads,
    Who hath uncovered the face of his garment?
    Or who will enter into his double jaw?

The "face of his garment" seems to mean the upper side or surface of his coat of scales, his armour; and the question is, Who has turned back, or removed this scaly covering? The question seems a general, preliminary one, as the scales are more particularly described in *v.* 15 *seq.* His "double jaw" is lit. *his double bridle,* the term "bridle" referring particularly perhaps to the corners of his jaws.

14. *who can open*] Or, **who hath opened.** The "doors of his face" is an expression for his "mouth" which has something artificial and forced in it.

his teeth are terrible] The jaws of the crocodile are very extended; the two rows of long, pointed teeth, thirty-six, it is said, above, and thirty beneath, being bare, as the mouth has no lips, present a formidable appearance.

15—17. His armour of scales.

15. *his scales are his pride*] Rather, **the rows of his shields are a pride.** Each of his scales is a shield, and they are disposed in rows, or courses, lit. *pipes* (ch. xl. 18), so called from their being curved or bossed. Of these rows there are said to be seventeen. The second clause describes the firmness and closeness with which each scale adheres to the body.

16, 17. These verses refer to the close coherence of the scales to one another.

18 *By* his neesings a light doth shine,
And his eyes *are* like the eyelids of the morning.
19 Out of his mouth go burning lamps,
And sparks of fire leap out.
20 Out of his nostrils goeth smoke,
As *out of* a seething pot or caldron.
21 His breath kindleth coals,
And a flame goeth out of his mouth.
22 In his neck remaineth strength,
And sorrow is turned into joy before him.
23 The flakes of his flesh are joined together:
They are firm in themselves; they cannot be moved.

18—21. The monster breathes smoke and flame.

18. The animal is said to inflate itself, as it lies basking in the sun, and then force the heated breath through its nostrils, which in the sun appears like a stream of light.

the eyelids of the morning] The reference may be to the shining of the reddish eyes of the animal, which are seen even under the water, before its head comes to the surface. In the Egyptian hieroglyphs the eyes of the crocodile are a symbol of the dawn.

19—21. These verses refer probably to the animal's emergence from the water, when the long-repressed hot breath is blown out along with water from his mouth, and shines in the sun like a fiery stream.

19. *burning lamps*] Or, burning **torches**.

20. *as out of a seething pot or caldron*] Rather perhaps, **like a seething pot with rushes**, i.e. with a fire of rushes.

22—24. His strength and hardness of muscle.

22. The verse means,

In his neck dwelleth strength,
And terror leapeth up before him.

His neck is the dwelling-place, the home of strength; and wherever he appears terror leaps up. The prosaic meaning in the last words is that in the presence of Leviathan every thing starts up affrighted and seeks escape.

23. The verse reads,

The flakes of his flesh cleave fast together;
It is firm upon him, it is not moved.

The "flakes" of his flesh are the parts beneath the neck and belly, which in most animals are soft and pendulous; in him they are firm and hard. In the second clause *it* refers to his flesh, which is "firm," lit. *cast* or *molten*, and does not move, or shake, with the motions of his body.

24. The second clause reads,

Yea, firm as the nether millstone.

His heart is as firm as a stone; 24
Yea, as hard as a piece of the nether *millstone*.
When he raiseth up *himself*, the mighty are afraid: 25
By reason of breakings they purify themselves.
The sword of him that layeth at him cannot hold: 26
The spear, the dart, nor the habergeon.
He esteemeth iron as straw, 27
And brass as rotten wood.
The arrow cannot make him flee: 28
Slingstones are turned with him into stubble.
Darts are counted as stubble: 29
He laugheth at the shaking of a spear.
Sharp stones *are* under him: 30
He spreadeth sharp pointed *things* upon the mire.
He maketh the deep to boil like a pot: 31

Gen. "as hard as the nether millstone." The term "firm," lit. *cast*, is repeated from the first clause (cf. *v.* 23). The nether millstone, bearing all the pressure upon it, needs to be harder even than the upper stone.
25. With his "firmness" of heart there naturally goes a corresponding courage and fierceness.

by reason of breakings] Rather, **by reason of terrors they are beside themselves**; lit. *they lose themselves*. The Geneva has: *for fear they faint in themselves*. The expression "lose themselves" seems more naturally said of mental confusion from terror, than of literally losing their way in their attempts to escape (Gesen.).

26—29. He can be subdued by no weapon.

26. *that layeth at him*] That is, that striketh at him; lit. *he that layeth at him with the sword,—it doth not hold*. The sword does not hold, or bite, but glances off his adamantine armour.

the habergeon] That is, the mail. "And be ye apparelled or clothed, saith Paul, with the habergeon, or coat armour of justice," Latimer, *Serm.* p. 29 (Wright, *Bible Word-Book*).

29. *darts are counted*] Rather, **clubs**.
30. The impression left where he has lien.

Under him he hath sharp potsherds,
He spreadeth a threshing-sledge upon the mire.

The scales of the belly, though smoother than those on the back, still are sharp, particularly those under the tail, and leave an impression on the mire where he has lien as if a sharp threshing-sledge with teeth had stood on it or gone over it (Is. xli. 15).

31. The commotion he raises in the deep.

The second clause of the verse hardly refers to fermentation in the pot of ointment, but rather to the foaming mixture of ingredients.

He maketh the sea like a pot of ointment.
32 He maketh a path to shine after him;
One would think the deep to be hoary.
33 Upon earth there is not his like,
Who is made without fear.
34 He beholdeth all high *things:*
He *is* a king over all the children of pride.
42 Then Job answered the LORD, and said,
2 I know that thou canst do every *thing*,
And *that* no thought can be withholden from thee.

32. The verse refers to the shining track which his swift darting through the water leaves behind him.
33, 34. He has no rival, he is king among the proud beasts.
33. *who is made*] That is, he who is made without fear—so as to fear nothing.
34. *he beholdeth all high things*] Or, **he looketh on all that is high**; he looks them boldly in the face without terror.
the children of pride] That is, the proud beasts; comp. ch. xxviii. 8.

CH. XLII. 1—6. JOB'S REPLY TO THE LORD'S SECOND ADDRESS FROM THE STORM.

The Lord's words make Job feel more deeply than before that greatness which belongs to God alone, and with deep compunction he retracts his past words and repents in dust and ashes.
2. *do every thing*] Or, *canst do all.*
no thought can be withholden] That is, **no purpose**. The meaning is that there is no purpose which the Almighty cannot carry out. Though literally the words seem merely an acknowledgement of power, they are also an admission of wisdom, the plans or purposes of which may be beyond the understanding of man (*v.* 3). Job does not, as might have been expected, acknowledge the Divine righteousness. His confession corresponds to the Almighty's address to him. That address did not insist on any one Divine attribute, but rather presented God in the whole circle of His attributes, power and wisdom but also goodness, for He refreshes the thirsty ground where no man is, He feeds the ravens, and presides over the birth-pangs of the goats of the rock; and His omnipotence goes hand in hand with His moral rule (ch. xl. 9 *seq.*). The Divine nature is not a segment but a circle. Any one Divine attribute implies all others. Omnipotence cannot exist apart from righteousness. Similarly Job's reply reflects the great, general impression of God now made on him. The exhibition of the Divine wisdom as it operates in nature has led him to feel that within his own history also there is a divine "thought" or "counsel," though he is unable to understand it. It can hardly, however, be the Author's purpose to teach the general principle that the "counsel" of God is incomprehensible, because he gives an explanation of it in the Pro-

Who *is* he that hideth counsel 3
Without knowledge?
Therefore have I uttered that I understood not;
Things too wonderful for me, which I knew not.
Hear, I beseech thee, and I will speak: 4
I will demand of thee, and declare thou unto me.
I have heard of thee by the hearing of the ear: 5
But now mine eye seeth thee.
Wherefore I abhor *myself*, and repent 6
In dust and ashes.

logue. He is not teaching general principles here, but shewing the position which just thoughts of God will induce a man to take, even when God's dealings may be beyond his understanding.

3. *who is he that hideth*] That is, that *obscures* counsel. The words of the Almighty (ch. xxxviii. 2) echo through Job's mind, and he repeats them, speaking of himself. The rest of the verse expands the idea of "obscuring counsel," or states its consequence. As one that obscured counsel Job had uttered that which he understood not. The reference is to his former judgments regarding God's operations in the world, and the rashness of his own language.

4. *hear, I beseech thee*] Or, *hear now*, and I will speak. The words are not an entreaty on the part of Job that the Almighty would further instruct him; they are a repetition of the words of the Lord (ch. xxxviii. 3, xl. 7). The verse is closely connected with *v.* 5, which suggests under what feeling Job repeats the words of God to him. He recites the divine challenge and puts it away from him—"Declare unto thee! (*v.* 4) that be far from me; I had heard of thee with the hearing of the ear, but now mine eye seeth thee" (*v.* 5). This is more natural than to suppose *v.* 4 uttered with a kind of self-irony, as if Job, in repeating the words of the divine challenge, also entered into the ironical spirit of it. In either case *v.* 5 has a half-apologetic meaning, accounting for Job's former rashness.

5. *I have heard*] Rather perhaps, I **had** heard. Job's former knowledge of God, though he had prided himself upon it (ch. xii.—xiii.), seems to him now only such a knowledge as one gets by hearsay, confused and defective. His present knowledge is that of eyesight, immediate and full (Is. lii. 8).

6. The effect of this deeper knowledge of God upon Job's heart.
I abhor myself] The word *myself* is not expressed; what has to be supplied as the object of "abhor" is rather *it*, that is, my former language and demeanour. The word means, I *retract*, or *repudiate*.

CH. XLII. 7—17. JOB, HAVING HUMBLED HIMSELF BEFORE GOD, IS RESTORED TO A PROSPERITY TWO-FOLD THAT WHICH HE ENJOYED BEFORE.

7—9. Job is commanded to intercede for his three friends lest

7 And it was *so*, that after the LORD had spoken these words unto Job, the LORD said to Eliphaz the Temanite, My wrath is kindled against thee, and against thy two friends: for ye have not spoken of me *the thing that is* right, 8 as my servant Job *hath*. Therefore take unto you now seven bullocks and seven rams, and go to my servant Job, and offer up for yourselves a burnt offering; and my servant Job shall pray for you: for him will I accept: lest *I* deal with you *after your* folly, in that ye have not spoken of me 9 *the thing which is* right, like my servant Job. So Eliphaz the Temanite and Bildad the Shuhite *and* Zophar the Naamathite went, and did according as the LORD com-

Jehovah should visit their folly upon them, because they spoke not that which was right concerning Him.

7. *the thing which is right*] The Lord blames the three friends for not speaking that which was right concerning *Him*, not concerning Job; He also commends Job for speaking what was right concerning Him. It is obvious that the three friends spoke many just and profound things concerning God, and that Job on the other hand said many things that were both blameworthy and false, things for which he was both rebuked by the Almighty, and expressed his penitence. The reference cannot be to such things as these. Neither can the charge made against the friends here be merely that brought against them by Job, that they did not speak in honesty and sincerity (ch. vi. 25, xiii. 7), though this may be included. Rather, the friends are blamed for speaking in regard to God that which was not right, or true, *in itself;* and the reference must be to the theories they put forth in regard to God's providence and the meaning of afflictions. On this point the friends spoke in regard to God what was not right, while Job spoke that which was right (ch. xxi., xxiii.—xxiv.). The Author puts the Divine *imprimatur* on his own theory of the meaning of suffering, or at least on Job's attacks on the theories advocated by the three friends.

The three friends "had really inculpated the providence of God by their professed defence of it. By disingenuously covering up and ignoring its enigmas and seeming contradictions, they had cast more discredit upon it than Job by honestly holding them up to the light. Their denial of its apparent inequalities was more untrue and more dishonouring to the divine administration, as it is in fact conducted, than Job's bold affirmation of them. Even his most startling utterances wrung from him in his bewilderment and sore perplexity were less reprehensible than their false statements and false inferences" (Green, *Book of Job*, p. 219).

10—16. Job is restored to a prosperity double that which he formerly enjoyed; his former friends gather around him; he is again blessed with children; and dies, old and full of days.

manded them: the LORD also accepted Job. And the 10
LORD turned the captivity of Job, when he prayed for
his friends: also the LORD gave Job twice as much as
he had before. Then came there unto him all his brethren, 11
and all his sisters, and all *they that had been of* his
acquaintance before, and did eat bread with him in his
house: and they bemoaned him, and comforted him over
all the evil that the LORD had brought upon him: every
man also gave him a piece of money, and every one an
earring of gold.

So the LORD blessed the latter end of Job more than his 12
beginning: for he had fourteen thousand sheep, and six
thousand camels, and a thousand yoke of oxen, and a
thousand she asses. He had also seven sons and three 13
daughters. And he called the name of the first, Jemima; 14
and the name of the second, Kezia; and the name of the
third, Keren-happuch. And in all the land were no women 15
found *so* fair as the daughters of Job: and their father gave
them inheritance among their brethren. After this lived 16

10. *turned the captivity*] The metaphorical use of the phrase would readily arise in a state of society like that in the East. The expression means that Job's afflictions were removed and his prosperity restored.

11. Comp. Job's sorrowful lamentations over the alienation of all his friends and acquaintances, ch. xix. 13 *seq.*

piece of money] The Heb. is *Kesita*, probably an uncoined piece of silver, of a certain weight, Gen. xxxiii. 19; Josh. xxiv. 32.

12. The exact doubling of Job's former possessions shews that we are not reading literal history here.

13—15. The former number of Job's children is restored to him. The name *Jemima* probably means *dove*, comp. Song, vi. 9, v. 2; *Kezia* is *cassia*, the aromatic spice, Ps. xlv. 8, Song, i. 3; and *Keren-happuch* means *horn* (or box) *of eye-paint*, *puch* being the paint or powder used by Oriental women to add lustre to the eye. The Sept. curiously renders *horn of Amalthea*, *cornu copiæ*, horn of plenty. A French commentator considers it important to remark that "les trois noms sont destinés à relever les grâces de ces filles, et pas le moins du monde leur coquetterie" (Reuss).

15. *inheritance among their brethren*] The Hebrew practice was that the daughters inherited only when there was no son, Numb. xxvii. 1 *seq*. The disposition of his property made by Job would retain the sisters in the midst of their brethren even after marriage, and allow the affectionate relations existing among Job's children to continue.

Job an hundred and forty years, and saw his sons, and
17 his sons' sons, *even* four generations. So Job died, *being* old and full of days.

17. Job dies, old and full of days. "Ye have heard of the patience of Job, and have seen the end of the Lord; that the Lord is very pitiful, and of tender mercy" (James v. 11).

APPENDIX.

ADDITIONAL NOTE ON CH. XIX. 23—27.

IN these verses Job anticipates that God will appear and interpose in his behalf to vindicate him, and that he shall see God, and he faints before the joyful vision. The meaning is sufficiently clear except in *vv.* 25, 26, in regard to which some difference of opinion prevails. The point on which interpreters differ is chiefly the question, When, according to Job's anticipation, shall this appearance of God on his behalf take place? Shall it be before or after his death?

The difference of view arises greatly from the ambiguity of the word *umibbesârî, and from my flesh*, *v.* 26 (see notes), though other points of construction are also involved. It is important to observe the connexion of ideas in the passage, and what the great thought is which fills Job's mind. In *vv.* 23, 24 he desired that his protestations of rectitude were written in a book or rather graven with an iron pen in the rock for ever, that all generations of men to come might read them and know that he died in innocence. Suddenly a higher thought takes possession of his mind, namely the assurance that this innocence shall yet be vindicated by God appearing to uphold it, and that he himself shall see God to his joy. This seeing of God includes all within it, for now God hides His face; and this is the main thought of the passage, as the impassioned reiteration of it, *v.* 27, indicates. The connexion of *vv.* 25 and 26 is: I know that my Goel liveth, and that he shall stand upon the dust, and......I shall see God. The bulk of *v.* 26 contributes nothing to the main idea of the passage, which is the assurance of seeing God; it merely describes the circumstances in, or rather, *after* which the vision shall take place. This makes it probable that the construction of *v.* 26 is light, and that its two clauses are parallel and not in antithesis to one another, in other words that the second clause begins with *and*, not with *yet*. The word *after*, too, is a prep. in the original, and this fact increases the improbability of the antithetical construction.

i. The words *from my flesh* might mean, (looking) *from my flesh I shall see God*, i.e. as A. V. *in* my flesh. Two interpretations are then possible, (1) that Job shall see God after his skin is destroyed and he is reduced to a mass of flesh; or (2) that endowed with flesh anew, in another (resurrection) body he shall see God. In the one case *skin* is opposed to *flesh;* in the other it is taken as denoting Job's present body. Both of these interpretations require the second clause of *v.* 26 to be taken in antithesis to the first, and are liable to the objections urged above. But in truth the first sense is nothing short of grotesque. A distinction between *skin* and *flesh* might be made, if the second expressed more strongly the same meaning with the first, but in the circumstances to put them in antithesis seems ludicrous. Considering the nature of Job's malady he could hardly express its worst ravages by saying that it would destroy his *skin*, leaving his flesh remaining. He had already said much stronger things than this of his actual condition, among others that he was become a skeleton of bones, ch. vii. 15; that all his members were a shadow, ch. xvii. 7; that his leanness bore witness to his face, ch. xvi. 8, as he says later that his clothes clung to his shrunken frame like the opening of his shirt, ch. xxx. 18; and that he was escaped with the skin of his teeth, ch. xix. 20. Besides, the word rendered *destroyed* is literally *struck off*, a meaning which suggests removal of the solid parts of the body. And that the word *skin* may be used in this general sense of the *body* appears from ch. xviii. 13. Where *flesh* is used along with *skin* the two words express the same general meaning, the accumulation of terms merely serving to intensify the expression, ch. x. 11, xix. 20; Lam. iii. 4; comp. Ps. cii. 5; Lam. iv. 8.

If therefore we understand the words "from my flesh" in the sense of *in* my flesh, we must suppose that Job anticipated being clothed in a new body after death; and this body is what he names his "flesh." Something may be said for this view. Undoubtedly in ch. xiv. 13 *seq.* Job already conceived the idea of being delivered from Sheol and living again, and fervently prayed that such a thing might be. And what he there ventured to long for he might here speak of as a thing of which he was assured. No violence would be done to the line of thought in the Book by this supposition. Nevertheless several things are against it. The great idea of the passage, as has been said, is that God shall appear and that Job shall see Him. The rest of the words in *v.* 26 seem unemphatic, and descriptive of something naturally to be understood. But it is highly improbable that the great thought of the resurrection of the body could be referred to in a way so brief. Even if this idea had been current and a commonplace of belief, a reference to it by the words *my flesh* would be singular and unnatural. But on Old Testament ground, and in the situation of Job, such a matter-of-course kind of reference is almost inconceivable. We may be certain, had such an idea been alluded to, that it would have been expressed in a manner much more formal and detailed.

A somewhat different view has been taken by some scholars. Finding it difficult to accept the meaning *without*, or, *away from* for the Heb. prep. here, they retain the sense *from* (i.e. *in*), and consider the words *skin* and *flesh* to be each used somewhat generally in the sense of the "body." Hence they translate: *and after my skin* (i.e. my body) *has been thus destroyed, yet from my flesh* (i.e. in this body of mine) *I shall see God*. Though not liable to the objections urged above, this view is rather unnatural. The words *skin* and *flesh* express a single general idea when coupled together by *and*, but that each of them should mean generally the body when separated by *yet* is little probable. Though this view agrees in rendering with i. above, it coincides in meaning with ii. (1) just to be mentioned, and is liable to the difficulties urged below.

ii. The words *from my flesh*, however, may mean *away from*, or, *without* my flesh. In this case the words "after this my skin has been destroyed" are taken up and their meaning repeated in a more intense form in the phrase *and without my flesh*. This is the natural construction. It is to be observed, however, that the language does not state *in* what condition precisely Job shall see God, but rather *after* what events, viz. after his skin has been destroyed and his flesh has been removed. Here, however, again a division of opinion exists. (1) By some the words are taken in a comparative sense, meaning that Job shall see God when his skin and flesh have been (virtually) destroyed by his disease and he is reduced to a skeleton of bones—though still in life. (2) By others the language is taken in an absolute sense, meaning that Job's vision of God shall be after his disease has wholly destroyed his body and brought him to death. The second view is the more natural, does most justice to the language, and is most in harmony with the elevated character of the passage. It is also supported by many considerations suggested by other parts of the Book.

Before these considerations are referred to another remark may be made. It is always to be remembered what is the main thought here in Job's mind; it is that God shall appear to vindicate his innocence, and that he shall see God to his joy. The question whether this shall be in this life or beyond this life is of subsidiary importance, and not the main point. At present Job's afflictions are proof to him of God's estrangement. God holds him guilty and hides His face from him. And his friends, arguing on his calamities, impute grievous sins to him. His misery was very aggravated in every view. His good name among men was sullied by shameful imputations, intolerable to his lofty mind; for the easy theory of his friends, that one might be a religious man and at the same time a great sinner, he repudiated with abhorrence, so far as his own life was concerned. Then, as a religious man, his heart was crushed by the loss of God's favour. And the inexplicableness of this loss, combined with his unbearable afflictions at God's hand, threw up before his mind great moral riddles which utterly baffled him. In this thick darkness he has nothing but his own consciousness to fall back upon. But his consciousness of his innocence assures him that God knows it also. And this assurance becomes the basis of the other assurance that God from His nature must yet make manifest the relation in which His servant stands to Him, and that he shall see God. Job's assurance is based on his own past experience, on his life with God, on his consciousness of being a God-fearing man, and on his ineradicable convictions in regard to the nature of God and His relations to men. Job's circumstances cause his principle to appear in its barest form: the human spirit is conscious of fellowship with God, and this fellowship, from the nature of God, is a thing imperishable, and, in spite of obscurations, it must yet be fully manifested by God. This principle, grasped with convulsive earnestness in the prospect of death, became the Hebrew doctrine of Immortality. This doctrine was but the necessary corollary of religion. In this life on earth the true relations of men and God were felt to be realized; and the Hebrew faith of Immortality—never a belief in the mere existence of the soul after death, for the lowest popular superstition assumed this (see notes on ch. xiv. 13 *seq.*)—was a faith that the dark and mysterious event of death should not interrupt the life of the person with God enjoyed in this world. Job's afflictions make his faith not so much an assurance of the continuation of his fellowship with God as of its renewal or manifestation, and, of course, this might take place in this life. The similarity of the passage, however, to many others in the Old Testament, uttered in the prospect of death, makes it probable that Job speaks with death in view. And the probability is heightened by many other considerations.

1. The whole of the chapters xvi., xvii. and xix. are spoken by Job under the feeling that he shall die with his innocence unrecognised. Hence in ch. xvi. 18 he appeals to the earth not to cover his innocent blood; and in ch. xix. 24 he desires that his protestations of his innocence might be graven in the rock for ever, that when he is gone men to all generations might read them. There is not the slightest ground to think that in the verses that follow these expressions in ch. xvi. and xix. Job retracts or corrects this anticipation that he shall die an unjust death. The verses that follow proceed on the same assumption, but they express the prayer (ch. xvi.—xvii.) or the assurance (ch. xix.) that, *though* he die with God's face hidden from him and under the reproach of being a transgressor, this perverse and cruel fate shall not for ever prevail over him; God shall yet appear to vindicate his innocence and he shall see Him to his joy.

On this view every word in ch. xix. 25 *seq.* becomes full of meaning. Job's *Goel* is he who shall vindicate him against his wrongful death. The word *liveth* derives its meaning from the fact that Job shall have died. The term *aḥaron*, however we render it, whether "he who shall come after me" or with Ewald an *after-man*, i. e. vindicator, equally implies Job's previous death. Similarly the word *dust*. On the supposition that Job's vindication shall be in this life, every one of those words is robbed of its just significance, and no account at all can be given of the use of the term *liveth*.

2. Further, it is certain that Job does not anticipate restoration to health and prosperity in this life. Neither in the lofty passages above referred to nor anywhere does he express such an opinion, but always and consistently an opposite one. He calls such a hope when held out by his friends "mockery," ch. xvii. 2; comp. ch. vi. 11, xvii. 10 *seq.* So certain is he that he shall die under his malady that he does not even pray for recovery, only for a little easing of his pain before he departs, ch. x. 20. If life is to be his portion at all, it must be a new life after this one comes to its rapid close, ch. xiv. 13 *seq.* This is his tone after ch. xix. as well as before it. In ch. xxiii. 14 he says that God "will perform the thing appointed for him," i. e. bring him to death through his malady. And almost his last words are, "I know that thou wilt bring me unto death," ch. xxx. 23. It seems clear therefore that God's intervention to declare Job's innocence, ch. xix. 23 *seq.*, if it take place in this life, will not be accompanied by Job's restoration

to health. His disease will in spite of it carry him to the grave. But could such a thought have occurred to Job? His disease was to him the seal of God's estrangement from him. It was God's witness to his guilt. It was this moral meaning which his death had that caused him so to wrestle against it (see notes ch. xvi. 18 *seq.*). It seems impossible that Job could have conceived God declaring to men and to himself his innocence *while* He continued to afflict him fatally with his disease. To "see God" and to be chastened to death by Him are two things which on Old Testament ground are contradictory of one another.

The theory that God's intervention in Job's behalf is looked for by him in this life is thought to derive support from the actual *dénouement* of Job's history (ch. xlii.). But the argument proves too much by a half. The author allows Job to be restored to prosperity in this life in contradiction to Job's uniform and contemptuous rejection of such a hope. And he may equally well have advanced Job's vision of God into this life, though Job pushed it back beyond his death. In truth, as has been said, the two things are inseparable. It would be a strange demand to make of a dramatic writer that he should make his personages express only opinions that coincide with his own, and allow them to anticipate the issue of the plot. Certainly the author of Job imposes no such restrictions on himself. He never allows Job to come within sight of the true cause of his afflictions, and as little does he permit him to foresee their issue. It was his purpose to bring into a focus the thoughts of men on the question of suffering, the great problem of his day; and some of the views expressed, particularly by Job, are those to which men were driven by the pressure of the time, or to which they rose out of the distress of their own hearts.

3. If, however, we must conclude that Job looked for this appearance of God on his behalf, and this vision of Him to his joy, not previous to his death, we must not attempt to fill up the outline which he has drawn. We must take care not to complete his sketch out of events that transpired long after his day, or out of beliefs, reposing on these events, that are now current among ourselves. The English Version has done so at the expense of the original. The great thought which filled Job's imagination was the thought that God would appear to manifest his innocence and that he should see Him in peace and reconciliation. This thought was so intense that it almost realized itself. Job's assurance of seeing God was so vivid that it virtually became a vision of God and he faints in the ecstasy of his faith. In such a condition of mind the preliminaries and the circumstances that would occur to a mind in a calmer state, or which immediately occur to us, do not obtrude themselves, and if we are rightly to conceive Job's state of mind we must entirely exclude them. We should be wrong to say that he contemplates a purely spiritual vision of God, and further wrong to say that he contemplates being invested with a new body when he shall see God. Neither thought is present to his mind, which is entirely absorbed in the idea of seeing God. The ideas of Old Test. saints regarding the condition of man after death were too obscure to permit of any such formal and precise conception as that which we call a spiritual sight of God. Besides, as the kind of half-ecstasy under which

Job here speaks has fallen on him when a living man, it is probable that, like all persons in such conditions, he carries over with him his present circumstances into his vision after death, and seems to himself to be such a man as he is now when he sees God; comp. ch. xix. 25, 26, 28, 29.

4. The above remarks suggest what elements of truth lay in the traditional interpretation of this passage, in spite of its hardy treatment of the text. The christology of the Book is indirect. There are no express references to the Messiah, though several passages may seem unconscious prophecies of Him, as those that express Job's desire to meet and see God as a man, ch. ix. 32, xxiii. 3 *seq.* Job's *Goel* or redeemer is God. A distinction of Persons in the Godhead was not present to his thoughts when he used this term; though the conception of God in the passage and many things said in it may find verification in God's manifestation of Himself in His Son. The strange distinction which Job draws between God and God, God who persecutes him and God who is his Witness and Redeemer, is, of course, not a christological distinction, nor one that corresponds to any distinction in the Godhead made known to us by subsequent revelation. To suppose so would be a gross perversion not only of this Book but of the whole of Scripture. The distinction was one which Job's ideas almost compelled him to draw. He believed that every event that occurred came immediately from God's hand; and he believed that every event that befell a man reflected the disposition of God's mind toward him: calamity indicated the anger and prosperity the favour of God. This second superstition is the source of all his perplexities; and the distinction which he draws between God and God is his effort to overcome it. God whom he appeals against is the rule and course of this world, the outer providence of God, to which Job can give no name but "God." God to whom he appeals is the inner mind of God towards His servants, the moral ideal of the human heart. This is God his Witness and Redeemer. Job succeeded in drawing this distinction; but the reconciliation which the distinction demanded he was only partially successful in effecting. He could not reach the idea that God, the heart of God, might be towards him, while God—the outer course of the world —afflicted him. These two things could not be at the same time. But they might succeed one another. Hence his reconciliation is temporal: God will bring him unto death, but after his body is destroyed God shall appear to vindicate him and he shall see God.

The doctrine of Immortality in the Book is the same as that of other parts of the Old Testament. Immortality is the corollary of Religion. If there be religion, that is, if God be, there is immortality, not of the soul but of the whole personal being of man (Ps. xvi. 9). This teaching of the whole Old Testament is expressed by our Lord with a surprising incisiveness in two sentences—"I am the *God* of Abraham. God is not the God of the dead but of the *living.*"

INDEX.

Abaddon, 183, 198, 215
abhor, 74, 287
aboriginal races, referred to, 174, 175, 207
Abraham, Mohammedan fable about, 218
Adam, as, = like common men, 219
adultery, a capital crime, 215
aharon, 294
Ahlwardt, referred to, 271
Ammianus, quoted, 90
Angels, 6, 7, 33, 35, 180, 230, 262
Arabian Nights, illustration from, 218
arms of the fatherless, 164
arrows of God, 43, 121, 151, 193, 234
ashes, 14, 96, 211
asses, 4, 173; wild, 174, 270, 271
astronomical allusions, 184, 267
Augustine, S., quoted, 15
authorship and date of Book of Job, lv—lxviii

Baal, 247
bahr, 103
balija, 73
bands of Orion, 266
bars of the pit, 130
base men, 208
Bedawin, 10, 37
before (not in temporal sense), 24, 33
behemoth, 279
belial, 236
belly, 130, 225
bemê)(*bemô*, distinction between, 73
betimes, = earnestly, 57, 60, 174
Bildad, comes to condole with Job, 17; his character, 25; his first speech, 58—64; his second, 130—136; his third, 180, 181
Bleek, referred to, xiii, xxvii
blood, = death, 123
boils, 13
book, 142, 220
booth, 192
bosses, 114
bottom of the sea, 252
bow, symbolical of power, 206
bowels, = the seat of feeling, 212
branch, 116, 135, 205
breasts, 158
bribery, 116
brooks, 47, 48
build desolate places 21
Burns, quoted, 47
Buz, 22

camels, 4
caravans, 47

Carlyle, quoted, 269
Catullus, quoted, 282
Chaldeans, 10
chambers of the south, 68, 254
chanelbone, a marginal reading, 217
changes and war, 78
check, 148
chief of the ways of God, 280
children of mine own body, xxxi, 140
children of the East, 4
Christology of the Book of Job, 296
Cicero, quoted, 5, 131
clapping of hands, token of malignant gladness or scorn, 193, 240
clay, in various figurative senses, 33, 77, 96, 191, 263
clouds, 184, 210, 252, 255, 268
cockle, 221
collar of my coat, 211
companions, = partners in occupation, 282
complaint, = complaining, 54, 73, 75, 154, 169
Conant, referred to, xlv, 13, 135, 217, 249
contend, a legal term, 66, 76, 95, 276
cords of affliction, 247
Coverdale's version quoted, 125, 156, 157, 223, 226, 228
Cox's *Comm. on Job* quoted, 177, 196
crocodiles, 20, 283
crooked serpent, 185
cruddled, = curdled, ch. x. 10
curse, 5, 9, 15, 20, 36

darkness, 79, 93, 114, 115, 129, 139, 151, 164, 172, 194, 256, 264
day, in various senses, 19, 53, 102, 115, 136, 173, 263
daysman, 74
death, = pestilence, 191; personified, 134, 135, 198
debtors, treatment of, 49, 175
declare, in various senses, 182, 199, 261
Delitzsch, referred to, xxii, xxxvi, l, lii, lx, 14, 68, 98, 146, 188, 190
De Sacy, referred to, 56
desolate, 21, 40, 115, 116, 207
destruction, = Sheol, 183, 198, 215 ;= misfortune, calamity, 212, 218
Dillmann, referred to, 14, 33, 190
discover, in A.V. = uncover, turn back, 93, 283
dogs, 207
double bridle, 283
Dragon, the, or Leviathan, of popular mythology, lxvi, 20, 54, 69, 185

INDEX.

drink, used metaphorically, 43, 157; drink...like water, 112, 234
dust, an image expressing plenty, 191
dust of gold, 195
dust, sprinkling of, a sign of grief, 18

eagles, 275
ear,=the understanding, 91, 229, 234
Egypt, referred to, 69, 196, 205, 220
elephantiasis, its symptoms described, 12, 13, 55, 122
Elihu, meaning of the name, 222; his speeches, xi, xl—lii, 221—258
Eliphaz, comes to condole with Job, 17; his character, 25, 41; his first speech, 27—42; his second, 108—116; his third, 162—168
Elohim, 6
end, in various senses, 45, 61, 194
enterprise, 39
Euripides, quoted, 160
Ewald, referred to, xiv, xxi, xxvii, xxxviii, lxiv, 138, 144, 146, 158, 165, 174, 175, 184, 189, 219, 294
excellency, 34, 96, 148, 253
extremity, 244
eyelids of the morn, 21, 284

face of his garment, 283
fash, 244
feasts of Job's children, 4
fetters, 247
filthy, in moral sense, 112
fire of God, 10
firmament, 67
firstborn of death, 134
flakes of his flesh, 284
flesh, 141, 218, 292
folly, 11, 33, 175
food, allusions to, in figurative sense, 24, 44, 50, 91, 149, 234, 243
fool, 15, 16, 36, 92, 208
foolishly, 11
forcible, 48

gall, 121
gate, place of rendezvous in Eastern cities, 36, 203, 216
Geneva version quoted, 15, 282, 285
Gesenius, referred to, 73, 84, 285
giant,=warrior, 121
girdles, 92, 93
glass, 197
glistering,=glittering, ch. xx. 25
goats, 270
go away,=be torn out, 34
Godet, referred to, xxxii, 8
goel, 143, 294, 296
Goethe, referred to, 122
gold, 257
grave,=*Sheol*, 53, 130, 155;=ruin, 212
great men,=old men, 224
Green, on *Book of Job*, quoted, 288
grief, in various senses, 18, 28, 43, 120

grin,=gin, ch. xviii. 9
grind unto another, 215
Grotius, referred to, xvii

habergeon, 285
Hamasa, the, quoted, 52
hand, in various senses, 90, 97, 156, 217, 228, 237, 254
Hauran, mining in the, 196
Havilah, of doubtful situation, 257
heart, in various senses, 55, 61, 67, 81, 85, 89, 93, 112, 188, 258, 268
hell,=*Sheol*, 84, 183
helpers, 69
Hengstenberg, referred to, xvii
hideth his face, 100, 238
hierodouloi, 247
hippopotamus, 279
hireling, 52, 102
hissing, a token of scorn, 193
historical allusions, lvi, lx, 69, 165
Hitzig, referred to, lxiv, 19, 83, 90, 119, 135, 156, 226, 252
Horace, quoted, 5, 252
horn, symbol of power, 122
horses, 4, 274
houses of clay, 33
hunger-bitten, 134
hypocrite, 62, 98, 116, 128, 148, 189, 247

Ibn Ezra, referred to, xiv, 47, 84
idolatry, practised in Israel, 217
immortality, Hebrew belief in, 103—104, 143, 291—296
imperatives, two co-ordinate,=a principal and consecutive clause, 15; used hypothetically, 35;=future, 83
influences of Pleiades, 266
inheritance, Heb. practice respecting, 289
iniquity in my tongue, 50
in my flesh, 144, 291
instruction, 229
inward friends, 141
inward parts, 268
island of the innocent, 168

jackals, 213
Jegar Sahadutha, 124
Jehovah, exceptional employment of the name, xxx, lv, 11
Jemima,='dove,' 289
Jerome, S., referred to, 13, 272
Job, his home, 1, 203; his name, 1, 2; his 'perfection,' 2; his family and wealth, 3, 4; sacrifices on behalf of his children, 5; his first trial, 9—12; his second, 12—18; his wife 'Dinah,' acc. to Targum, xx, 15; visited by friends. 17; opens the debate by 'cursing his day,' 18; his universal respect, 204; his Oriental hospitality, 218; restored to twofold prosperity, 288; dies, 290
Jordan, 281
Josephus, referred to, xiii

INDEX. 299

judgment, of God contrasted with that of man, 248
juniper roots, 208
keemah, 68
Keren-happuch, xv, 289
keseel, 68
kesita, lvi, 289
Kezia, = 'cassia,' 289
king of terrors, 135
knees prevent me, 21
Koran, referred to, 2, 62, 111, 218
Kuenen, referred to, xxviii, xxxvi, lxvii

landmarks, 173
Lane, referred to, 138, 244
Latimer, quoted, 285
latter day, 143, 291
lay...hand upon...mouth, signifying respect or awe-struck silence, 154, 204, 276
Layard, quoted, 274
lead, 143
Lebanon, mining in the, 196
legal customs in the East, lvi, 36, 84, 99, 116, 124, 216, 220
Leviathan, = the Dragon or storm-cloud, personified in popular mythology, 20, 54, 69, 185 ; = the crocodile, 20, 281
light, in various senses, 133, 176, 181, 232, 252, 256, 263, 264, 265, 284
lions, 30, 269
Locman, quoted, 73
lots, casting of, 49
Lowth, Robert, Bp, referred to, xvii
Lucan, quoted, 73
Luther, referred to, xiv, xv, lx, 188

magicians, 20
makâm, 1
mallows, 208
mantles, 11
Maimonides, referred to, xiv
mark, = obstacle, 57
mark (vb.), 165, 176
Mazzaroth, 267
Messianic references, 296
Michaelis, J. D., referred to, xvii
Michaelis, J. H., referred to, xvi
Michie, referred to, 136
midnight, at, = suddenly, 237
mighty, in various senses, 48, 92, 164, 179, 237
Milton, quoted, 41, 79, 262
mining operations, 194—196
mirrors, 256
misprint in present text of A.V., 208
Mohammed, referred to, 3, 62, 73, 111, 217
money, weighed not counted, 197, 289
moth, before the, 33
mouth, 39, 91, 115, 119, 149, 217, 253
my Maker, 246
my mother's womb, 11
mythological ideas, 20, 54, 68, 69, 180, 185, 196

Naamah, 17
naked, 164, 174
nephew, 136
night, in various senses, 19, 32, 52, 249
north, the, 183, 254, 257
Nukra, the traditional home of Job placed in the, 1
number of...days, 264 ;...months, 20, 102, 157 ;...years, 113, 251
number of my steps, 220
numbers, symbolism of round, xviii, 3, 18, 25, 40, 138

occasions, = grounds of enmity, 228
organ, = pipe, 155, 213
ostriches, 213, 272 ; Arab proverb regarding, 273
oxen, 4, 173, 279

papyrus, 62
perfect, = righteous, 2, 63, 71
perfection, 83, 194
perverse things, 50
Phœnicians, 282
Phœnix, fable respecting the, 205
piece of money, 289
pillars of heaven, 185
pleasure, = concern, 157, 163 ; = good, 158
plenty of silver, 167
Pliny, referred to, 13, 73, 217
Plumptre's *Ecclesiastes* referred to, 22
post, = courier, 72
prepositions, ambiguity in rendering of Hebrew, 144
present tense, graphic use of, 32 ; gnomic, 36
pride, = ungodliness, xlv
priests, ancient dignity of, 92
prince, 159, 220
proud helpers, 69
punishments of the sword, 146

Rahab, = the mythological Leviathan or Dragon, lxvi, 69, 185
Ram, 222
ransom, 231, 249
ravens, 269
recompence, = exchange, 115
record, = sponsor, 124
redeemer, i.e. *Goel*, 143, 294—296
reêm, 271
re/âim, 183
reins, = vital parts, 121, 145
remembrances, = maxims, 96
remnant, 166
Renan, referred to, xlix, lvii
Reuss, referred to, xvii, 17, 82, 289
rich, = wicked, 192
rivers, = channels or galleries, 195
robber, = snare, 37, 133

Saadia, referred to, 62
Sabeans, 10
sackcloth, 121
salutations, Oriental, 5

INDEX.

samoom, the, 10
sanctification, preparatory to sacrifice, 5
sand, image of weight, 43; of countless number, 205
sapphires, 195
sarcophagus, Sidonian, described, 160
Satan, ix, xxxi, 7, 135
Schlottmann, referred to, 110, 265
Schultens, A., referred to, xvi
scorning, = impiety, 234
sea, personified as Leviathan, 20, 54, 69, 185
seal (vb.), 229, 254
seal (subst.), 263
secret of God, 203
Septuagint, referred to, xv, 1, 14, 15, 33, 34, 39, 57, 92, 169, 185, 192, 196, 205, 244, 267, 272, 289
serpent, = Dragon or Leviathan, 20, 54, 69, 185
shadow of death, 19, 79, 93, 122, 176, 194, 237, 264
Shakespeare, quoted, 5, 43, 46, 54, 134, 141, 144, 148, 160, 177, 181, 194, 266
Sheol, 53, 84, 103, 106, 130, 135, 155, 178, 183, 184, 198, 211, 215, 264
Shuah, 17
Simon's *History of the O. T.*, ref. to, xvii
skin of my teeth, 141
skin for skin, 13
snares, 133
snow water, 73, 178
son of man, 125
sons of God, 6, 262
Sophocles, quoted, 21
Spanheim, F., referred to, xvi
speak wickedly for God, 95
Spenser, quoted, 74, 136
spider's web, 62
spirit, in various senses, 32, 112, 125, 147, 183, 223
spitting in the face, 127, 128, 209
spoiled, = stripped of clothing, 92
spreadings of the clouds, 252
stars, ideas respecting the, 180, 262, 266
storks, 272
straitness, Oriental figure for adversity, 133, 248, 249
Streane's *Jeremiah* referred to, 273
strike hands, = undertake suretyship, 126
Studer, referred to, xxix, 54
swallow down my spittle, 56
swift ships, 72
sword, in various senses, 39, 114, 146, 151, 230, 247, 280

tabrets, 128
Talmud, referred to, xiii, lviii
Targum, referred to, 12, 13, 15
Tema, 47
Teman, xix, lvii, 17

Tennyson, quoted, 52, 198
tents, 34
Theodore, Bp of Mopsuestia, ref. to, xv
thieves, 176
Thomson's *Land and Book* quoted, 256
thorns, = thorn-hedge, 37
thoughts of my heart, 129
threshing-floors, 156
timbrels, 128, 155
time, in various senses, 71, 115, 165, 173
toholah, 33
toph, = timbrel, 128
topheth, = spitting, 128
trees, frequent objects of comparison, 115, 116, 135, 139, 178, 205
Tristram, referred to, 271, 273
Tyndale's version quoted, 283

umibbesārt, 291
understanding, = discretion, 89, 92
unicorn, = wild ox, 167, 271
Uz, 1

vain, in various senses, 84, 109, 118, 190
vanity, in various senses, 52, 55, 115, 116, 214, 243
Vergil, quoted, 90, 135
vile, not in moral sense, 276
vines, 116
vineyards, 174, 175, 177
vision of Eliphaz, 32
vows, in connection with requests in prayer, 167
Vulgate, referred to, 13, 98, 114, 169

wardrobes, element of Oriental wealth, 191
waters, in figurative sense, 24, 164, 177, 192; = rain, 199, 265
way, in various senses, 23, 63, 139, 170, 198, 206, 209, 214
ways of their destruction, 209
wealth, = prosperity, 155
Wetzstein, referred to, 1, 14, 63, 192, 271
white of an egg, 44
wicked, in various senses, 150, 174, 236
wilderness, = perplexity, 93
wisdom, in various senses, 39, 45, 82, 92, 163, 197, 200
wise, in various senses, 16, 67, 84, 258
woman, Oriental ideas respecting, 3, 15
worm, Hebrew words signifying, 144, 181
wrath, in various senses, 36, 146, 247, 249
Wright's *Bible Word-Book* referred to, 74, 217, 272, 285

Zophar, comes to condole with Job, 17; his character, 26; fails to come forward in the last round of speeches, 27, 186; his first speech, 80—86; his second, 146—152

CAMBRIDGE UNIVERSITY PRESS.

THE PITT PRESS SERIES.

⁂ *Many of the books in this list can be had in two volumes, Text and Notes separately.*

I. GREEK.

Aristophanes. Aves—Plutus—Ranæ. By W. C. GREEN, M.A., late Assistant Master at Rugby School. 3s. 6d. each.
—— **Vespae.** By C. E. GRAVES, M.A. [*Nearly ready.*
Aristotle. Outlines of the Philosophy of. By EDWIN WALLACE, M.A., LL.D. Third Edition, Enlarged. 4s. 6d.
Euripides. Heracleidae. By E. A. BECK, M.A. 3s. 6d.
—— **Hercules Furens.** By A. GRAY, M.A., and J. T. HUTCHINSON, M.A. New Edit. 2s.
—— **Hippolytus.** By W. S. HADLEY, M.A. 2s.
—— **Iphigeneia in Aulis.** By C. E. S. HEADLAM, M.A. 2s. 6d.
Herodotus, Book V. By E. S. SHUCKBURGH, M.A. 3s.
—— **Book VI.** By the same Editor. 4s.
—— **Books VIII., IX.** By the same Editor. 4s. each.
—— **Book VIII. Ch. 1—90. Book IX. Ch. 1—89.** By the same Editor. 3s. 6d. each.
Homer. Odyssey, Books IX., X. By G. M. EDWARDS, M.A. 2s. 6d. each. **Book XXI.** By the same Editor. 2s.
—— **Iliad. Book VI.** By the same Editor. 2s.
—— —— **Book XXII.** By the same Editor. 2s.
—— —— **Book XXIII.** By the same Editor. 2s.
Lucian. Somnium Charon Piscator et De Luctu. By W. E. HEITLAND, M.A., Fellow of St John's College, Cambridge. 3s. 6d.
—— **Menippus and Timon.** By E. C. MACKIE, B.A. 3s. 6d.
Platonis Apologia Socratis. By J. ADAM, M.A. 3s. 6d.
—— **Crito.** By the same Editor. 2s. 6d.
—— **Euthyphro.** By the same Editor. 2s. 6d.
Plutarch. Life of Demosthenes. By Rev. H. A. HOLDEN, M.A., LL.D. [*Nearly ready.*
—— **Lives of the Gracchi.** By the same Editor. 6s.
—— **Life of Nicias.** By the same Editor. 5s.
—— **Life of Sulla.** By the same Editor. 6s.
—— **Life of Timoleon.** By the same Editor. 6s.
Sophocles. Oedipus Tyrannus. School Edition. By R. C. JEBB, Litt.D., LL.D. 4s. 6d.
Thucydides. Book VII. By H. A. HOLDEN, M.A., LL.D. 5s.
Xenophon. Agesilaus. By H. HAILSTONE, M.A. 2s. 6d.
—— **Anabasis.** By A. PRETOR, M.A. Two vols. 7s. 6d.
—— **Books I. III. IV. and V.** By the same. 2s. each.
—— **Books II. VI. and VII.** By the same. 2s. 6d. each.
Xenophon. Cyropaedeia. Books I. II. By Rev. H. A. HOLDEN, M.A., LL.D. 2 vols. 6s.
—— —— **Books III. IV. and V.** By the same Editor. 5s.
—— —— **Books VI. VII. VIII.** By the same Editor. 5s.

London: Cambridge Warehouse, Ave Maria Lane.
25/9/92

II. LATIN.

Beda's Ecclesiastical History, Books III., IV. By J. E. B. MAYOR, M.A., and J. R. LUMBY, D.D. Revised Edition. 7s. 6d.
—— **Books I. II.** *[In the Press.*
Caesar. De Bello Gallico, Comment. I. By A. G. PESKETT, M.A., Fellow of Magdalene College, Cambridge. 1s. 6d. COMMENT. II. III. 2s. COMMENT. I. II. III. 3s. COMMENT. IV. and V. 1s. 6d. COMMENT. VII. 2s. COMMENT. VI. and COMMENT. VIII. 1s. 6d. each.
—— **De Bello Civili, Comment. I.** By the same Editor. 3s.
Cicero. De Amicitia.—De Senectute. By J. S. REID, Litt.D., Fellow of Gonville and Caius College. 3s. 6d. each.
—— **In Gaium Verrem Actio Prima.** By H. COWIE, M.A. 1s. 6d.
—— **In Q. Caecilium Divinatio et in C. Verrem Actio.** By W. E. HEITLAND, M.A., and H. COWIE, M.A. 3s.
—— **Philippica Secunda.** By A. G. PESKETT, M.A. 3s. 6d.
—— **Oratio pro Archia Poeta.** By J. S. REID, Litt.D. 2s.
—— **Pro L. Cornelio Balbo Oratio.** By the same. 1s. 6d.
—— **Oratio pro Tito Annio Milone.** By JOHN SMYTH PURTON, B.D. 2s. 6d.
—— **Oratio pro L. Murena.** By W. E. HEITLAND, M.A. 3s.
—— **Pro Cn. Plancio Oratio,** by H. A. HOLDEN, LL.D. 4s. 6d.
—— **Pro P. Cornelio Sulla.** By J. S. REID, Litt.D. 3s. 6d.
—— **Somnium Scipionis.** By W. D. PEARMAN, M.A. 2s.
Horace. Epistles, Book I. By E. S. SHUCKBURGH, M.A. 2s. 6d.
Livy. Book IV. By H. M. STEPHENSON, M.A. 2s. 6d.
—— **Book V.** By L. WHIBLEY, M.A. 2s. 6d.
—— **Book VI.** By H. M. STEPHENSON, M.A. 2s. 6d.
—— **Book IX.** By H. M. STEPHENSON, M.A. 2s. 6d.
—— **Book XXI.** By M. S. DIMSDALE, M.A. 2s. 6d.
—— **Book XXII.** By the same Editor. 2s. 6d.
—— **Book XXVII.** By Rev. H. M. STEPHENSON, M.A. 2s. 6d.
Lucan. Pharsaliae Liber Primus. By W. E. HEITLAND, M.A., and C. E. HASKINS, M.A. 1s. 6d.
Lucretius, Book V. By J. D. DUFF, M.A. 2s.
Ovidii Nasonis Fastorum Liber VI. By A. SIDGWICK, M.A., Tutor of Corpus Christi College, Oxford. 1s. 6d.
Ovidii Nasonis Metamorphoseon Liber I. By L. D. DOWDALL, LL.B., B.D. 1s. 6d.
Quintus Curtius. A Portion of the History (Alexander in India). By W. E. HEITLAND, M.A., and T. E. RAVEN, B.A. With Two Maps. 3s. 6d.
Vergili Maronis Aeneidos Libri I.—XII. By A. SIDGWICK, M.A. 1s. 6d. each.
—— **Bucolica.** By the same Editor. 1s. 6d.
—— **Georgicon Libri I. II.** By the same Editor. 2s.
—— —— **Libri III. IV.** By the same Editor. 2s.
—— **The Complete Works.** By the same Editor. Two vols. Vol. I. containing the Introduction and Text. 3s. 6d. Vol. II. The Notes. 4s. 6d.

London: Cambridge Warehouse, Ave Maria Lane.

III. FRENCH.

Corneille. La Suite du Menteur. A Comedy in Five Acts.
By the late G. MASSON, B.A.   2s.
—— **Polyeucte.** By E. G. W. BRAUNHOLTZ, M.A., Ph.D.
[*Nearly ready.*
De Bonnechose. Lazare Hoche. By C. COLBECK, M.A.
Revised Edition.   Four Maps.   2s.
D'Harleville. Le Vieux Célibataire. By G. MASSON, B.A.   2s.
De Lamartine. Jeanne D'Arc. By Rev. A. C. CLAPIN,
M.A.   New edition revised, by A. R. ROPES, M.A.   1s. 6d.
De Vigny. La Canne de Jonc. By H. W. EVE, M.A.   1s. 6d.
Erckmann-Chatrian. La Guerre. By Rev. A. C. CLAPIN,
M.A.   3s.
La Baronne de Staël-Holstein. Le Directoire. (Considérations sur la Révolution Française. Troisième et quatrième parties.) Revised and enlarged. By G. MASSON, B.A., and G. W. PROTHERO, M.A.   2s.
—— —— **Dix Années d'Exil. Livre II. Chapitres 1—8.**
By the same Editors. New Edition, enlarged.   2s.
Lemercier. Fredegonde et Brunehaut. A Tragedy in Five
Acts.   By GUSTAVE MASSON, B.A.   2s.
Molière. Le Bourgeois Gentilhomme, Comédie-Ballet en
Cinq Actes. (1670.)   By Rev. A. C. CLAPIN, M.A.   Revised Edition.   1s. 6d.
—— **L'Ecole des Femmes.** By G. SAINTSBURY, M.A.   2s. 6d.
—— **Les Précieuses Ridicules.** By E. G. W. BRAUNHOLTZ,
M.A., Ph.D.   2s.   **Abridged Edition.**   1s.
Piron. La Métromanie. A Comedy. By G. MASSON, B.A.   2s.
Racine. Les Plaideurs. By E. G. W. BRAUNHOLTZ, M.A.   2s.
—— —— **Abridged Edition.**   1s.
Sainte-Beuve. M. Daru (Causeries du Lundi, Vol. IX.).
By G. MASSON, B.A.   2s.
Saintine. Picciola. By Rev. A. C. CLAPIN, M.A.   2s.
Scribe and Legouvé. Bataille de Dames. By Rev. H. A.
BULL, M.A.   2s.
Scribe. Le Verre d'Eau. By C. COLBECK, M.A.   2s.
Sédaine. Le Philosophe sans le savoir. By Rev. H. A.
BULL, M.A.   2s.
Thierry. Lettres sur l'histoire de France (XIII.—XXIV.).
By G. MASSON, B.A., and G. W. PROTHERO, M.A.   2s. 6d.
—— **Récits des Temps Mérovingiens I.—III.** By GUSTAVE
MASSON, B.A. Univ. Gallic., and A. R. ROPES, M.A.   With Map.   3s.
Villemain. Lascaris ou Les Grecs du XVe Siècle, Nouvelle
Historique.   By G. MASSON, B.A.   2s.
Voltaire. Histoire du Siècle de Louis XIV. Chaps. I.—
XIII.   By G. MASSON, B.A., and G. W. PROTHERO, M.A.   2s. 6d.   PART II.
CHAPS. XIV.—XXIV.   2s. 6d.   PART III.   CHAPS. XXV. to end.   2s. 6d.
Xavier de Maistre. La Jeune Sibérienne. Le Lépreux de
la Cité D'Aoste.   By G. MASSON, B.A.   1s. 6d.

London: Cambridge Warehouse, Ave Maria Lane.

IV. GERMAN.

Ballads on German History. By W. WAGNER, Ph.D. 2s.
Benedix. Doctor Wespe. Lustspiel in fünf Aufzügen. By KARL HERMANN BREUL, M.A., Ph.D. 3s.
Freytag. Der Staat Friedrichs des Grossen. By WILHELM WAGNER, Ph.D. 2s.
German Dactylic Poetry. By WILHELM WAGNER, Ph.D. 3s.
Goethe's Knabenjahre. (1749—1761.) By W. WAGNER, Ph.D. New edition revised and enlarged, by J. W. CARTMELL, M.A. 2s.
—— **Hermann und Dorothea.** By WILHELM WAGNER, Ph.D. New edition revised, by J. W. CARTMELL, M.A. 3s. 6d.
Gutzkow. Zopf und Schwert. Lustspiel in fünf Aufzügen. By H. J. WOLSTENHOLME, B.A. (Lond.). 3s. 6d.
Hauff. Das Bild des Kaisers. By KARL HERMANN BREUL, M.A., Ph.D., University Lecturer in German. 3s.
—— **Das Wirthshaus im Spessart.** By A. SCHLOTTMANN, Ph.D. 3s. 6d.
—— **Die Karavane.** By A. SCHLOTTMANN, Ph.D. 3s.
Immermann. Der Oberhof. A Tale of Westphalian Life, by WILHELM WAGNER, Ph.D. 3s.
Kohlrausch. Das Jahr 1813. By WILHELM WAGNER, Ph.D. 2s.
Lessing and Gellert. Selected Fables. By KARL HERMANN BREUL, M.A., Ph.D. 3s.
Mendelssohn's Letters. Selections from. By J. SIME, M.A. 3s.
Raumer. Der erste Kreuzzug (1095—1099). By WILHELM WAGNER, Ph.D. 2s.
Riehl. Culturgeschichtliche Novellen. By H. J. WOLSTENHOLME, B.A. (Lond.). 3s. 6d.
Schiller. Wilhelm Tell. By KARL HERMANN BREUL, M.A., Ph.D. 2s. 6d. **Abridged Edition.** 1s. 6d.
—— **Geschichte des Dreissigjährigen Kriegs.** By the same Editor. 3s.
Uhland. Ernst, Herzog von Schwaben. By H. J. WOLSTENHOLME, B.A. 3s. 6d.

V. ENGLISH.

Ancient Philosophy from Thales to Cicero, A Sketch By JOSEPH B. MAYOR, M.A. 3s. 6d.
An Apologie for Poetrie by Sir PHILIP SIDNEY. By E. S. SHUCKBURGH, M.A. The Text is a revision of that of the first edition of 1595. 3s.
Bacon's History of the Reign of King Henry VII. By the Rev. Professor LUMBY, D.D. 3s.
Cowley's Essays. By the Rev. Professor LUMBY, D.D. 4s.
Discourse of the Commonwealf of thys Realme of Englande. First printed in 1581, and commonly attributed to W. S. Edited from the MSS. by the late ELIZABETH LAMOND. [*In the Press.*
Milton's Comus and Arcades. By A. W. VERITY, M.A., sometime Scholar of Trinity College. 3s.
Milton's Ode on the Morning of Christ's Nativity, L'Allegro, Il Penseroso and Lycidas. By the same Editor. 2s. 6d.
Milton's Samson Agonistes. By the same Editor. 2s. 6d.
Milton's Paradise Lost. Books I. II. By the same Editor.
[*In the Press.*

London: Cambridge Warehouse, Ave Maria Lane.

THE CAMBRIDGE UNIVERSITY PRESS. 5

Milton's Paradise Lost. Books V. VI. By the same. 2s.
Milton's Paradise Lost. Books XI. XII. By the same. 2s.
More's History of King Richard III. By J. R. LUMBY, D.D. 3s. 6d.
More's Utopia. By Rev. Prof. LUMBY, D.D. 3s. 6d.
The Two Noble Kinsmen. By the Rev. Professor SKEAT, Litt.D. 3s. 6d.

VI. EDUCATIONAL SCIENCE.

Comenius, John Amos, Bishop of the Moravians. His Life and Educational Works, by S. S. LAURIE, A.M., F.R.S.E. 3s. 6d.
Education, Three Lectures on the Practice of. I. On Marking, by H. W. EVE, M.A. II. On Stimulus, by A. SIDGWICK, M.A. III. On the Teaching of Latin Verse Composition, by E. A. ABBOTT, D.D. 2s.
Stimulus. A Lecture delivered for the Teachers' Training Syndicate, May, 1882, by A. SIDGWICK, M.A. 1s.
Locke on Education. By the Rev. R. H. QUICK, M.A. 3s. 6d.
Milton's Tractate on Education. A facsimile reprint from the Edition of 1673. By O. BROWNING, M.A. 2s.
Modern Languages, Lectures on the Teaching of. By C. COLBECK, M.A. 2s.
Teacher, General Aims of the, and Form Management. Two Lectures delivered in the University of Cambridge in the Lent Term, 1883, by F. W. FARRAR, D.D., and R. B. POOLE, B.D. 1s. 6d.
Teaching, Theory and Practice of. By the Rev. E. THRING, M.A., late Head Master of Uppingham School. New Edition. 4s. 6d.

British India, a Short History of. By E. S. CARLOS, M.A., late Head Master of Exeter Grammar School. 1s.
Geography, Elementary Commercial. A Sketch of the Commodities and the Countries of the World. By H. R. MILL, D.Sc., F.R.S.E. 1s.
Geography, an Atlas of Commercial. (A Companion to the above.) By J. G. BARTHOLOMEW, F.R.G.S. With an Introduction by HUGH ROBERT MILL, D.Sc. 3s.

VII. MATHEMATICS.

Arithmetic for Schools. By C. SMITH, M.A., Master of Sidney Sussex College, Cambridge. 3s. 6d.
Elementary Algebra (with Answers to the Examples). By W. W. ROUSE BALL, M.A. 4s. 6d.
Euclid's Elements of Geometry. Books I.—IV. By H. M. TAYLOR, M.A. 3s. Books I. and II. 1s. 6d. Books III. and IV. 1s. 6d. [Books V. and VI. In the Press.
Solutions to the Exercises in Euclid, Books I—IV. By W. W. TAYLOR, M.A. [Nearly ready.
Elements of Statics and Dynamics. By S. L. LONEY, M.A. 7s. 6d. Or in two parts. Part I. Elements of Statics. 4s. 6d. Part II. Elements of Dynamics. 3s. 6d.
Mechanics and Hydrostatics for Beginners. By S. L. LONEY, M.A. [In the Press.
An Elementary Treatise on Plane Trigonometry. By E. W. HOBSON, Sc.D., and C. M. JESSOP, M.A. 4s. 6d.

Other Volumes are in preparation.

London: Cambridge Warehouse, Ave Maria Lane.

The Cambridge Bible for Schools and Colleges.

GENERAL EDITOR: J. J. S. PEROWNE, D.D.,
BISHOP OF WORCESTER.

"*It is difficult to commend too highly this excellent series.*—Guardian.

"*The modesty of the general title of this series has, we believe, led many to misunderstand its character and underrate its value. The books are well suited for study in the upper forms of our best schools, but not the less are they adapted to the wants of all Bible students who are not specialists. We doubt, indeed, whether any of the numerous popular commentaries recently issued in this country will be found more serviceable for general use.*"—Academy.

Now Ready. Cloth, Extra Fcap. 8vo. With Maps.

Book of Joshua. By Rev. G. F. MACLEAR, D.D. 2s. 6d.
Book of Judges. By Rev. J. J. LIAS, M.A. 3s. 6d.
First Book of Samuel. By Rev. Prof. KIRKPATRICK, D.D. 3s. 6d.
Second Book of Samuel. By the same Editor. 3s. 6d.
First Book of Kings. By Rev. Prof. LUMBY, D.D. 3s. 6d.
Second Book of Kings. By Rev. Prof. LUMBY, D.D. 3s. 6d.
Book of Job. By Rev. A. B. DAVIDSON, D.D. 5s.
Book of Psalms. Book I. By Prof. KIRKPATRICK, D.D. 3s. 6d.
Book of Ecclesiastes. By Very Rev. E. H. PLUMPTRE, D.D. 5s.
Book of Jeremiah. By Rev. A. W. STREANE, B.D. 4s. 6d.
Book of Ezekiel. By Rev. A. B. DAVIDSON, D.D. 5s.
Book of Hosea. By Rev. T. K. CHEYNE, M.A., D.D. 3s.
Books of Obadiah & Jonah. By Archdeacon PEROWNE. 2s. 6d.
Book of Micah. By Rev. T. K. CHEYNE, M.A., D.D. 1s. 6d.
Haggai, Zechariah & Malachi. By Arch. PEROWNE. 3s. 6d.
Book of Malachi. By Archdeacon PEROWNE. 1s.
Gospel according to St Matthew. By Rev. A. CARR, M.A. 2s. 6d.
Gospel according to St Mark. By Rev. G. F. MACLEAR, D.D. 2s. 6d.
Gospel according to St Luke. By Arch. FARRAR, D.D. 4s. 6d.
Gospel according to St John. By Rev. A. PLUMMER, D.D. 4s. 6d.
Acts of the Apostles. By Rev. Prof. LUMBY, D.D. 4s. 6d.
Epistle to the Romans. By Rev. H. C. G. MOULE, M.A. 3s. 6d.
First Corinthians. By Rev. J. J. LIAS, M.A. With Map. 2s.
Second Corinthians. By Rev. J. J. LIAS, M.A. With Map. 2s.

London: Cambridge Warehouse, Ave Maria Lane.

THE CAMBRIDGE UNIVERSITY PRESS. 7

Epistle to the Galatians. By Rev. E. H. PEROWNE, D.D. 1s. 6d.
Epistle to the Ephesians. By Rev. H. C. G. MOULE, M.A. 2s. 6d.
Epistle to the Philippians. By the same Editor. 2s. 6d.
Epistles to the Thessalonians. By Rev. G. G. FINDLAY, B.A. 2s.
Epistle to the Hebrews. By Arch. FARRAR, D.D. 3s. 6d.
General Epistle of St James. By Very Rev. E. H. PLUMPTRE, D.D. 1s. 6d.
Epistles of St Peter and St Jude. By Very Rev. E. H. PLUMPTRE, D.D. 2s. 6d.
Epistles of St John. By Rev. A. PLUMMER, M.A., D.D. 3s. 6d.
Book of Revelation. By Rev. W. H. SIMCOX, M.A. 3s.

Preparing.

Book of Genesis. By the BISHOP OF WORCESTER.
Books of Exodus, Numbers and Deuteronomy. By Rev. C. D. GINSBURG, LL.D.
First and Second Books of Chronicles. By Very Rev. Dean SPENCE.
Books of Ezra and Nehemiah. By Rev. Prof. RYLE, B.D.
Book of Isaiah. By Prof. W. ROBERTSON SMITH, M.A.
Epistles to the Colossians and Philemon. By Rev. H. C. G. MOULE, M.A.
Epistles to Timothy & Titus. By Rev. A. E. HUMPHREYS, M.A.

The Smaller Cambridge Bible for Schools.

"*We can cordially recommend this series of text-books.*"—Church Review.

"*The notes elucidate every possible difficulty with scholarly brevity and clearness, and a perfect knowledge of the subject.*"—Saturday Review.

"*Accurate scholarship is obviously a characteristic of their productions, and the work of simplification and condensation appears to have been judiciously and skilfully performed.*"—Guardian.

Now ready. Price 1s. each Volume, with Map.
Book of Joshua. By J. S. BLACK, M.A.
Book of Judges. By J. S. BLACK, M.A. [*In the Press.*
First and Second Books of Samuel. By Rev. Prof. KIRKPATRICK, D.D.
First and Second Books of Kings. By Rev. Prof. LUMBY, D.D.
Gospel according to St Matthew. By Rev. A. CARR, M.A.
Gospel according to St Mark. By Rev. G. F. MACLEAR, D.D.
Gospel according to St Luke. By Archdeacon FARRAR, D.D.
Gospel according to St John. By Rev. A. PLUMMER, D.D.
Acts of the Apostles. By Rev. Prof. LUMBY, D.D.

London: Cambridge Warehouse, Ave Maria Lane.

The Cambridge Greek Testament for Schools and Colleges,

with a Revised Text, based on the most recent critical authorities, and English Notes.

Gospel according to St Matthew. By Rev. A. CARR, M.A.
With 4 Maps. 4s. 6d.

Gospel according to St Mark. By Rev. G. F. MACLEAR, D.D.
With 3 Maps. 4s. 6d.

Gospel according to St Luke. By Archdeacon FARRAR.
With 4 Maps. 6s

Gospel according to St John. By Rev. A. PLUMMER, D.D.
With 4 Maps. 6s.

Acts of the Apostles. By Rev. Professor LUMBY, D.D.
With 4 Maps. 6s.

First Epistle to the Corinthians. By Rev. J. J. LIAS, M.A. 3s.

Second Epistle to the Corinthians. By Rev. J. J. LIAS, M.A. 3s.

Epistle to the Hebrews. By Archdeacon FARRAR, D.D. 3s. 6d.

Epistles of St John. By Rev. A. PLUMMER, M.A., D.D. 4s.

Book of Revelation. By Rev. W. H. SIMCOX, M.A.
[*In the Press.*

London: C. J. CLAY AND SONS,
CAMBRIDGE WAREHOUSE, AVE MARIA LANE.
Glasgow: 263, ARGYLE STREET.
Cambridge: DEIGHTON, BELL AND CO.
Leipzig: F. A. BROCKHAUS.
New York: MACMILLAN AND CO.

THE CAMBRIDGE BIBLE FOR SCHOOLS AND COLLEGES.
GENERAL EDITOR, J. J. S. PEROWNE,
BISHOP OF WORCESTER.

Opinions of the Press.

"*It is difficult to commend too highly this excellent series.*"—Guardian.

"*The modesty of the general title of this series has, we believe, led many to misunderstand its character and underrate its value. The books are well suited for study in the upper forms of our best schools, but not the less are they adapted to the wants of all Bible students who are not specialists. We doubt, indeed, whether any of the numerous popular commentaries recently issued in this country will be found more serviceable for general use.*"—Academy.

"*One of the most popular and useful literary enterprises of the nineteenth century.*"—Baptist Magazine.

"*Of great value. The whole series of comments for schools is highly esteemed by students capable of forming a judgment. The books are scholarly without being pretentious: and information is so given as to be easily understood.*"—Sword and Trowel.

"*The notes possess a rare advantage of being scholarly, and at the same time within the comprehension of the average reader. For the Sunday-School Teacher we do not know of a more valuable work.*"—Sunday-School Chronicle.

The Book of Judges. J. J. LIAS, M.A. "His introduction is clear and concise, full of the information which young students require."—*Baptist Magazine.*

II. Samuel. A. F. KIRKPATRICK, M.A. "Small as this work is in mere dimensions, it is every way the best on its subject and for its purpose that we know of. The opening sections at once prove the thorough competence of the writer for dealing with questions of criticism in an earnest, faithful and devout spirit; and the appendices discuss a few special difficulties with a full knowledge of the data, and a judicial reserve, which contrast most favourably with the superficial dogmatism which has too often made the exegesis of the Old Testament a field for the play of unlimited paradox and the ostentation of personal infallibility. The notes are always clear and suggestive; never trifling or irrelevant; and they everywhere demonstrate the great difference in value between the work of a commentator who is also a Hebraist, and that of one who has to depend for his Hebrew upon secondhand sources."—*Academy.*

I. Kings and Ephesians. "With great heartiness we commend these most valuable little commentaries. We had rather purchase these than nine out of ten of the big blown up expositions. Quality is far better than quantity, and we have it here."—*Sword and Trowel.*

II. Kings. "The Introduction is scholarly and wholly admirable, the notes must be of incalculable value to students."—*Glasgow Herald.*

"It would be difficult to find a commentary better suited for general use."—*Academy.*

The Book of Job. "Able and scholarly as the Introduction is, it is far surpassed by the detailed exegesis of the book. In this Dr DAVIDSON'S strength is at its greatest. His linguistic knowledge, his artistic habit, his scientific insight, and his literary power have full scope when he comes to exegesis...."—*The Spectator.*

"In the course of a long introduction, Dr DAVIDSON has presented us with a very able and very interesting criticism of this wonderful book. Its contents, the nature of its composition, its idea and purpose, its integrity, and its age are all exhaustively treated of.... We have not space to examine fully the text and notes before us, but we can, and do heartily, recommend the book, not only for the upper forms in schools, but to Bible students and teachers generally. As we wrote of a previous volume in the same series, this one leaves nothing to be desired. The notes are full and suggestive, without being too long, and, in itself, the introduction forms a valuable addition to modern Bible literature."—*The Educational Times.*

"Already we have frequently called attention to this exceedingly valuable work as its volumes have successively appeared. But we have never done so with greater pleasure, very seldom with so great pleasure, as we now refer to the last published volume, that on the **Book of Job**, by Dr DAVIDSON, of Edinburgh.... We cordially commend the volume to all our readers. The least instructed will understand and enjoy it; and mature scholars will learn from it."—*Methodist Recorder.*

Psalms. Book I. "His commentary upon the books of Samuel was good, but this is incomparably better, shewing traces of much more work and of greater independence of scholarship and judgment.... As a whole it is admirable, and we are hardly going too far in saying that it is one of the very ablest of all the volumes that have yet appeared in the 'Cambridge Bible for Schools'."—*Record.*

"Another volume of this excellent Bible, in which the student may rely on meeting with the latest scholarship. The introduction is admirable. We know of nothing in so concise a form better adapted for Sunday-School Teachers."—*Sunday-School Chronicle.*

"It is full of instruction and interest, bringing within easy reach of the English reader the results of the latest scholarship bearing upon the study of this ever new book of the Bible. The Introduction of eighty pages is a repertory of information, not drily but interestingly given."—*Methodist Recorder.*

"For a masterly summary of all that is known and much that is hazarded about the history and authorship of this book of religious lyrics we can point to that with which Mr KIRKPATRICK prefaces his new volume. From a perusal of this summary the student will be unimpressionable indeed if he rise not convinced of the vitality imparted to the Psalter by a systematic study of its literary character and historical allusions....In conclusion, we may say that for a work which is handy, and withal complete, we know none better than this volume; and we await with considerable interest the next instalment."—*Education.*

"It seems in every way a most valuable little book, containing a mass of information, well-assorted, and well-digested, and will be useful not only to students preparing for examinations, but to many who want a handy volume of explanation to much that is difficult in the Psalter. ......We owe a great debt of gratitude to Professor Kirkpatrick for his scholarly and interesting volume."—*Church Times*.

"In this volume thoughtful exegesis founded on nice critical scholarship and due regard for the opinions of various writers, combine, under the influence of a devout spirit, to render this commentary a source of much valuable assistance. The notes are 'though deep yet clear,' for they seem to put in a concentrated form the very pith and marrow of all the best that has been hitherto said on the subject, with striking freedom from anything like pressure of personal views. Throughout the work care and pains are as conspicuous as scholarship."—*Literary Churchman*.

Job—Hosea. " It is difficult to commend too highly this excellent series, the volumes of which are now becoming numerous. The two books before us, small as they are in size, comprise almost everything that the young student can reasonably expect to find in the way of helps towards such general knowledge of their subjects as may be gained without an attempt to grapple with the Hebrew; and even the learned scholar can hardly read without interest and benefit the very able introductory matter which both these commentators have prefixed to their volumes. It is not too much to say that these works have brought within the reach of the ordinary reader resources which were until lately quite unknown for understanding some of the most difficult and obscure portions of Old Testament literature."—*Guardian*.

Ecclesiastes; or, the Preacher.—" Of the Notes, it is sufficient to say that they are in every respect worthy of Dr PLUMPTRE's high reputation as a scholar and a critic, being at once learned, sensible, and practical....Commentaries are seldom attractive reading. This little volume is a notable exception."—*The Scotsman*.

Jeremiah, by A. W. STREANE. "The arrangement of the book is well treated on pp. xxx., 396, and the question of Baruch's relations with its composition on pp. xxvii., xxxiv., 317. The illustrations from English literature, history, monuments, works on botany, topography, etc., are good and plentiful, as indeed they are in other volumes of this series."—*Church Quarterly Review*.

Malachi. "Archdeacon Perowne has already edited Jonah and Zechariah for this series. Malachi presents comparatively few difficulties and the Editor's treatment leaves nothing to be desired. His introduction is clear and scholarly and his commentary sufficient. We may instance the notes on ii. 15 and iv. 2 as examples of careful arrangement, clear exposition and graceful expression."—*Academy*.

"**The Gospel according to St Matthew**, by the Rev. A. CARR. The introduction is able, scholarly, and eminently practical, as it bears on the authorship and contents of the Gospel, and the original form in which it is supposed to have been written. It is well illustrated by two excellent maps of the Holy Land and of the Sea of Galilee."—*English Churchman*.

"**St Mark**, with Notes by the Rev. G. F. MACLEAR, D.D. Into this small volume Dr Maclear, besides a clear and able Introduction to the Gospel, and the text of St Mark, has compressed many hundreds of valuable and helpful notes. In short, he has given us a capital manual of the kind required—containing all that is needed to illustrate the text, i.e. all that can be drawn from the history, geography, customs, and manners of the time. But as a handbook, giving in a clear and succinct form the information which a lad requires in order to stand an examination in the Gospel, it is admirable......I can very heartily commend it, not only to the senior boys and girls in our High Schools, but also to Sunday-school teachers, who may get from it the very kind of knowledge they often find it hardest to get."—*Expositor*.

"With the help of a book like this, an intelligent teacher may make 'Divinity' as interesting a lesson as any in the school course. The notes are of a kind that will be, for the most part, intelligible to boys of the lower forms of our public schools; but they may be read with greater profit by the fifth and sixth, in conjunction with the original text."—*The Academy*.

"**St Luke.** Canon FARRAR has supplied students of the Gospel with an admirable manual in this volume. It has all that copious variety of illustration, ingenuity of suggestion, and general soundness of interpretation which readers are accustomed to expect from the learned and eloquent editor. Anyone who has been accustomed to associate the idea of 'dryness' with a commentary, should go to Canon Farrar's St Luke for a more correct impression. He will find that a commentary may be made interesting in the highest degree, and that without losing anything of its solid value....But, so to speak, it is *too good* for some of the readers for whom it is intended."—*The Spectator*.

The Gospel according to St John. "The notes are extremely scholarly and valuable, and in most cases exhaustive, bringing to the elucidation of the text all that is best in commentaries, ancient and modern."—*The English Churchman and Clerical Journal*.

"(1) **The Acts of the Apostles.** By J. RAWSON LUMBY, D.D. (2) **The Second Epistle of the Corinthians**, edited by Professor LIAS. The introduction is pithy, and contains a mass of carefully-selected information on the authorship of the Acts, its designs, and its sources. ......The Second Epistle of the Corinthians is a manual beyond all praise, for the excellence of its pithy and pointed annotations, its analysis of the contents, and the fulness and value of its introduction."—*Examiner*.

"The Rev. H. C. G. MOULE, M.A., has made a valuable addition to THE CAMBRIDGE BIBLE FOR SCHOOLS in his brief commentary on the **Epistle to the Romans**. The 'Notes' are very good, and lean, as the notes of a School Bible should, to the most commonly accepted and orthodox view of the inspired author's meaning; while the Introduction, and especially the Sketch of the Life of St Paul, is a model of condensation. It is as lively and pleasant to read as if two or three facts had not been crowded into well-nigh every sentence."—*Expositor*.

"**The Epistle to the Romans.** It is seldom we have met with a work so remarkable for the compression and condensation of all that is valuable in the smallest possible space as in the volume before us. Within its limited pages we have 'a sketch of the Life of St Paul,' we have further a critical account of the date of the Epistle to the Romans, of its language, and of its genuineness. The notes are numerous, full of matter, to the point, and leave no real difficulty or obscurity unexplained."—*The Examiner.*

The First Epistle to the Corinthians. Edited by Professor LIAS. Every fresh instalment of this annotated edition of the Bible for Schools confirms the favourable opinion we formed of its value from the examination of its first number. The origin and plan of the Epistle are discussed with its character and genuineness."—*The Nonconformist.*

Galatians. "Dr PEROWNE deals throughout in a very thorough manner with every real difficulty in the text, and in this respect he has faithfully followed the noble example set him in the exegetical masterpiece, his indebtedness to which he frankly acknowledges."—*Modern Church.*

"The introductory matter is very full and informing, whilst the Notes are admirable. They combine the scholarly and the practical in an unusual degree....It is not the young students in 'schools and colleges' alone who will find this Commentary helpful on every page."—*Record.*

"This little work, like all of the series, is a scholarly production; but we can also unreservedly recommend it from a doctrinal standpoint; Dr E. H. PEROWNE is one who has grasped the distinctive teaching of the Epistle, and expounds it with clearness and definiteness. In an appendix, he ably maintains the correctness of the A. V. as against the R. V. in the translation of II. 16, a point of no small importance."—*English Churchman.*

The Epistle to the Ephesians. By Rev. H. C. G. MOULE, M.A. "It seems to us the model of a School and College Commentary—comprehensive, but not cumbersome; scholarly, but not pedantic."—*Baptist Magazine.*

The Epistle to the Philippians. "There are few series more valued by theological students than 'The Cambridge Bible for Schools and Colleges,' and there will be no number of it more esteemed than that by Mr H. C. G. MOULE on the *Epistle to the Philippians.*"—*Record.*

Thessalonians. "It will stand the severest scrutiny, for no volume in this admirable series exhibits more careful work, and Mr FINDLAY is a true expositor, who keeps in mind what he is expounding, and for whom he is expounding it."—*Expository Times.*

"Mr FINDLAY maintains the high level of the series to which he has become contributor. Some parts of his introduction to the Epistles to the Thessalonians could scarcely be bettered. The account of Thessalonica, the description of the style and character of the Epistles, and the analysis of them are excellent in style and scholarly care. The notes are possibly too voluminous; but there is so much matter in them, and the matter is arranged and handled so ably, that we are ready to forgive their fulness....Mr FINDLAY'S commentary is a valuable addition to what has been written on the letters to the Thessalonian Church."—*Academy.*

"Of all the volumes of this most excellent series, none is better done, and few are so well done as this small volume....From beginning to end the volume is marked by accurate grammatical scholarship, delicate appreciation of the apostle's meaning, thorough investigation of all matters open to doubt, extensive reading, and deep sympathy with the spiritual aim of these epistles. It is, on the whole, the best commentary on the Thessalonians which has yet appeared, and its small price puts it within reach of all. We heartily recommend it."—*Methodist Recorder.*

"Mr FINDLAY has fulfilled in this volume a task which Dr Moulton was compelled to decline, though he has rendered valuable aid in its preparation. The commentary is in its own way a model—clear, forceful, scholarly—such as young students will welcome as a really useful guide, and old ones will acknowledge as giving in brief space the substance of all that they knew."—*Baptist Magazine.*

Hebrews. "Like his (Canon Farrar's) commentary on Luke it possesses all the best characteristics of his writing. It is a work not only of an accomplished scholar, but of a skilled teacher."—*Baptist Magazine.*

The Epistles of St John. By the Rev. A. PLUMMER, M.A., D.D. "This forms an admirable companion to the 'Commentary on the Gospel according to St John,' which was reviewed in *The Churchman* as soon as it appeared. Dr Plummer has some of the highest qualifications for such a task; and these two volumes, their size being considered, will bear comparison with the best Commentaries of the time."—*The Churchman.*

Revelation. "This volume contains evidence of much careful labour. It is a scholarly production, as might be expected from the pen of the late Mr W. H. SIMCOX....The notes throw light upon many passages of this difficult book, and are extremely suggestive. It is an advantage that they sometimes set before the student various interpretations without exactly guiding him to a choice."—*Guardian.*

"Mr SIMCOX has treated his very difficult subject with that conscious care, grasp, and lucidity which characterises everything he wrote."—*Modern Church.*

The Smaller Cambridge Bible for Schools.

"*We can only repeat what we have already said of this admirable series, containing, as it does, the scholarship of the larger work. For scholars in our elder classes, and for those preparing for Scripture examinations, no better commentaries can be put into their hands.*"—Sunday-School Chronicle.

"*Despite their small size, these volumes give the substance of the admirable pieces of work on which they are founded. We can only hope that in many schools the class-teaching will proceed on the lines these commentators suggest.*"—Record.

"*We should be glad to hear that this series has been introduced into many of our Sunday-Schools, for which it is so admirably adapted.*"—Christian Leader.

"*All that is necessary to be known and learned by pupils in junior and elementary schools is to be found in this series. Indeed, much more is provided than should be required by the examiners. We do not know what more could be done to provide sensible, interesting, and solid Scriptural instruction for boys and girls. The Syndics of the Cambridge*

University Press are rendering great services both to teachers and to scholars by the publication of such a valuable series of books, in which slipshod work could not have a place."—Literary World.

"For the student of the sacred oracles who utilizes hours of travel or moments of waiting in the perusal of the Bible there is nothing so handy, and, at the same time, so satisfying as these little books...... Nor let anyone suppose that, because these are school-books, therefore they are beneath the adult reader. · They contain the very ripest results of the best Biblical scholarship, and that in the very simplest form."—Christian Leader.

"Altogether one of the most perfect examples of a Shilling New Testament commentary which even this age of cheapness is likely to produce."
—Bookseller.

Samuel I. and II. "Professor KIRKPATRICK'S two tiny volumes on the First and Second Books of Samuel are quite model school-books; the notes elucidate every possible difficulty with scholarly brevity and clearness and a perfect knowledge of the subject."—*Saturday Review.*

"They consist of an introduction full of matter, clearly and succinctly given, and of notes which appear to us to be admirable, at once full and brief."—*Church Times.*

Kings I. "We can cordially recommend this little book. The Introduction discusses the question of authorship and date in a plain but scholarly fashion, while the footnotes throughout are brief, pointed, and helpful."—*Review of Reviews.*

Matthew. "The notes are terse, clear, and helpful, and teachers and students cannot fail to find the volume of great service."—*Publishers' Circular.*

Mark. Luke. "We have received the volumes of St Mark and St Luke in this series....The two volumes seem, on the whole, well adapted for school use, are well and carefully printed, and have maps and good, though necessarily brief, introductions. There is little doubt that this series will be found as popular and useful as the well-known larger series, of which they are abbreviated editions."—*Guardian.*

Luke. "We cannot too highly commend this handy little book to all teachers."—*Wesleyan Methodist Sunday-School Record.*

John. "We have been especially interested in Mr PLUMMER'S treatment of the Gospel which has been entrusted to his charge. He is concise, comprehensive, interesting, and simple. Young students of this inimitable book, as well as elder students, even ministers and teachers, may use it with advantage as a very serviceable handbook."—*Literary World.*

John. "A model of condensation, losing nothing of its clearness and force from its condensation into a small compass. Many who have long since completed their college curriculum will find it an invaluable handbook."—*Methodist Times.*

Acts. "The notes are very brief, but exceedingly comprehensive, comprising as much detail in the way of explanation as would be needed by young students of the Scriptures preparing for examination. We again give the opinion that this series furnishes as much real help as would usually satisfy students for the Christian ministry, or even ministers themselves."—*Literary World.*

THE CAMBRIDGE GREEK TESTAMENT
FOR SCHOOLS AND COLLEGES
with a Revised Text, based on the most recent critical authorities, and English Notes,

"*Has achieved an excellence which puts it above criticism.*"—Expositor.

St Matthew. "Copious illustrations, gathered from a great variety of sources, make his notes a very valuable aid to the student. They are indeed remarkably interesting, while all explanations on meanings, applications, and the like are distinguished by their lucidity and good sense."—*Pall Mall Gazette.*

St Mark. "Dr MACLEAR'S introduction contains all that is known of St Mark's life; an account of the circumstances in which the Gospel was composed, with an estimate of the influence of St Peter's teaching upon St Mark; an excellent sketch of the special characteristics of this Gospel; an analysis, and a chapter on the text of the New Testament generally."—*Saturday Review.*

St Luke. "Of this second series we have a new volume by Archdeacon FARRAR on *St Luke*, completing the four Gospels....It gives us in clear and beautiful language the best results of modern scholarship. We have a most attractive *Introduction*. Then follows a sort of composite Greek text, representing fairly and in very beautiful type the consensus of modern textual critics. At the beginning of the exposition of each chapter of the Gospel are a few short critical notes giving the manuscript evidence for such various readings as seem to deserve mention. The expository notes are short, but clear and helpful. For young students and those who are not disposed to buy or to study the much more costly work of Godet, this seems to us to be the best book on the Greek Text of the Third Gospel."—*Methodist Recorder.*

St John. "We take this opportunity of recommending to ministers on probation, the very excellent volume of the same series on this part of the New Testament. We hope that most or all of our young ministers will prefer to study the volume in the *Cambridge Greek Testament for Schools.*"—*Methodist Recorder.*

The Acts of the Apostles. "Professor LUMBY has performed his laborious task well, and supplied us with a commentary the fulness and freshness of which Bible students will not be slow to appreciate. The volume is enriched with the usual copious indexes and four coloured maps."—*Glasgow Herald.*

I. Corinthians. "Mr LIAS is no novice in New Testament exposition, and the present series of essays and notes is an able and helpful addition to the existing books."—*Guardian.*

The Epistles of St John. "In the very useful and well annotated series of the Cambridge Greek Testament the volume on the Epistles of St John must hold a high position... The notes are brief, well informed and intelligent."—*Scotsman.*

www.ingramcontent.com/pod-product-compliance
Lightning Source LLC
Chambersburg PA
CBHW030359230426
43664CB00007BB/661